Tax Justice and the Political Economy of Global Capitalism, 1945 to the Present

Tax Justice and the Political Economy of Global Capitalism, 1945 to the Present

Edited by
Jeremy Leaman
and
Attiya Waris

berghahn
NEW YORK · OXFORD
www.berghahnbooks.com

Published in 2013 by
Berghahn Books
www.berghahnbooks.com

Library of Congress Cataloging-in-Publication Data

Tax justice and the political economy of global capitalism, 1945 to the
present / edited by Jeremy Leaman, Attiya Waris.
    p. cm.
    ISBN 978-0-85745-881-0 (hbk. : alk. paper) -- ISBN 978-0-85745-
882-7 (ebook) 1. Taxation. 2. Tax incidence. 3. Fiscal policy. 4. Social
justice. 5. Distributive justice. 6. International trade. I. Leaman, Jeremy,
1947- II. Waris, Attiya.
    HJ2305.T173 2013
    339.5'25--dc23

                                                                    2012032902

British Library Cataloguing in Publication Data
A catalogue record for this book is available from the British Library

Printed in the United States on acid-free paper

ISBN 978-0-85745-881-0 (hardback)
ISBN 978-0-85745-882-7 (institutional ebook)

Contents

List of Tables and Figures

Tables

Figures

Why Tax Justice Matters in Global Economic Development

JEREMY LEAMAN AND ATTIYA WARIS

The concept of tax justice has become a part of social and political currency in recent years. It reflects an increased awareness of the centrality of taxation to the affairs of the individual state – as a fiscal jurisdiction – and to the relationship between states within the global political economy. It has arguably moved up the agenda of the powerful block of developed states in the wake of the global crises which erupted in 2008 and which exposed the fiscal vulnerability of those states to the costs of structural and cyclical crisis management. Substantial budget deficits and growing accumulated sovereign debt have alerted the leaders of the major G8 states and of other OECD countries to the fundamental problem of maintaining the supply of public goods over time against the background of increased military expenditure, stagnating or dwindling revenues and increasing debt-servicing costs.

Several state leaders of the G8 have, recently, drawn attention to the problems posed by corporate tax avoidance and by tax competition with low-tax jurisdictions, problems largely ignored prior to the outbreak of the crisis. The discovery of these problems and the damage they inflict on 'normal' tax jurisdictions is surprising inasmuch as they had existed for several decades. They have now only been deemed worrying because their contribution to the global crises and their associated destruction of wealth and social equilibrium has become palpable. They were tolerated – within the G8 and the European Union – firstly, because budgetary bottlenecks were used, by and large, as vehicles for reducing state expenditure in the spirit of neoliberal roll-back programmes and debt-reduction rather than as problems to be examined from the revenue side. Secondly, the tax administrations of the major OECD states had comparatively few difficulties raising revenue via their long established channels of both direct and indirect taxation and, in the event of temporary shortfalls, treasuries have been able to borrow money relatively cheaply via sovereign bond sales; in this, they differed significantly from many developing and emerging economies and from several peripheral European states. In many developing states, there are many factors that play a part in unjust tax systems: firstly, globalisation and the effects of being bound to the global economy has possibly muted domestic discourse on taxation. Secondly, the distinct absence of the existence of well-established social welfare processes has not posed the same dilemma to populations that are still mainly concerned with daily survival and alleviation of their poverty: citizens' awareness of taxation at times simply does not register as a cause for concern. Thirdly, the inability of developing and emerging states to fully harness their resources through a just tax system is partly due to a poorly constructed system. Finally, this is compounded by the absence of policy capacity which forces reliance on both domestic and international entities and lobby groups for whom justice and fairness are not key concerns.

The recent invocation of 'fairness' in taxation by the leaders of the world's powerful capitalist states therefore reflects a degree of political and/or electoral expediency, inasmuch as anger within civil society over the recklessness of financial institutions coincided with revelations of their complicity in large-scale tax avoidance, but it also reflects a belated acknowledgement of critical contradictions in the management of fiscal affairs: Barack Obama's citing of Ugland House in the Cayman Islands, postal address of 18,857 international corporations (c.f. *The Economist* 2009); or Gordon Brown's call for a crackdown on tax havens (c.f. Watt 2009); or Nicholas Sarkozy's earlier questioning of the need for net EU transfers to any state that was 'rich enough to allow itself the luxury of a "flat tax"' (Evans-Pritchard 2005) betoken arguably an insight into the fiscal damage caused by corporate tax arbitrage and tax competition between states. However cynical we may deem the motivation behind the sudden thematisation of tax by leading politicians to be, the rhetorical outrage also betokens a real sense of the indispensable element of perceived 'justice' in the maintenance of legitimacy in advanced democracies. Such perceptions are clearly malleable and context-dependent, but – in the world of interdependent, technically savvy international think tanks, NGOs and campaign groups – political and economic elites ignore them at their peril.

'Justice' and 'tax justice' are self-evidently political constructs which are rooted not in any theocratic certainties but in the collective structures of human language, the usage of which is varied and frequently highly nuanced but which nevertheless has a significance that is identifiable in all social formations. Whatever the evolutionary pathway towards modern usages of the term 'justice', its usage suggests a general anthropological appeal to the 'social brain' (Wilkinson and Pickett 2009: 202f) which is reinforced by the social experience of coexistence, parenting, friendship, work and shared mortality, and by an aesthetics of symmetry and sympathy. It is no coincidence that the dominant Western image of justice involves the metaphor of balanced measuring scales in the hands of a female figure, frequently with sword in hand, implying a preparedness to defend militantly the right to fair treatment before collective (state) law, and indifference to prejudice in the form of the blindfold. The normative concepts of social justice and tax justice would thus seem to benefit from the enduring and positive images of social interdependence and symmetry, notwithstanding the threats that have historically beleaguered human attempts to establish stable, peaceful and viable social arrangements.

The particular form that concepts of tax justice take is nevertheless very varied, beyond its general emotional appeal. Murphy and Nagel in *The Myth of Ownership* (2002) provide a valuable analytical survey of the variety of approaches to issues of tax justice which above all questions any concept of tax justice that is not rooted in a broader conception of social justice. *Vertical equity* is eliminated from serious consideration as a guiding principle because it demands an equal tax burden (as in a simple head tax) from each individual, regardless of income and ability to pay, and is seemingly rooted in a 'naive . . . libertarianism' which 'assumes that pretax market incomes are presumptively just' (Murphy and Nagel 2002: 15). Similar reservations can be directed at the *benefit principle* or the *equal sacrifice principle* which, while distinct from a crude libertarianism, operate according to a fundamental yardstick of proportionality without reference to the distributional outcome of the subsequent use of fiscal resources in state expenditure (ibid.: 16ff, 24ff). *Horizontal equity*, which is given wide coverage in the conventional literature on tax theory, is also problematic in that it ignores the overall social distribution of income and observes merely the principle of fairness of tax burdens within given categories of taxpayers (companies, trusts, households) or income bands. Murphy and Nagel make a persuasive case for the principle that 'tax justice must be part of an overall theory of social justice and of the legitimate aims of government' (ibid.: 38). This case is founded in particular on the 'denial that property rights are fundamental' (ibid.: 175) and the perception that ownership is a social construction that could not exist without the legal framework provided by the collective phenomenon which is the state. In consequence, taxation is not expropriation – as commonly assumed by many tax theorists and by popular culture – but a political means of determining the shape of ownership within a given society (ibid.: 176f). This conception of tax justice – as applied to a single jurisdiction – still allows a wide variety of interpretations as to what constitutes a fair distribution of income and wealth, but it removes from serious consideration the notion of individual ownership as an ontological given.

Tax justice cannot simply be a yardstick that is applied to single sovereign jurisdictions, however. The extensive internationalisation of economic affairs, but in particular of financial transactions, has rendered individual nation states increasingly vulnerable to 'tax competition' between states as a means of encouraging transnational corporations to (re)locate their operations (Genschel et al. 2011; Rixen 2011) through foreign direct investment projects or simple profit-shifting (Rixen 2011). The necessary international dimension of campaigns for tax justice, as pursued by the Tax Justice Network, Global Financial Integrity and by NGOs like Oxfam, Christian Aid and Actionaid, relates above all to the ruinous effect of tax competition, of low-tax jurisdictions and of weak fiscal governance on the economic development of less developed and emerging economies. All the contributions in this volume share the perception that the tax arrangements of states and the corporations of OECD states have a critical effect on the development prospects of the less powerful states in Africa, Asia, Latin America and in Europe's own periphery. Justice in tax affairs must therefore consider the fundamental interdependence of the global economy and the very specific disadvantages facing poorer states with weaker institutions of tax governance, deriving from the sophisticated tax and regulatory arbitrage strategies of highly mobile transnational corporations. The social justice of decent, humane conditions of life for all citizens in less developed economies is thus heavily dependent on the preparedness of the dominant states of the developed world to outlaw the 'free rider' practices of TNCs, global banking corporations, hedge funds and accountancy firms, *as well as* the corruption of kleptocratic elites, i.e., to remove the loopholes which allow the 'legal' avoidance of tax liabilities by economic agents who nevertheless take advantage of the infrastructural facilities and legal protection provided by states to whom they deny revenue. The corrosive effect of low-tax jurisdictions ('tax havens') continues to represent a major obstacle to a recalibration of global economic affairs which would allow the sustainable modernisation and development of poorer states, combined with social justice. Several of the contributions to this volume therefore address the wider issues of international tax governance and multilateral harmonisation.

Another significant obstacle to the realisation of a progressive and internationally beneficial reform of taxation is to be found in the not uncommon resistance to the taxing state among many social cultures. This resistance to 'Leviathan' (c.f. Daunton 2001) has deep cultural roots and reflects above all the historical function of capitalist states in maintaining the economic disparities and social hierarchies which are essential constitutive preconditions for capitalist relations of production and distribution. The way in which the early capitalist state gathered and deployed its revenues was for a long time more self-evidently clientelist, favouring ruling-class economic interests and repressing the opposition of subaltern classes; the financing of the physical and social infrastructures of domestic economies and the conduct of dynastic wars, colonial expansion and international diplomacy had little to do with the promotion of social or indeed tax justice; the most reliable source of state revenue was consistently found to be duties levied on articles of mass consumption or on imports – on salt, bread, meat, sugar, coal, wine, etc. (Sabine 1980; Daunton 2001), i.e., it was regressive in nature. Quasi-progressive sources of taxation (graduated property taxes or the famous window tax in Britain, for example) were the exceptions that proved the rule before the beginning of the twentieth century.[1] In repressive, undemocratic states, economic and social disparities compounded by indirect taxes were thus more likely to reinforce mass resentment towards the fiscal state.

The shared subversive resistance to the expropriating 'Leviathan' survives to varying degrees in contemporary political cultures, despite the transition to more obviously redistributive forms of the capitalist state in the twentieth century. More tellingly perhaps, neoliberal propaganda was able to capture the public imagination of the electorates of most OECD countries by appealing to this spirit of resistance to the misuse of expropriated social wealth by 'extravagant' and 'wasteful' states. Cheating the taxman was implicitly sanctioned by a doctrine which could appeal to an 'everyday libertarianism' (Murphy and Nagel 2002) and the jokey cynicism of the powerless. The disingenuous generalisation that tax revenue is plunder – when this applies to states in the past or to some states today – is lazy and dishonest, but it continues to make very effective electioneering.[2] As Murphy and Nagel note:

> Pretax economic transactions are so salient in our lives that the governmental framework that determines their consequences and gives them their real meaning recedes into the background of consciousness. What is left is the robust and compelling fantasy that we earn our income and the government takes some of it away from us, or in some cases supplements it with what it has taken from others. This results in widespread hostility to taxes, and a political advantage to those who campaign against them and attack the IRS as a tyrannical bureaucracy, trying to get its hands on our hard-earned money. (Murphy and Nagel 2002: 176f)

The generalised critique of the taxing state is used to justify the dishonest claims of trickle-down economists that lower top marginal rates, or indeed a proportional flat tax, would benefit all citizens (thus Edwards and Mitchell 2008), where neoliberal tax cuts have demonstrably benefited top-earners disproportionately and trickle-down effects have been risible (Chang 2010: 144f). More perverse, perhaps, is the use by state treasuries of the cultural appeal of cheating the taxman when selling particular treasury savings bonds with rhetorical flourishes like: 'why pay tax to the state?' (1996 advert for UK National Savings Certificates). In other words, one revenue section of the UK Treasury induces its citizens to put sizeable tranches of their financial assets at its disposal for a fixed term by invoking the spirit of tax resistance to the demands of another revenue section in the same ministry.

It is therefore by no means surprising that we can observe in the present collection of world states very different and complex tax cultures (Sandford 2000; Ganghof 2006) which reflect both distinct levels of economic and political development but also varying levels of knowledge about tax affairs (Sheffrin 1996: 311ff) as well as fluctuating sentiments among taxpayers.

- The tax compliance behaviour of individuals has been shown to vary markedly between different tax jurisdictions both within specific categories of taxpayer (PAYE and retroactive Assessed Income Tax) and between those categories (Eissel 1997: 136; Sandford 2000: 142ff); the variability of compliance will be determined by numerous factors: the (perceived) legitimacy of the state (democracy, autocracy, kleptocracy, colonial), the real and/or perceived disparities in the gross/net distribution of national income, the administrative 'style' of the revenue authorities (authoritarian, disciplinarian, arbitrary, vigilant, conciliatory), as implied by Adam Smith (1904: 472f) and Sandford (2000: 152ff) among others.
- The tax compliance behaviour of enterprises has also been shown to vary according to jurisdiction and between the legal forms of enterprise (incorporated, unincorporated, limited partnership, etc.) and to the marginal utility of tax 'efficiency' management/tax avoidance (Eissel 1997: 137; Sanford 2000: 142ff), in addition to the above factors of legitimacy and the behaviour of fiscal authorities. Several studies relate the intensity of administration by the tax authorities as a determinant, where the reduced regularity of tax inspections correlates with both lower compliance levels and lower effective rates of taxation (Galbiati and Zanella 2011).
- The tax-raising motivations of states or governing parties have always been manifestly varied, influenced by class/party/ethnic/regional interest, by clientelist considerations, by religious or sociopolitical principles and much more; the history of the emergence of income taxation in Britain and elsewhere illustrates this variety and/or the path dependency of tax policy preferences very adequately (Sabine 1980; Adams 1993; Daunton 2001): from the exceptional, temporary measure to finance the Napoleonic wars to the modest reform to stimulate growth by compensating for the removal of customs and excise duties in the 1840s to the administrative convenience of a mode of taxation involving the 'minimum of irritation' (Daunton 2001: 180ff); to the construction of a new 'fiscal constitution' (ibid.: 330ff) and finally to the primary pillar of a welfare state based on fiscal redistribution.

These few examples illustrate the problem of limiting theories and models of taxation to the narrow dimensions of micro- or macro-economic rationalities: even if such rationalities could be distilled for the purposes of improving the accounting efficiency of the individual enterprise or the sustainability of family budgets, in the real operational context of economic, social, political and cultural history; of asymmetrical international economic and political relations; of rival normative rationalities; of (sometimes crass) disparities of income, wealth and resource distribution; of demographic, climatic and environmental 'externalities', they – the comforting quantifiable rationalities – become entangled in an impenetrable intellectual thicket which prevents meaningful progress. Methodologically, much of the Western traditional academic literature on taxation is weakened by narrowness of focus and/or analytical assumptions, while among developing country academics, the analysis and discussion of taxation is a traditionally ignored area. Given that taxation, together with the state's monopoly of violence, occupies a central position in the relationship between the citizens and the public authorities of a territorial jurisdiction, it is arguably inadequate to define, explain and justify that relationship in terms of a limited set of rationalities: neither the evolution nor the reform of a given tax system can be sensibly analysed by reference to corporate cost 'efficiency', rational taxpayer interest, administrative logic or indeed the logic of a putative general interest and modelled accordingly. The relationship between citizens/taxpayers and state is too multidimensional to be thus reduced. Rather, a survey of taxation literature reveals either directly or by default that particular dimensions operate according to different and frequently colliding logics and rationalities, the ignoring of which paralyses understanding. The most cursory acquaintance with the history of taxation will provide examples of such collisions in the concrete form of tax revolts (Sabine 1980: 82ff; Adams 1993: 227ff, 293ff), legislative compromises (Daunton 2001), tax avoidance, or the kleptocratic expatriation of fiscal resources (Shaxson 2011), to name just a few.

The contributions to this volume broadly share the conviction that an *interdisciplinary* approach to the multi-dimensional character of taxation as a phenomenon of human society to account for the behavioural mechanisms involved in its practice and to develop half-way adequate prescriptive models for achieving social justice at national and international level. The case for a holistic, interdisciplinary approach to the analysis of taxation is above all to be found in the extraordinary mess that has developed in the global political economy over recent decades (in large measure as a result of one-eyed orthodox economics) and in the acute dangers that threaten the nature and function of the democratic state in the twenty-first century. The true extent of the mess has been partly revealed by the global financial crisis in the autumn of 2008, by the resulting global recessions of production and trade and by the ongoing fiscal crises of most OECD states and many others besides. One can add to these major crises of the global political economy the *intellectual crisis* that befell the community of scholars and practitioners that made up the dominant policy elites of the developed world, as they surveyed the debris of their 'scientific' paradigm and desperately recommended reversing the 'roll-back' of state functions to prevent the complete meltdown of neoliberal capitalism. The sudden rediscovery of both national state crisis management and the virtues of international political coordination of macro-policy was long overdue but it is by no means secure at the time of writing (2011). It needs, above all, to be supported by a thoroughgoing re-examination of past failures and the still unresolved contradictions in the institutions and processes of global capitalism. Taxation, as this volume seeks to demonstrate, constitutes a key area in which these contradictions are manifested. Without their internationally coordinated resolution – along with the resolution of other crucial areas of international political weakness – the global economy is very likely to experience a further destructive episode of destabilisation.

The motivational point of departure of this volume is thus unashamedly political inasmuch as it proceeds from the conviction that the democratic/ collective resolution of social and economic problems is preferable to autocratic or oligarchic solutions, and from the diagnosis that democratic institutions and processes are being increasingly threatened by oligarchic structures of power. No volume that invokes the principles of social justice and justice in taxation affairs can pretend political neutrality. A shared perception of the contributions is thus that transnational (i.e., territorially *unbound*) capital has increased its political leverage to the extent that it can and does deploy regulatory and tax arbitrage to influence territorially *bound* political jurisdictions. Transnational corporations pressurise states directly through threats of relocation or indirectly through exploitation of the ensuing 'location competition' between states; in corrupt states, moreover, it is not simply rent-seeking TNCs that secure optimal supply-side conditions but political oligarchs who exploit their right of seignorage to demand tributes and to expatriate their own rents.

The analyses below are thus informed by a regulatory reform agenda rooted in a shared insight into the hegemonic character of transnational capital and the subordination of national/regional polities to that hegemony and the unequal interdependence it represents. It is logically counterposed to the political point of departure of the advocates of regulatory liberalisation and their deeply ideological generalisation of 'freedom' which masks the very specific and privileged freedoms of vested interest and power.

The centrality of tax 'justice' as an objective of policy reform and economic development is rooted in a set of shared perceptions:

1. that, historically, perceptions of the 'injustice' or unfairness of taxation have been a key driver of both popular uprisings against political elites or of pre-emptive action by political elites to avoid revolution or social upheaval;
2. that the political legitimacy of a state is strongly associated with the degree to which it conforms to the norms of equity, answerability and transparency;

3. that successful, modern states are generally characterised by both higher ratios of taxation to GDP and by relatively narrow disparities of income and wealth distribution, in part achieved through fiscal redistribution measures;

4. that the task of promoting tax justice has been made more problematic by the partial reversal of Keynesian welfarism within the OECD group of nations as a result of global capital market deregulation and associated opportunities for companies and wealthy individuals to circumvent the taxation laws of particular states while enjoying the commercial benefits provided by those states;

5. that 'public understanding of tax matters is the precondition for international tax justice' (Tax Justice Network 2005); for the legitimacy of progressive tax policies to be maintained, restored or developed, civil society must engage in a constantly renewed discourse on the role of the fiscal state for ensuring the overall welfare of citizens and on the benefits of social justice and relative equality for peace and the future of humanity.

The collection of chapters is organised into three distinct but interrelated sets. The first four chapters focus on tax affairs in Europe, in relation to both individual states and the European Union. This initial focus derives in large measure from the position of European states in the history of global economic and political development; they constitute the majority of advanced welfare states within the OECD and are characterised by refined, if not highly complex taxation systems. Both as single jurisdictions and as members of a strong regional grouping of states, they have tended to function as models of governance in tax affairs and general administrative systems for developing states and groups of states. The importance of European administrative cultures as the basis for political legitimacy, trust and levels of compliance is key to an understanding of the model character of its tax arrangements, but it cannot allow the observer to neglect the deficiencies, the historical anomalies and the contradictions of these arrangements as they have accumulated over time. In particular, the problems associated with the most recent wave of tax reform programmes both at national and at EU level need to be highlighted as indicators of the pitfalls of tax reform in a global political economy dominated by mobile corporations, with particular reference to the consequences of these reforms for social inequalities and for justice in taxation. The three individual cases – Britain, Germany and Portugal – provide valuable contrasts in terms of the very different trajectories to which their tax cultures have been subject: Britain, the relatively stable, older centralised capitalist democracy with a longish tradition of progressive income taxation and a dominant financial services sector; Germany, the latecomer to industrialisation, nationhood and democracy, with a fiscal architecture strongly influenced by defeat and the containment preferences of the victors; Portugal, a maritime and colonial power which made a very late transition to democracy (1974–5) and a correspondingly late exit from colonial rule and which gained relatively late membership of the European Community (1986).

George Irvin's analysis uses the results of the neoliberal reforms conducted by Margaret Thatcher, John Major and Tony Blair as the backdrop to a critique of the fiscal plans of the Conservative/Liberal coalition government under David Cameron and George Osborne, with a particular focus on increased income inequality since 1979 and the likelihood of a further worsening of post-transfer income disparities as a consequence of fiscal austerity. Irvin makes explicit recommendations for a radical tax reform, notably for a reversal of policy trends and the reinforcing of progressivity in income taxation, along with measures to limit the widening disparities in market incomes. Dieter Eissel's account of the recent history of tax reform in the unified Germany identifies a similar continuity between the centre-right Kohl governments of the 1980s and 1990s and the 'Red-Green' administrations under Gerhard Schröder (1998–2005), but underscores that the incisive neoliberal, supply-side tax reforms in the Federal Republic were enacted not by Kohl but by Schröder after 1999. The decisive Schröder/Eichel reforms built on the liberalisation, privatisation and deregulation measures adopted after 1982 but were supplemented by further labour market reforms (Hartz) and reforms to German pensions (Riester). The policy trajectory of flattening curves of progressivity and reductions in capital taxes shows a clear neoliberal continuum, according to Eissel, with an unsurprising widening of both market income disparities and post-transfer distribution ratios. Eissel makes a set of specific recommendations to reverse these trends, and like Irvin proposes the adoption of a Tobin tax on international financial transactions. Miguel Glatzer describes the fluctuating fortunes of taxation policy in post-revolution Portugal, which initially defied the trend in other OECD countries by introducing very high marginal rates and a correspondingly steep curve of progression which were subsequently modified but at a later date. The comparative framework of Glatzer's analysis allows a closer understanding of a tax culture which was obliged to cope with the challenges of democratization, economic modernisation, European integration and the development of a welfare state within a fairly narrow timescale. Additionally, these transitions did not enjoy the luxury of a favourable global economic environment, such as existed for earlier members of the European Community in the 1950s and 1960s. Stagflation, structural unemployment and severe external imbalances dogged Portuguese reformers, rendering their achievements all the more remarkable, according to Glatzer. Portugal's potential vulnerability to exogenous shocks was nevertheless already fairly evident in its comparatively low tax ratio (a weakness shared with Greece, Spain and Ireland) even before the outbreak of the global crisis in 2008. Glatzer also underscores the relatively high level of income inequality compared to the other members of the EU15, even before the process of austerity-driven debt-reduction was initiated in 2009.

The need for a regional framework covering taxation policy is the message of the last contribution to the first section of this volume by Leaman. The record of the European Union in the field of tax harmonisation has been very disappointing, inasmuch as the *acquis communautaire* contain strict minimal standards only in relation to indirect taxation (VAT) and the principle of progressive taxation has been extensively eroded by the unhindered introduction of flat tax regimes in a majority of the post-2004 member states and the inter-state tax competition this has promoted. Leaman takes the specific case of the global financial crisis to illustrate the effect of EU decisions and non-decisions on the conduct of crisis management after September 2008, the contradictions in Commission priorities and the dangers for the future coherence of the European project and for tax justice in general.

The weaknesses of both the national systems of taxation examined in Part I and of the European regional approach form the backdrop to the five chapters in the second part of the book, which focus on less developed countries, firstly in their relationships with developed states and then in the specific issues affecting the management of their national systems of taxation. The first chapter in this set – by Paul Sagar, John Christensen and Nick Shaxson – examines Britain's critical contribution to the shaping of global tax affairs in the emergence of low-tax jurisdictions in its post-colonial satellite dependencies during the late 1950s up until the 1970s. It seeks thereby to illuminate the evolution of the extraordinary and destructive system of offshore jurisdictions that permit the criminal evasion of tax liabilities by companies, organisations and individuals and the free-rider 'legal' avoidance of tax liabilities by a large number of corporations, shell trusts, hedge funds and others. The picture revealed by their predominantly archival research is of conflicting preferences between the UK Inland Revenue, which was very concerned about both the haemorrhaging of revenues and the legality/morality of tax avoidance through tax haven shell accounts, and the Bank of England, which took a benign view of tax haven status in Crown Dependencies as a means of generating income for these often isolated, small settlements and as a conduit for foreign capital flows. The Bank's benign neglect prevailed, and overruled the concerns of the Inland Revenue, of several ministers and of other British politicians. The damaging consequences of this neglect are evident in the calculations of groups like Global Financial Integrity, which estimates that the average annual outflow of illicit money from developing countries to offshore locations between 2000 and 2008 was $810 billion. The anatomy of tax haven abuse is tellingly captured in Nicholas Shaxson's recent publication, *Treasure Islands* (Shaxson 2011).

Alberto Vega's chapter on 'Tax Treaties between Developed and Developing Countries' takes a close look at the evolution of the two main models of bilateral tax agreements in the context of attempts to solve the problems of double taxation of multinational companies and corporate transparency. The older OECD model, which sought to establish the core principle of taxing companies in their country of residence, is compared to the later UN model which sought to favour developing countries through encouraging the taxation of profits generated in the host country. The UN model is predicated on the perceived need for developing countries to generate the critical mass of state revenues sufficient to promote the modernisation of their economies and to construct the appropriate administrative systems and regulatory framework to conduct tax policy effectively. The picture which emerges is one of incremental improvements in some developing countries as well as changes to the treaty preferences of some emerging economies – notably the so-called BRICS – that have themselves become significant exporters of capital.

The persistent problems of developing countries as fiscal states are well illustrated by the case studies of two former British colonies in Africa: of 'Taxation and State Legitimacy in Kenya' by Attiya Waris, and of 'Tax Avoidance Practices in Nigeria' by Olatunde Julius Otusanya. Waris' analysis of the Kenyan Constituency Development Fund (KCDF) is set against the background of the difficulties faced by a country upon which the fiscal state structures of a developed state were imposed during the colonial period and which was unable to construct organically the kinds of institutions best suited to economic and political modernisation. The mismatch of institutions and policy instruments left a legacy of a political economy which 'faces a crisis of legitimacy' and is characterised in part by corruption and a lack of accountability and corresponding problems of trust and compliance in tax affairs. Waris assesses the advantages of a new funding system, the KCDF, which links state expenditure to specific development aims and which improves institutional trust and legitimacy through the measurable results deriving from targeted fiscal measures. While acknowledging the weaknesses of the comparatively young funding system, Waris concludes that it is a 'noble initiative' which has brought many benefits to communities around the country and which merits refining and developing as a source of improved legitimacy.

Olatunde Otusanya's chapter examines the 'inter-company transfers of intangible assets' and the effect of these tax avoidance practices on the fiscal state in Nigeria. The author explores the mechanics of these common programmes of 'tax management' which involve primarily shifting taxable profits through royalties and technical fees paid by their affiliates in developing countries to a subsidiary in tax havens and the consequent denial of tax revenue to the Nigerian state. Otusanya's findings suggest that the ability of corporations to roam the world facilitates the migration of intangibles and the use of 'non-residence' rules to challenge the taxation law of the host country. The relocation of intangible property to low-tax region affiliates is one of the biggest challenges facing governments in developing nations, because this practice encourages tax avoidance, capital flight and also shifts the tax burden to less mobile capital and undermines the social fabric. The case studies of Cadbury Nigeria Plc, Cadbury Schweppes Overseas Limited and Shell Petroleum International Mattschappij B.V provide compelling evidence of systematic abuse by large corporations and the consequent negative impacts on both Nigeria's revenues and its tax cultures, underscoring the centrality of 'tax justice' and popular perceptions of tax justice for the legitimacy of this and other states in similar situations of unequal interdependence.

The final chapter of the second part of this volume is derived from research by an eight-country consortium and examines the gender dimension of taxation in predominantly emerging states, namely South Africa, Ghana, Uganda, Mexico, Argentina, India, Morocco and the United Kingdom. In many of these countries, the tax system continues explicitly to discriminate against women. This is especially so in areas such as the taxation of joint income. The results for indirect taxes are more encouraging and show that well-designed indirect tax policies can go some way to alleviating the burden on poor women. For many developing countries trying to increase their tax/ GDP ratio, VAT is an attractive form of taxation – it is relatively easy to collect, relatively easy to administer and it is difficult for taxpayers to evade. A number of commentators have expressed concern about the burden that VAT may place on those with low incomes, in particular women, and high-light the regressive nature of an over-reliance on indirect taxation. However, within the limitations that the economic cultures of rural or semi-rural economies place on fiscal policy, the authors suggest that it is possible to design VAT in a manner that addresses some of these concerns.

The third and final part of the volume proceeds from the diagnoses and conclusions of the chapters in the first two parts, namely that global tax arrangements have become dangerously skewed towards the interest of highly mobile enterprises and that the fiscal power of *all* jurisdictions has been weak-ened by this asymmetry between states and dominant market agents. Low-tax jurisdictions as well as their high-tax counterparts, developed and less devel-oped states are to a greater or lesser extent beholden to the fiscal preferences of large international companies when they consider the options for reform-ing their tax systems. A relatively borderless market for capital transactions, foreign direct investments and profit-shifting poses a formidable challenge to the fragmented set of sovereign tax regimes, both to achieve or sustain ade-quate revenue flows and, above all, to ensure the social justice of equitable tax burdens and equitable access to income, wealth, public goods and a fulfilling social existence.

The four chapters in the final part examine a variety of options for recast-ing taxation policy, with a predominant focus on international tax governance and the harmonisation of national taxation. Paolo Ermano provides a theo-retical defence of the principles of progressive taxation in his examination of the debates surrounding the relationship between efficiency and equity and the limitations of neoclassical accounts of optimal systems of taxation. Ermano proposes a different approach to taxation which allows us to focus more adequately on equity and liberty issues. He consequently widens his analysis to include theoretical features of the labour market and social inclusion. In particular, apart from the impact of recessions on government finances, one of the most problematic aspects of many political economies is the failure of market systems to provide certain individuals with jobs that fulfil their personal aspirations, notwithstanding that they demonstrate specific abilities in non-market sectors that are important ingredients for our social and political life. Ermano concludes that, for this group of individuals only a strong redistributive policy based on greater progressivity in direct taxation can permit them to invest their resources without being excluded from economic life. Furthermore, this enhanced progressivity would also act as an automatic stabilizer against economic shocks.

Douglas Bamford's chapter – on comprehensive lifetime taxation, tax avoidance and international citizens – presents a proposal for a new form of international taxation. The proposal is a holistic response and, in the context of the recorded failures outlined in other chapters, revolutionary in nature. The focus of the proposal is on the comprehensive income of individuals rather than numerous disjointed taxes. The system proposes to determine the tax rate for individuals based on their *proportional economic allegiance* to different states and the tax rates they would face within each state. It would then share out the tax collected for the individual to states, according to both their allegiance and the level of taxation in those states. This would require the creation of a World Tax Organisation to administer the information and payments required. The proposal is presented here as a solution to the problem of international tax competition and avoidance. Comprehensive taxes being unavoidable, a weighting element in the calculation provides a counterincentive to race-to-the-bottom tax competition. The author suggests many further advantages to this proposal, such as the implementation of fair internation and inter-individual taxation and compensation for brain drain. The proposal respects the constraints placed on any international tax regime; to allow states to set their own tax rates, and to enable an efficient world economy.

The penultimate chapter by Dries Lesage and Yusuf Kaçar addresses the model of country-by-country reporting (CBCR), first proposed by Richard Murphy of the Tax Justice Network and currently being actively considered by several bodies, in particular by the European Union, the OECD, the IMF and the World Bank. CBCR aims to establish a new duty on the part of multinational corporations, whereby, in their annual public financial statements, they would have to record the company names under which the group operates; total sales, purchases and financial costs, split between third parties and intra-group transactions; total labour costs and employee numbers; pre-tax profits, and related further details. Correct compliance with this new reporting duty would be enhanced by the obligation for the firms' accountants and auditors to deliver correct data and by the threat of prosecution and sizeable fines in cases of fraud. Lesage and Kaçar describe a 'remarkable' and 'successful' journey for the idea of CBCR and suggest that its realisation, in the wake of the global financial crisis and the sovereign debt crisis, is perfectly feasible. The current breadth of support for the proposal among European states and within the US administration would seem to indicate that it might make meaningful progress, improving the chances of countering the malign influence of low-tax jurisdictions and tax competition.

The final contribution by Margit Schratzenstaller – 'International Taxes – Why, What and How?' – seeks to summarise the current state of the political discussion on international taxes and to provide a theoretical basis for that discussion. After defining and clarifying the concept of international taxes, Schratzenstaller presents the most important theoretical arguments and the factors that support their implementation. She then establishes a catalogue of criteria for identifying tax bases and those activities which appear to be particularly suited to internationally organised taxation. The chapter also provides an overview of the most important suggestions for international taxes brought forward in the ongoing political discussion and their rationale, and we try to identify relevant economic effects of these taxes.

While the likelihood of the successful introduction of some kind of Tobin tax may have receded since the outbreak of the global economic crisis – in contrast to CBCR – there remains a strong body of international opinion that would favour such an innovation, in particular if the revenue raised were to be deployed to promote the modernisation of economic infrastructures and governance in the developing world. It is hoped that the contributions to this volume will help to advance the case for a reform of national and international systems of taxation that are rooted in a commitment to peace and social justice. The recent global crisis illustrates above all the degree to which the citizens of this fragile planet are bound within an interdependent and dynamic political economy. It provides us with an ideal opportunity to reflect on the current chronic asymmetries of that political economy and on the corresponding need to ensure that we bequeath future generations a more equitable, more just and sustainable framework of existence.

Notes

1. Henry VIII's 1535 tax on beards was graduated according to wealth, in contrast to the unitary beard tax imposed by Peter 1 in Russia in 1705.
2. Thomas Paine's description of the specific development of British sovereign power

and the origins of its government in *The Rights of Man* (2009 [1791], Chapter 2) is frequently peddled as a call to arms by conservative critics of the welfare state, as a cursory trawl of the internet demonstrates. Perversely, Paine's argument against arbitrary monarchy was intended to justify the introduction of representative government with legitimate powers to tax, albeit modestly (ibid., Chapter Three).

PART I

Taxation, Tax Culture and Taxation Reform in European Countries

CHAPTER I

Dismantling Slasher Osborne

Why Britain Needs Tax Reform, not Cuts

GEORGE IRVIN

Writing in *The Guardian*, George Monbiot has bemoaned the fact that the TUC and other organisers of the anti-cuts demonstration on 26 March 2011 failed to spell out a succinct alternative (Monbiot 2011). That's not quite true. A myriad of books, pamphlets and journalistic articles have been written about how the financial crisis became a recession and setting out alternatives to Osborne's vicious wielding of the budgetary axe.[1] Below, I elaborate on these alternatives once more. The main points can be summarised as follows:

- Rebutting 'handbag economics' is not difficult; crucially, the notion of the 'structural budget deficit' is highly misleading; the UK's debt/GDP ratio (60 per cent) is one of the lowest in the OECD and, of course, we are nothing like Greece.
- UK inequality is serious: the social costs of inequality are well known and cuts will make inequality worse. The burden of Osborne's cuts is borne by the poorest.
- Total taxation is itself now regressive; greater weight falls on the poorest. Remember that 'Mandelson [was] relaxed as long as [the rich paid] their taxes' but the rich don't pay their fair share.
- There is plenty of 'slack' in the UK tax system – both for more revenue and for greater progressiveness! We show how reform of the tax system could bring in an extra £45bn each year, avoiding the need for any social service cuts.

Handbag Economics and the Structural Deficit

Margaret Thatcher famously preached what is sometimes called 'handbag economics': the notion that the nation's finances work exactly like that of the housewife, that the nation's budget must balance and that public borrowing is a bad thing. This view is, of course, nonsense. But it has become part of the conventional wisdom and, thanks to a largely conservative media, has had a stranglehold on the public.

We are nothing like Greece since we can devalue sterling, nor was there ever any significant chance of being unable to place our bonds. Most UK government bonds are held by the British private sector (for whom they are assets), the 10-year benchmark bond rate has remained low and, even after the banking crisis, our debt-to-GDP ratio has remained around 60 per cent, lower than even Germany or France. The only danger perceived by the City was that there might be a run on sterling. Because many of our banks hold liabilities in the Euro-dollar (Euro-yen or whatever) market, the City would suffer from a weaker pound.

In 2010, I co-authored a Compass pamphlet called *The £100bn Gamble: On Growth without the State*.[2] Our main argument was two-fold: first, Osborne's cuts were far too large and entirely without serious justification; secondly, they wouldn't work. Britain's problems, both in 2011 and at the time of writing the pamphlet, can be characterised thus: while domestic private savings at present are (once again) positive, domestic public savings are negative (the budget is in deficit) while foreign savings (the current account deficit) are high. So if both the government and current accounts are to move to zero, as Osborne wishes, export growth must recover strongly and private investment must shoot up by 2015 to match the pool of domestic private savings.

Consider the current (external) account. By 2015, Osborne forecasts that the overseas trade deficit will have shrunk to near zero (i.e., foreign savings will be negligible). For the period from the beginning of 2011 to the end of 2015, exports are assumed to grow by 33 per cent and imports by only 18 per cent. The forecast for the current account in 2015 is the most favourable since 1983. This is totally at odds with the current trend. In the past decade, imports have grown faster than exports. Moreover, despite a nominal devaluation of 23 per cent since 2008, export growth in 2010 was still negligible.

Next consider domestic savings. With the budget assumed to be in balance by 2015, government savings are zero. Household savings decline somewhat as a percentage of GDP. Although corporate savings do not appear explicitly, these can be calculated and their GDP share is seen to fall by about 10 per cent. Such a result is important since corporate savings are such a large proportion of total domestic savings. But corporations have been busy 'deleveraging'; i.e., rebuilding savings. In reality, it is difficult to see why corporate savings would fall for the period in question.

Crucially, it will be seen that investment is assumed to rise by 44 per cent between 2011 and 2015. UK gross investment (including public investment) at present is slightly less than 14 per cent of GDP, sufficient to maintain the capital stock intact but insufficient for strong growth. The Treasury assumes that it will reach over 19 per cent of GDP by 2015. This is higher than at any time in the past decade, and is to be achieved despite cuts in public sector investment. The resulting annual GDP growth rate forecast for the period 2011–2015 is 2.7 per cent, higher than the underlying trend growth rate in the past decade.

In summary, if private investment does not grow as rapidly as forecast, if export growth does not quickly outpace that of imports and if domestic savings do not fall enough, it will not be possible to balance the budget. This is not a matter of conjecture but of national accounting definitions.

I (and lots of others) said this a year ago. Since then, GDP has actually fallen in the final quarter of 2010 and is expected to be stagnant in much of 2011 and probably beyond. The current account position has hardly improved and, crucially, total gross fixed capital formation has remained at about 13 per cent of GDP, far below the level on which Osborne's Treasury forecasts are predicated. It is becoming increasingly obvious that the cuts, far from helping the economy, are harming it. And of course, the 'economy' is not some abstract textbook concept – it is all about the jobs and welfare of ordinary people. It is those people who are now starting to suffer – and they will suffer far more as the cuts begin to bite in 2011–12.

The reader should notice something else too: the so-called 'structural' deficit. Not only can one argue that the budget is being balanced too quickly, one can make the far stronger point that the deficit is mainly cyclical and that the notion of reducing the 'structural' component is highly misleading. Why? A 'structural' deficit is defined as one not associated with recession. And here is the key point. The view that the budget gap is mainly structural – as opposed to cyclical – has allowed Mr Osborne to argue that it was Labour's spending, not the recession, which 'caused' the budget gap. In the words of Robert Chote, then Director of the Institute of Fiscal Studies (IFS) and main author of their 2009 Green Budget:

> Labour entered the current crisis with one of the largest structural budget deficits in the industrial world and a bigger debt than most OECD countries, having done less to reduce debt and – in particular – borrowing than most since 1997.[3]

It should be added that the IFS, though often characterised in the media as one of Britain's most influential independent think tanks, played a key role in promoting the notion that Britain's structural deficit had grown far too large. The Office of Budget Responsibility (OBR), initially under Alan Budd but currently under Chote, has peddled the same argument.[4] But the most pessimistic view of all has come from the Treasury, which has argued that the structural deficit accounts for as much as two-thirds of the total deficit (cited in Webb 2010).

What is the difference between the so-called 'cyclical' and 'structural' components of the deficit? During a downswing in the business cycle, tax receipts fall and social spending on items such as unemployment benefit increases, thus giving rise to the so-called cyclical component of the deficit. This component is self-liquidating since the opposite happens during the business cycle upswing. So the budget should balance over the cycle as a whole unless – and this is the crux of the matter – there is a further 'structural deficit'; i.e., a gap between current receipts and revenue which remains even when the economy returns to growth with full employment.

At this point, the argument gets a bit more complicated. During a run-of-the-mill recession, the economy may turn down for a period but soon recovers its previous path – the so-called 'potential output' path. In a serious and prolonged downturn such as the one we are experiencing in Britain, part of the country's productive capacity is lost forever, thus permanently shrinking the tax base and reducing the employment and output potential. When this happens, economists have serious difficulty predicting both by *how much* potential output has fallen, and *how long* it will take to get back to the (now lower) full-employment non-inflationary growth path, sometimes abbreviated as NAIRU. Moreover, the story is even more complicated if any external inflationary pressure exists since it is claimed the non-accelerating rate of unemployment (NAIRU) may be higher than that which prevailed before the recession. For example, the Treasury and the OBR differ in their respective forecasts of the 'recovery' rates of growth the UK will experience between now and 2015. And on the Monetary Policy Committee (MPC), Andrew Sentance has recently argued that firmer action must be taken to combat the inflationary danger, *inter alia*, because the gap between current output and potential output, or the output gap, may be smaller than we think.[5]

Nevertheless, there are serious reasons for believing that the notions of structural deficit, output gap, and NAIRU are all quite shaky.

Firstly, NAIRU is notoriously difficult to quantify, particularly at present when inflation is largely imported and wage pressure on prices is negligible.

Secondly, how large is the output gap? If the pre-2008 trend-line for output is taken as the reference point, the gap measured as a share of GDP is currently 11 per cent. But the Treasury now thinks that 6.5 per cent of GDP has been permanently lost, leaving the (reduced) output gap at 4.5 per cent. If Britain's output, employment and tax base has shrunk that much, it helps explain why the Treasury believes that two-thirds of Britain's deficit is now structural; i.e., the reduction in full capacity output means that Britain can no longer 'afford' to spend as much as it could in 'normal' times.

Thirdly, the budget gap (or 'government savings') cannot be separated analytically speaking from the other national accounting savings identities. For simplicity, assume that the external current account remains constant – in reality, a tenable assumption. For a given level of national income, if the private sector decides to save more (say in order to rebuild its savings), the public sector must spend more by definition. In short, policy makers lack the autonomy to reduce public spending without having an impact on other variables – in particular, the level of national income (as the Irish and Greek cases clearly demonstrate). Fourthly, the structural deficit argument depends on assuming a fixed structure of revenue. But the tax-revenue response to each percentage point rise in income is not carved in stone; it can be changed through tax reform. In 2010, another study undertaken for Compass indicated that nearly an extra £50bn per annum in tax (about 4 per cent of GDP) could be raised merely by raising the tax paid by the top decile group whose overall percentage tax contribution is currently smaller than that of the bottom 10 per cent of households. Indeed, a worldwide Tobin tax of only 0.05 per cent on sterling transactions would bring in even more.[6]

Finally, the obvious rejoinder to the argument that the structural deficit is higher because potential output (and output gap) is now lower is to call for more public investment directed towards increasing the economy's output potential. Such investment – say in modernising infrastructure – would have two effects. It would both help to 'crowd in' private investment while, through the multiplier effect, raising national income and employment and thus tax receipts.

Chris Dillow, a columnist for the *Investors' Chronicle*, has summed up the case against the structural deficit concept admirably. As he argues, there are some countries with large structural deficits but low debt-to-GDP ratios in which the bond markets still have confidence, while there are others with much smaller structural deficits which the bond markets have turned against:

I fear, then, that the idea of a structural deficit serves a political rather than analytical function. It is a pseudo-scientific concept which serves to legitimate what is in fact a pure judgment call – that borrowing needs cutting. By all means, make this call. Just don't think that talk of a structural deficit helps enlighten us. (Dillow 2010)

So much for the budget-cutting rationale!

Towards a More Unequal Britain

Much has been written about the social costs of inequality, particularly by academics such as Michael Marmot and, perhaps best-known, Richard Wilkinson and Kate Pickett.[7] What these academics have shown is that it is not just absolute poverty that matters but rather the degree of inequality.

The next point on the agenda, one which will have escaped few people's notice, is that the weight of the government's fiscal consolidation package will fall disproportionately on the poor. Britain's income distribution is already one of the least equal amongst the OECD countries. The most familiar measure of inequality is the Gini coefficient (the smaller the coefficient, the more equal the country). The left-hand side of Figure 1.1 shows how inequality has grown in Britain over the period 1979–2008, while the right-hand side shows recent Gini values for major countries:

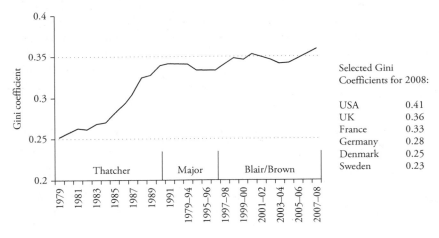

Figure 1.1 Rise of Income Inequality in UK and Selected Gini Coefficients for 2008
Note: The Gini coefficient has been calculated using incomes before housing costs have been deducted.
Sources:
Authors' calculations using Family Expenditure Survey and Family Resources Survey, various years.
Hills, Brewer et al. (2010)

As one would expect, although income distribution in the UK is somewhat more equal than in the USA, it is less equal than in Germany and France and much less equal than that in the Nordic countries. It is worth noting that in the 1960s and 1970s, the income Gini in Britain was about 0.25. Britain's inequality has thus become structurally ingrained (Dorling 2010).

The distributional impact of the Osborne cuts and the VAT rise has been discussed in various publications, and almost all agree that the impact is regressive. Here we look at the Horton and Reed estimate of the combined effect of a £48bn cut in public services and an £18bn cut in tax/welfare benefits for the period 2011–2015. The effects of the 2011 VAT rise are not included, but these are also regressive when measured as a proportion of income. The above £64bn in cuts are regressive both in that they have a greater proportional impact on the poorest households than on the richest, and equally because they hit women far harder than men. Figure 1.2 shows the estimated impact on the income of different decile groups starting (on the left) with the poorest.

In the words of the authors:

> The regressive nature of [Spending Review] SR2010 is exacerbated by three factors. First, the Coalition government has relied more heavily on spending cuts than tax increases to address the fiscal deficit. Second, the tax and benefit changes which have been announced as part of the deficit reduction package are also regressive overall, albeit to a lesser extent than the cuts in public services. Finally, social care and social housing – which are the two areas of public services spending which are most heavily weighted towards the poorest households – have suffered particularly deep cuts which make the distributional effects of the overall package more regressive than if cuts had been applied more evenly across the board. (Horton and Reed 2010a; 2010b)[8]

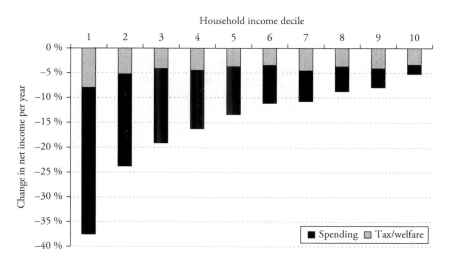

Figure 1.2 Overall Impact of Fiscal Consolidation: Spending Cuts and Tax/Welfare Measures
Source: Horton & Reed (2010b: 9)

Moreover, the authors argue that the impact of the cuts is proportionately greater for families with children (who lose child benefits) and pensioners (who are highly dependent on social services) as well as for certain regions of the country dependent on public sector jobs (e.g., the West Midlands). Finally, fiscal consolidation will hurt women more than men. For example, the TUC is concerned that as women represent 65 per cent of the public sector workforce, they will bear the brunt of the estimated 400,000 public sector job losses over the next four years.[9]

Although major academic economists, from Robert Skidelsky to Joseph Stiglitz, have warned about the consequences of Osborne's reckless gamble, it is only now that the results of the 2010 Spending Review and subsequent emergency budget are beginning to bite that one can begin to appreciate the irreversible nature of the deed. It was David Blanchflower who put it most succinctly in *The Guardian* on 18 October 2010: 'The austerity package is likely to turn out to be the greatest macro-economic mistake in a century'. Osborne has pursued his goal of emasculating the welfare state with unswerving determination and ruthlessness. According to a YouGov poll, nearly half the electorate believe that the last Labour government was responsible for Britain's current economic plights – less than one-fifth blame the Coalition. Cameron et al. have endlessly chanted the mantra of Labour's irresponsible spending as the cause of the crisis, which flies in the face of everything we know about the origins of the banking collapse, the OECD-wide recession following the credit crunch and the collapse of Britain's fiscal balance, which until 2008 had been reasonable.

The Coalition's message may be totally at odds with most economists' take on the need to react to an economic slump by stimulating aggregate demand, but Osborne has capitalised on the widespread belief that when times are bad, everybody – starting with government – must tighten their belts. The Tories have put right-wing Liberal Democrats like Nick Clegg and Danny Alexander in key positions, marginalised Vince Cable and kept out the rest. It has been an object lesson in the *realpolitik* of the Thatcherite legacy.

It is often argued that the cuts are unnecessary – that they conceal the true Tory agenda, that of shrinking the welfare state and reversing the post-war social democratic settlement. Ironically, although this argument was set out in Parliament by Harriet Harman, successive New Labour governments since 1997 have been deeply complicit in this agenda.[10]

The National Health Service in Britain provides an excellent example of 'privatisation from the inside', a process by which health provision, while retaining the outward appearance of a publicly funded service, is gradually turned over to private sector firms from any member-state to be run on a 'for profit' basis. New Labour (1997–2010), far from reversing John Major's introduction of a pseudo-market in health care (the so-called internal market), sped up the process, decentralising the National Health Service (NHS) and reorganising hospitals into regionally based 'primary care trusts' (PCTs) while 'contracting in' everything from managers to cleaning services. At present, the Conservative/Liberal Democrat coalition in Britain is in the process of abolishing the Primary Care Trusts and handing over their funds to general practitioners (GPs), who in turn will be free to hand on management operations to private conglomerates, often headed by US-style Health Maintenance Organisations (HMOs). In the words of the *Guardian* columnist, Polly Toynbee:

> GPs are camouflage for the true Cameron revolution. Consortiums must now commission services from 'any willing provider'. Naive GPs who fondly imagine they can choose where to send patients may get a nasty shock. Monitor, whose role was limited to scrutinising foundation hospitals, has been re-born as a regulator whose first task is 'to promote competition'. For the first time the NHS is opened to EU competition law. If a consortium keeps a relationship with a trusted local hospital, it may find itself challenged in court by any private company claiming the right to outbid. Neither GPs nor patients will control who is treated where: the law will decide. (Toynbee 2011)

Much the same can be said of the financial services industry. When, famously, Northern Rock was taken under UK government control in 2008 after the housing bubble burst, the new publicly owned company was prevented from offering cheap mortgages to stricken households on the grounds that to do so would constitute 'unfair competition' with the private sector.

One can also cite the example of state pensions in which the squeeze on government budgets has been used as a reason for either reducing pension provision, increasing the pensionable age, or both. French street protests in 2010 provide a good example of just how volatile an issue pension entitlement has become. But neoliberal logic dictates that we can 'no longer afford' generous pensions, and thus that entitlements must be reduced – or more precisely, that individual responsibility must replace state responsibility as far as possible.

Or again, take higher education. Budgetary austerity has been cited as the reason for raising the cap on university fees from £3,000 per annum to £9,000 per annum. It is argued that such increased fees, particularly when repaid over a number of years, are justified because university education provides access to higher future income for graduates. What is notable is that the notion of 'public good' – i.e., that access to higher education should be available to all as a matter of principle – has been replaced by the instrumental notion of education as a means of promoting economic efficiency and faster growth.

There is a real sense in which Labour shares the blame for all this. For a decade Brown boasted of his 'fiscal prudence', attempting to offset what New Labour perceived as the damaging legacy of its tax-and-spend image. The Brown/Darling response to the credit crunch was as Friedmanite as it was Keynesian, while the economic downturn which followed produced a puny stimulus package. Earlier this year, Alistair Darling caved in to the IFS-led chorus of deficit-cutters and proposed cuts 'deeper than Thatcher'. Nor does the change in leadership appear to have radicalised Labour; within the shadow cabinet the row continues over the proportion of spending cuts and tax rises in Labour's own deficit reduction plan.

In truth, the economic crisis presented both Labour and the Tories with an opportunity for radical change – an opportunity which Labour squandered and which the Tories were quick to capitalise on. If Labour had been the party of social democracy, it would have taken the bailed-out banking sector into genuine public ownership, reintroduced mutualisation, thoroughly reformed the tax system using the proceeds for publicly led investment in sustainable growth, and reversed the creeping privatisation of public services. In Brussels, Britain would have called for an EU-wide stimulus package and backed improved economic governance and better financial regulation.

The single-mindedness with which the Tories have capitalised on the crisis to drive through draconian measures stands in stark contrast to Labour's inability to seize the moment. In a decade's time, history may judge Osborne's cuts with the same disdain as it does the poll tax and similar Thatcherite policies. But by then it will be too late – Slasher Osborne will have killed the welfare state.

Double-dip?

As if the cuts were not enough, pressure is building for the Bank of England to tighten monetary policy in order to combat the 'danger' of rising inflation. However circumspect Mervyn King may be about raising interest rates in the Bank of England's (BoE) quarterly inflation report issued in February 2011, it is clear that the City wants him to do so. Indeed, judging from the fact that twelve-month interest rate futures are now 1.4 per cent, it is generally thought that there will be three to four quarter-point hikes over the next twelve months, while over the coming two years the rise may be twice that figure. One must ask, first of all, is such a rise justified by inflation; and secondly, if not, what damage will raising UK interest rates do?

The proximate cause of the problem is that the Retail Price Index (RPI) has jumped to just over 5 per cent in the UK, mainly reflecting rising world food and energy prices, but also the effect of a sterling devaluation of over 20

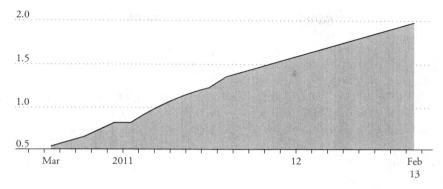

Figure 1.3 Expectations for UK Bank Rate (Per Cent)
Source: N. Cohen, 'King denies interest rate rise certainty', *FT*, 16 February 2011

per cent in 2008 working its way through the economy, as well as the VAT rise in January 2011. Even the Consumer Price Index (CPI), which strips out housing costs, stands at nearly 4 per cent, above the BoE's 2 per cent target.

Of course, stripping out food and energy, core inflation is well below the BoE's target, but inflation hawks would argue that several other factors must be taken into consideration. First, inflation is rising not just in the UK but in the US and the core Eurozone countries such as Germany and France, in part reflecting strong inflationary pressures in countries such as China and Brazil. Secondly, UK firms may be raising prices to recoup the profits lost during the credit squeeze, or even in anticipation of lower future profits. Finally, the fact that the recession has pulled down UK trend growth means that the weight of the structural deficit is all the greater; i.e., a return to (lower) trend growth would leave a larger proportional gap between public spending and receipts than would have been the case before the recession. On this view, the larger the structural deficit, the higher are domestic inflationary expectations.

The counter-argument goes roughly as follows. First of all, the main domestic culprits – devaluation and the VAT rise – are once-and-for-all events, so their inflationary impact can be expected to decline over time. Secondly, with regard to the key imported components, mainly food and energy, it is not so much a case of gradual price inflation; rather, these prices have exhibited strong fluctuations. Energy prices peaked in 2008, then fell and have now risen again; there is every reason to believe that they will fall again. And even if imported inflation continues to rise, raising domestic interest rates will not seriously arrest this rise. Thirdly, there is no sign of wage inflation in the UK economy – indeed, with unemployment at 2.5 million and rising, real wages are falling. Moreover, with the bulk of government spending cuts still in the pipeline, unemployment will rise (and real wages fall) further. This being the case, 'inflationary expectations' are groundless. As one academic colleague put it, 'there has been no Phillips curve [expectations augmented or otherwise] in the UK for a generation'.[11]

Little wonder then that Mervyn King, governor of the Bank of England, was being circumspect about raising interest rates when the prospects for UK growth are so poor and their impact on inflation was likely to be negligible. Nevertheless, it is equally clear that George Osborne wants higher rates and that the MPC, which has been dovish on the matter, is now split and edging towards hawkishness (Blanchflower 2011). Such hawkishness will come at a cost; in the words of one commentator writing for the *Financial Times*:

> [C]harts in the Inflation Report suggest the Bank now believes the UK economy must grow by about 0.25 percentage points less than it thought in November [2010] to avoid sparking inflation. That is a loss to economic output which accumulates by roughly an additional £4bn every year, making fiscal consolidation even more difficult. (Giles 2011)

Indeed, such a loss would come on top of the cuts. A recent report by the IMF suggests that, even if interest rates remain near zero, public sector cuts equivalent to 1.5 per cent of GDP per annum over the next four years will subtract an equivalent amount from growth, or about £20bn every year (Weldon 2011).

According to the IFS Green Budget, between 2010 and 2015, the UK is forecast to have the third largest reduction (behind Ireland and Iceland) in the share of government borrowing in national income among twenty-nine high-income countries (Brewer et al. 2011). As Martin Wolf has noted, using the OBR's latest figures, the implicit (compound) rate of growth of GDP between 2007 and 2015 is just 1.2 per cent per annum (Wolf 2011). And if interest rates rise in response to a perceived inflationary threat, the growth rate will be even less. In a word, Britain, under the Tory-led government, faces years of not merely stagnation, but quite possibly of something worse: stagflation.

The Alternative: Tax Reform and Investment for Growth

Unlike the US, the overall incidence of direct and indirect tax on gross income in the UK is regressive – i.e., the poorest 10 per cent pay a higher proportion of their income in tax than the richest 10 per cent – a state of affairs which even Adam Smith would have abhorred.

Table 1.1 is based on the work of Byrne and Ruane (2008) showing the effective incidence of both direct and indirect personal taxation on (standard-

Table 1.1 Effective Household Total Tax Incidence by Decile, 2008

Decile Group	Effective Tax Rate	Post-tax Income (£/annum)
Poorest	46.1%	£4,891
2nd	33.7%	£9,033
3rd	32.9%	£11,294
4th	33.0%	£13,635
5th	34.6%	£16,858
6th	35.1%	£19,435
7th	36.6%	£23,538
8th	36.7%	£28,313
9th	36.0%	£34,961
Richest	34.2%	£62,243

Source: Byrne and Ruane 2008: Table 2

ised) household income. It will be noted that the richest (10th) decile group pays an effective rate of just over 34 per cent, a figure considerably lower than the rate of 46 per cent paid by the poorest (1st) decile group. Were the data for the richest decile further disaggregated into percentile groups, the degree of regressiveness would be even more striking since the higher up the income pyramid one goes, the lower the percentage of income paid as tax. Two factors help explain this regressive incidence; first, the proportion of indirect tax in the total paid (VAT, NIC, council tax) has risen; secondly, the rich have got very much richer. Crucially, the Byrne and Ruane study does not look at the degree to which tax avoidance affects tax receipts from the upper end of the distribution.[12]

The 'tax gap' in Britain has been analysed *inter alia* in Irvin, Byrne et al. (2009). The regressive nature of overall household tax incidence is detrimental to the economy in a number of ways. For one thing, it promotes and sustains inequality. For example in Britain, although Labour since 1997 has attempted to lift the very poorest out of poverty with some degree of success – notably in reducing its incidence amongst groups most at risk such as the pensioners and children – income inequality has not declined largely because the top of the richest decile has seen its income rise, particularly the 'super-rich'.

Moreover, a regressive tax incidence hampers the operation of fiscal stabilisers since, in good times, 'tax buoyancy' will be low; i.e., tax revenue will not increase as quickly as it otherwise would were taxation more progressive, thus making it harder for government to 'save for the bad times'. Most importantly, in the upswing real wages and thus aggregate consumer demand grow more slowly, making growth increasingly dependent on an unsustainable expansion in credit.

While it has become standard practice for economists to suggest that the widening gap between the 'haves' and 'have-nots' can be explained by the rise

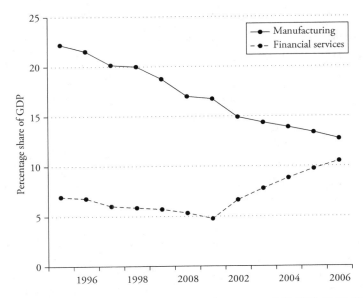

Figure 1.4 Changing Shares of Manufacturing and Finance in UK GDP, 1996–2006
Source: Lansley 2008: 15

of the knowledge economy and the higher premium attached to high levels of skill and education, this is far from being either a satisfactory or a comprehensive explanation. In practice, the rich have grown richer and Britain has become more unequal largely not because of any 'skill premium', but because of the country's changed occupational structure. Britain's workforce was once employed in industry where wages and benefits were protected by strong trade unions; it has been increasingly dispersed to low-wage, non-unionised employment in services. In the 1960s, nearly 40 per cent of GDP originated in industry, many times the share of financial services. Under Margaret Thatcher, industry declined – and financial services rose – and the trend continued under New Labour to such an extent that, today, their relative shares in output (and employment) are nearly equivalent, as shown in Figure 1.4.

Table 1.2 shows tax reforms and certain spending cuts that could be introduced to reduce the deficit in a way that is progressive.[13] Britain does not lack the capacity to reduce its deficit and a combination of cuts to unnecessary projects and tax rises could significantly reduce the deficit in the medium to long term, supplementary to growth. We outline below a set of alternative measures to those adopted by Osborne, which could help put Britain's finances back on the path not merely to growth, but to growth with greater fairness.

Table 1.2 Tax Reform

Reforms	Extra revenue pa (£ billion)
1. 50% income tax band at £100,000	2.3
2. Uncap NICs and make payable on investment income	9.1
3. Minimum income tax bands (40% 100K; 50% 150K)	14.9
4. Reintroduce 10p tax band and 22p basic rate	−11.5
5. Higher council tax bands	1.7
6. Abolish tax havens; tax 'non-doms'	10.0
7. Currency transactions tax (0.05% tax on sterling trades)	17.0
8. Bankers' bonus tax	2.0
TOTAL	45.5

Source: Irvin et al. 2009

First, the government could introduce a 50 per cent income tax band for gross incomes above £100,000. This reform introduces a new 50 per cent band of income tax for *taxable incomes* above £94,000 per year (approximately £100,000 a year gross income). This would raise £4.7 billion compared with the current (2009/10) tax system, or an extra £2.3 billion compared with introducing this band at £150,000 as proposed by the previous chancellor, a proposal that the Tories may well scrap.

Second, National Insurance Contributions (NICs) could be 'uncapped' so they are paid at 11 per cent all the way up the income scale (continuing to exempt pensioners). George Osborne proposes to increase NICs, but to retain their highly regressive character. Currently, employee NICs are payable at 11 per cent from £100 a week up to £884 per week – and at 1 per cent above this level, but self-employed NICs have an equivalent structure based on annual profits, paid at 8 per cent up to profits of £43,875 and then at 1 per cent above this. Also, unearned income (for example, income from investments and savings) is not subject to NICs. This reform removes the upper threshold so that employee NICs are payable at 11 per cent on all earnings above £884 per week for employees and at 8 per cent on all profits above £5,715 per year for the self-employed. Additionally, all investment income above £110 per week (or the annualised equivalent) is made liable to NICs at 11 per cent. This results in further revenue of £9.1 billion; thus uncapping NICs would rake in a great deal of money. It would turn NICs into a flat tax, making it 'merely regressive' rather than 'über regresssive'.

Third, the government could introduce minimum tax rates. This reform would introduce a lower limit to effective rates of income tax above certain levels of gross income, a principle suggested by the TUC in its 2008 report *The Missing Billions* (Murphy 2009a). As gross income approaches each threshold, the personal allowance and other forms of relief (for example, tax relief on pension contributions) are 'clawed back' at a high marginal rate until the average tax rate – as well as the marginal tax rate – on income above each threshold is equal to tax rates of 40 per cent and 50 per cent on incomes of above £100,000 and £150,000 respectively. Such a reform would raise an additional £14.9 billion.

Fourth, while reducing the deficit may be important in the long term, it is important that tax rises don't hit the poorest hardest – which is why we would introduce a special lower tax band of 10 per cent below the poverty line (below £13,500 per annum), while restoring the 'basic rate' to 22 per cent. This costs £11.5 billion, far less than the extra tax take outlined above.

Fifth, the tax payable (higher multipliers) for houses in council tax bands E to H should be raised. This would raise a further £4.2 billion.

Sixth, personal and corporate tax avoidance could be minimised by requiring tax havens to disclose information fully and changing the definition of 'tax residence'; these two reforms together are estimated minimally to yield £10 billion.

Seventh, a financial transactions tax (FTT) could be introduced at a rate of 0.05 per cent, applicable to all sterling transactions. This would raise minimally a further £4.2 billion – maximally, it would raise £34 billion, or about 2.5 per cent of UK GDP.[14] In the above table we split the difference and assume that such a tax would raise at least £17 billion per annum. Most of the major EU countries are favourable to such a tax, and on 18 July 2010 the head of the IMF, Dominique Strauss Kahn, announced he would back it.[15]

Eighth, reintroduce the Bankers' bonus tax introduced by Alistair Darling in 2009, which raised £2 billion.

We have not counted here various alternative cost-cutting measures such as scrapping Trident which we believe could save an additional £10–15bn per annum, raising the annual total to perhaps £60bn – or over 4 per cent of GDP. In any event, such extra revenues from tax reform would ensure that in the medium to long term there would be no need, if ever there was one, to cut public expenditure on essential services.

Conclusions

The bursting of the bubble in 2007–9 exposed the institutional fragility of the City, massively leveraged, over-exposed to risk and even to criminality in high places (c.f. Shaxson 2011). Despite government efforts to rescue the banks, contagion spread on a worldwide scale impacting on the real economy. Recovery from the economic downturn in the major industrial countries is at present faltering, and it seems probable that the UK (and possibly many of the major OECD countries) will enter into a period of prolonged stagnation.

While a return to the *status quo ante* should not be ruled out, recovery is unlikely to produce long-term growth unless a more active state role finds widespread political acceptance. This will be the responsibility of a Labour government, either in coalition or on its own. Not only will recovery need to be carefully managed by government, but so too will any prolonged period of growth in average living standards if the dangerous cycle of financial crisis is not to be repeated. At the heart of such a recovery need to be economic policies which foster high levels of education and innovation and which translate renewed growth into decent wages, not just for a few but for all.

A new welfare settlement in Britain – as important as that which followed the Second World War – will contain not just the promise of jobs and just rewards, but of better education for children, universal crèche provision, secure employment for the workforce, decent pensions for the old and an end to gender wage differentials. It will be based not on 'financial wealth creation' but on sustainable growth. Achieving this state of affairs need not entail reinventing the wheel, but it will entail the wholehearted adoption of a new model in which incomes policy, regulated credit and decentralised finance will play a crucial role.

Palley (2009) has rightly distinguished between 'narrow microeconomic' and 'broad macroeconomic' fixes. The former involve little more than improved financial regulation while the latter entail rethinking the changed nature of the growth model underlying the current crisis. This is not to say that improved financial regulation will not be a feature of the new welfare component; rather, it is but one of several components. The key building blocks of the new settlement are: (a) high wages; (b) new sustainable industrial growth, and (c) the provision of public goods.

The most important strategic change in government policy will be reversing the growth of super-rich rewards, re-establishing the link between productivity and wages growth. This will involve recognizing two things. First of all, the key to the distribution problem lies not just in shoring up the bottom of the income distribution but capping the top; i.e., not just tackling poverty but reversing inequality. Secondly, although tax reform is important, tackling inequality is not purely a matter allowing the free market to generate the wealth while using taxation to improve its distribution. Re-establishing a high wage economy depends crucially on industrial innovation; on developing the new processes and product lines underpinned by an industrial strategy (see Irvin 2010). The neoliberal notion that the state has no role to play in industrial strategy has been shown to be false in economies as diverse as France and Finland (Chang 2010). An important concomitant of a new industrial model will be a far stronger trade union movement. Indeed, part of the inequality story has been the casualisation of labour and the virtual exclusion of unions from any significant role in policy making. Higher minimum wages, better employment protection legislation and an end to gender differentials are doubtless part of the solution, but the crucial ingredient is a return to full employment. Employment cannot return to pre-recession levels without growth, and there cannot be growth unless current neoliberal policies to achieve immediate budget balance are jettisoned.

While it may be possible to reduce public borrowing through tax reform of the sort outlined above, the aim of government fiscal policy must be to use public investment to 'crowd in' private investment. Nor are candidates lacking: the renewal of public infrastructure, high-speed public transport, modernised hospitals and schools, new forms of sustainable energy generation, a major insulation programme for residential and commercial property – the list goes on and on.

To deal with climate change alone, the Stern Report of 2006 estimated that annual investment equivalent to 1 per cent of GDP would be required; his estimate has since doubled (Jowett and Wintour 2008). Such an investment-driven programme may not be 'shovel-ready', but a delayed resumption of sustainable growth is preferable to decades of possible stagnation implied by adhering to the strictures of the deficit hawks.

Above all, it is simply not true that the current financial crisis condemns us to lower public spending on better education, on affordable housing, on decent pensions and even on overseas aid. If anything, as a society grows richer, it requires more public goods, not fewer. The success of neoliberal economics over the past generation is very largely explained by a private consumption boom driven at different times by a financial bubble, a housing boom and negative net private savings. While increments in growth were distributed to the very wealthy leaving the working and middle classes increasingly hard-pressed, growth was maintained by what one writer has aptly described as 'private Keynesianism'; i.e., the switch from public to private spending as the motor of pump-priming (see Crouch 2008).

If that model has now imploded, it does not mean that we can no longer afford to finance public goods. It simply means that the motor of such provision must once again become the public sphere. Thomas Palley has summarized the current dilemma admirably:

> While the economics are clear, the politics are difficult, which partially explains the resistance to change on the part of policymakers and economists aligned with the neoliberal model. The neoliberal growth model has benefited the wealthy, while the model of global economic engagement has benefited large multinational corporations. That gives these powerful political interests, with their money and well-funded captive think tanks, an incentive to block change. (Palley 2009: 38)

In essence, achieving a new welfare settlement is not a matter of economic policy alone; it demands radical political change.

Notes

1. On the TUC's own home page are various links to sucking explanations of 'why the cuts are wrong'; e.g., <http://falseeconomy.org.uk> (accessed 14 August 2010); this includes short pieces by David Blanchflower, Christopher Pissarides, Paul Krugman, Sue Himmelweit, Joseph Stiglitz, Robert Skidelsky and others. Otherwise, there are a whole series of TUC Touchstone pamphlets dealing with various aspects of the economy.
2. See <http://www.compassonline.org.uk/publications/item.asp?d=3265> (accessed 16 August 2010); the other authors were Howard Reed and Zoe Gannon.
3. See <http://www.ifs.org.uk/publications/4623> (accessed 16 August 2010);
4. See <http://socialisteconomicbulletin.blogspot.com/2010/06/fake-independence-of-office-for-budget.html> (accessed 28 June 2010);
5. See <http://www.bankofengland.co.uk/publications/speeches/2011/speech476.pdf> (accessed 16 November 2011);
6. See <http://www.guardian.co.uk/commentisfree/2011/mar/02/deficit-cuts-banks-robin-hood-tax?> (accessed 3 March 2010);
7. On the 'Marmot Review' (*Fair Society, Healthy Lives*), see Ramesh (2010). Although Wilkinson has two excellent prior books, see Wilkinson and Pickett (2010) *The Spirit Level: Why Equality is Better for Everyone*, London: Penguin Books. My own review of the book can be found at <http://www.social-europe.eu /2010/08/the-spirit-level-political-wobble/> (accessed 19 November 2010).
8. Figure 1.2 and the quote are from Horton and Reed (2010b: 20–23); this source is more detailed and looks at the distributional impact of all the October 2010 budget cuts on disposable household income. For a discussion of the impact of the VAT rise, see Brown (2010).
9. See <http://www.tuc.org.uk/equality/tuc-18888-f0.cfm> (accessed 14 March 2011); also <http://www.social-urope.eu/2011/02/austerity-promotes-gender-hierarchies/> (accessed 5 March 2011).
10. See <http://www.bbc.co.uk/news/10377159> (accessed 16 October 2012).
11. In private correspondence with Martin Hoskins.
12. For work on this see Richard Murphy's work published in TUC (2008) in which it is estimated that personal and corporate tax avoidance together costs the UK Treasury some £25bn per annum. Also see Leigh (2009), an excellent series of investigative articles for *The Guardian* looking at tax avoidance schemes used by individuals and companies, and the resulting losses to the UK Treasury. Most recently see Shaxson (2011) cited below.
13. The tax discussion below is based largely on Irvin, Reed and Gannon (2010).
14. The lower estimate is Richard Murphy's; the higher is the author's. See Irvin (2009).
15. See <www.guardian.co.uk/business/2010/jul/18/tobin-taxfinancial-transactions> (accessed 18 July 2010).

CHAPTER 2

Social and Economic Aspects of Tax Policy in Germany

DIETER EISSEL

This chapter provides an overview of the development of tax policy in Germany, exploring the publicly stated logic behind official policy, but showing rather that the assertion of its positive function for growth and jobs was without any substance. The redistributive policy was not simply a flop economically but also contributed to a widening gap between rich and poor, and endangered the public sector's capacity to ensure future public investments – in the physical and social infrastructure, including education, and in sustainable energy – because of the increasing poverty of the central state as well as of the Länder (regional states) and municipalities. Thus, the two objectives of budgetary policy, which are focused on an efficient allocation of resources subject to a fair distribution of income and a stable macro-economic environment, were not realised.

Constitutional Allocation of Revenue

The German constitution (Basic Law) is quite specific in regard to issues of fiscal federalism. Separate articles of the Basic Law assign competency for legislation, for administration, for revenue-raising, and for expenditure to different levels of government. In general, legislative power lies at the federal level, administrative responsibility primarily at the Land level, and revenue-raising and expenditure powers are shared. The exclusive federal power to legislate on taxes is restricted to customs duties and fiscal monopolies (Article 105). The power to legislate on all taxes, the revenue from which is shared, is concurrent; in practice, this means that the Länder can use the Federal

Council (Bundesrat) as their vehicle for shaping federal tax legislation. The major feature of German revenue-raising arrangements is the constitutionally mandated sharing of tax revenues. All of the most important revenue sources are shared. Together, wage (PAYE) and assessed income taxes, corporation tax, and value added tax (VAT), make up about three-quarters of total tax revenue, and the proceeds of all these taxes are shared. While the Basic Law distinguishes between the right of each layer of government to legislate on specific taxes, and the right to appropriate the proceeds of taxes, in practice the two are tied together.

We must therefore bear in mind that Germany has a varied tax system guaranteeing the federal system of shared and separated public policies at each level based on the principle of connexity. This principle is designed to safeguard the independence of local authorities and the Länder governments from the federal level following the prescriptions of the Basic Law by providing enough financial means to maintain the stable funding of their distinct tasks.

In 2009 the federal level received 42.5 per cent of income tax revenues, 50 per cent of corporation tax revenues and, since 2007, about 55 per cent of all VAT. The regional states' share amounts to 42.5 per cent of income taxes, 50 per cent of corporation tax and 43 per cent of VAT. The local authorities receive 15 per cent of income tax revenues and currently 2.2 per cent of all VAT.[1] This share of revenue must take into account that municipalities, Länder and federal government have to meet specific challenges. For instance, since the last reform of Germany's federal system, the Länder have virtually sole responsibility for the organisation and funding of education, whereas the local level accounts for about two-thirds of all public investments. For the last ten years, the cities in particular complain about a widening gap between new legal obligations, like increased institutional care for children, on the one hand, and diminishing tax receipts and financial support on the other (see below).

Background: Shift from Keynesianism to Market Dogmatism

Because of the relatively generous system of social services, in the past Germany's tax rates on corporations, individuals, and goods and services were relatively high in comparison with other countries. However, far-reaching reforms have taken place since the 1980s, reaching their height during the period of the Red-Green governments (1998–2005), when tax relief measures in the spirit of supply-side theories were implemented (Leaman 2009).

The shift to neoliberalism in Germany can be explained by the rising influence of employers' organisations, the right-wing mass media, and a majority of economic advisers and political parties making use of the new

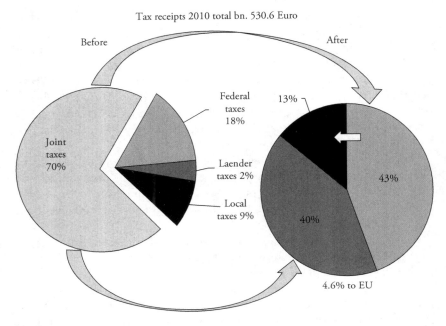

Tax receipts 2010 total bn. 530.6 Euro

Figure 2.1 Total Tax Receipts in Germany 2010
Source: Federal Statistical Office of Germany: Statistical Yearbook 2011: 574

uncertainties of global competition by urging governments to deregulate the existing labour market arrangements and to minimise the tax burden on profits. Additionally, trade unions were put under pressure to reduce wage costs. The growing dominance of this new economic philosophy was fuelled by a profound economic crisis of so-called Fordism (including mass production by assembly-line technology, high growth rates, rising wages, acceptance of trade unions, development of the welfare state and state interventionism in the spirit of Keynes). This crisis is rooted in the lower GDP growth rates in the early 1970s in most Western countries where record levels of supply in many market segments was confronted with a deceleration in the dynamic of post-war demand. This downward demand-side was worsened in the 1970s by the dramatic upsurge in oil prices in 1973–74. West Germany's GDP in 1975 fell by 1 per cent (in real terms), the first time since the founding of the FRG that it had fallen so sharply; it was accompanied by a rise in unemployment to more than one million people. The West German trade balance also fell as global demand declined and as the terms of trade deteriorated because of the rise in petroleum prices.

The price increases emanating from OPEC countries led to rapid breakdowns in consumption and intensified the so-called stagflation (stagnation with simultaneous inflation). The USA, as 'engine of the world economy', experienced additional inflationary effects through the Vietnam War. This wave of price increases, together with other factors, brought about the end of the so-called Bretton Woods system of fixed exchange rates. This in turn caused a change in economic policy, generating the first wave of a worldwide liberalisation of financial markets and confronting the nation states and export-oriented companies with the new situation: exchange rates were determined by the operations of free capital markets. The reaction of transnational corporations to fiercer global competition after the end of the post-war boom and to the new uncertainties of floating exchange rates, together with the assistance of the US government, brought about the end of Fordism.

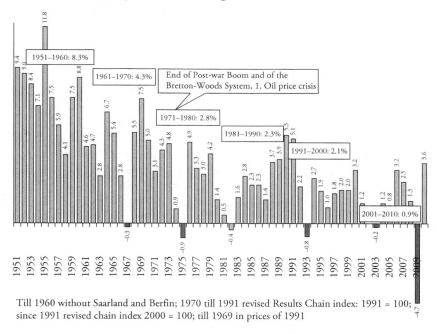

Till 1960 without Saarland and Berfin; 1970 till 1991 revised Results Chain index: 1991 = 100; since 1991 revised chain index 2000 = 100; till 1969 in prices of 1991

Figure 2.2 Economic Growth Rates in Germany, 1951–2009
Source: Statistical Office of Germany: Statistical Yearbook 2011: 630–31

This coincided with the rebirth of market dogmatism or the economic ideology of supply-sidism favoured by its idols like Milton Friedman (1962) and his Chicago school. Market-radical thinkers like Friedman and von Hayek have always either ignored or denied any threat to social cohesion and the resulting consequences for undisturbed economic growth. According to their view, freedom can only be secured through the limitation of the state to merely guaranteeing the free market order and stable prices and the liberation of economic dynamics. As early as 1944 Friedrich August von Hayek warned in his work *The Road to Serfdom* (Hayek 1944) against redistribution of the social product in the name of equality. Indeed, Hayek and others strictly demand that, in order to promote progress and economic growth, the rich should be treated moderately while the poor should not be supported. For Friedman, welfare systems are the worst type of state intervention, being a fraud at the expense of all those who still go to work and pay taxes. Progressive income taxation with the aim of redistributing income is, according to him, an imposition and diametrically opposed to personal freedom. From this perspective he advocates low proportional income tax (Friedman 1971: 207). From the perspective of market dogmatism, union wage demands in addition endanger any improvement in employment opportunities, even if these demands remain within the boundaries of neutral distribution provided by inflation and the development of productivity. Accordingly, Hayek rather sees inequality itself as an incentive for the poor to achieve more, with the luxurious lifestyle of the rich as a goal to which they can strive. If the rich are visibly better off than the poor, an 'evolutionary process' is set in motion, since the poor also wish to acquire riches. For this reason, tax burdens imposed on large fortunes are vehemently rejected as economically and socially senseless measures of redistribution. High rates of taxation are adjudged to paralyse the preparedness of individuals and businesses to invest, and hence hinder economic activity; furthermore they would produce a flight from taxation and into the black economy. The freeing of the principle of profit-maximisation as the individual impetus for wealth creation was thus supposed to take priority over any commitment by the state to satisfy the needs of the masses.

This message was received with considerable enthusiasm by governments. The Reagan administration as well as Thatcher in Britain and, in the end, German administrations, orientated their economic policy according to this supply-side advice, starting in the 1980s, with the result that state redistribution, mainly the effect of tax policy, favoured capital and produced a stagnation of wage income positions. Cutting back the welfare state, privatising public enterprises, deregulation and minimising production costs through wage and tax reductions were henceforth considered adequate strategies for surmounting the economic crisis caused by low GDP-rates and high unemployment.

The transnational corporations became the key economic actors after the mid 1980s, as they could obtain substantial cost savings through worldwide outsourcing. This produced a new dimension of globalisation, because TNCs were increasingly able to escape any form of political control. A purely national framework of taxation and also labour market regulation will invariably fail if the players assess the costs and risks as too high and instead take advantage of their 'exit' options. International institutions like the European Union (EU), the Organisation for Economic Cooperation and Development (OECD), the International Monetary Fund (IMF) and the World Trade Organisation (WTO) were weighty promoters of this process. Their measures have raised globalisation of the economy to new levels, which no nation state can ignore. Increased competition among companies and locations took place, exposing regions and even cities increasingly to the international economy, subjugating governments through the apparently neutral interplay of market forces and limiting increasingly the possibility for countries to develop their national economies independently. On the whole, the new politico-economic strategies since the mid 1970s have spurred world economic integration and the international division of labour. Market opportunities have increased, but competition is also growing. Therefore this form of economic globalisation highlights a shift of decision-making power from the state to the market, and from the welfare state to the 'competition' state.

Because of the worsening economic conditions, the conservative-liberal federal coalition which came to power with Chancellor Helmut Kohl in 1982 and governed for sixteen years, began to direct what was termed the 'turn-around' (*Wende*). The government proceeded to implement new policies to reduce its role in the economy, following neoliberal concepts. The broad policy included several main objectives: to reduce the federal deficit by cutting both expenditures and taxes, to reduce government restrictions and regulations, and to improve the flexibility of the labour market. Although the policies of this neoliberal turn-around or supply-side revolution changed the mood of the West German economy, the figures for growth and inflation improved only slowly; the average growth rate remained at 2.3 per cent in the 1980s, and the number of unemployed doubled to 2 million people. However, the daily brain-washing oriented towards supply-sidism was somehow successful. It persuaded the electorate that maintaining existing levels of tax on capital and relatively high wage levels would mean that capital would shun Germany and go to cheaper locations with ongoing harmful effects for employment security.

Tax Gifts for Capital

The political class in Germany pursued its neoliberal preferences, reflecting the demands of employers, and reduced taxes on income from capital and helped build an extensive low-wage sector, whilst the problem of a weak domestic market, stemming from stagnating wages over more than a decade, was neglected. It is a (sad) extraordinary truth that it was the Red-Green coalition which came to power in 1998 that was most effective in converting the supply-side strategy into practice. On the other hand the political orientation of the ruling SPD under Chancellor Schröder towards the centre and towards implementing the neoliberal strategy for solving Germany's economic problems had its price: the traditional support from trade unions was considerably weakened and this provided room to the left of the SPD left-side to strengthen the successor party to the Democratic Socialists, Die Linke (The Left), even in Germany's western states.

The top marginal rates on income tax in Germany, for most of post-war period up until the 1990s, had remained at 53 per cent or even before at 56 per cent. Since 1998 this top rate was reduced incrementally to 42 per cent (see Figure 2.3). Big businesses and trusts benefitted even more, because in the Schröder era their tax load was reduced by 20 percentage points, a trend that has persisted (Eissel 2008).

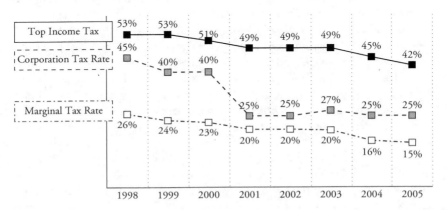

Figure 2.3 Tax Reductions in Germany 1998–2005
Source: Federal Ministry of Finance

In comparison to other EU member states Germany produced the highest level of tax relief on big business, namely of 27 percentage points (see Table 2.1).

Table 2.1 Changes in Top Statutory Tax Rate on Corporate Income, 1995–2011

Hungary	1.0	Luxembourg	−12.1
Finland	1.0	Portugal	−10.6
Sweden	−1.7	Greece	−20.0
France	−2.3	Italy	−20.8
Spain	−5.0	Czech Republic	−22.0
United Kingdom	−6.0	Poland	−21.0
Belgium	−6.2	Slovakia	−21.0
Austria	−9.0	Germany	−27.0
Denmark	−9.0	Ireland	−27.5
Netherlands	−10.0	*EU-27*	*−12.2*
USA	*−1.0*	Japan	−9.6

Source: European Commission 2011a: 130, 131

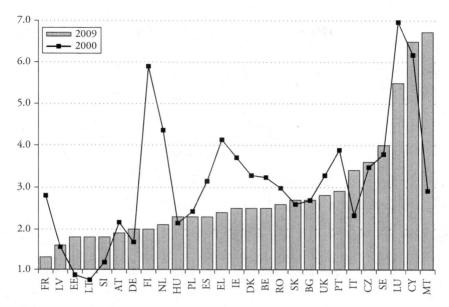

Figure 2.4 Share of Corporation Tax as Percentage of GDP, EU27, 2000–2009
Source: European Commission 2011a: 340

Germany's corporation tax ratio (as a percentage of GDP) was the lowest of all EU member states in 2009 at only 2.0 per cent.

This race to the bottom of taxation on profits was publicly announced as necessary to protect the competitive position of Germany as a location for global capital flows and to guarantee further investments in employment. Examining the results, the effects remained nevertheless poor.

There is empirical evidence that the top-down redistribution, favouring capital returns, was a flop. The so-called 'reforms' (which is a reinterpretation of the former positive meaning of the word) during the Schröder era had no clear positive effect on improving the sluggish economy. Low growth rates and high unemployment persisted, despite massive tax reductions for the better off and for companies.

From an economic perspective, the poor results are not surprising: faced with the stagnation of domestic private and public demand, entrepreneurs behaved as could have been expected: there was no obvious reason to increase capacity through investments to meet static demand. Furthermore, despite rising rates of return overall, investments in real capital yielded increasingly lower returns than financial investments. The alternative then was to use additional accumulated profits for speculative purposes (qua casino capitalism), which was ultimately one of the factors behind the current finance crisis.

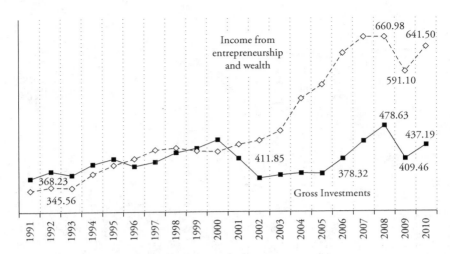

Figure 2.5 Profits and Investments in Germany, 1991–2010

Sources: SVR, Jahresgutachten 2009/2010; Federal Statistical Office, Statistical Yearbook 2011: 619

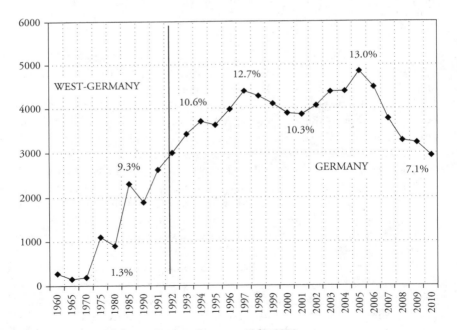

Figure 2.6 Unemployment Rates in Germany, 1960–2010

Source: Federal Statistical Office: Statistical Year Book 2009; 2011

So far, tax policy and redistribution favouring top incomes and incorporated businesses has clearly compounded the crisis. The German case shows that the government's tax gifts helped to increase the net returns of capital, but failed to encourage investments in jobs, favouring capital market investments instead. In 2006 Germany ranked second only to China in terms of capital exports to the US market with $169 billion or 5.8 per cent of GDP (China: $217 billion or 8.2 per cent of GDP), thus contributing significantly to the real estate bubble (see EEAG Report 2008 [Ifo-Institut 2008]; McKinsey Global Institute 2008).

Redistribution from Bottom to Top – The State's Contribution to a Widening Gap between Rich and Poor

With regard to different income groups, the benefits of the tax reform in the period 1998–2005 clearly indicate that millionaires were the great winners, whereas the mass income groups gained only marginally. Furthermore, in contrast to the objectives of the German welfare state and the traditional model of the social market, redistributive policy did not prevent a widening gap between rich and poor, which would have required more adequate social transfers and a corresponding tax policy.

Table 2.2 Tax Reductions in Germany, 1998–2005
Married Couple without Children

Yearly income in €	Benefits
20,000	590
30,000	1,563
50,000	2,305
100,000	4,178
1,000,000	102,500*

Source: Federal Minister of Finance, Monthly Report 12/2004, p. 57
*own calculation

As Müller-Armack, a German economist who had a strong influence on the conception of the social market economy, put it: 'Without doubt the market-economic formation of income leads to income differences which for us appear socially undesirable' (Müller-Armack 1947: 109). Therefore, he suggested that 'a direct income balancing between high and low incomes should be carried out through the direct diversion of income' (ibid.). This concept does not aim to provide an economic argument for redistribution, but what is important here is the question of social justice as the basis and the measure which can indicate how far the disadvantaged accept social capitalism or the social market economy as formulated by Müller-Armack and Ludwig Erhard. Erhard, in addition, insisted on wage growth reflecting the rise of productivity in real prices. Otherwise the supply-side would not match domestic demand (Erhard 1957: 211).

After the 1980s this 'social market' concept lost its weight and was replaced by a 'market' concept without the adjective social. The Gini-coefficient data, using the socioeconomic panel, clearly show rising inequality: from 1991 to 2007 the specific data for West Germany show a rise from 0.396 to 0.461 and in East Germany from 0.370 to 0.512 (SVR 2009: 313, Table 39).

Table 2.3 Change of Income* and Wealth** Positions of Households in Germany

	Adjusted equivalent market income of households; (new OECD scale)		Net income of households		Net wealth
	1991	2009	1991	2009	2007
1. decile	0.2	0.1	4.1	3.6	–1.6
2. decile	2.2	1.2	5.8	5.2	0
3. decile	4.7	2.8	6.8	6.3	0
4. decile	6.7	5.1	7.7	7.3	0.4
5. decile	8.3	7.2	8.5	8.2	1.2
6. decile	9.7	9.2	9.5	9.3	2.8
7. decile	11.5	11.3	10.6	10.3	6.0
8. decile	13.7	13.6	12.0	11.9	11.1
9. decile	17.0	17.7	17.3	14.2	19.0
10. decile	25.9	31.7	20.7	23.7	61.1

Sources: *SVR 2009: 316, Table 40; SVR 2011: 340, Table 32 – socioeconomic panel
** Frick and Grabka 2009: 54–67

The data specify that the lower half of all households in 2009 accounted for only 16.4 per cent of market income, whilst the top 10 per cent received 31.7 per cent. In comparison: in 1991 the lower 50 per cent of households shared 22.1 per cent and the top decile 25.9 per cent. Even after redistribution the disparity between the richest decile and the lower income groups has grown: the top decile gained 23.7 per cent of total net income in 2009 (1991: 20.7 per cent) whilst the lower half lost ground from 32.9 per cent to 30.6 per cent.

With regard to wealth, the development was even more unequal: in 2007 the top 10 per cent of income groups owned 61.1 per cent of all assets, an increase of 3.2 percentage points since 2002. The lower half of the income groups had more or less no property. Taxes on properties, inheritance and donations are nevertheless very low. In 2007 their contribution to total state revenue was only 2.5 per cent, less than half the OECD average of 5.7 per cent. Inevitably, Germany's increasing poverty had to be officially acknowledged. It affected predominantly jobless people, single parents (mostly mothers) and children. Following the two reports on 'Poverty and Wealth in

Germany' published by the federal government in 2001 (www.bmgs.bund.de) and in 2005 (www.bmas.bund.de), the number of those living under the poverty line was seen to have increased.[2]

On the other hand, not only private but additionally public poverty grew over this period, because the state forewent too much revenue, which enforced further cuts in the social security system. This led to increasing privatisation of former publicly run enterprises (like water works, local energy supplies and traffic systems), and worsened the state's ability to invest in future infrastructure (above all in education).

Table 2.4 Increasing Poverty* in Germany

Proportion of poor as a percentage of particular population groups

	1997	2007–2009
All	10.9	12.7
Men	10.2	11.9
Women	11.6	13.3
Children below 10 years	12.9	12.3
Single parent, one child	33.9	36.4
Married couples without children	7.2	6.8
Unemployed	30.6	53.3

*Poverty line 60 per cent median
Source: Federal Statistical Office 2006, 2011b

Following the neoliberal credo, the government reduced the tax burden on the rich and thus increased both private and public poverty. Because of lower state revenues, further state expenditure to safeguard the social net would have led to rising indebtedness, which on the other hand would contravene the Maastricht criteria. Under these conditions the political class looked for ways to cut social expenditure, being additionally under stress because of high unemployment and the exploding costs of the health system. The so-called Hartz reforms of the labour market (named after the commission chairperson) which aimed to increase the contribution ratio of insurees in the compulsory health insurance fund, were the outcomes of these efforts. One of the effects was that the low-wage sector in Germany grew to nearly a quarter of the total workforce.

Wage Earners and Mass Income Had to Foot the Bill

As already stated, it was the Red-Green coalition which initiated the massive reduction in tax burdens on capital income and the personal income tax of top earners. After 2005, when a grand coalition came to power, this anti-social trend continued. In the end the outlook for the state's capacity to act was perceived to be so endangered that the grand coalition (2005–2009) decided to raise VAT by 3 percentage points to boost revenue, even if both parties had promised during the election campaign not to do so. This promise reflected the acknowledgement that sales taxes have a regressive function because poorer families, having no savings, pay VAT on their total income/expenditure, whilst the rich have a relatively lower tax burden because of their savings.

Comparing the growth of revenue after reunification in 1990, 80.1 per cent of tax increases (1991–2009) are attributable to higher wage tax (PAYE) and VAT paid by the masses whilst taxes on profits were eased in relative terms.

Table 2.5 Tax Revenue in Germany, 1990–2010 by Category of Tax

Important Taxes 1990–2010 in € billions

	1991	*2000*	*2010*	*1991–2010*
Wage tax*	109.5	166.7	166.7	57.2
Assessed income tax	21.2	12.2	31.2	10.0
Corporation tax	16.2	23.6	12.0	-4.2
Taxes on capital gains**	5.8	20.8	13.0	7.2
Tax on industry and trade	21.1	27.0	35.7	14.6
Wealth tax	3.4	0.4	0	-3.4
Inheritance tax	1.3	3.0	4.4	3.1
VAT	91.9	140.9	136.5	44.6
Energy tax	24.2	37.8	46.0	21.8
Total receipts from taxes	338.4	467.3	530.6	192.2

* Before reduction of child allowance (since 1996) ** since 1993 incl. Duties on Interest Income

Source: Federal Statistical Office 2011a: 574 <www.destatis.de>; BMF 2011

The overall consequence was that between 1990 and 2008 the net income from capital and wealth rose by 96.2 per cent whilst net wages increased by only 33.3 per cent (BMAS 2009: 1.10, 1.14). If we look at the real purchasing power of the mass of wage earners, then we have to recognise that it stagnated: the average real net wage remained virtually the same, when comparing average yearly income in 1992 with 2009. This is not only due to the weaker position of the trade unions in their negotiations with capital organisations but in addition it is the consequence of the tax policies pursued by successive governments. Hit by mass unemployment and declining membership, the weaker trade unions have abandoned high wage demands since the mid 1990s (Eissel 2006). In addition, gross wage increases were neutralised by faster higher taxes and social contributions.

So far, this does not represent a new phenomenon in the German tax system. If we explore the last fifty years we can identify – despite all tax reforms – a clear trend: whilst taxes on capital (assessed income tax, corporation tax and the local tax on industry and trade) went down, the wage tax remained above the 30 per cent line of total revenue since the beginning of the 1980s and, importantly, VAT increased.

Table 2.6 Income Position before and after Deductions per Wage Earner and Year in Germany, 1980–2009

	Gross wage	Wage tax	Social contributions	Net wage	Real net wage
WEST GERMANY					
1980	15,065	2,372	1,920	10,792	16,275
1990	20,603	3,289	2,874	14,480	17,005
GERMANY					
1992	21,742	3,732	3,156	14,853	17,251
1998	24,428	4,764	4,066	15,598	15,916
2009	27,746	4,948	4,930	17,868	16,699
change 1992–2009	27.6%	32.6%	56.2%	20.3%	−3.2%

Source: BMAS 2010: 1.13–1.15

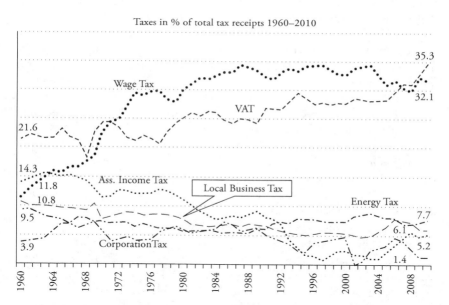

Figure 2.7 Individual Taxes in Germany as a Proportion of all Tax Revenue
Source: own calculation on basis of Federal Statistical Office; Wage before reduction of child allowance; 2010 ass. by Working Group Tax Assessment May 2010

By simply comparing direct taxes on profits and wages, the data confirm what Marx had suggested, namely that the class formation of a society can be primarily demonstrated by its tax system.

The permanent reduction of tax burdens on capital and the forfeiting by wage earners of real net wage increases failed to boost investment in secure, full-time employment.

Threats to Necessary Public Provision of Infrastructure and Services

In the face of lower state revenue and driven by the ideology 'private is better than public', many formerly publicly funded activities were divested through denationalisation and privatisation. The sale of public businesses and also the considerable restriction of public investments was a consequence of the financial crisis, essentially caused by the described impacts of tax policy, albeit the ideological effect of free market orthodoxy should not be overlooked. As a consequence, many areas of provision with necessary goods and services were privatised, like the local provision of affordable accommodation for socially disadvantaged families, of water services, public transportation systems, and waste disposal. In the context of denationalisation, the assumption of greater efficiency from competition between private operators has been proven in many cases to be an illusion. Where a local monopoly was replaced by a private monopoly, as happened in many areas, this assumption can be regarded as absolutely questionable. The pressure to generate short-term profitability often encourages private operators to undertake only absolutely necessary investments. The share-holders insist on high profits realised through low costs – often through dismissals, low wages, price increases and the postponement of necessary investments. Altogether, outsourcing to private enterprises or even public–private partnerships is accompanied by a loss of political and democratic control. Critics therefore demand that local self-administration, with its extensive competencies and responsibilities in relation to the local community, should keep its core functions and handle privatisation proposals very cautiously.

However, because of the severe crisis of local finance this cannot easily be achieved. The municipalities are burdened by the largest deficits and the prospect of the largest household crisis since the establishment of the Federal Republic. The Federation of Municipalities (Der Deutsche Städtetag) expects municipal debts to rise to €15 billion. This is double the historic record of the crisis year 2003. Swimming pools and theatres remain closed, road surfaces are not repaired. Many citizens experience day after day how acute the emergency of Germany's town halls has become.

Petra Roth, president of the Städtetag and Christian Democrat mayor of Frankfurt, has criticised the extent of the catastrophe: 'Our budgets are completely overstretched'. Roth at the same time warned against 'experiments' with the tax on industry and trade, which is very important for the cities. Accordingly she described the plans of Finance Minister Wolfgang Schäuble (CDU) to reform municipal finances as generally unacceptable. The Commission on Local Finance, she argued, should rather concentrate on modernising the existing local business tax rather than abolishing it. Addressing the federal government, Roth asked for a stronger consideration of the interests of the municipalities. Approximately half the income decreases of the municipalities were based not on the economic situation, but on reductions in tax revenues.[3] German municipalities provide two-thirds of public investments, which are preconditions for the future social and economic development and the well-being of citizens. Public expenditure affects not only our future prospects, but also our quality of life. Therefore we should carefully emphasise sustainable financing in order not to allow local finance problems to succumb to central political diktats.

The Outlook: Austerity Policy Endangering Future Competitiveness

Of course, reduced rates of income and profit taxes certainly can have a positive effect on demand and production. However, the resulting additional revenues for treasury and social security do not necessarily match the original tax receipt losses. Reductions of taxes erode public budgets but hardly stimulate economic growth. These findings are the results of a study of the Institut für Makroökonomie und Konjunkturforschung (Institute for Macroeconomics and Economic Research, IMK) when exploring the results of the tax revisions of 2000, which was the most extensive in the post-war period. The Institute has analysed the consequences of the tax policy of the years 2001 to 2005 in combination with a strict consolidation policy aligned to the Maastricht Criteria. Although the basic economic conditions were at that time much better than today, the calculation of the Red-Green government's fiscal policy was not realised. IMK tax expert Achim Truger estimates that a lowering of direct taxes is only 25 per cent self-financing. No positive effect remains if the state reduces expenditure at the same time, in order to avoid the higher indebtedness that would compensate for tax reductions.

If austerity strategies are put into practice, fiscal policy has negative impacts on economic growth, instead of promoting it. As a rule of thumb: if the state reduces wage and income taxes by approximately €10 billion, then economic performance rises by only approximately €5 billion. At the same time the gross domestic product sinks by more than €10 billion, if the state finances the shortfall in revenue by expenditure cuts. The tax reduction thus either intensifies the recession or the pressure for consolidation. From the experience of the past, it is quite clear that the consolidation strategy 'failed dramatically', according to Truger (Hans-Boeckler-Stiftung 2010: 21.4). For the year 2005 the IMK comes to this conclusion: the tax revision led to receipt losses of approximately €43bn, the deficit of the public households was about €32bn higher than it would have been without reductions in taxes; however, the extensive tax relief afforded to enterprises and households let the gross domestic product rise by a mere €1.1bn.

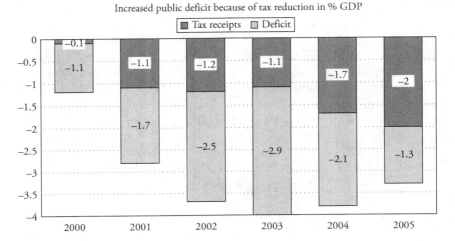

Increased public deficit because of tax reduction in % GDP

Figure 2.8 Effects of Tax Cuts on Public Sector Borrowing in Germany, 2000–2005
Source: IMK, Hans-Boeckler-Stiftung

The trade union Verdi has complained that without the tax gifts of both Red-Green and Black-Yellow governments, the federal state, the Länder and local authorities would have received alone in 2011 over €50 billion more in revenue. With property tax it could be as much as €70 billion more. Many municipalities urgently need a cash infusion to avoid bleeding to death. The property tax is very suitable as a means to boost revenues. It is a Länder tax, which could be passed in part to the municipalities. This would be fairer in contrast to the unfair way of insisting on less expenditure and would represent appropriate support for the economic situation.

Nothing should be said against deficit spending as an anti-cyclical strategy in the spirit of Keynes. However, it is bizarre firstly to relieve rich individuals and corporations from tax burdens and then ask them for loans to cover public expenditures in exchange for interest payments.

The outlook is rather threatening when, in addition to the Maastricht criteria, a new regulation to contain debt was introduced in 2011 following a decision by the Federalism Commission. As the previous fiscal rule had failed to sufficiently restrain the build-up of government debt over the past decades, the government introduced a new – also constitutionally enshrined – fiscal rule in 2009, constraining the structural budget deficit to 0.35 per cent of GDP by 2016 for the federal government and requiring balanced structural budgets for the Länder by 2020. A transition path will ensure steadily decreasing structural deficits in the meantime. Exceptions are permitted in the case of natural catastrophes or heavy recessions.

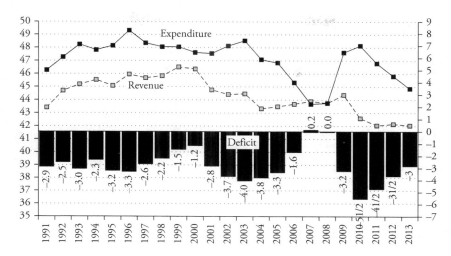

Figure 2.9 State Expenditure, Revenue and Annual Deficit in Percentage of GDP
Source: BMF-Monatsbericht 2/2010, S. 37

The new fiscal rule is likely to help bring public finances back to a sustainable path, but it should ensure through proper prioritisation that an appropriate level of public investment is made while implementing the rule. With respect to this harder regulation it is clear that the government will look for areas in which expenditure cuts will not mobilise strong and powerful opponents or harm the interests of its specific electorate. That is why the Liberals demanded further tax rebates for the high performers in businesses, which are identified as their special clients. It represented almost the only point in their election campaign, and they managed to include this policy in the coalition contract with the Conservatives. However, the harsh loss in the recent regional election in North Rhine-Westphalia, and the bitter data of the tax assessment in May 2010 together with the new far-reaching state guarantees for loans in the case of an insolvent Greece persuaded the Liberals to postpone their agenda or even give it up.

Precisely the opposite to further tax reductions is necessary: realistically, even as economies emerge from recession, it is likely to be necessary to raise additional revenues. Cyclical recovery of tax revenues through the operation of the automatic stabilisers is unlikely to be sufficient, given for instance the rise in debt service costs. In this context it could prove vital that governments are ready to restructure tax systems to promote long-term economic growth. Thus, the focus after the crisis could be a shift towards taxes that have been shown to be least harmful to growth, such as recurrent taxes on immovable property and at the same time widening the tax base to achieve a fairer sharing of the tax burden. For Germany, there is considerable scope for raising more revenue, because

56 | *Dieter Eissel*

together with Austria it is far below the average in tax burdens on property in the OECD countries. The state revenues from taxes on real estate, wealth, donations and inheritance are in Germany firmly around 0.9 per cent of GDP and thus less than half of the OECD average of 1.9 per cent. Only Mexico, the Czech Republic and Slovakia, i.e., states with a clearly lower financial status than Germany, as well as Austria, obtain less revenue from this tax type (OECD 2006a). In case the German political class fails to decide massively in favour of tax hikes, the Damocles sword of giant debt would then lead to harmful cuts in expenditures, as the former prime minister of Hesse, Roland Koch, announced, even concerning expenditures on education and public institutions for childcare which are written into the coalition contract of the federal government.

Sustainable Tax Policy and State Revenues

International comparison indicates that a higher state share of GDP does not obstruct economic performance like the market theorists want us to believe. The Nordic EU member states, for instance, which have state revenue ratios of over 50 per cent of GDP, did not suffer from lower growth rates than for example Germany with a revenue ratio of 43.7 per cent: the average real growth rate of GDP from 2000 to 2008 in Sweden was 2.6 per cent, in Denmark 1.6 per cent, in Finland 3 per cent and in Germany during the same period only 1.5 per cent.

Obviously the state share of GDP is not a proven indicator for the level of economic growth. It is obvious that public infrastructure, mainly expenditure for education and training, is a precondition for economic performance.

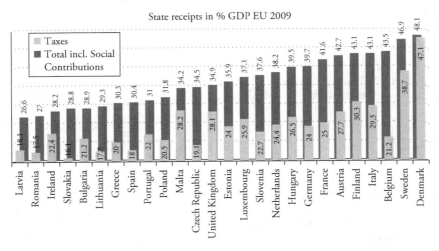

Figure 2.10 Total Revenue for EU States in 2009 from Taxes and Social Contributions
Source: Eurostat: Taxation Trends in the EU 2011, S. 282, 284

What we therefore need is an adequate tax system which is fair and sufficient to cover wanted and needed public expenditures without a permanent increase in debt. Any plan to lower taxes will inevitably raise future consolidation needs. Especially wealthier income earners and corporations should pay enough with regard to their higher income and returns. Under the current circumstances this restructuring of a sustainable tax system would only minimise the savings of the rich and therefore would not be harmful to the demand-side. Despite this fair requirement, the neoliberal argument is then that this will be a 'punishment' of the rich which would stimulate migration to tax havens. Surely, that might be the consequence in some cases, however not all capital would and could flee because there are other factors which are positive for Germany as a location, like its well-trained workforce and the high level and high quantity of research institutes, all of which are in many cases of higher importance than taxes as a cost factor (BDI et al. 2008). Last but not least, all personal services, which need face-to-face provision, can't move without losing their consumers, and the service sector is by far the largest one.

The Alternative Economic Policy Working Group (Arbeitsgruppe Alternative Wirtschaftspolitik) therefore demands an active financial policy, as well as an increase in tax revenues on the basis of a fair distribution. The demand for a future investment programme lies at the centre of a national policy strengthened by tax revenues. Besides financing through increasing revenues, public borrowing should also be used for financing (Arbeitsgruppe Alternative Wirtschaftspolitik 2010: 33).

These alternative economists insist on the principle of equality in relative tax burdens oriented to incomes, which means that large incomes, fortunes and enterprise should pay more. With such a concept approximately €80 billion annually could be generated, this time redistributed from top to bottom.

In detail, the following measures are needed:

- The top rate of the income tax must be raised from 42 per cent to 48 per cent (plus solidarity duties). Starting with a lower marginal tax rate of 14 per cent, tax rates should rise linear-progressively to the top.
- All incomes (also unearned income and dividends) must be uniformly subject to the individual income tax tariff. The withholding tax of 25 per cent on interest income is to be abolished again.
- The wealth tax which has been in abeyance since 1997 because of a Supreme Court decision must be levied immediately again. Starting from net assets of €500,000, private households but also the enterprise sector are to be included in this levy.
- The inheritance and donation taxes must be basically amended. In 2007 the state received only approximately €4 billion from both taxes. Huge

inheritances must be taxed more substantially and the fiscal special treatment of the transmission or donation of an enterprise where its operation is to be continued, operated by the Federal Government, is to be rejected. Even the Council of Economic Advisors point out: 'The resolutions for the reform of the inheritance tax failed in the beginning. Anticipated payments from 85% to sparing for business assets, agrarian and forest assets and for shares of finance companies, of which the testators or donors hold more than 25% of the nominal capital, is unjustified in each regard' (SVR 2008: 193).

- In order to prevent excessive speculation in the international financial markets, there must be a deceleration, i.e., a decrease in the extent and speed of the transactions on capital markets. That is why the Alternative Economic Policy Working Group is not alone in suggesting an international financial transaction tax (Tobin tax). Even with a small tax rate of only 0.1 per cent on the basis of the transaction data of 2007 the German state would receive €27 billion more in revenue. In addition, as discussed in the USA, it is indispensable that banks and insurance companies share in the bail-out costs in the context of the financial crisis.
- Last but not least, tax evasion must be seen no longer as a 'harmless crime', from which one can escape by 'self-declaration'. Immediate control reports from banks – also transnational – are to be introduced, and the personnel in the tax offices supplemented substantially (Arbeitsgruppe Alternative Wirtschaftspolitik 2010: 37–39).

To be realistic, there is not much hope that these proposals will be implemented by the ruling political class. Conservative politicians and their supporters in society would rather raise VAT from 19 per cent to over 20 per cent and minimise the number of goods which today are taxed at the lower VAT rate of 7 per cent. It will depend on a change in power whether socially and economically required tax policies would have a chance of being implemented.

All in all, the current financial misery has causes which go back to the decisions of the Red-Green government under Chancellor Schröder. Within the last ten years the repetitive reduction of taxes has led to shortfalls in revenue of together approximately €300 billion. Above all, enterprises, wealthy citizens, top earners and rich heirs have benefitted from these measures. As a share of GDP, state revenue fell in the last ten years from over 46 per cent to under 43 per cent. That means approximately €80 billion less in tax receipts and social contributions per year. In 2011 there followed a further lowering to just 42 per cent. The constitutional amendment to the Basic Law in 2009, concerning the reduction of public debts, is forcing the public authorities to institute a rapid dismantling of annual federal borrowing by 2016 and that affecting the Länder by 2020. The policy-makers of the conservative-liberal coalition have thus blocked the way to a long-term and more compatible dismantling of indebtedness. Instead of cutting back expenditure, which is the plan of the conservative-liberal government, Germany needs to guarantee welfare state measures, counteracting the social costs of the crisis and meeting the demands for qualitative growth and employment. This can be attained only by means of a clear stabilisation of domestic demand: by the expansion of public investments in education, by ecological change, a modern infrastructure, and by the promotion of private consumption. The government coalition, however, wants to cut social benefits for the unemployed and for parents – more than 30 per cent of the total sum of about €82 billion in the next four years – which would not only contribute to an increase in poverty but furthermore weaken the private demand of groups which spend their money nearly completely on the domestic market. Even the additional tax burdens which are expected through increased levies on the banks, aviation enterprises and energy suppliers can be passed on to customers (DGB 2010b).

However, what we need, above all, is an alternative to the list of Federal Government cuts, in the form of a socially and ecologically balanced programme of economic recovery and sustainable growth.

Notes

1. Federal Minister of Finance: Results of the Working Group 'Tax Assessment', May 2010.
2. For 2001, see <http://www.bmgs.bund.de> and for 2005 <http://www.bmas.bund.de> (accessed 3 September 2010).
3. 'Kommunen in der Haushaltskrise. Das gigantische Loch', in *Süddeutsche Zeitung*, 14 May 2010; see <www.sueddeutsche.de> (accessed 17 May 2010).

CHAPTER 3

Tax Reform, Income Inequality and the Welfare State

The Case of Portugal

MIGUEL GLATZER

Portugal, Spain and Greece are among the world's most recent welfare states. Democratisation in the 1970s, followed by accession to the European Community in the 1980s, is central to most accounts of the rise in social spending in these three countries. Democratisation provided an impulse for greater social spending as the political systems responded to unmet needs. It is true that the dictatorships, particularly in the 1960s and early 1970s, had paid some attention to social policy, but these initiatives tended to cover only the civil service and core sectors of the workforce. Large portions of the population survived without social protection and the total budgetary outlays, both as a percentage of GDP and of the budget, remained low. For these three countries, universal coverage and the take-off in spending are democratic phenomena. The Portuguese case is symptomatic.

Table 3.1 Social Expenditure in Portugal 1950–2008

Social Transfers % GDP	1950	1970	1980	2000	2008
	2	3.7	9.5	17	16.1

Number of Recipients	1960	1970	2000	2008
	120,000	260,000	2,700,000	Close to 3,000,000

Source: Silva Lopes 2004: 83 and Rosa and Chitals 2010: 27–28

Under democracy, a mixture of workers' movements, civil society organisations and unions provided voice to previously stifled needs. Political parties on the left, but also centre-right parties, found that paying heed to these needs provided political benefits. Socialist parties were by no means the sole protagonists in the construction of these welfare states.

The European Union is frequently seen as an additional cause of the growth of these welfare states. Here the causal mechanism is less direct. The *acquis communautaire* does not by itself require substantially increased social spending. Rather, it was Europe as an ideal, as a 'model of society', along with the institutional forums and information flows the EU provided, that further facilitated the growth of these welfare states. To be modern, to be European, meant having a system of social protection.

Entry into the European Union also meant market making and market opening. Policies of autarchy, which had characterised these countries through the 1950s, were no longer tenable and were now illegal. If Spain and Portugal had started to liberalise their trade regimes with membership in EFTA, strategies of openness pursued by the democratic governments, and then anchored by the EU, committed these countries strongly to economic globalisation. Goods, capital and labour would now flow freely.

The Southern European countries thus underwent a triple transition – to democracy, to economic openness and to a welfare state. The construction, durability and indeed continued growth of these welfare states is a notable phenomenon. They were built not during the Golden Age of post-war capitalism when growth was high and relatively steady and unemployment low. Instead they were built during a very volatile period that certainly saw periods of very substantial growth but also periods of negative growth, inflation, balance of payments crises, declining real wages and high unemployment. From an economic point of view, the oil shocks of the 1970s were not the most propitious time for the birth of democracy. In the words of one Portuguese analyst, the country went from a lack of a welfare state to the crisis of the welfare state, skipping the Golden Age.

Two big lessons emerge from this triple transition. First, welfare states can be built during turbulent economic times. Second, and contrary to a once-prevalent view, globalisation, including in its modern form, is compatible not only with mature welfare states but with the building of new ones. In Portugal, Spain and Greece, the turn towards economic openness and the increase in social spending were contemporaneous.

Inequality and Poverty

Welfare states socialise risk and redistribute income. But the redistribution of income is often inter-temporal or cross-generational as much as it is across income groups. Pure Bismarckian pension systems, for example, move income from workers to retirees, but replicate in pensions the distribution of income among wage earners. Under conditions of low unemployment, social transfers flow overwhelmingly to the elderly and to the young (via their parents' child credits). As a result, large welfare states are compatible with both a poor distribution of income (as measured by Gini-coefficients, for example) as well as high levels of poverty. When this is the case, the welfare state's large transfers are, in effect, replicating or even reinforcing existing inequalities of income. Think of a country with a thicket of public retirement schemes, some of which provide earlier retirement ages and a more generous rate of replacement of earned income than others. In addition, part of the population is simply not covered by a public pension scheme. Under such circumstances, the welfare state is likely to increase inequality, not reduce it.

Compared to other EU countries, Portugal, Spain and Greece all have poor income distributions and high poverty rates.

Table 3.2 Inequality in Europe (EU15)

	Gini coefficient total income % early 2000s	Gini coefficient mid 2000s	Quintile ratio S80/S20 early 2000s	Quintile ratio S80/S20 mid 2000s
Portugal	37	39	7.1	5.6
Spain	33	32	5.7	6.9
Greece	34	32	6.3	5.6
Austria	26	27	3.9	3.7
Belgium	28	27	4.4	3.9
Denmark	23	23	3.3	4.4
France	29	29	4.4	4.5
Germany	28	29	4.5	4.5
Ireland	33	31	5.4	5.3
Italy	33	35	5.8	5.2
Luxembourg	28	26	4.1	4.1
Netherlands	29	28	4.5	3.7
United Kingdom	33	33	5.5	5.4

Source: OECD 2003: 95 (Gini coefficient and quintile ratio for early 2000s); OECD 2011 (Gini coefficient, mid 2000s); Eurostat 2011 (Quintile ratio mid 2000s)

There are many reasons for this. Educational achievement tends to be low, which places a greater income premium on those segments of the population with greater educational credentials. The skills premium is relatively high. Wage compression, which in some Northern European countries is achieved via union strength and meso- or macro-level bargaining arrangements, is also low. Norms may also play a role in compensation differentials. In addition, the Bismarckian features of the welfare state result in social spending that has historically been tilted towards pensions and that largely replicates market inequalities in those pensions. Despite the growth of substantial welfare states, these countries continue to be marked by high inequality and high poverty.

Attention to the problem of poverty has led to a number of programs meant to reduce it. The *Rendimento Mínimo Garantido* tries to alleviate some of the more extreme forms of poverty. The minimum wage has been the focus of special attention, both because of its direct effects on wage income and because it is frequently used as an index or anchor in the determination of other social benefits. The minimum pension is also a frequent object of attention. Because of the high number of beneficiaries who never contributed or contributed insufficiently to a pension scheme, the number of elderly on a minimum pension is high. Because these pensions are paid through a non-contributory fund, increasing them can have a significant budgetary impact. Nonetheless, they have been increased at rates higher than inflation, but because the base is so low they remain meagre.

Poverty and income inequality can also be affected by the tax system, however, and it is to this that we now turn.

Tax Systems

The rise of the welfare state in Portugal, Spain and Greece, with its very significant increases in social spending, required very considerable increases in taxation. Table 3.3 shows the increase in total taxation in these countries and compares it to the EU12. While the EU12 increased their tax take substantially during the 1973–1985 period, reaching a relatively stable 40–42 per cent of GDP, the growth in taxation was even greater in Portugal, Spain and Greece and continued through the 1990s. As a result, by 2005 these three

Table 3.3 Total Tax Revenue as a Percentage of GDP, 1973–2010

Portugal, Spain and Greece Compared with EU12

	1973	1980	1985	1990	1995	2000	2005	2008	2010
Portugal	17.5	22.9	25.2	27.7	31.7	34.1	34.7	35.7	34.4
Spain	17.7	22.6	27.6	32.5	32.1	34.2	35.8	34.2	33.5
Greece	18.1	21.6	25.5	26.2	28.9	34.1	31.3	33.9	32.1
EU 12	33.6	38.0	40.5	40.6	41.0	42.2	39.9	41.0	40.5
Gap PT/EU 12	16.1	15.1	15.3	12.9	9.3	8.1	5.2	5.3	6.1
Gap SP/EU 12	15.9	15.4	12.9	8.1	8.9	8.0	4.1	6.8	7.0
Gap GR/EU 12	15.5	16.4	15.0	14.4	12.1	8.1	8.6	7.1	8.4

Note: EU12 consists of Austria, Belgium, Denmark, Finland, France, Germany, Ireland, Italy, Luxembourg, the Netherlands, Sweden and the United Kingdom

Source: OECD 2008 and Eurostat 2011 (for 2008 and 2010 data)

countries narrowed their gap with the EU12 by about half in the case of Greece and by about two-thirds in the case of Portugal and Spain. Since then, with varied depths of and responses to the crisis, the gap has widened somewhat for Portugal and more so for Spain.

Tax systems typically have a number of goals, some of which conflict with one another. These include:

- **horizontal equity**: individuals with similar incomes should have equivalent tax burdens, regardless of the source of their income;
- **vertical equity**: individuals with higher incomes should pay higher (or at a minimum equal) shares of their income in taxes than individuals with lower incomes;
- **market conformity**: taxes should not be distortionary;
- **simplicity and efficiency**: the tax system should be easy to understand and the costs of compliance should be low;
- **promotion of beneficial behaviour** and **reduction of harmful behaviour**: e.g., tax incentives promote retirement savings or donations to non-profits; carbon taxes promote energy efficiency; 'sin' taxes reduce drinking and smoking;
- **raising enough revenue without hurting other goals such as economic growth and employment**: although the academic literature on taxation and growth is by no means univocal, high unemployment rates in Europe have led many to focus on the tax wedge on labour. Too big a gap between an employer's costs and an employee's take-home pay are thought to discourage work and employment. A partial solution to this is to tax consumption rather than income.

The trade-offs are many. Progressive taxation might lead to punishing marginal taxes on income, for example. A concern with horizontal equity often leads to calls to tax capital income at similar rates to wage income, but tax shifting from personal income to corporate income, which is taxed at a lower rate, is often the result. Consumption taxes are easy to administer, but are rarely progressive. Tax deductions or tax incentives might increase fairness, but reduce tax simplicity. Given the multiple trade-offs in tax design, it is not surprising that analyses such as those of the OECD (2008a) or of Bernardi and Profeta (2004) find considerable variation in tax systems and in the direction of change. In the words of a leading analyst:

> The tax systems of the European countries are still widely different from one another. There seems to have been relatively little movement toward tax harmonisation except in a few areas. Furthermore, there is no obvious, ideal or theoretical system that is acting as a reference point for tax reforms. In some ways the situation has changed for the worse in recent

decades. While three or four decades ago there was some convergence of views among tax experts on how a good system should look, there is now no system that gets the approval of the majority of tax specialists. (Tanzi 2004: xxii)

Although the passage above might suggest considerable freedom of action for policy makers, this freedom is constrained by several forces. For Portugal, Spain and Greece, the growth of the welfare state, the European Union and globalisation placed significant pressures on the reform of the tax system.

The growth in social spending required considerable increases in taxation. This was facilitated by general support for increased social spending. Economic growth in many (but not all) years also facilitated increased taxation by avoiding zero-sum games between increased revenue and take-home pay. In a survey of a number of the advanced industrialised democracies, Kato finds that large welfare states rely more heavily on regressive taxation than meagre ones. At first glance this is puzzling and counterintuitive, as the larger welfare states of Northern Europe tend to be more committed to income equality. While they generate large revenues to be used in redistribution they reject a reliance on progressive taxation. A counterintuitive result, as Prasad and Deng note, is that the United States is likely to be one of the few countries with a globally progressive tax system (Prasad and Deng, 2009). This stems both from the progressive nature of the US income tax system along with the relatively low weight of regressive consumption taxes in the overall tax mix. In the words of an early observer of this phenomenon, 'Strangely enough, progressive taxes in the traditional sense turn out to be a conservative instrument of policy in that they often support smaller, not larger, government' (Steurle 1995: 258).

These findings raise the following question with respect to Portugal, Spain and Greece. As these countries embarked on massive welfare state building, did they shift away from a reliance on progressive taxation? In other words, did they follow a Northern European model in which an extensive welfare state is made possible by regressive taxation? Clearly, none of these countries have levels of taxation and spending equal to those of their Northern European counterparts, but these countries are already above the levels of social spending in the United States, Canada, Japan and, for Spain and Portugal, above the level of the UK. Whether the Southern European countries have tax mixes that divide along Kato's categories, or that shift from one to another, sheds light on the affinities and links between taxation systems and welfare states.

The European Union influenced tax policy in two principal ways. The first was the requirement that countries develop a VAT system. VAT rates have risen in many countries to rates well above 20 per cent. A frequent explanation for this is that indirect taxation is less visible and thus more politically palatable. However, relying on the rise in VAT rates often overstates the growth of consumption taxes in the tax mix. This is because in many countries the VAT has a large substitutive effect, replacing other, previously existing consumption taxes.

The second way in which the EU has affected tax policy is through the requirements for EMU, set out first in the convergence criteria and then in the Growth and Stability Pact. Budget deficits above 3 per cent are problematic and can give rise to official excessive deficit procedures from Brussels. By restricting budget deficits, the EU forces member states to confront the issue of fiscal consolidation. For Southern European countries with weak controls over public spending, this forces politically difficult choices between reductions in expenditure and increases in revenue, particularly when the exercise is conducted under conditions of low or even negative economic growth. Examining these periods of fiscal consolidation allows one to determine the degree to which success was achieved through revenue growth or through expenditure control. In addition, one can examine what happens to the growth in social transfers in these rapidly evolving welfare states.

Globalisation and Taxation

The effects of globalisation on the size of government and on income inequality are the subject of a large academic literature and have given rise to several debates. On the one hand, a long-standing line of thought finds that openness is correlated with larger government size (Cameron 1978; Ruggie 1987; Rodrik 1997). In this view large government size makes possible social stabilisers that make political openness – and its real or feared volatility and increased risk – politically viable. On the other hand, a number of studies have suggested either that globalisation increases the cost of taxation (because capital and high-earners can go abroad and, increasingly, even purchases can be made in low-tax jurisdictions) or that it alters the tax mix. There is little evidence so far that the overall tax take is declining significantly, or that high-tax jurisdictions are failing to attract investment, but there is some evidence that the tax mix is changing. Some evidence suggests that taxes on capital, which is more mobile than labour, have been reduced. Certainly, tax rates on capital have been lowered in many countries but exemptions have also been narrowed, leading to an increase in the tax base and revenue neutrality in many cases. Progressive taxation has been flattened as high earners are among the most mobile of all taxpayers. There is also evidence in some cases of a greater reliance on consumption taxes.

In a related vein, Hines and Summers find that countries with small open economies 'rely much less heavily on corporate and personal income taxes than do other countries' and instead rely on 'consumption-type taxes, including taxes on sales of goods and services and import tariffs' (Hines and Summers 2009: ii). They report that 'a ten percent smaller population in 1999 is associated with a one percent smaller ratio of personal and corporate income tax collections to total tax revenues' (ibid.: ii). They conclude by saying that if 'the rapid pace of globalisation implies that all countries are becoming small open economies, this evidence suggests that the use of expenditure taxes is likely to increase, posing challenges to governments concerned about recent changes in income distribution' (ibid.: ii).

For Slemrod and Bakija, globalisation appears to produce countervailing and indeterminate effects. On the one hand, openness is associated with increased demands for social insurance, larger governments and thus higher rates of taxation. On the other hand, openness increases the costs of taxation and of some forms of taxation, notably progressive taxation on high earners, more than others. While noting a secular downward trend in progressive taxation, they argue that the consequences of globalisation for progressivity 'are thus not entirely clear' (Slemrod and Bakija 2000: 21).

Appraisals of these effects vary from the deeply concerned to the sanguine. For Kenneth Messere 'vertical equity has been thrown out of the tax policy door' (quoted in Panitch 1993). Vito Tanzi argues that for much of the post-war period the idea of a global income tax, in which individuals' total or global income is subject to progressive rates, was popular among economists and governments. Surveying the current period, however, he asks 'whether globalisation will eventual kill completely the global income tax' (Tanzi 2004: xvii). Stephan Ganghof, although concerned about the problem, argues that it is technically possible for a modified form of progressive taxation to coexist with globalisation and that whether this happens depends on political choice (Ganghof 2008).

The Evolution of the Portuguese Case

We now turn to an analysis of progressivity and to charting changes in taxation in Portugal. Progressivity in taxation was initially proposed and introduced during Portugal's first experiment with democracy, the First Republic (1910–1926). It appeared in a very weak form in inheritance and donations tax in 1911 (although progressivity didn't apply to direct descendants) and then in 1913 in property tax. The 1922 introduction of an income tax contained progressive rates, but implementation was extremely weak (Silva Lopes 2005).

The Salazar dictatorship was initially hostile to progressive taxation. A commission formed in 1926 to study tax reform called the very principle of progressivity 'unjust' and argued that its practical effects are 'to confiscate the wealth of the best taxpayers'.[1] Three decades later the Salazar dictatorship changed its mind, introducing progressivity in 1958 in the *imposto complementar*. Later, the dictatorship would add a degree of progressivity to the *imposto profissional*.

In the first few years of democracy following the 1974 revolution Portuguese governments markedly increased the degree of progressivity in these income taxes, and the principle itself became enshrined in the constitution. The multiple increases resulted in cases with absurdly high marginal rates that reached 84 per cent, but even so analyses pointed to the likely regressivity of the overall system (Brown and Beleza 1976; Tanzi and de Wulf 1976; de Carvalho 1976; Fernandes Ferreira 1976).

Far-reaching reform of the tax system arrived in 1989, five years after Anibal Cavaco Silva became prime minister and two years after his party, the centre-right PSD, won an absolute majority of the vote (50.2 per cent) and a strong absolute majority in parliament (148 of the 250 seats). Committed to economic liberalisation and market making in many policy areas, the Cavaco Silva government introduced a 'modern and more rational' tax system (Castel-Branco Borges 1991). The reform reduced top tax rates. It also excluded progressivity from sources of income that are particularly important to wealthier strata of the population. Capital income, such as interest and dividends, would now be taxed on a proportional base. Under many situations, such as holding stocks for more than twelve months, capital gains were excluded from taxation altogether.

In his writings Cavaco Silva has made several arguments in favour of these reforms. 'In the context of globalisation and economic integration, traditional means of redistributing income – such as progressive income taxation on high earners and social transfers – are no longer viable' (Cavaco Silva 2001: 127). In his view there are three reasons why globalisation and demographic change, namely population ageing, place strong pressure on the European countries' fiscal systems and budgets. First, 'because capital is mobile and because high wage-earners are so as well, globalisation forces governments to reduce taxation rates on capital income and to reduce progressivity in taxation on earned income'. Note that this results in an argument against the old idea of progressive taxation on an individual's global income, which was the classic means of satisfying the requirements of both horizontal and vertical equity. Taxation on capital income is now decoupled from taxation on wage income. And wage income is now taxed at less progressive rates. A smaller share of total income is now subject to progressivity, and the steepness of the different progressive rates has been reduced.

Second, globalisation and international competition increase the costs of inefficiency and dead-weight losses produced by high levels of taxation and other public policies. This is an argument largely directed to the red tape and low productivity of the system of public administration in Portugal. Its low efficiency is exacerbated by its large size (Portugal has a relatively high ratio of government employment to private employment) and the public wage bill is a large component of the budget. Under conditions of economic openness, this is likely to lead to lower net inflows of investment, and lower rates of economic growth.

Third, tax systems serve goals other than equity, and these other goals have been seen as increasingly important. In the context of population ageing and the budgetary pressures affecting social security systems, the need of the tax system to encourage private savings is all the more important. Likewise, tax systems can be used to encourage technological investment for growth (or, Cavaco Silva might add if he were writing this passage today, for environmental reasons). Modifying the tax system to add credits or deductions for savings, investment or technological innovation interferes with the equity principle and reduces the progressivity of the system.

For Cavaco Silva, the decreasing sustainability of the post-war states' traditional instruments of income redistribution – progressive taxation and social transfers – does not mean that the goal of an equitable distribution of income is doomed. Rather, the solution is to adjust the goal and to develop new policy instruments (Cavaco Silva 1999). Concern should shift somewhat to the problem of poverty rather than with the distribution of income per se. This involves a concern with both absolute poverty as well as relative poverty (as a percentage of median income, for example). Public policy should concentrate on inequality and dispersion of income in the low and middle ends of the distribution. Globalisation has increased the costs of curtailing the increasing dispersion of income at the high end of the income distribution but this is now considered a less important policy goal.

If progressive taxation and social transfers are increasingly costly to sustain, and if the goal is to focus relatively more on the problem of poverty rather than merely on a narrowing of the income distribution, what are the new policy instruments with which to achieve social equity? Cavaco Silva argues that in addition to a focus on anti-poverty spending, public policies that jointly serve the goals of economic growth and social equity should be embraced. This means less emphasis on social transfers and more on employment and human capital policies, designed in such a way as to pay particular attention to the disadvantaged. Policies that tackle long-term unemployment or youth unemployment through employment subsidies or that reduce the social costs of low-wage employment by, for example, reducing taxes on low incomes, are to be encouraged. So are policies that make it easier to open a business. General public investments in education and training along with targeted spending on programs that reduce the educational drop-out rate, that make it easier for single parents to access the educational system or that improve access to life-long learning, especially for people with low levels of educational attainment, are also encouraged. In sum, the shift is from 'passive' social transfers to active social policy.

As a corollary, Cavaco Silva argues that responsibility for social equity in European countries should shift from the Ministries of Finance (tax progressivity) and Ministries of Social Affairs (social transfers). On the one hand, more ministries (employment, education, economic development) will be involved, widening the number of state institutions involved. On the other hand, the leadership and attention of the prime minister becomes all the more important as this is necessary to develop and coordinate the new active equity strategy.

Returning to the Ministry of Finance, what effects did the 1989 tax reform have on progressivity? Certainly, the lowering of top rates of progressive taxation and the exclusion of capital income from such taxation (to be taxed proportionally or not at all) reduced progressivity. Tax deductions, tax shifting of personal income to corporate income, tax evasion, non-reporting and tax fraud further reduced the progressivity of the Portuguese tax system although, it should be noted, many of these problems were long-standing and pre-dated the 1989 reform. Non-reporting was common among the self-employed. The self-employed constitute a large category of total Portuguese employment and include many high-earners in the 'liberal professions' such as doctors, lawyers and accountants. It was hard for the state to accurately track income and many in this category reported very low incomes. Tax shifting from personal to corporate income also reduced the tax take. Common strategies for high earners included the partial use of in-kind compensation, such as the supply of a company car or the payment of children's private school tuition fees, which would be taxed at low rates if at all.

For Silva Lopes, these factors all contribute to a lack of overall progressivity in the Portuguese tax system. Income taxation was clearly progressive only for wage earners in the low and middle sections of the income distribution. Income taxation was regressive at the top end of the distribution, where income from capital is important, opportunities for non-reporting abounded and income could be shifted from the personal to the corporate category. If income taxation was progressive only for a subset of income earners (wage earners at the low to middle end of the income distribution), it is abundantly clear that the overall system of taxation (including social security taxes, VAT and other sources of taxation) was regressive.

Other analysts largely agree with this assessment. Using what it calls a 'crude measure' of progressivity, which compares the marginal 'all-in' tax rate faced by a top wage earner and the rate faced by an average production worker, the OECD found that progressivity in Portugal is average (OECD 2001: 75). However, after refining the analysis by taking into account tax deductions and credits, reduced taxation of capital income and tax evasion, the same OECD report finds that 'income taxation achieves little in the way of income redistribution' (ibid.: 77). It also notes that Portugal has one of the widest after-tax income distributions in the OECD. Two years later the OECD was blunter, arguing that 'if the wide range of tax credits and deduction of personal income tax is taken into consideration, the fiscal system probably exacerbates the inequality of income distribution' (OECD 2003: 90).

Statutory declines in the number of tax brackets and in the top marginal rates of progressive income structures can overstate the decline in progressivity, however. There are two principal reasons for this. The first is fiscal drag. Unless adjusted for inflation and wage growth, higher rates will eventually apply to greater numbers of taxpayers. (This is seen on a regular basis in the US case, where, unless adjusted, the alternative minimum income tax dips into upper-middle-class incomes.) In Portugal, adjustments to the tax brackets have sometimes only partially offset inflation and wage growth. Fiscal drag in such cases has been reduced but not eliminated. This results in higher revenues without the need for legislated tax increases.

The second reason why statutory declines in rates can overstate declines in progressivity involves incentives for tax fraud and evasion. Visco's comments on Italy, a Southern European country whose experience in income tax policy parallels the Portuguese case in some respects, are instructive in this regard. Like Portugal, Italy in the mid 1970s increased the progressivity of its income tax system. Under the tax reform of 1973, the personal income tax (Irpef) was spread over thirty-two brackets. The lowest rate was 10 per cent and the highest was 82 per cent. Again like the Portuguese case, the 1980s saw tax reforms that reduced progressivity. The major year of reform in the Italian case is 1983; in Portugal it was 1989.

With respect to the 1973 reforms, Visco reports that 'the progression of rates was more apparent than real. Due to legal erosion, tax avoidance and tax evasion, very few incomes were (or are) placed in the higher brackets' (Visco 1992: 114). If reductions in rates are combined with increased tax collection efforts, the incentives to cheat on taxes go down and the cost of doing so goes up. Simpler tax codes can also lead to a widening of the tax base. In such cases, lower tax rates on larger taxable incomes can result in revenue-neutral or even revenue-increasing reforms. As Visco writes:

> Reduction of the rates would not pose problems from the point of view of equity either (the highest marginal rates envisaged would be slightly more than 30%). On the contrary, the progression of the income tax, defined as the share of revenue paid by higher-income earners, would increase considerably since at present a large portion of the typical income earned by the wealthier classes is exempt, or subject to substitute taxation, or benefits from generous erosion or numerous possibilities of avoidance. (Visco 1992: 140)

The 1989 tax reforms in Portugal reduced top marginal rates but also set in motion a process of more effective tax collection. The following years, right up to the present point, would see many measures introduced to combat tax fraud and evasion. These include better computerisation and cross-matching of records, increased judicial penalties for tax fraud, increased filing of court cases and public listing of high profile cases of tax arrears.

Fiscal Consolidation

In the 1990s and 2000s tax issues have been inextricably linked to issues of budgetary consolidation. This issue, important in its own right, came to the fore of government decision making as a result of EU constraints, first in the form of the convergence criteria required to join the Euro and then in the Growth and Stability Pact. These rules stipulate a maximum budget deficit of 3 per cent of GDP. Democratic Portugal has long had difficulty controlling the public budget, with public expenditure often exceeding targets and forecasts. These have been exacerbated by the low rates of economic growth experienced in the 2000s, when Portugal's catch-up with EU average GDP per capita reversed. Twice before the current crisis, Portugal was subject to the EU's excessive budget deficit procedure, first in 2002 and then in 2005/6.

Episodes of fiscal consolidation, where revenue and expenditure need to be brought into balance, present governments with difficult choices. The solutions – increases in taxes, cuts in spending or a combination of the two – are painful. This is especially so when fiscal consolidation takes place under conditions of low or negative growth. In an analysis of fiscal consolidations in the 1980s and 1990s the OECD found that 30 per cent of cases involved fiscal balance achieved fully or mostly by revenue increases, 50 per cent involved primarily expenditure cuts, and in 20 per cent revenue increases and expenditure cuts played roughly equal roles in achieving fiscal balance (OECD 2006a).

The OECD classifies Portugal's fiscal consolidation in 2002/3 as fitting in the first category, where balance is primarily achieved by higher revenues. As in many countries, revenue increases frequently relied on one-off measures. These ranged from standard measures such as the privatisation of state-owned enterprises to more creative techniques such as the sale and leasing-back of state assets or the shifting of post office pension surpluses to the general account. However Portugal was also able to engage in substantial modernisation of the tax collection apparatus, allowing it to reduce tax fraud and tax evasion and improve tax collection.

The tax changes that were part of the budgetary consolidations of the early and mid 2000s had mixed effects on the overall progressivity of the tax system. It is hard to detect a clear direction of change. In response to concerns about excessive budget deficits in 2005, the Socialist government of Prime Minister Jose Socrates tightened fiscal policy. Measures decreasing progressivity of the overall tax system included two comprehensive increases of the VAT rate as well as multiple raises of taxes on tobacco, fuel and automobiles. Reductions in the corporate tax rate initiated by the previous PSD government of Pedro Santana Lopes were maintained.

However, income taxation moved in the opposite direction. In 2006, the top rate was actually increased, from 40 to 42 per cent, and the bottom rate declined from 12 to 10.5 per cent, suggesting greater progressivity.

Social transfers continued to grow during the early to mid 2000s. Writing about the 2005 budget, for example, the Economist Intelligence Unit noted that from 1997 to 2004, social transfers (which include pensions and unemployment benefits) grew at an average rate of 9.7 per cent a year. In 2004, social security payments increased by 11.4 per cent. Given this trend, as well as the promise of higher pensions, the EIU found the budgeted increase of only 2.7 per cent in social transfers unrealistic (Economist Intelligence Unit 2005). Nonetheless, the 2006 reform of the social security system aimed to slow the increase in social spending, but this was to be done over a relatively long period of time.

How could social spending continue to increase during the lost decade of the 2000s, when economic growth was weak and GDP per capita convergence with the richer countries of Europe reversed? The explanation has several components. Declines in interest rates stemming from entry into the Euro freed up several points of GDP from debt service to other uses. In 1995, for example, public expenditure on interest consumed 5.8 per cent of GDP. By 2008, as a result of extraordinarily low rates set by the European Central Bank and after a two budgetary consolidations earlier in the decade, interest consumed only 3 per cent of GDP (Banco de Portugal 2009: 350).

Transfers from Brussels in the form of cohesion or structural funds were another way in which budget deficits could be closed and spending maintained. In budgetary consolidations increases in revenue (sometimes stemming from better collections rather than increases in taxes and frequently relying on one-off measures such as privatisations or balance-sheet transfers) tended to predominate over expenditure cuts. And spending cuts tended to fall on capital expenditures or on the public payroll rather than on social policy.

Many of these tools have now run their course. Even if a return to low pre-crisis rates were possible, it would be a long time before interest payments consumed so little of GDP. With the Eastern enlargements of the European Union, structural and cohesion funds for Portugal have been trimmed. Even had their value remained the same, economic growth, even if slow, would have reduced their weight as a proportion of GDP. And one-off revenue measures may temporarily make up for expenditure overruns but are no permanent solution.

The Current Crisis

Despite low economic growth, in the immediate run-up to the current crisis Portugal made steady progress in correcting a high budget deficit of 5.9 per cent of GDP in 2005. The deficit was reduced to 4.1 per cent in 2006 and to 3.1 per cent in 2007. The financial and economic crisis that started that year led to rapid increases in both budget deficits and government debt. Portugal's budget deficit in 2009 soared to 10.1 per cent. This was the result not only of an 11 per cent drop in tax receipts and increased spending as a result of the welfare state's automatic stabilisers but also a result of stimulus actions undertaken by the government, which included easing the rules on unemployment benefits. Efforts to shore up the labour market introduced in 2007/8 included targeted reductions in non-wage costs, expansions in job search and short-time working opportunities as well as training and income support for the unemployed. By 2009/10, the Socialist government of Prime Minister Socrates decided to reverse course. Most of the labour market support measures introduced a year or two earlier were withdrawn as budgetary containment became the order of the day. The austerity measures implemented up to June 2011, when the new PSD-led government of Prime Minister Coelho took office, included a mix of increases in taxes, cuts in public sector pay and reductions or freezes of social benefits. Listed in a European Commission Social Situation Observatory Research Note (European Commission 2011b: 37), the mix of austerity measures tracked to investigate changes in household income included the following:

Increases in Direct Taxes:
Tax rates were increased by 1 and 1.5 percentage points depending on income level. A new bracket for incomes above 153,300 EUR was introduced, raising the highest tax rate from 42 to 46.5 per cent.
Increases in Indirect Taxes:
In January 2011, the standard VAT rate was increased from 20 per cent to 23 per cent. At the same time the reduced VAT rate was increased from 12 per cent to 13 per cent and the base rate from 5 per cent to 6 per cent.
Reductions in Tax Credits and Tax Allowances:
The reference indicator for tax credits was reduced by replacing the 2011 minimum wage of 485 EUR with the 2010 minimum wage of 475 EUR or the 2011 social benefit index of 419.22 EUR. The pension tax allowance was reduced.
Reductions in Social Benefits:
The nominal value of the social benefit index used for most social benefits was frozen at the 2009 level. The nominal value of benefits not linked the social benefit index (such as pensions) was frozen from 2010 to 2011. The social assistance benefit was frozen from 2010 to 2011. Family benefit was frozen and eligibility conditions tightened.

Public Sector Pay
Public sector pay was cut by 10 per cent.

When compared to Spain, Greece, Estonia, the UK and Ireland, simulations of the effects of Portugal's austerity measures produced the second highest increase in the risk of poverty, defined as household income below 60 per cent of the pre-crisis median. Ireland had the highest increase in the risk of poverty among the countries studied but the size of its austerity cuts (8.1 per cent of total household disposable income) was more than 2.5 times the size of the austerity cuts in Portugal (3.0 per cent of total household disposable income). As a point of comparison, Spain and Greece's austerity measures during this period amounted to 2.7 per cent and 2.2 per cent of total household disposable income. If the poverty threshold is changed to 60 per cent of the median of the new post-austerity distribution of income, the risk of poverty increased the most in Portugal (European Commission 2011b).

The study also simulated the distributional effects of the austerity measures on household incomes and found that Portugal was the only one of the countries studied where the distribution was clearly regressive. A number of caveats need to be kept in mind. First, as mentioned by the authors of this study, the analysis focuses solely on the distributional effects of the austerity measures listed above. It excludes the very large distributional effects of the crisis itself (through increases in unemployment, for example, which were significantly larger in Spain and Greece than in Portugal). It also excludes cuts to public services that are not easily tractable in terms of the distribution of household income but which might have significant effects. Finally, the study only looks at what might be called the first wave of austerity measures implemented by June 2011. Nonetheless, the study raises important questions about not only the different size but also different design – and impacts – of austerity measures across countries.

The shift from initial stimulus to austerity as well as the shifting European economic outlook led to significant variation in Portuguese GDP growth rates during the crisis. Growth of 2.7 per cent in 2007 on the eve of the crisis shifted to contractions of 0.35 per cent in 2008 and 2.1 per cent in 2009. GDP grew by 0.91 per cent in 2010 but contracted by 1.6 per cent in 2011 and is expected to contract by 3.2 per cent this year. Difficulties in many of Portugal's most important European export markets, most notably Spain, deleveraging of debt at home, difficulty accessing credit, increasing unemployment, and the effects of new austerity measures agreed with the troika (the European Commission, the European Central Bank and the International Monetary Fund) all play significant roles in explaining the contraction.

In May 2011, the Socialist caretaker government agreed to the terms of a 78 billion EUR bailout package with the EC/ECB/IMF troika. The package required Portugal to not only implement additional austerity measures but to also engage in structural reforms. These included privatisation of state-owned enterprises as well as reform of the labour market and justice system. The PSD government of Prime Minister Coelho that took office in June 2011 has vowed to fully implement the troika's prescriptions and indeed to make faster progress in reducing the budget deficits than is envisioned in the plan. In contrast to Greece, where both political will and the track record of implementation have been questioned, Portugal has been cast as the 'good student' of Europe, embracing and implementing the policy prescriptions it is being asked to carry out. Nonetheless, it is increasingly doubtful that austerity and structural reform will by themselves place Portugal back on a track of sustainable debt, economic growth and international competitiveness. Many think not only that a return to the financial markets by 2013 or 2014 is unlikely but that a haircut on the debt will be needed. The debt to GDP ratio was 107 per cent at the time of the May 2011 bailout but is likely to reach 113 per cent over the next two years due to the debts of regional governments as well as of some state-owned enterprises (Stratfor 2012).

To reduce Portugal's budget deficit to 4.5 per cent of GDP this year from 5.9 per cent in 2011 and to comply with the troika's terms, the new PSD government implemented its first set of austerity measures in November 2011. These include reductions in welfare spending and the health budget and cuts in pension spending. In addition, further cuts to public sector pay have been implemented. Proposals have included a reduction in the number of holidays and the elimination of holiday pay (thirteenth and fourteenth months of pay, traditionally paid in August and December) for the next two years. Combined with earlier public sector wage cuts and increases in income tax, the take-home pay of many public sector workers is declining by over 22 per cent.

In the wake of the 2007 onset of the crisis, a number of structural reforms were implemented by the Socialist government. More are envisaged under the troika agreement and planned or carried out by the current government. These include privatisation of state-owned enterprises, reductions in the public administration workforce through adoption of a rule specifying a 2:1 ratio of job leavers to job hires, reduced administrative burdens on business, including the lifting of licensing for some services, and the liberalisation of regulated professions. Heavy emphasis is placed on labour market reforms to dualism and insider/outsider divides as well as reform of the court system and the rental market in housing (Europa 2012).[2] Crucially for the purposes of this chapter, actions have been taken to simplify the tax system. These include broadening the tax base in consumption and income taxes while reducing tax expenditures.

Conclusion

The current crisis notwithstanding, the Portuguese case demonstrates that welfare state development, and the tax increases that go with it, are possible well after the end of the Golden Age. From the mid 1970s to the mid 2000s Portugal opened its markets, grew wealthier, built a substantial welfare state and generated the tax revenues to pay for most of it. The vast majority of revenue was generated by substantial tax increases and improved tax collection. It is important to remember that on the eve of the current crisis Portugal was not running high budget deficits or carrying high debt.

The increased cross-border flows of capital, trade and labour that define globalisation and that are anchored by the EU's single market are thus compatible with very significant increases in a country's tax take. However, concerns about globalisation's impact on the tax mix and on the progressivity of income taxes seem well-placed and are given voice by important political actors, including the prime minister. There is evidence that the contribution of consumption taxes to the tax mix has increased and that the progressivity of income taxes has gone down. Nonetheless, movement in this direction is by no means constant. Episodes of fiscal consolidation, where the government is forced to confront imbalances between revenues and expenditures, include cases where income tax progressivity appears to increase.

Despite the dramatic increases in social spending and taxation that characterise democratic Portugal, post-tax and transfer inequality remains high. If the tax system is regressive and if heavily pension-focused social transfers replicate earnings inequalities, large increases in taxation and the creation of a welfare state will do little to reduce income inequality.

More recently the current economic and financial crisis is putting Portugal under severe stress. Fundamental mistakes in the architecture of the Euro, the imposition of severe austerity cuts from the troika and a decision by the Portuguese government to reduce budget deficits faster than the troika demanded have thrown Portugal into a deep recession. However, the crisis has also placed centre-stage the need for Portugal to address the issues of growth and economic competitiveness. High social spending during recent years of low growth was sustained through one-off measures and mechanisms such as declines in interest that are no longer available. Structural reforms, if successful, will take time to bear fruit. Internal devaluation is slow and grinding. Unilateral debt defaults or exit from the Euro carry wrenching costs. Until a new road to growth is found, the goal of a fairer society and a more equal distribution of income that a welfare state in principle makes possible will remain elusive. As austerity bites and structural reforms take shape, debate about the appropriate role for progressive taxation will continue.

Notes

1. Report of the 1926 Commission, cited in Silva Lopes 2005: 299.
2. See also 'The Uncertainty Society', *The Economist*, 3 March 2012.

CHAPTER 4

The Fiscal Lessons of the Global Crisis for the European Union

The Destructive Consequences of Tax Competition

JEREMY LEAMAN

> Within a single market and major trading bloc like the EU, it makes good sense to coordinate national economic policies. This enables the EU to act rapidly and coherently when faced with economic challenges such as the current economic and financial crises. (European Commission: webpage for Economic and Monetary Affairs)[1]

The global crash of 2008/9 revealed many hidden fault lines in the edifice of finance capitalism and in the policy architecture of the states called upon to sort out its mess. Many of these fault lines were programmed into the operational mindset of the most recent generation of policy makers in the so-called 'advanced economies'. One such fault line is evident in the Balkanisation of macro-economic policy making, in particular the neutralisation of policy coordination in the adoption of autonomous central banks and the associated imposition of a debt-avoidance imperative on treasury departments and individual spending ministries/agencies in most states. The real fragmentation of the political governance of macro-economic affairs stands in stark contrast to the popular image among European electorates, for example, of an incremental arrogation of power in policy making to public officials at both state and, in particular, at EU level. This illusion of the overweening 'insatiable' (Bessard 2008: 6ff) political behemoth is arguably one of the main strategic achievements of the neoliberal media campaign to blacken the name of state administrations/bureaucracies at the same time as these bureaucracies were being subordinated to, and instrumentalised by, the corporate controllers of markets and international capital flows.

The fragmentation of state macro-economic policy making was a key element in the neoliberal/monetarist revolution which overwhelmed Western political elites and their academic allies in economics research institutes so rapidly at the end of the 1970s and beginning of the 1980s. It was rooted in a fundamental rejection of the post-war Keynesian orthodoxy of coordinated, counter-cyclical and structural economic management, indeed it blamed Keynesian interventionism for the 'fiscal crisis' of stagflation and structural unemployment. The attempts by Keynesian 'technocrats' to fine-tune the development of aggregate demand and to ensure the stable social foundations of organised capitalism via welfare measures were accordingly replaced through both the withdrawal of the state from direct ownership and control of productive assets (privatisation) and the strategic abandonment of the perceived delusion of informed/refined state compensation for market weaknesses The neoliberal narrative sees the state rather as the source of market distortions; the efficient market hypothesis accordingly postulates the superior allocatory function of market forces, which the state can best optimise by removing supply-side obstacles to the competitive interactions of private enterprises through deregulation and liberalisation.

While the intellectual debris of the 'efficient market' hypothesis now lies exposed to wide sections of both political and intellectual elites and the electorates of the world, and while the salutary powers of state crisis management have been invoked by the same economic elites that had publicly eschewed them over the last thirty years, the institutional structures that underpinned the neoliberal revolution remain worryingly intact, to the extent that they threaten the medium- to long-term reform of both capitalism and the capitalist state, not to mention the progress of humanity to a socially and ecologically just future.

Fiscal Policy in the European Union: Fragmented and Asymmetrical

This danger is most clearly observable in the failure of the European Union to harmonise and coordinate the fundamental macro-economic policies of its member states and to prevent a destructive beggar-thy-neighbour competition between those states to attract foreign direct investment and employment, or simply paper profits (Rixen 2011). Where the case for national and international coordination and cooperation in short- and long-term crisis management was so overwhelming in the last months of 2008 and through 2009, the EU has arguably shown a worrying lack of leadership in both global multilateral forums (G20, WTO) and in its own regional affairs. The initial combined – if not coordinated – response of the larger developed states to the cardiac failure of banking and the resultant global contraction of production and trade, did not – as hoped – produce a new wave of concerted and refined strategies aimed at supporting all EU states. Rather, an extraordinary and anarchic process set in, involving on the one hand national counter-cyclical stimulus packages in the core member states of the old EU15 and, on the other, immediate pro-cyclical austerity measures in several of the newer central European member states.

Table 4.1 Recessionary Slump in the EU27 in 2009: Development of GDP and Domestic Demand Factors in Per Cent over Previous Year

	GDP	Private Consumption	State Consumption	Investment
Austria	−3.9	1.3	0.4	−8.8
Belgium	−2.8	−0.3	0.6	−5.3
Bulgaria	−5	−6.3	−5.5	−26.9
Cyprus	−1.7	−3	5.8	−12
Czech Republic	−4.1	−0.2	4.2	−9.2
Denmark	−4.9	−4.6	2.5	−12
Estonia	−14.1	−18.5	−0.5	−34.4
Finland	−8	−1.9	1.2	−14.7
France	−2.6	0.6	2.7	−7.1
Germany	−4.9	−0.1	3.4	−9
Greece	−2	−1.8	9.6	−13.9
Ireland	−7.1	−7.2	−1.8	−29.7
Italy	−5	−1.7	0.6	−12.1
Hungary	−6.3	−7.5	−1.1	−6.5
Latvia	−18	−24	−9.2	−37.3
Lithuania	−14.8	−16.8	−1.2	−39.1
Luxembourg	−4.1	−0.7	2.7	−14.5
Malta	−1.5	1.3	−0.7	−18.8
Netherlands	−3.9	−2.5	3.2	−13
Poland	1.7	2.3	1.2	−0.3
Portugal	−2.6	−1	3	−11.9
Romania	−7.1	−10.5	0.8	−25.3
Slovakia	−4.7	−0.7	2.8	−10.5
Slovenia	−7.8	−1.4	3.1	−21.6
Spain	−3.6	−4.9	3.8	−15.3
Sweden	−5.1	−0.8	1.7	−14.7
United Kingdom	−4.9	−3.3	1.2	−15
EU15	*−4.4*	*−1.9*	*2.3*	*−13.1*
EU27 Average	*−5.5*	*−4.2*	*1.3*	*−16.3*
EU10 (CEECs) Average	*−8*	*−8.4*	*−0.5*	*−21.1*
Hungary + Baltic States Average	*−13.3*	*−16.7*	*−3*	*−29.4*

Source: Eurostat 2010

The figures assembled in Table 4.1 above reflect in part the contradictory messages relayed from Brussels to individual member states during the 2008/9 crisis. On the one hand, the Commission publicly sanctioned the bank salvage programmes of the core EU states (Germany, France, UK, Belgium,

Netherlands) and convened a number of meetings of Finance Ministers to discuss anti-cyclical stimulus packages to prevent a further deterioration of the pan-European slump. Indeed, in the retrospective *General Report on the Activities of the European Union 2009*, the Commission even ascribes itself a key role in crisis management:

> By late 2008 the EU had designed an economic recovery plan that included initiatives to stimulate the real economy, and this was approved by the European Council in December 2008. During 2009, the European economic recovery plan started to come into effect. Its priorities were restoring business and consumer confidence, kick-starting lending and investments, and supporting and creating jobs. Central to the plan was the ability of the European Union to catalyse cooperation. The EU could exert its influence because it was able to harness Member States' and Union action, using the strengths of each part of Europe to best effect. This allowed the EU to help in shaping the global response to the crisis. (European Commission 2009b: 10)

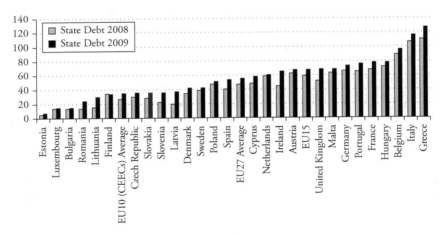

Figure 4.1 EU27 State Debt as a Percentage of GDP, 2008–2009
Source: Eurostat

This account is, however, an extremely selective view of the EU's role in the 2009 recessionary slump. In its 2009 *Spring Report*, the Commission (2009a) can be seen consistently to invoke the need for budgetary consolidation in a number of the newer member states of Central and Eastern Europe. Even in the case of Bulgaria which had a PSBR of only 0.5 per cent of GDP and an overall state debt ratio of 17.3 per cent of GDP in 2009, the Commission lamented the fact that 'discipline has not been maintained' and urged 'strict expenditure control'. In the case of Estonia, the Commission applauded the budget cuts by the Estonian state as a means 'to mitigate the risk of breaking the 3% threshold in 2009', even though Estonia's accumulated state debt was only a paltry 4.8 per cent of GDP (Stability Pact Ceiling: 60 per cent) and all the Western member states mounting anti-cyclical recovery programmes were set to exceed both PSBR and overall debt ceilings (see Figure 4.1)![2] Similar demands for (pro-cyclical) budgetary restraints were expressed in relation to Hungary, Latvia and Lithuania and supported by the IMF in conjunction with its emergency assistance to Hungary and Latvia; IMF assistance had been applied for, precisely because there was no coordinated plan for assisting all EU27 member states in the manner described so fulsomely in the above quotation. While EU15 states were encouraged to increase their expenditure – as evidenced in the 1.3 per cent average increase in state consumption for this group (Table 4.1), newer member states – particularly those with high structural current account deficits – were encouraged *to cut back pro-cyclically*; the average reduction of state consumption for the EU10 was –0.5 per cent, while for the Baltic states and Hungary it was –3 per cent.

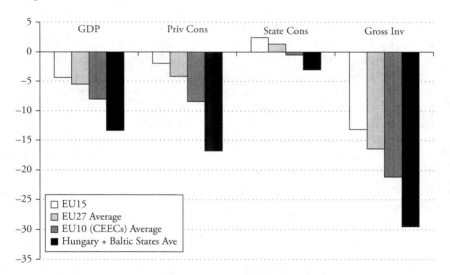

Figure 4.2 Development of Components of Domestic Demand in the EU in 2009 in Per Cent
Source: Eurostat, own calculations

An unequivocal causal link between budgetary retrenchment and extreme cyclical fluctuations in the newer member states is impossible to deduce, but it is arguably more than circumstantial that the contraction of GDP, of private consumption and of investments was far higher in the states urged to slash budgets during a recession (see Figure 4.2). Thus the worst recession for eighty years in the old EU15 (average for 2009: –4.4 per cent) is eclipsed in ferocity by the slump which hit CEECs (–8 per cent) or the smaller crisis group of Hungary and the Baltic states (–13.3 per cent); similarly, the collapse of investment, while dramatic in the EU15 (–13.1 per cent), was catastrophic in the crisis group (–29.4 per cent). The severity of the contraction was further reflected in marked increases in unemployment (Table 4.2).

Table 4.2 Rate of Total Adult Unemployment* and Youth Unemployment in the European Union, 2008–2009 in Per Cent

	EU15	EU27	EU10	Hungary	Estonia	Latvia	Lithuania	H + Balt
TAU 2008	6.3	7.0	6.3	7.8	5.5	7.5	5.8	6.6
TAU 2009	8.3	8.9	10.1	10	13.8	17.1	13.7	13.6
YU 2008	15.6	14.9	14.6	19.9	12.0	13.1	13.4	14.6
YU 2009	19.9	20.7	23.1	26.5	27.5	33.6	29.6	29.3

*Percentage of total labour force aged 15–74

Source: Eurostat 2010

While the rise in the rate of unemployment in the EU15 was limited to 2 percentage points both by fiscal stimulus packages and by labour 'hoarding' through various short-time arrangements (subsidised in Germany and elsewhere), unemployment in the EU10 rose by 3.8 percentage points to 10.1 per cent and by 7 percentage points in the crisis group to 13.6 per cent. The deflationary imperative of pro-cyclical deficit reductions is evident in the particular weakening of the labour market in the Baltic states, but also in the particular decline in the rate of consumer price inflation; while the recession produced a marked fall in EU27 inflation from an average of 5.3 per cent in 2008 to 1.3 per cent in 2009, the Baltic states, with the compounding influence of swingeing expenditure cuts and the currency peg to the euro, saw their average inflation rate drop from 12.3 per cent to 2.8 per cent.

Incoherence

In relation to the EU27 as a whole, therefore, there is no evidence of the Commission responding 'coherently' (see the quotation above) to the global crisis. At no stage was there a serious suggestion of applying harmonised EU-wide support for the vulnerable, peripheral countries outside of the EU15 or the Eurozone. Where there was evidence of member states having the fiscal wherewithal to finance stimulus packages through triple-A rated sovereign bonds, the Commission was happy to endorse such programmes. Where, on the other hand, member states had neither the fiscal strength in depth nor a healthy current account balance – the situation of most CEE states – the European Commission pursued an essentially ruthless policy of *sauve qui peut*, obliging Hungary and Latvia to make early approaches to the IMF.

Dilatoriness

Equally absent in the Commission's response to the crisis was the virtue of timeliness (also stressed in the quotation above); there was nothing very 'rapid' about the mobilisation of the counter-cyclical programmes in the core EU15 countries following the cardiac arrest of global banking in mid September. This was in large measure due to the initial resistance on the part of some member-state leaders to the idea that the crisis was more than a sectoral problem, confined to financial services. Peer Steinbrück, the German federal finance minister in Merkel's grand coalition, poured scorn on the British prime minister's call for coordinated deficit-financed stimulus measures as late as December 2008, dubbing Brown's approach 'crass Keynesianism'.[3] Steinbrück was deemed 'stupid' by the economist Paul Krugman, who at an early stage drew attention to the dangers of non-cooperation within the EU: 'If Germany prevents an effective answer on the part of Europe, it will make the global downturn worse'.[4] While Germany belatedly acknowledged the comprehensive and global nature of the slump with the implementation of a €50 billion stimulus package in January 2009, its dilatoriness became evident once again in the Eurozone's sovereign debt crisis of early 2010. The long delay in agreeing the Stabilisation Fund encouraged widespread short-selling of Greek, Portuguese and Spanish sovereign bonds and produced a dramatic widening of the bond-yields (bond-spreads) between these and German bonds. The cost of this failure, informed to a considerable degree by the neoliberal posturing of the German Free Democrats within the new centre-right coalition, will be felt acutely in the medium term. A more timely agreement would have prevented the divide-and-conquer speculation by hedge funds and currency dealers and ensured a much less expensive and more secure stabilisation of the Eurozone. Even more effective would have been the promotion of Eurozone bonds, guaranteed by all sixteen member states, as proposed by both Barroso and Van Rompuy among others earlier in 2010.[5]

The claim to timely coordination on the part of the EU is thus specious. Commission president, José Manuel Barroso, came close to acknowledging this in his 'state of the union' address in Strasbourg in May 2010, when he warned of the 'disintegration of the Union' and spoke of the lesson of the global crisis being the need for national economic disparities within the EU to be reduced: 'we swim together or we sink separately'.[6] What is or should actually be coordinated, is another matter. The Euromemorandum group argues that the very particular failure of the EU to achieve real progress in the coordination/harmonisation of fiscal affairs, most notably in matters of taxation, has seriously hampered effective crisis management in the short term and re-regulation in the medium to long term (Euromemorandum Group 2011).

A principal point of departure of the argument set out below is that taxation is the primary means within advanced capitalism for (a) reducing the disparities generated by the market determination of incomes and (b) achieving levels of income distribution which are deemed fair and which permit the maintenance of a solidaristic, democratic culture. What the European Commission has demonstrated in the area of taxation in the last two decades is at best culpable neglect of the redistributive potential of fiscal policy, at worst the deliberate promotion of widening disparities.

The Fatal Toleration of a Fragmented Tax Culture in Europe

Advanced states with a complex division of labour, with refined physical and social infrastructures and with democratic commitments to the social welfare of their citizens require high levels of revenue from sustainable sources. High tax ratios (as a proportion of GDP) are a consistent characteristic of prosperous and stable societies. Low tax ratios, particularly in times of severe economic crisis, make states more vulnerable to cyclical and structural shocks. This is particularly clear in the developments over the last two years. Figure 4.3 reveals marked disparities in the tax ratios of the larger, core states of the EU15 and the vast majority of the transition states that joined the EU in 2004 and 2007. It is significant that Greece, with an overall tax ratio of 32.6 per cent of GDP (including social security contributions), is almost

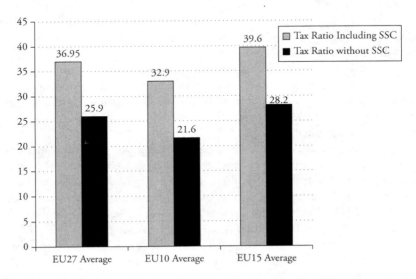

Figure 4.3 Tax Ratios as Percentage of GDP with and without Social Security Contributions, 2008

Source: European Commission 2010a; own calculations – the averages are arithmetic not weighted

exactly in line with the average for the EU10 (32.9 per cent), but more than 7 percentage points below the average for the EU15 (39.6 per cent). Ireland, long the EU15's most dynamic 'tiger' economy and flagship of neoliberal deregulationism, has an even lower tax ratio of 29.6 per cent of GDP; its 2009 budget deficit of 14.3 per cent was the highest in the EU27 and was set to exceed 20 per cent in 2010.

The EU's 2010 report, *Taxation Trends*, notes Greece's and Ireland's attempts to solve their budgetary problems by increasing their tax revenue (European Commission 2010a: 202ff) but does not draw the obvious conclusion from its extensive comparative data that low tax ratios in advanced states by and large weaken their ability to respond effectively to exogenous shocks; it is significant that the statistical annex to the annual report does not include weighted averages for the new member states but only for the EU27 and Eurozone states. When figures are aggregated for the EU10 and the EU15, it is hard to ignore the obvious fact that the only EU states that were able to mount counter-cyclical programmes, financed by increased borrowing, were the larger states with higher than average tax ratios and consequently the ability – acknowledged by credit rating agencies – to meet sovereign debt obligations through future revenue flows. None of the EU10 states were able to mount reflationary programmes, precisely because they lacked the critical mass of (taxation) revenue characteristic of the larger core states.

There is therefore a fundamental lesson that the EU and its member states need to draw from the global crisis if they wish to achieve an appropriate level of economic convergence, enhance the region's competitiveness (Lisbon Agenda) and avoid the disintegration of the European project:

- Advanced states need high levels of revenue in order
    1. to ensure an adequate provision of public goods and services;
    2. to ensure the social and economic security of all their citizens through measures of fiscal redistribution;
    3. to maintain the commitment of the population to democracy and social justice;
    4. to assist less developed states in their political and economic modernisation;
    5. to combat severe structural and cyclical economic crises.
- Low tax ratios are likely:
    1. to hinder modernisation through weaker provision of economic and social infrastructures;
    2. to render states dependent on (foreign) corporate interests that will not (necessarily) match the modernisation requirements of the wider economy;
    3. to weaken the ability of states to reduce disparities in market incomes through redistribution;

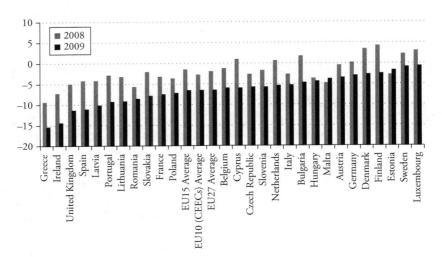

Figure 4.4 State Deficits in the EU27 in 2008 and 2009: Public Sector Borrowing Requirements as a Percentage of GDP
Source: Eurostat

4. to raise the Gini-coefficients of income and wealth distribution;
5. to weaken states' potential for effective crisis management.

Pre-programming Fiscal Vulnerability in the Newer Member States 1990–2008: Tax Competition and the Erosion of Progressive Taxation in the EU

The integration of twelve new member states – ten of them post-communist transition states – into the European Union proceeded according to a central condition of *convergence*: convergence of political, economic and social statutes and norms. 'Conditionality' involved, in the first instance, the preparedness to absorb the so-called *acquis communautaire* into the statute books of individual state jurisdictions. Secondly, and in contrast to previous enlargements, conditionality entailed the fulfilment of the Copenhagen Criteria of 1997, specifying particular commitments to democracy, market economics and human rights. While the *acquis* contained the requirement for all member states to adopt a minimum standard rate of 15 per cent for Value Added Tax (the primary source of indirect taxation), the failure of the European Union to produce a harmonised approach to direct taxation has meant that no such minimum standards (for rates and tax base) were applied to either Personal Income Tax (PIT) or Corporation Tax (CT); nor was there even an explicit commitment required to progressive taxation, i.e., to the principle of rates of direct taxation rising with increased gross incomes. All EU15 member states have maintained systems of progressive PIT but these represent no more than implicit parts of individual fiscal cultures rather than an explicit norm for membership of the European Union. This deficiency was evident at an early stage of the enlargement process involving Central and Eastern European countries when, in 1994 and 1995 the three Baltic states established systems of proportionate direct taxation ('flat tax' systems); the European Commission raised no objection to this deviation from the implicit norm of the EU15, even though progressive taxation is a key political vehicle for achieving a more favourable distribution of private household income through targeted state welfare transfers.

Table 4.3 Corporation Tax Rates in the EU10 and the EU15, 1990–2009

	1995	2000	2009
Czech Republic	41	35	21
Estonia	26	26	21
Hungary	18	18	16
Latvia	25	25	15
Lithuania	29	29	20
Poland	40	28	19
Slovakia	40	40	19
Slovenia	30	25	22
	1990		
Austria	30	34	25
Belgium	41	39	33.99
Denmark	40	32	25
Finland	25	29	26
France	37	33.3	33.3
Germany	50	45	15
Greece	46	40	25**
Ireland	43	24	12.5
Italy	36	37	31.4
Luxembourg	34	30	25.5
Netherlands	35	35	25.5**
Portugal	36.5	32	27.5**
Spain	35	35	30**
Sweden	40	28	26.3
UK	35	30	28**

Sources: World Tax Database; **denotes top rates

Of the seven remaining EU10 states, four subsequently introduced similar 'flat tax' regimes for personal income tax (Slovak Republic 2005, Romania 2005, Bulgaria and the Czech Republic 2008); only Poland, Hungary and Slovenia have retained progressive systems, i.e., higher marginal rates for higher earners. While all EU27 states have been affected by the acceleration of tax competition within the region, only one EU15 state has seen any discussion of a similar reform to its PIT system, namely during the 2005 election campaign by the Christian Democratic Union in Germany, but then only fleetingly because of doubts over its voter appeal. The effects on all tax systems in the EU of the abandonment of progressivity on the new Eastern periphery have nevertheless been significant, with a marked flattening of the curve of progressivity – i.e., a narrower difference between bottom and top marginal rates – and significant reductions in capital tax rates, most notably corporation tax.

As Table 4.3 shows, thirteen out of the fifteen 'old' member states have corporation tax rates that are considerably lower in 2009 than they were in 1990; all fifteen have lower rates today than in 2000. The average rate of CT for the EU15 was 42.7 per cent in 1980, 37.5 per cent in 1990, 33.5 per cent in 2000 and just 26 per cent in 2009. While German capital taxes also include local business taxes, its new, common 15 per cent CT rate is almost as low as Ireland's much criticised 12.5 per cent rate and represents the most dramatic reduction in all EU15 countries since 2000. Average CT rates for the 2004 Central European accession states have fallen from 31 per cent in 1995 to just 19 per cent in 2009. Significantly, the CT rates in the two 2007 Balkan accession states (Bulgaria, Romania) and in the applicant states of the western Balkans are even lower on average. With several Balkan states (Albania, Bulgaria, Macedonia, Serbia and Srpska within Bosnia-Herzegovina) levying a standard 10 per cent, and Montenegro an even lower 9 per cent, the regional average for the Balkans is just 14 per cent.

There is a 'revenue paradox' relating to CT inasmuch as revenues from this tax Europe-wide have not fallen significantly as a proportion of total tax revenue, a fact taken by some to assert that tax competition is benign. There are, however, reasons for this paradox: firstly, rate reductions have been accompanied by the removal of some allowances and the broadening of the tax base; secondly, and more importantly, there is clear evidence of 'income shifting' as non-incorporated businesses change their legal form to avoid the generally higher marginal rates of PIT, normally applied to SMEs; thirdly, profits from capital as a proportion of national income expanded markedly in the 1990s and the recent decade, increasing the volume of taxable corporate income (Sørensen 2006; Mooij and Nicodème 2008; Piotrowska and Vanborren 2008).

Top rates of PIT have been reduced since the middle of the 1990s; Figure 4.5 shows the arithmetic average for the EU27 falling from 47.3 per cent in 1995 to 37.5 per cent in 2010; the average for the EU10, the countries of Central and Eastern Europe, has fallen to just 28.5 per cent in 2010, in large measure as a result of the flat tax regimes in seven of the ten states.

Although the revenue losses from reduced top marginal rates were in part compensated by the reduction in allowances and thus the broadening of the tax base, this was insufficient to halt the gradual decline in the share of direct taxes in total taxation. This is particularly marked in the EU10, where the arithmetic average share of indirect taxes in total taxation rose from 38.5 per cent in 1995 to 41.4 per cent in 2007 (EU27: 37.1 per cent) while the share

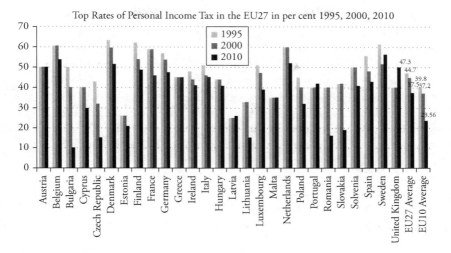

Figure 4.5 Declining Rates of Income Tax in Europe, 1995–2010
Source: European Commission 2010a

of direct taxes in the EU10 fell from 27.1 per cent to 24.6 per cent in the same period (EU27: 32.3 per cent).[7] Indirect taxation (VAT, excise duties) has a regressive effect on the distribution of income as poorer households spend a higher proportion of their disposable income on consumption, save a much smaller proportion of that income and benefit disproportionately from basic allowances on PIT (Ganghof 2004, 2006, 2008).[8] While the European Union acknowledges the higher dependency of the transition states on consumption taxes (European Commission 2010a: 19) as well as the downward trend of CT and PIT rates in this region and the EU27 as a whole, it does not acknowledge the regressive nature of recent taxation trends. Rather, in a bizarre and very brief paragraph on 'tax fairness', the 2010 survey of taxation trends even suggests a shift towards greater progressivity:

> The fairness of the tax system has been a major concern. Several countries have introduced measures to safeguard lower incomes, usually by raising allowances or, in a few cases, raising the top PIT rate. This seems to point towards some increase in progressivity in the coming years. (European Commission 2010a: 28–29)

This conclusion is entirely delusional. Four EU27 states have indeed raised top marginal rates as crisis measures (Greece, Latvia, Hungary and the UK) but two others have lowered theirs (Denmark, Finland); seven have reduced CT rates during the crisis and eight have made reductions in PIT regimes, in part providing particular relief for SMEs and the self-employed. By the same token, the EU notes a rise in standard VAT rates in eight countries, reductions in three (temporary in the UK) and increases in excise duties in sixteen EU27 states (ibid.: 28–29). The average top rate of PIT in 2010 was still almost ten percentage points lower than in 1975. How an 'increase in progressivity in the coming years' can be extrapolated from these indicators is entirely mysterious, since the trend continues to be self-evidently in the opposite direction, i.e., towards an increase in 'regressivity' and unfairness in the distribution of tax burdens. What also emerges from an analysis of the specific tax measures recorded by the EU report is the high concentration of PIT and CT stimulus measures in the core Western states of the EU27; these PIT/CT measures totalled a full 1.6 per cent of GDP in Denmark, 1.5 per cent in France, 1.4 per cent in Germany, 1.25 per cent in Austria and 1.1 per cent in Sweden. In contrast, there was an overall contractive effect of tax measures in Hungary (–0.5 per cent of GDP), Estonia (–3.12 per cent) and Latvia (–4.57 per cent) (figures calculated from EU's own data in ibid.: 30–48).

The Persistence of Neoliberal Fiscal Imperatives

Against the background of the worst global economic crisis in living memory, the European Commission's most recent 430-page report on the EU's tax affairs is astonishingly unreflective, as well as lacking in scientific rigour. The absence of a coherent programme of coordination and harmonisation in the field of taxation and a toleration of the colossal disparities in tax systems and tax cultures within the EU27, contrast markedly with the Commission's persistent and painstaking focus on the *other* key features of fiscal policy, namely public expenditure and the reliance of Europe's state authorities on borrowing to cover revenue shortfalls. The policy architecture of the European Monetary Union and the overall mindset within the wider Union is characterised by the old monetarist imperative of the primacy of deflation, the control of the money stock by an autonomous central bank, using short-term interest rates and open-market trading, and the 'crowding-in' of private demand for credit through strict limits on public borrowing, i.e., state demand for credit. This deflationary imperative dominated the Maastricht Convergence Criteria, it dominates the Stability and Growth Pact and it has dominated the debate about the Eurozone's Stabilisation Fund. The totally arbitrary ceilings set for annual borrowing (3 per cent of GDP) and overall state debt (60 per cent) have, for the guardians of this architecture – in particular successive German administrations and the European Central Bank – taken on totemic significance as primary macro-economic targets, sidelining other objectives, like job creation, a sustainable, healthy environment and social well-being. Crucially, in this context, the monetarist discussion of sovereign debt as a means of bridging revenue shortfalls does not thematise the adequacy of customary revenue sources (taxes and excise duties) in a systematic way: that is, the chronically low tax ratios of Ireland, Greece and most CEECs are not identified as possible causes of fiscal weaknesses. Up until 'the crisis', the colossal leakage of potential revenue through the systematic use of private and corporate tax avoidance schemes, through inadequate policing by revenue authorities, non-compliance by wealthy taxpayers, through corruption and tax evasion, and the scandalous nonsense of tax havens within Europe and beyond its shores, were the object of an extraordinary conspiracy of silence among the European policy-making community (Shaxson 2011). The remarkable zeal with which the sin of 'excessive' public sector borrowing was exposed and criticised stands in stark contrast to the blithe neglect of the industrial scale 'off-shoring' pursued by banks and global accountancy firms on behalf of their clients, and the consequent haemorrhage of tax revenues in the 'onshore' jurisdictions.

Since September 2008, admittedly, EU state leaders did start to draw attention to the anomalies of 'off-shoring', tax avoidance and tax havens, given both the suddenly newsworthy scandals of Madoff, Stamford and others and the unprecedented cost of bank salvage operations. It was, after all, blindingly obvious that the key agents in global financial services – the big banks and the 'big four' accountants – that were co-responsible for the sectoral crisis, were also centrally involved in the culture of systematic concealment that is represented by tax avoidance programmes. However, three years on from the outbreak of the crisis, surprisingly little has been done to address either the issue of destructive intra-European tax competition or the continuing scandal of programmatic tax avoidance on the part of Europe's economic elites.

In relation to tax havens, both the European Union and the OECD have developed an analytical approach which seeks to identify 'unfair tax competition' and which – in the case of the OECD – involves an Internationally Agreed Tax Standard (IATG) and contrasting categories of tax jurisdiction, measured by the respective level of compliance with this standard (OECD 1998). A 'white list' consists of states that both recognise and comply with the standard; a 'grey list' includes states that have signed up to the standard but have yet to comply with its requirements – centrally of information exchange between tax authorities – and, finally, there is a 'black list' category of jurisdictions which do not recognise the standard.

Implicit in the notion of 'unfair' or 'harmful' tax competition is the clear understanding that there are forms of tax competition that are not harmful, that are indeed benign. The history of the OECD listing programme has, consequently, been sadly predictable (c.f. Rixen 2011: 22). With its emphasis on bilateral information exchange between the tax authorities of all jurisdictions in the 'white' category, the primary target has not been tax avoidance – which continues to be legal under international law – but 'tax evasion'. It is therefore not surprising that, by the end of September 2010, the vast majority of tax jurisdictions addressed by the OECD programme had both signed up to the IATG and implemented their compliance (OECD 2010a: 14ff). The 'white' list thus includes jurisdictions which can still be classed as tax havens and continue to belong to the extensive network of offshore locations through which tax avoidance programmes operate: e.g. Andorra, Bermuda, British Virgin Islands, Cayman Islands, Guernsey, Jersey, the Isle of Man, Liechtenstein, Monaco, Switzerland and the Turks and Cacos Islands are adjudged 'white' by dint of their agreement to exchange information on the serious, but still comparatively minor problem of tax evasion.

Tax competition between national jurisdictions in a globalised world without exchange controls is fundamentally corrosive of sustainable fiscal systems (Genschel, Kemmerling and Seils 2010; Rixen 2011). It is absurd to equate the progressive reduction of fiscal sustainability through the successive underbidding of one tax authority by another with competition on commercial markets. Martin Wolf, the *Financial Times* commentator, correctly asserts that 'the notion of the competitiveness of countries, on the model of the competitiveness of companies, is nonsense' (Wolf 2005: 268).[9] Even before the outbreak of the current crisis, a *Financial Times* editorial underlined the need for the urgent global regulation of taxation:

> A world in which a global plutocratic class pays little or no tax, while benefiting from the stability generated by taxes imposed on the 'little people', will prove unsustainable.[10]

The lack of any coordinated approach to the fundamental problems of tax competition allows tax avoidance agencies to continue their regulatory and tax arbitrage, as evidenced by the recent but separate national initiatives to negotiate bilateral agreements with low tax jurisdictions or to impose separate bank levies (France, Germany, UK) or a temporary increase in the top marginal rate of PIT to 50 per cent (UK). The response to the latter move has been a set of corporate decisions to shift their locations to lower tax jurisdictions.[11] Grey lists and white lists will do nothing to alter this situation. A blockade of tax havens, as recommended by Willem Buiter would be a more effective way to end the destructive beggar-thy-neighbour tax competition throughout Europe:

> The vast majority of European countries – all those that lose out because of the existence of these tax havens – should unite in a determined effort to end these countries' ability to offer safety to tax evaders by granting anonymity, confidentiality and secrecy. (Buiter 2008)

Eliminating the corrosive effect of low tax jurisdictions would also provide a basis for tackling the increasing inequality in European societies.

Taxation, Crisis and Increasing Inequalities

Europe is the most populous advanced region of the world, with a politically unified population of almost 500 million and a 'neighbourhood' of some 250 million. As a political region, the EU unites twenty-seven democratic states with relatively high tax ratios and, by international comparison, higher levels distributional justice; they make up a clear majority of the fifty nation states with a Gini coefficient of 0.36 or below; of the ten states in the world with the statistically most favourable Gini coefficient of income distribution, seven are EU member states.[12] This is no coincidence. Democratic legitimation, distributional equity and high levels of taxation are strongly correlated (Boix 2003; Acemoglu and Robinson 2006; Profeta and Scabrosetti 2010). More recently, Wilkinson and Pickett (2009) have argued persuasively that 'more equal societies almost always do better'; the central tenet of their study has been reinforced in the public imagination by the revelations of elite greed and stupidity in media coverage of the global slump.

Wilkinson and Pickett actually pay more attention to synchronous comparisons between countries and less to international developments over time. For students of economic history, it is the erosion of Europe's relatively high levels of equality over time that should arguably be regarded as the most significant developments, as these help to account for the scale and intensity of the global slump as it affected the region and also give some indication of the particular dangers inherent in the crisis-management strategies favoured by the EU and its member states. The role of tax systems in the evolution of the social distribution of income and wealth is of central importance, as there is clear evidence that 'tax competition causes inequality within and between countries' (Rixen 2011: 7).

If one takes the functional distribution of national income (Figure 4.6 overleaf), that is, income from wages and salaries compared with income from capital, the period 1980–2005 shows an extraordinary decline in the gross wages ratio, without precedent in the modern history of capitalism; this decline matches an equivalent rise in the profits ratio, such that the share of profits in national income in Europe rose by 9.36 percentage points in the twenty-five years up to 2005 as the wages ratio declined by the same proportion. The development of the gross wages ratio provides the best illustration of the increasing inequality of the market-determined distribution of income, i.e., the inequality that advanced states have historically sought to reduce through fiscal transfers, a process which requires appropriate revenues. A widening of market-determined income disparities logically places increased demands on fiscal authorities if they want to prevent a deterioration of net per capita disparities in the personal distribution of income.

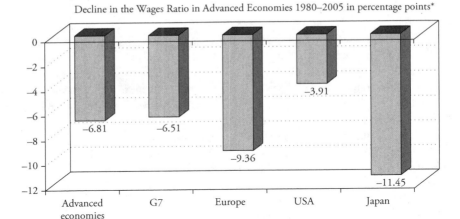

Decline in the Wages Ratio in Advanced Economies 1980–2005 in percentage points*

Figure 4.6 The Rise in Inequality before the Global Crisis
*The gross wages ratio is the share of wages and salaries of gross national income
Source: IMF 2007, data for Figure 5.7

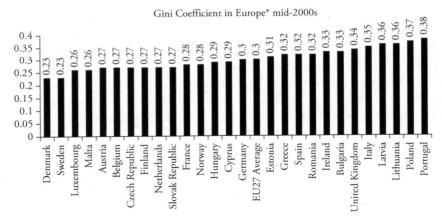

Gini Coefficient in Europe* mid-2000s

Figure 4.7 Distribution of Personal Income in Europe: Gini Coefficient after Taxes and Transfers
*EU27 plus Norway
Source: OECD; CIA World Factbook

The net personal distribution of income, as measured by the Gini coefficient, has become demonstrably less equal since the 1970s. The most recent dataset from the OECD shows a rise in the average Gini index for OECD countries from 0.296 in the 1970s to 0.31 in the mid 2000s; the average for the European members of the OECD rose 20 basis points from 0.275 to 0.295 between the mid 1980s and the mid 2000s; when one adds the newer EU

Table 4.4 Development of Income Distribution in Europe 1980s to Mid 2000s

Gini Coefficient*	Mid 1980s	Around 1990	Mid 1990s	Around 2000	Mid 2000s
European OECD members (av)**	0.275	0.283	0.286	0.291	0.295
EU 27 (av)				0.296	0.30

*After taxes and transfers **Arithmetic average
Source: OECD 2011, CIA World Factbook; own calculations

member states that are not members of the OECD (Bulgaria, Cyprus, Estonia, Latvia, Lithuania, Malta and Romania) the most recent average for the EU27 stands at 0.3.

While such Gini scores are still low by global standards, the trend towards greater income inequality is clear and to be expected, given the thrust of the neoliberal 'tax reform movement' of the 1980s (Sandford 2000: 158ff) and the tax relief this afforded both corporations and non-incorporated businesses. The average figures also conceal significant differences between individual countries, where typically the Scandinavian and Benelux countries show markedly lower Gini scores (0.23–0.28) and Baltic, Mediterranean and Anglo-Saxon economies (UK and Ireland) show significantly higher levels of income inequality (0.32–0.38). There is also an identifiable correlation between tax ratios and Gini scores: low Gini scores are associated with higher tax ratios (average for the Benelux/Scandinavia group: 46.3 per cent of GDP); high Gini scores generally correspond to lower tax ratios (average for Baltic, Med and UK group: 34 per cent of GDP). However, the case of the United Kingdom illustrates an additional and critical contradiction in the political economy of welfare regimes in the context of fiscal supply-sidism.

In its 2007 survey of poverty and inequality in the UK (Brewer et al. 2007: 21), the Institute for Fiscal Studies asserted that tax and benefit reforms under the Labour administration since 1997 had 'clearly been progressive, benefiting the less-well-off relative to the better off'; it also asserts that these reforms 'have had very little impact on overall levels of inequality' (ibid.: 23). Rather, the very considerable increase in welfare benefits (aimed at poor households with children in the main) had succeeded only in preventing a further significant rise in the Gini coefficient: the widening disparities of market incomes (gross incomes before taxes and transfer payments) had thus required increasingly expensive compensatory welfare payments in order for net distribution to stand still. All welfare regimes are confronted by this dilemma: poverty in advanced political economies is defined – rightly – as a relative phenomenon, measured by the degree to which households are deprived of the means to participate fully in the life of a given society. Deprivation of or exclusion from those means is defined in terms of household incomes which lie below a percentage threshold of median income (usually 60 per cent). In a situation where the market incomes of particular sections of society (be they quintiles or percentiles in the distribution) grow at divergent rates, the distance between the lowest quintile/percentile and the median increases and the need for compensatory fiscal transfers rises. Because the New Labour (Blair/Brown) regime had committed itself, firstly to halve and then to eliminate child poverty and also address pensioner poverty, while at the same time boosting profit income through PIT and CT reductions, it created a self-defeating dynamic of rapidly declining marginal utility.

A number of recent studies have demonstrated the disproportionately small group of top households – the top 1 per cent or even top 0.1 per cent of households – that have benefited from the general shift in favour of capital incomes (Atkinson and Piketty 2007). The period of relative equalisation of household incomes in the thirty years following the end of the Second World War has, according to these and other studies, given way a period of regression where levels of inequality have risen to those reminiscent of pre-modern times. Göran Therborn (2009) asserts that: 'The gap in income between those at the top and the average worker is now much wider than it was in pre-modern times'.[13] In 1688, English baronets had an annual income about one hundred times higher than that of labourers and out-servants, and 230 times that of cottagers and paupers. In 2007/8, chief executives of the FTSE top 100 companies received remuneration 141 times higher than the median income of all full-time employees in the UK, and 236 times higher than those of people in 'sales and customer service occupations' (Therborn 2009).

Levels of poverty have accordingly risen within European states over the last three decades. Recent figures from Eurostat show that, in 2009, the percentage of the population 'at risk of poverty', i.e., with a disposable income below 60 per cent of median income, stood at 23.1 per cent, with marked differences between the old EU15 (20.5 per cent) and the EU10 (30.1 per cent). Figure 4.8 also shows a general correlation between low tax ratios and a higher risk of poverty. There is nevertheless a clear danger that the 'race to the bottom' and the flattening of progressivity within the EU27 as a whole will weaken the ability of all states to adopt redistribution measures to counteract the effects of market-determined income disparities.

Two processes of redistribution become evident therefore, the first by capitalist corporations through financial 'engineering' and assisted by political deregulation up to 2008, and the second by the state/taxpayer in the extraordinary salvage operations of late 2008/early 2009. Jean-Claude Trichet, current president of the ECB, conceded in a *Financial Times* interview in 2010 that on both sides of the Atlantic taxpayers 'put approximately 27 percent of GDP on the table to stabilise the system and avoid a major global depression' (Trichet 2010a). Even if some of the EU states' surety for the banks' toxic assets is not in the end required and even if there is some return

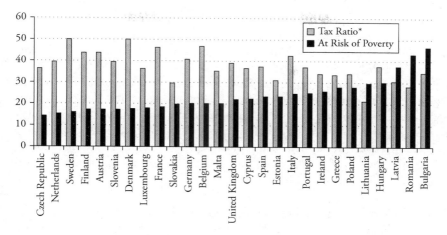

Figure 4.8 Taxation as a Correlate of the Risk of Poverty**
**Share of persons with equivalised disposable income below 60 per cent of median income
Source: Eurostat, OECD, CIA, own calculations; *Taxation as a proportion of GDP

from the reprivatisation of nationalised banks, the scale of the salvage operation remains staggering: if one takes the Eurozone countries and the United Kingdom, their nominal GDP in 2008 was just over €11 trillion, the volume of state expenditure and guarantees therefore just short of €3 trillion (€2.99 trillion). Trichet rightly emphasises the magnitude of the bank salvage operations – the most unprecedented programme in peacetime in the modern era – but he does so in the context of repeated demands from himself and other members of the ECB board for all EU states to end stimulus measures and concentrate on reducing budget deficits and overall debt levels (Trichet 2010a; see also Stark 2009). It is significant that the demand for retrenchment (July 2010) was couched in slightly different terms:

> The growth of public debt has been driven by three phenomena: a dramatic diminishing of tax receipts due to the recession; an increase in spending, including a pro-active stimulus to combat the recession; and additional measures to prevent the collapse of the financial sector. (Trichet 2010b)

Rhetorically, here, Trichet focuses on state expenditure as anti-cyclical stimulus and not on the 'additional measures to prevent the collapse of the financial sector'. However, these 'additional measures' dwarf the debt-financed stimuli of the German, French, British and other governments. What Trichet also neglects to point out is that fiscal retrenchment and the accompanying austerity measures will further cement the level of inequality reached as a result of reckless casino operations. 'Accompanying the market as it progressively gets back to normal' (Trichet 2010a) sounds ominously complacent in terms of the 'normal' propensity of 'the market' to fail and the distributional factors which contributed to that failure.

There are two fundamentally flawed assumptions in the reasoning behind Trichet's and others' argumentation: The first is that, by reducing the contribution of the public sector to aggregate domestic demand, the state will ensure sustainable levels of social prosperity and lower deficits in the short, medium or long term, irrespective of timing. The second is that, by restoring the 'normality' of the market, the latter's 'allocatory efficiencies' would emerge, despite all the historical evidence to the contrary.

1) The global slump is not just a normal, if severe, cyclical weakening, nor even a normal structural crisis, like the sectoral shifts of the nineteenth and twentieth centuries. Rather, it represents a fundamental crisis of accumulation, in which the rent-seeking dynamic of credit-driven fictitious capital came to a shuddering halt in a manner similar to the Ponzi schemes it ultimately resembled. The 'normal' expectation of rates of return on capital far in excess of the real rate of economic growth proved delusional; the expectation that state treasuries could rely on profit-rich financial institutions providing a constant revenue stream, despite the systematic abuse of tax avoidance schemes, was delusional.

The market 'normality' of the last thirty years has resembled the collective stupidity of the fairy-tale courtiers persuaded to deny the tailors' swindle and the emperor's nakedness rather than be judged ignorant. Trichet cannot be allowed to 'accompany' this market back to normality; tinkering with Tier One capital ratios will certainly not ensure sustainability of either GDP growth or fiscal health. Only a recalibration of demand nationally, regionally and globally in the direction of fairer distribution will achieve anything remotely resembling stability.

2) The austerity measures announced by the major economies of the EU – Germany, France, Italy, Spain and the UK – amount to cutbacks of 0.47 per cent of total EU27 GDP for each of the subsequent four years, or 1.9 per cent of current GDP. If one adds to this the cutbacks planned for Ireland, Denmark, Latvia, Lithuania, Estonia, Poland, the Czech Republic, Romania, Portugal and Greece, the combined negative multiplier effect on aggregate domestic demand will be considerably greater than 0.5 per cent for each of the next four years. With the rate of unemployment forecast to rise from 7.5 per cent to over 10 per cent in 2010/11 and public sector salaries set either to stagnate or – as in the case of Ireland, Spain, Portugal, Romania and Greece – to be significantly reduced, the prospects for increased consumer spending are also weak in the short term. There is strong evidence of households seeking to reduce their credit card

debts, pay off their mortgages and increase their savings (European Commission 2010b: 20). Such contingency measures appeared entirely justified as the ratio of unemployed people to job vacancies rose from 6:1 prior to the crisis to almost 12:1 in the third quarter of 2009 (Hijman 2010: 7).

With aggregate unemployment set to rise to 9.75 per cent in the EU27 and to 10.5 per cent in the Eurozone (European Commission 2010b: 23), it is unlikely that the competition for jobs will ease. Arguably more significant is the effect that the rise in structural unemployment is having and will continue to have on young people. Between 2008 and 2009, youth unemployment in the EU27 rose from 14.9 per cent to 20.7 per cent; in the EU10 from 14.6 per cent to 23.1 per cent. In five CEECs more than a quarter of the younger labour force are out of work; in Latvia (33.6 per cent) and in Spain (37.8 per cent) the situation is even more critical. The individual and macro-economic consequences of this early exclusion of so many younger members of society from paid labour can be at the very least estimated in terms of the proven 'wages scar' suffered by workers at later stages of their working life compared to those who have enjoyed continuous employment (Gregory and Jukes 2001; Gregg and Tominey 2004; Leaman 2010: 61f).

The long-term sociopolitical consequences of one fifth of all young Europeans experiencing unemployment – while a mere tenth of all adults are so affected – can also be guessed at in terms of established and fairly robust correlations between social exclusion, delinquency, drug and alcohol dependency, criminality, imprisonment, mental ill-health and anti-social behaviour, particularly in societies with greater inequality (Wilkinson and Pickett 2009). One can add to this the negative consequences for home countries of the migration of sections of the younger population, particularly the better qualified and more enterprising, as noted by a recent ILO report (Ha et al. 2010).

1) Depoliticisation and social alienation among young people also risk weakening democratic culture still further.
2) There is a danger that young people will turn their backs on their labour market (Ha et al. 2010: 8).
3) Government austerity measures will have a direct negative effect on inequality in EU countries (Heise and Lierse 2011) because they reflect a reduction in the core redistributive function of fiscal policy; the severe cuts to a variety of welfare benefits already begun in Ireland, Greece, Spain, Portugal, Latvia, Estonia, Lithuania, Hungary and Romania are set to be followed by similar cuts in the core economies, most notably in Germany and the UK.

Conclusions

There is fairly robust evidence of 'location competition' within Europe driving down rates of direct taxation and flattening the curve of progression (Ganghof 2004; Genschel et al. 2011; Rixen 2011). The associated reduction in the progressive, redistributive function of direct taxation is compounded by the shift of overall tax burdens from direct taxation to regressive indirect taxation. The deterioration of the 'vertical equity' of taxation, indeed the widespread use of tax reductions for wealthy taxpayers, in turn increases overall levels of income inequality, and with particular reference to the poorest deciles/percentiles of the income distribution. The 'horizontal equity' of taxation – for example in relation to company taxation – has been further compromised by the differential treatment of corporations compared to non-incorporated businesses: where corporation tax rates are consistently below top marginal rates of personal income tax – particularly in the EU15 – SMEs that cannot choose the option of incorporation are faced with considerably higher tax burdens than their corporate counterparts; incorporation conversely has compounded the problem of vertical equity (Sørensen 2006; Mooij and Nicodème 2008; Piotrowska and Vanborren 2008). By the same token, the widespread use of tax avoidance schemes by the corporate sector skews the real distribution of income within national European jurisdictions still further away from notions of vertical and horizontal equity.

The problems of tax competition and tax avoidance are international problems. Such problems cannot be solved at national level through bilateral arrangements, not even by quasi-hegemonic states. The continuing potency of corporate threats to relocate for influencing legislative processes is clear evidence of the relative powerlessness of individual jurisdictions to resist (Brooks 2011). They are therefore of necessity only soluble on a multilateral level and in consequence an obvious and urgent task for the European Union. Its record hitherto has been disappointing, particularly in relation to its failure to prevent seven of the twelve new member states from abandoning progressivity in direct taxation and its inability to find common ground in combatting the corrosive effect of low tax jurisdictions and corporate tax avoidance. The snail's pace of progress towards a Common Corporate Tax Base (CCTB) augurs very badly for any meaningful harmonisation of direct taxation as a whole.

Above all, the fiscal policy architecture of the European Union and key member states like Germany and the UK remains fixated on state expenditure and debt ratios as problems, ignoring the critical disparities in state revenue ratios and the not unrelated disparities in external balances. The one-eyed obsession with state borrowing is a relic of the simple-minded monetarism which failed to ensure either macro-economic stability or growth and which presided over the catastrophic farce of light-touch regulation and the hugely expensive debacle of financial meltdown, recession and sovereign debt crises. Fiscal sustainability cannot be achieved in Europe simply by leaning on state expenditure and state debt; a European fiscal union which reinforced the German preference for 'crowding-in' through debt brakes and austerity would fail, if it neglected to establish common rules for revenue generation and tax justice. States like Ireland, Greece and Portugal which either deliberately choose to have lower tax ratios or only achieve low tax ratios because of avoidance and non-compliance cannot reasonably expect the taxpayers of countries with more appropriate tax ratios and tax rates to subsidise their sovereign debt and finance their current account deficits.

The most recent sovereign debt crisis does not therefore simply reveal the consequences of over-exposure to casino capitalism but, above all in this context, the folly of tax competition. Companies which fail to generate sufficient cash-flow and/or sustainable bridging finance will, *ceteris paribus*, be liquidated or at best acquired and asset-stripped by larger companies. Democratically legitimated states do not have this option. They are obliged to maintain both the loyalty of voters and of enterprises to the social and economic by ensuring the viability of its institutions and processes. Members of a currency union and/or participants in a regulated single market can only reasonably expect the support of fellow participants if there is a politically defined framework of horizontal equity and mutual support. The European Union has signally failed to provide such a framework in the field of taxation and consequently runs a very serious risk of fragmentation and marginalisation in the medium term.

Notes

1. European Commission (no date): <http://europa.eu/pol/emu/index_en.htm> (accessed 12 September 2010).
2. The PSBR/Debt figures for 2009 were: Belgium: 6.0 per cent/96.7 per cent of GDP; Germany 3.3/73.2; France 7.5/77.6; Italy: 5.3/119; Netherlands: 5.3/60.9; Spain: 11.2/53.2; UK: 11.5/68.1.
3. Quoted in *Die Welt*, 11 December 2008.
4. *Focus Online*, 11 December 2008, available at: <http://www.focus.de/politik/ausland/ briten-kritik-nobelpreistraeger-empoert-ueber-steinbrueck_aid_355277.html> (accessed 16 January 2009).
5. It is significant that José Manuel Barroso singled out Germany for criticism in relation to the Stabilisation Fund, ascribing the popular scepticism towards the package to Germany's exaggerated fears of Greek default and the demands of some leading German commentators that Greece should leave the Eurozone.
6. Quoted in *Die Welt*, 25 May 2010.
7. 2007 is more representative of the trend as the crisis which set in in 2008 distorted individual revenue streams significantly
8. In its annual report, *Social Trends*, the UK Office for National Statistics calculate

that indirect taxes consume 31 per cent of household income in the poorest fifth of households, while the wealthiest fifth spends just 13 per cent (Office for National Statistics 2009: 73).

9. It should be added that Martin Wolf in *Why Globalisation Works* (2005: 249ff) takes a more benign view of the effects of globalisation and tax competition on the manoeuvrability of the state; the current sovereign debt crisis that has hit the very states that have lower than average tax ratios – in part because of low tax regimes designed to attract FDI – should be sufficient evidence to suggest that tax competition in Europe has indeed weakened states.

10. *Financial Times*, 25 June 2007.

11. The British plumbing specialist, Wolsey, announced the shift of its tax base to Switzerland in September 2010, following the media company Informa earlier in the year. United Business Media and WPP have both shifted their tax base to Ireland (*New Statesman*, 27 September 2010); see also the recent report by the British Institute of Directors, 'How Competitive is the UK Tax System?' (Institute of Directors 2010).

12. Germany, Austria, Malta, Slovakia, Czech Republic, Luxembourg, Sweden.

13. Available at: <http://www.eurozine.com/articles/2009-10-02-therborn-en.html>.

PART II

Taxation, Taxation Policy and Less Developed Economies

CHAPTER 5

British Government Attitudes to British Tax Havens

An Examination of Whitehall Responses to the Growth of Tax Havens in British Dependent Territories from 1967–75

PAUL SAGAR, JOHN CHRISTENSEN
AND NICK SHAXSON

Introduction: The Rise and Rise of the British Tax Haven Empire

Britain has close political and economic ties to thirty of the sixty tax havens ranked in the Financial Secrecy Index.[1] The British tax haven empire, including former colonies of the British state such as Hong Kong and Ireland, has captured a massive share of the market for offshore financial services, accounting for 37 per cent of global banking liabilities and 35 per cent of paper assets (Palan, Murphy and Chavagneux 2010).

Several factors might explain the rise of Britain's tax haven empire. Firstly, the growth of Britain's imperial power during the nineteenth century was driven to a significant extent by global trade in financial services, including banking, insurance and shipping (Cain and Hopkins 1993). Second, the extension of English Common Law practices to colonial territories provided a favourable legal milieu for developing tax haven activity, particularly for creating offshore trusts and non-resident companies. Third, during the course of its imperial expansion, Britain colonised an astonishing number of small islands and microstates where colonial financial and commercial elites could shape local polities to their interests. Fourth, anxious to avoid building up long-term liabilities during its period of imperial decline the British state seemed happy enough that its colonial outposts, some of which were not prepared to opt for outright independence, were being used as conduits for capital from outside the sterling area headed towards the City of London. Finally, the emergence of what became known as the Euromarket in London in the late 1950s played a significant part in reversing the decline of the fortunes of the banks of the City of London, which were more than happy to exploit the lax regulation and low-tax environment provided by what Tom Nairn has labelled 'the flotsam and jetsam' of Britain's former empire (Nairn 1997: 146).

The development of tax havens in British colonies preceded post-war decolonisation. In the 1930s Canadian and US citizens started to use Bahamian offshore companies and private trusts for tax avoidance purposes (Hampton 1996: 98). During the same period organised criminal networks in the US pioneered the use of tax havens in the Caribbean to hide and launder their ill-gotten assets. Jersey, in the British Channel Islands, was also attracting wealthy tax exiles as early as the 1920s, to the extent that in 1927, during Winston Churchill's period as Chancellor of the Exchequer, UK Treasury officials and Channel Island authorities convened in London to negotiate an agreement, the so-called Bailiff's Clause, preventing Jersey-incorporated companies from being used to hold assets of UK residents who would otherwise be liable to UK estate duty (ibid.: 149). The 1920s also saw the emergence of transnational companies using offshore captive insurance companies for aggressive tax avoidance, with Bermuda becoming a market leader in this sector (ibid.: 31).

The spectacular rise of London's Euromarket activity in the early 1960s quickly spread to the City's offshore satellites. During the 1960s and early 1970s many US banks established branches in the Caribbean to act as offshore booking centres (ibid.: passim). Likewise, London banks started relocating their private client banking activities and Euromarket booking offices to the Channel Islands. In Jersey, as in the Bahamas, the driving force behind the early development of tax haven activity consisted largely of a local, but outwardly connected, financial and legal elite who spotted opportunities to attract foreign portfolio capital, much of it illicit, in either its origins, its manner of transfer, or its final use. They were helped in this project by the rather extraordinary nature of their relationship with Britain. Although apparently autonomous in key respects, not least their ability to decide domestic tax rates, they were closely tied in others, for example, being in monetary union with sterling and having strong laws to protect property rights backed by the British judicial system as the final court of appeal. More importantly, behind the façade of local democracy senior officials appointed by the British government exerted powerful controls over domestic politics, discreetly protecting Britain's (and the City's) interests (Shaxson 2011). These perceptions of stability were reinforced by other attractions, such as generally weak or non-existent regulation, minimal or non-existent direct taxes, and strict laws protecting client data from external investigation. It was not surprising, therefore, that financial and business elites in British colonies saw opportunities for attracting offshore financial services. It is also not surprising that British colonial officials were alarmed by some of the characters coming ashore in the Caribbean. On 3 November 1961, for example, W.G. Hullard of the Colonial Office, stationed in the Bahamas, wrote a memorandum to B.E. Bennett at the Bank of England noting:

> We feel that this [lack of provision of an effective regulatory system] might be a grave omission, since it is notorious that this particular territory, in common with Bermuda, attracts all sorts of financial wizards, some of whose activities we can well believe should be controlled in the public interest.[2]

Our research at the National Archives in London did not reveal a response to Mr Hullard's memorandum. Nor have we been able to trace any clear evidence that during the period of decolonisation the British government actually had a coherent policy regarding the development of its Crown Dependencies and former colonies as tax havens. This is consistent with Payne, who concludes: 'In short, a British policy towards its Caribbean dependencies can hardly be said to have existed' (Payne 1991: 26). Perhaps this is not surprising since more pressing events, such as the Suez Crisis, developments in the ongoing Cold War, and the Malayan and Kenyan insurgencies, would have taken precedence around the Cabinet table. But this does not necessarily mean that the development of Britain's tax haven empire occurred spontaneously in a political environment of benign neglect. Other explanations can be posited. We know, for example, that the Foreign and Commonwealth Office at times encouraged tax havenry in certain Caribbean territories in order to reduce potential future liabilities. On the other hand we also know that British colonial officials were alarmed by tax haven activities happening under their noses and, as we shall see, Britain's Inland Revenue was increasingly concerned at revenue loss arising from British residents using offshore structures to evade estate duties, capital gains and income taxes. But what of other major departments like the Treasury or the Bank of England? This chapter explores some of the evidence collected from archival research in London. But as we make clear, much more investigation is needed before we can begin to understand the full history of the astonishing growth of Britain's tax haven empire.

'Increasingly Concerned'

On 18 October 1967, the British Inland Revenue wrote their Treasury civil service colleagues a memorandum whose exasperation is still palpable today.

The note opens pessimistically, with the Revenue stating that they 'do not suppose that the Treasury will be able to help us in this, but we feel we must leave no stone unturned'. Specifically, the Revenue were 'increasingly concerned about the avoidance of tax through "tax havens"', for it is proving 'very difficult for us to extract any information from those we suspect, or even to know who is engaged in the traffic'. The memo continues:

> A variety of sophisticated and elaborate services are no doubt employed. If we had complete information our existing anti-avoidance measures would probably catch some cases; others might well escape, but until we know more about what goes on, we cannot tell. Death duties may be involved, as well as taxes on income. Tax havens are mostly within the sterling area. Press reports suggest that in Bermuda and the Bahamas in particular the provision of the avoidance facilities is one of the major industries and that members of the local government are involved in the business.[3]

Such was the Revenue's desperation for information the Treasury might supply, that 'Even a piece of gossip that Mr X. was thought to have made such a transfer would be some help, because we might not hitherto have suspected Mr X. and we can then at any rate launch an attack on him by requesting information'. The Revenue acknowledged that there would probably be little or no information available on territories within the sterling area, but that if they were 'too pessimistic about this', then discussion between the departments at working level might usefully be arranged.[4]

Although the Revenue's statement of 'increasing' concern indicates it may have had an eye on the tax haven problem for some time, it is reasonable to speculate that by October 1967 domestic political and economic pressures brought the issue to prominence. Whilst Harold Wilson would not be forced into the humiliation of devaluing sterling until 18 November, any issues pertaining to the sterling area would already have been high in the minds of civil servants by October of that year. More generally, the Revenue in particular may have been under increasing pressure to recoup tax losses as the Wilson government attempted to bring down a large current account deficit inherited from the previous Conservative government (Newton 2010). Newton states that by 1967 the current account deficit was estimated at £800m, but later revised down to £300m (ibid.: 912).

Initially the Treasury showed little sympathy with the Revenue's concerns. A Mr Glover replied for the Treasury, referring to an earlier report on the Bahamas which 'noted that the Bahamas were a tax haven, but concluded that it would not be appropriate to exclude them from the Scheduled Territories on that account. In other words we deliberately decided then that Exchange Control considerations and Revenue considerations were separate and should be kept separate'. Accordingly, 'It must be supposed that Parliament does not wish to close the loopholes. Unless the resulting situation damages the balance of payments, there is no reason for us to intervene'.[5] Similar sentiments are expressed by a Mr Walker (also of the Treasury), who notes that the Bank of England has never reported cases of tax evasion to the Treasury and that very sensitive issues about information disclosure are raised by cooperation with the Revenue: 'The fact that Parliament has refused to give the Revenue powers for perhaps potentially the most powerful method of avoidance detection leads me to conclude that we should proceed with great caution in using any of our or the Bank's information for this purpose'.[6]

Yet despite this initial hesitancy, figures within the Treasury soon came around to sharing the Revenue's concerns. Specifically, the potential for tax haven abuse to seriously undermine sterling exchange controls and thus the UK balance of payments, made them a live issue for the Treasury. This concern would produce a short period of fascinating correspondence, report writing and conflict within and around Whitehall. Examining the records from this period offers insights into both the bureaucratic decision-making processes of the period, and also into understanding and explaining the nature and extent of the involvement of the British state and other British institutions in the growth and spread of offshore tax haven activity in dependent territories. This chapter attempts to begin that process of understanding and explanation, in the hope of stimulating further research into an essential, but largely neglected, area of British (and global) financial and economic history.

On 13 November 1967, Treasury attitudes to Revenue concerns began to soften. A Mr A.K. Rawlinson indicated that whilst the Treasury would not wish to disclose information regarding avoiders of tax (sticking thereby to the view that 'avoidance' constitutes legal activity but 'evasion' crosses the line into criminality), it would be happy to cooperate regarding evaders. He also remarked, intriguingly, that it is 'no accident that there are tax havens in the sterling area'.[7] Following a memorandum expressing concern that tax haven activity potentially harms the UK balance of payments, a meeting between the Treasury and Inland Revenue was held in mid December.[8] Revenue representatives stressed that they were increasingly concerned about tax havens being used to evade and avoid tax, and that the number of havens was rapidly increasing (especially in the Caribbean), expressing further concerns over the ease with which funds were being moved. Still wary of disclosing sensitive information, Treasury officials reiterated that whilst they were willing to cooperate regarding evasion, they were reluctant to do so regarding avoidance.[9]

However, as 1968 progressed, Treasury attitudes towards tax haven activities hardened. On 29 April, A.J. Gower Isaac of the Treasury wrote to the Bank of England, stating that 'Some of my colleagues here are investigating, with the Inland Revenue, the present and possible future movement of capital to so-called "tax havens" abroad'. Isaac stated that he would be 'very grateful if, for this purpose, you could let me have . . . any figures available to you about the gross cash flows for private investment other than direct investment in each of the following countries', before listing sixteen such 'tax havens'. Isaac, however, betrayed no naivety about the availability of data: 'I realise that hard information in this detail is very limited at present . . . But anything which you do have, even of a qualitative nature, would be welcome'; the sixteen tax havens were: Andorra, Antigua, the Bahamas, Barbados, Bermuda, Cayman Islands, the Channel Islands, Gibraltar, the Isle of Man, Jamaica, Lichtenstein, the Netherlands Antilles, Monaco, St Vincent, Switzerland 'and (prospectively) the Virgin Islands'.[10] Even so, he must have been disappointed with the Bank's response:

> As you suspect, our information about portfolio investment in the 'tax havens' you mention is very scanty. So far as the overseas sterling area is concerned, such figures as we have relate only to net changes in investment; and the country detail, which is admittedly far from comprehensive, does not show up any change of significance in 1967 in any of the countries you list. The Channel Islands and the Isle of Man are not covered at all by our survey as they are treated as part of the United Kingdom. There are a few unit trusts based in the Channel Islands who presumably get some money from UK investors, but we are unable to say how much.
>
> Exchange control sources give us a little better information about portfolio investment in the non-sterling area – but from the list of countries you mention there are only two where the figures are large enough to show up. [Figures are then given for the Netherlands Antilles and 'Switzerland (including Liechtenstein)']['[11]

Isaac's hopes that we 'shall be in a much better position when [the Bank's] new inquiry gets under way' were clearly misplaced.[12]

By June 1968, however, the Treasury was taking seriously the prospect of acquiring information for the (joint) use of the Revenue. In a striking correspondence, J.G. Littler of the Treasury wrote to his colleagues Walker and Isaac:

> Whether we can score any success with this exercise will depend on our ability to persuade the Bank of England to provide, or obtain and provide information which the Inland Revenue can use, and we shall obviously need to tread wearily. My impression after talking with Mr Isaac is that we may not be up against quite the brick-wall I had originally expected to meet at the Bank of England. We are unlikely to succeed with requests for comprehensive detailed information, but Mr Isaac thought it not impossible that certain kinds of specific information, of particular value, might ultimately be obtained.

Littler goes on to suggest that the Revenue be prompted to ask a narrow range of specified questions 'in an overall form which, by prior enquiry, we might know to be just possibly acceptable to the Bank'. The message was clear: progress must be attempted 'piecemeal, by trying to work up specific questions which can be put acceptable to the Bank of England'.[13]

This correspondence alone is startling. It indicates the extent to which information essential to the sovereign British revenue collector was held not by government departments, but by the Bank of England (nationalised in 1946, but still clearly acting autonomously) – and the degree to which the Bank was perceived as being uncooperative by the affected Government departments. As we shall see, the impression of the Bank as a recalcitrant guardian of secret information only deepens.

By July 1968 the Treasury and Revenue convened a joint working party 'On the Balance of Payments aspects of Tax Questions'. A minute states that 'tax havens may involve not only tax losses to the Exchequer, but also losses to the balance of payments'. It continues:

> The extent of these losses is at present unknown, and one of the objects of the current exercise is to establish as closely as possible the size of these tax/balance of payments gaps. If further examination suggests that the amounts at stake are large, the conjuncture of balance of payments and tax interest might make it appropriate for the Revenue to aim to devote more resources to the problem, though on tax grounds alone the problem would probably not warrant this.

The working party was initially optimistic that Section 30 of the Exchange Controls Act 1947 could be used to extract necessary information from individual companies, but decided that this would in fact not be so. Instead the tenor of the mid July report is that the Bank of England holds crucial information (though attention at this stage is directed especially to non-sterling area havens).[14]

Commenting on the situation, a Mr Draper of the Revenue aptly represented his department's apparently permanent cynicism vis-à-vis their chances of success: 'Although, like the poor, these tax avoidance problems will always be with us we should, I think, try and dispose of these comparatively straightforward information problems fairly quickly now'.[15] The following day Draper wrote to Isaac at the Treasury and laid his department's problems out clearly:

> [The Treasury] say that the 'Revenue have very considerable powers of investigation when they know where to look'. This is true but I am not sure they will be of much use unless you were able to direct us to particular individuals and companies. There is, nevertheless, something to be gained

from more detailed Balance of Payments information and perhaps the way to deal with this point is simply to delete the sentence referred to.[16]

Lack of information – not governmental powers – emerges as the main stumbling block to Revenue (and Treasury) action against tax havens. The point was understood by Littler at the Treasury, who observed that the Revenue 'are not entirely sure what it is they need to stop, what its scale is, and how best to set about tackling the problem'; 'what the Inland Revenue are therefore searching for is some guiding information'. He drew the obvious conclusion in September 1968: 'what we really need is a meeting between Bank of England and Inland Revenue' at which the Revenue could explain their requirements and the Bank could indicate where it would be able to help and what 'would be quite impossible to touch'. Littler acknowledged that this 'is probably going to mean trespassing rather near ground of confidentiality on both sides', but suggested that the Treasury would be willing to play 'honest broker'.[17]

Yet the Bank was cool towards Littler's advances. Responding to the Treasury's earlier request for information on companies operating in non-sterling area tax havens, the Bank claimed that due to 'pressures of work' they were able to do only a 'sample analysis' rather than the usual one quarter of the three hundred companies on their list – thus reducing the usefulness of any results. The Bank then provided just four short bullet-points of information,[18] before remarking tersely that 'We are not particularly anxious to continue this exercise'.[19] Following further Treasury correspondence urging the Bank to attend a joint meeting with the Revenue, a reply was sent in late October. The author (the signature is illegible) at the Bank remarks: 'I am very glad to note that you accept the unsuitability of using information acquired in the course of administering exchange control'. Nonetheless a meeting with the Revenue was agreed to, for which the 'appropriate people' would be made available. But a warning was also imparted: 'I might add that I am far from sure whether we can make any significant contribution to the kind of assessment which you evidently have in mind, although of course we shall do our best to help'.[20]

The Bank/Revenue meeting went ahead on 10 December 1968, in the room of Mr Littler at the Treasury. The Revenue's position was that tax-avoidance activities had increased substantially since 1965 (though proving to what extent was difficult). Although the Revenue possessed 'extensive' powers to bring abuse under control, these pre-required much information which it was ordinarily too laborious to justify collecting unless a substantial loss to the British state was already known to be taking place – the 'catch 22' of the situation is clearly evident. The Revenue was therefore seeking information which would help it estimate the scale of the problem, and it believed that 'the Bank was probably in a better position to give a provisional view on this than either

Treasury or Revenue'. Yet the Bank was lukewarm in its response, claiming that any help it could offer was limited by the fact that British West Indian tax havens were all in the sterling area, and therefore the most they could probably achieve was an estimate of the magnitude of balance of payment flows. 'The other limiting factor was the lack of detailed knowledge on tax matters in the bank'. Yet despite this confession of official ignorance, a possible course of action was mooted, one fitting with the shady nature of the topic under discussion. The Revenue suggested that: 'the Bank might feel able to have informal discussion on a confidential basis with a few bankers who were willing to cooperate to get their view of the size of the problem'; 'The matter would obviously need much tact, but it could be put to those concerned that their help was being sought on an informal basis as the alternative to a much more far-reaching probe by the Revenue which . . . could turn out to be unnecessary'. As the minutes note 'the object was to avoid using a sledge-hammer to crack what could be a possible nut'. Perhaps unsurprisingly the Bank was highly reluctant, 'plainly' needing to consider this possibility 'very carefully' and claiming it would be imprudent to take any initiative for at least two or three months. However, the Bank did offer to do some preliminary work comparing the UK balance of payments to that of tax havens as a 'useful starting point'.[21]

Yet any cheer the Revenue and Treasury might have taken from this meeting was not to last. On 24 January 1969, the Bank wrote to both departments regarding the possibility of informally approaching UK bankers to gauge the scale of tax haven activity, and rejected this possibility. Firstly, it claimed that it would be in danger of contravening Section IV(iii)(a) of the Bank Act which debarred it from requesting information of any banks regarding the affairs of particular customers. Secondly, the Bank claimed the approach simply would not work because the information sought was not discernable through informal enquiry, and '[f]or these reasons we would prefer not to pursue this request'.[22] Although some basic information was provided by the Bank about direct and portfolio investments (relating to the request regarding balance of payment flows made at the earlier meeting), the tone of the Bank's correspondence is one of attempting to bring matters to a close.

The declassified Treasury file which carries the correspondence and documentation examined so far ends here – except for one newspaper clipping included at the final page. The article recorded is by Charles Raw, financial editor of the *Sunday Times*, and already established as a vociferous proponent of financial deregulation. Raw's article is entitled 'Why not turn the City into a Tax Haven?' with an argument to precisely that effect. That this possibility had crossed the minds of the Bank's key players is, in turn, an intriguing one. Especially in light of the institution's recalcitrance vis-à-vis the offices of the state and, as we shall see, its later enthusiasm for cooperation with British tax havens.

Despite the Bank's reluctance to engage, the Treasury and Revenue continued to pursue the tax haven issue into 1969. In March that year Littler wrote to both the Revenue and the Bank, as well as a Mr O'Brien of the Foreign and Commonwealth Office, and a Mr Rednal at the Ministry of Overseas Development, alerting all to a discussion being held between the accountants Price, Waterhouse and Co. and the government of Montserrat, apparently aimed at establishing the latter as a tax haven:

> The developing of tax havens, particularly those within the sterling area . . . is already damaging to the UK balance of payments and revenue. We have estimated outflows to tax havens resulting in direct loss to our balance of payments as being as much as £10–20 million per year recently. And there are signs that these arrangements will gradually become more damaging if we do not take steps to prevent this.

Littler expressed further concern at developments in the Cayman Islands, and an apparent trend for tax havens to compete with each other to offer the best deal, enhancing the opportunities to avoid UK tax and move capital out of the UK. He further flagged particular concern regarding the 'tinier islands', who unlike well-established Bermuda and the Bahamas cannot be expected to support a 'complex and effective exchange control system, and which may well be more inclined to compete in the offer of inducements'.[23]

O'Brien of the FCO replied to the Treasury stating that 'we share your concerns about these developments'. He noted that the FCO had been engaged in discussions with the St. Vincent administration in 1968 about tax haven issues, and that the department was being approached by a Mr McAlpin, 'a U.S. citizen who wishes to take over the Turks and Caicos Islands and run them as a base for brass-plate financial activities, largely U.S.-orientated'. O'Brien goes on to inform the Treasury that regarding Price, Waterhouse's involvement with Montserrat, this was done in the full knowledge of both the FCO and Ministry for Overseas Development (ODM), with the aim of reducing the subsidy paid by Britain to that territory – and that apparently the Revenue were kept informed throughout. However O'Brien stated that:

> Our recent experience over a number of developments in the Caribbean . . . has led us to the conclusion that we should attempt to draw up a set of general principles for the guidance of dependent administrations in dealing with developers and other commercial organisations who wish to set themselves up in business in the smaller territories in return for tax concessions of various kinds. There are some pretty fly operators about, particularly in the Caribbean (? Anguilla) [sic], and it is up to us to ensure as far as possible that the smaller territories in particular are not done down.[24]

Following this correspondence a meeting was arranged between the Treasury, Revenue, FCO, ODM and the Bank of England. The FCO provided a note – 'Tax Havens and Tax Concessions in the Dependent Territories' – made available to all departments, which makes the following observations: that tax havens are bad for the British Revenue; that they are a drain on the balance of payments due to the capital outflow they facilitate; that they create exchange-control loopholes and leakages; that they are increasingly characterised by being in territories where the local administration lacks the financial expertise for effective management (e.g., Turks and Caicos); and that the United States revenue authorities are very concerned about proliferation of Caribbean tax havens and the attendant American revenue loss.[25] Accordingly the note recommends that Britain discourage the growth of tax havens, whilst observing that territories themselves will tend to suffer from setting up as tax havens.[26]

More striking, however, are the minutes of the meeting itself. O'Brien of the FCO argues that an inter-departmental study is required, and that whilst the Government can do little regarding independent countries, many tax havens in the sterling area are amenable to Bank of England influence. Littler, speaking for the Treasury, is characteristically concerned about the impact of tax haven capital outflows on the UK balance of payments, describing the capital outflow and the aid given to territories as a 'double burden' on the balance of payments. Green of the Revenue, unsurprisingly, sounds opposition to all new tax havens and expresses existing frustration towards the established ones, claiming that losses to UK revenues were increasing. He also points specifically to the Cayman Islands, which had introduced new trust law apparently designed to specifically undermine that of the UK. He adds that the USA was very unhappy about the proliferation of Caribbean tax havens, and that other European nations were increasingly affected, before expressing a desire to amend some of the UK's double taxation agreements accordingly. The Bank of England, however, was quite clearly concerned primarily with loopholes in the exchange control system created and/or exploited by tax havens. The rise of small territories – e.g., Cayman Islands – was apparently causing serious concern to the Bank (but only insofar as it undermined exchange control). The Bank's priority was thus not to stop tax havens being tax havens, but simply to ensure they possessed the sufficiently sophisticated administrations required to be *reliable* financial centres for exchange control purposes.

However, as the meeting developed, fissures appeared when discussing the impact of tax haven activity on dependent territories themselves, with concerns raised that in the longer term Caribbean islands in particular might be made *worse* off. Mainly, this was because costs tended to rise quite quickly after a financial centre was established; as most of the business was really taking place elsewhere – the territories simply providing 'brass plate' locations – profit was limited in the long run, with territories quickly undermined by neighbours offering better deals. Accordingly, the 'meeting agreed that brass plate activities tended to build up an artificial impression of wealth which was not based on actual resources and that dependent territories should be warned that it might not be in their long-term interests to attract these activities'. However, it was also observed that many such territories lacked any apparent alternative to economic development, due to possessing small populations and limited resources, as well as suffering geographical isolation. The Treasury at this stage suggested that 'in some cases it might be appropriate to increase development aid in order to deter territories from setting themselves up as tax havens'; specifically, the level of aid 'could be used either as a stick or a carrot in negotiations with the territories concerned'. Yet the ODM opposed this, saying it was 'not in favour of threatening the cessation of development aid as a deterrent in a matter of this kind'. As we shall see, growing divisions between departments (and the Bank) can be traced back to this March 1969 meeting.[27]

It is important to note that during this period two dependent territories in particular were causing alarm and concern to the Treasury and Revenue. First, the Cayman Islands had recently pursued an extremely aggressive policy of introducing legislation apparently designed to frustrate the tax arrangements of the UK.[28] However in this period the territory that caused most alarm appears to be the Turks and Caicos Islands, insofar – and especially – as these islands were apparently intent on emulating the practice of not just long-established havens like the Bahamas and Bermuda, but the more aggressive and fast-moving financial activities of Cayman. As a result, much attention is given over to the Turks and Caicos by the Treasury especially, and the territory became a sort of case-study for newly emerging tax havens – the focus point of debate on the extent to which overseas dependent territories should be allowed, or even encouraged, to pursue tax haven status as an alternative to dependency on British aid.[29] Unsurprisingly, the Treasury in this period was opposed to the creation of tax havens within the sterling area, insofar as it was predominantly concerned with balance of payments issues. However, the Treasury was alive to the dilemma faced by both the territories who wished to develop economically, and the FCO (and ODM) who were keen to find ways of no longer needing to support their 'colonial pensioners' in the Caribbean.[30] That financial services offered only short-term opportunities for many dependent territories to develop away from UK-dependence made the situation particularly difficult. Nonetheless, the proposals being put forward by the Turks and Caicos Islands – including the granting of 'sweeping' tax exemptions to potential developers – are described as 'preposterous' in the British documentation, and great scepticism was frequently expressed about such plans by the Treasury especially.[31] Yet the FCO in this period admitted to being under considerable pressure, particularly from the domestic populations of territories which demanded the opportunity to emulate tax haven neighbours and set up brass-plate bases in a gambit to achieve rapid economic development.[32] As we shall see, preoccupation with the Turks and Caicos would lead to an inter-departmental party being sent to the Islands to assess the situation there and report on how it could best proceed. But it is first necessary to return to the Whitehall of 1969, in the wake of the March FCO meeting.

On 11 April the Bank of England wrote to the Treasury and FCO, reiterating worries about exchange control leakage through tax havens, with especial concern at the behaviour of the Cayman Islands. The Bank cited not just lack of expertise or infrastructure for proper exchange controls, but also concern about 'expatriate operators who aspire to turn [dependent territories] into their own private empires'. Concerned at the outflow of UK capital to places like Cayman and the Turks and Caicos, the Bank proposed to send its own experts in order to assist in establishing proper exchange controls. The aim was not to stop tax haven activity, just to make sure it took place in a manner not damaging to UK exchange controls – although the Bank still claimed the 'action we are proposing . . . is first and foremost to help the UK'.[33]

Littler of the Treasury replied, and given his department's concern with exchange control unsurprisingly backed the Bank's suggestion to 'send a man' to provide financial expertise, a move supported by his departmental colleagues.[34] Yet when the Revenue and Ministry of Overseas Development become involved, divisions soon emerged. First, Green of the Revenue wrote to the other departments, asking that stronger wording be added to an advice document being prepared for circulation amongst the dependent territories, particularly regarding the downsides of attracting 'brass plate' companies.[35] However, at the start of May the ODM wrote – partly in response to the Revenue – a remarkable letter best quoted at length:

> [W]e may be in danger of looking at this too much from the point of view of the British Government and not sufficiently from the point of view of the interests of the dependent territories themselves. I do not think that it would be wise to dismiss out of hand the possible indirect benefits which 'brass plate' companies may bring to the dependent territories in the form of commercial entrepreneurship that might not otherwise be attracted to the area. It can be argued that tax havens which are mainly aimed at North American companies may have little adverse effect on the United Kingdom and could even benefit sterling area reserves.

Accordingly, the ODM suggested that any warning in the planned circular about brass plate companies should be tempered by a subsequent paragraph stating that 'although the direct benefits of brass plate activities may be small they may bring indirect benefits through attracting to the territory entrepreneurs and financiers who may themselves embark upon commercial enterprises of value to the territory that would not otherwise be undertaken'.[36]

This position was not greeted kindly by the Revenue. Green responded to Rednall, stating that whilst the proposed circular drew attention to the harmful impacts upon the British revenue of tax haven activities, 'this is not I would have thought a matter for which we need apologise'. He continued: 'Most, if not all, of the territories to which this document will be sent are receiving significant budgetary aid and in addition, no doubt, large amounts of development aid' – and the UK risked giving the further impression that it turned a 'blind eye' or gave 'tacit approval' to tax haven activity. Indeed, some of the activities of 'the smaller developing countries in the tax haven field are inimical to the interests of the UK Revenue, and where this is so we are bound to take action to protect ourselves', especially from the Cayman Islands, which has introduced legislation which 'blatantly seeks to frustrate our own law for dealing with our own taxpayers'. Green suggested that such legislation was introduced at the insistence of 'UK operators', and that action of this kind was 'to say the least, unfriendly', and that it was 'deplorable that we should encounter it in territories which still derive a considerable amount of assistance from the UK'. As for Rednall's claim that brass plate enterprises bring 'indirect' benefits to territories, the Revenue viewed such benefits are 'overrated', and they would be very interested 'to know what evidence there is' that brass plate legislation 'has attracted any worthwhile development' in long-established tax havens. Drawing on experience in the Bahamas, Green claimed: 'A brass plate company can have literally no more connection with the territory in which it is "resident" than the brass plate indicating its place of registration and the services for a few minutes a year of a local bank manager, accountant or solicitor. All the financial transactions of the company can take place outside the island'. Suffice to say, the Revenue strenuously opposed the ODM's proposals.[37]

The Bank of England, however, did not side with the Revenue; instead it expressly backed Rednall's position and claimed that 'experience elsewhere has shown that the ability to establish a tax free company generates activity and employment – particularly in the development of tourism. All of this would look pretty attractive to some of the undeveloped islands around the world'.[38] Further correspondence shows the Revenue and Bank continuing to hold these contrasting positions,[39] and Green in particular writes to O'Brien at the FCO that it 'is in our view highly regrettable that a study financed by the UK exchequer should . . . have led to the . . . substantial loss to the UK Exchequer through the opening up of new opportunities of avoidance of UK income tax'.[40]

A draft for circulation to the administrators of dependent territories was prepared by September 1969. Although the draft's opening page stresses at some length the risks of 'brass plate' strategies for attracting growth – because 'brass plate' companies themselves bring little development to a territory, and hence little financial or economic activity will actually take place there and anyway firms will quickly relocate to more competitive neighbours – it none-theless notes that, "Brass plate companies can of course sometimes help to promote local development since they bring to the territories entrepreneurs and financiers who may assist with the provision of finance when a worth-while local project comes along'.[41] The document then proceeds to give a fairly comprehensive overview of 'do's and don'ts' when dealing with prospec-tive developers, entrepreneurs and financiers seeking to locate in dependent territories. Hence, the document is much what we would expect: a compro-mise between affected departments in Whitehall. Revenue warnings and concerns are included – but tempered by the ODM and Bank's insistence of 'indirect' benefits to 'brass plate' tax haven activity. The bulk of the document ultimately tracks the dominant concerns of the Bank and the Treasury, pos-sibly reflecting these two institutions' relative power: that if dependent terri-tories *are* going to engage in tax haven activities, then they should do so in a manner favourable to UK exchange controls.

In late 1969 and early 1970, government departments became increas-ingly alarmed by activities in the Turks and Caicos Islands. A proposal by the developer Morris Wigram Ltd. to invest in the islands in exchange for exten-sive tax relief caused concern amongst the Treasury, Revenue and FCO, with the latter worried about the Islands becoming 'yet another tax haven' in the sterling area.[42] However, the departments also acknowledged pressure from the Islands' residents – envious of apparent economic developments in Cayman – to allow them to pursue 'tax haven' activities. But Whitehall offi-cials were also concerned that the long-term interests of the territories would in fact be undermined by such policies, a tension that manifests itself frequently in official documents over this period.[43]

In early 1970 an official government party, led by Derek Jakeway, was sent to the Turks and Caicos Islands to make an assessment of the Islands' develop-ment needs and potential, and reported in March alongside another official report undertaken by private contractors – the 'TTT' Report. The Jakeway Report concluded that a judicious mix of tourism and property development were the only solution to the Turks and Caicos's economic problems.[44] Noting that the Islands government had succeeded to a remarkable extent in interest-ing private enterprise in the development of the Islands, the report noted 'an urgent desire to raise the standard of living' and achieve 'development whatever the cost'.[45]

Interestingly, the Jakeway Report did not shy away from considering the possible downsides of 'tax haven' development. As well as an appendix includ-ing a section entitled 'The arguments for and against the setting up of a "tax haven" in the Turks and Caicos',[46] the main report acknowledged 'undesirable dangers in development', especially the risk of creating a 'state within a state'.[47] Furthermore, social tensions would be risked if tax haven status led to a 'rapid, uncontrolled influx of foreigners'.[48] Nonetheless, the report concluded that despite the dangers of tax haven-style development, the Turks and Caicos exhibited 'considerable potential'.[49] The authors thus concluded 'that there are good prospects for the territory to achieve a balanced budget by the mid-seventies, with the consequent elimination of budgetary aid' by pursuing tax-haven policies.[50] And even though there were considerable social and political implications – in particular an influx of North Americans who might quickly outnumber present inhabitants – the 'Islanders say they are prepared to accept this; and indeed we see no alternative but a continuation of the present state of stagnation, impoverishment and dependence on British dole'.[51] Perhaps the most striking aspect of the Jakeway Report is the extent to which it offers precisely this relatively strict dichotomy, between either dependency on the 'British dole', or tax haven development. On balance the report concludes that tax haven activities offer the best prospects for the Turks and Caicos, and even goes so far as to suggest establishing an offshore trust system 'similar to that now operating in the Cayman Islands – i.e., exemption from taxation for a maximum period of 50 years dating from a fixed base year'.[52]

Unsurprisingly, the conclusions of the report were not greeted kindly in all Whitehall departments. The Revenue in particular felt that Jakeway focused excessively on exchange controls and neglected the potential tax-loss impacts to the UK. Whilst Jakeway indicated that the Turks and Caicos could attract reserves of £75,000 a year from company and trust fees, the Revenue objected that it could lose this and more from just one single avoidance scheme using the Turks and Caicos. 'It follows therefore that we would not be at all happy with the proposed 50 year exemption for trusts'. The Revenue further pointed out that 'if a territory is looking for a substantial measure of material support from the UK – which can only come from UK taxation – legislation should not be implemented which has as its objective the facilitating of schemes for the avoidance of our tax'.[53] Responding, the Treasury stated that whilst it considered some of the Jakeway proposals 'not unreasonable', and hoped that the Turks and Caicos could become non-dependent upon budgetary aid by 1975/6, it nonetheless 'strongly support[ed] the Inland Revenue's line'.[54] The FCO also expressed alarm. Whilst the department was certainly in favour of financial independence for the Turks and Caicos, setting up financial trusts could mean significant costs to the UK and it 'would be crazy if we were to agree to the use of Islands for tax avoidance purposes which might result in the loss of say £1m of UK revenue for every £10,000 which accrued to the Island Government'. Furthermore, 'as regards the "one more haven" argument' (i.e., 'what's the harm in one more haven?'), the FCO noted that 'the only other island offering what was being envisaged [for the Turks and Caicos] was Cayman and we are about to launch with them a review of this subject'. In general, 'It would be very much more expensive for the UK to allow the Island to set up as a tax haven than to continue budgetary aid for a few years longer at whatever is the level which the islands need'.[55] Clearly, the relatively pro-tax haven conclusions of the Jakeway report were not straightforwardly endorsed by all the players back in Whitehall.

Accordingly, and apparently as at least a partial response to Jakeway, the Treasury, Revenue and FCO proceeded from 1970–71 to establish an inter-departmental working party on tax havens. This working party culminated in the issuing of a report – 'British Dependent Territories and Tax Haven Business' – which was very much a joint and compromise document between the three departments.[56] It appears that at least part of the report's intended purpose was to establish the groundwork for understanding the situation regarding tax havens in British dependent territories, so as to avoid future generations having to reinvent the wheel. Furthermore, the report clearly aimed at building government *policy* for dealing with territories which had become, or were attempting to become, tax havens. The report consists of a fourteen-page main section, plus three lengthy appendices by each of the departments focusing on tax matters (the Revenue), exchange control (Treasury) and case-studies of relevant dependent territory tax havens (FCO). The main report – containing some striking passages – repeats the observation already encountered in the correspondence of this period: that if the Revenue 'knew of the transactions, they would be half way (though not more than halfway) to recovering the tax through powers which Parliament has given them'.[57] However, when discussing the question of British aid and tax haven dependency the working party report exhibits more nuance than the either/or dichotomy characterised by Jakeway: '[That] some of the . . . tax havens are also those least dependent on U.K. aid does not mean that . . . tax haven benefits would provide an alternative to continued aid in the short or medium term', for indeed 'the issue is not a simple choice of methods of finance'.[58]

Things were made more complicated, however, by the fact that 'pure tax haven operations bring in relatively little direct benefit to the territories and involve substantial costs to the UK'.[59] The report explicitly notes that in certain cases the ability of the British state to intervene in the tax haven activities of dependent territories may be limited. For although 'H.M.G. are still ultimately responsible for all aspects of their [the dependent territories] government . . . the degree of internal self-government in some territories precludes direct intervention in matters of financial policy, or severely inhibits the extent to which this would be practicable'. Nonetheless, in less independent territories 'there may be scope for preventing or limiting the development of tax haven facilities'. However, another constraint also emerges: that the British authorities must be seen 'to give equitable treatment' to all concerned territories, so even though it may be prudent to discourage activities in one place, there could be 'political repercussions' if similar activities had been previously permitted in a neighbouring territory.[60] And the working party was not blind to the considerable international pressures being risked if Britain's dependent territory tax havens continued to expand: 'the USA . . . deplores the United Kingdom's "encouragement" of tax havens, and France . . . has animadverted on the prevalence of "paradis fiscaux" as yet another undesirable feature of the sterling area'.[61]

The impression which emerges is of a complex and somewhat shady relationship between the British government and the administration of dependent territories. Indeed the manipulative dimensions of this relationship are especially well brought out by a 1972 letter from Kenneth Crook, then-governor of the Cayman Islands:

> Caymanians don't want independence . . . They don't want internal self-government either – they are very unwilling to trust each other with effective power . . . they quite well understand that the British connection gives them a status which they would otherwise not command. Hence they are delighted to have a Governor around; apart from anything else he's very handy for taking unpopular decisions . . . They realise that if the Governor is seen to have effective power then the others appear to be essentially cyphers. The elected politicians among them find this bad for their image. What they want is to make the Constitution look as if it obliges the Governor to do what they want, even though they know it doesn't. I think we are in the world of semantics here. The more Caymanians we can put in positions of power, the better; they will act as lightning conductors for political dissent.[62]

Juggling these myriad and complex concerns, the report concludes that it could not be denied that tax haven policies had, in the short term, brought significant benefits to territories that would otherwise likely have experienced no development at all – and in the process saved the British state some costs in terms of reduced need for development aid. Nonetheless, the situation was leading to 'heavy and increasing losses' for the UK revenue and reserves, and increased tax haven activity would only exacerbate the situation. Already 'in absolute money terms the loss to the UK far exceeds the gain to the tax haven territories', and increased aid payments to these territories as a result of ending their tax haven activities would be far less costly. Yet the working party concluded that 'in general it would be difficult to curtail and impracticable to eliminate existing tax haven facilities' – although in particular cases 'it may be possible to negotiate modification of existing legislation which provides excessive opportunities for tax avoidance'. The report ended by establishing the general principle that 'a competitive scramble between territories for tax haven business is to be avoided', and measures to protect UK revenue should be undertaken, with particular objection to legislation designed to undermine UK tax collection. However, the report conceded that in the case of 'the smaller West Indian territories' it 'may not be practicable to discourage reasonable moves towards tax haven status similar to their neighbours' even though this would likely lead to 'marginal increase in the total volume of tax haven business'. Hence, although it would – in terms of cost – be more afford-able for the UK to simply finance development projects to encourage tourism and infrastructure than have these things paid for by pursuing tax haven policies, insofar as territories opted to take the tax haven path, exchange control concerns must be prioritised: 'Where a tax haven exists or is develop-ing, or where the territory is involved in complex tax and exchange control transactions, it is in the UK interest to provide, by technical assistance or other means, adequate qualified staff to ensure that reliable controls are maintained'.[63]

Following the publication of the working party report, Littler of the Treasury wrote to the Bank of England, introducing the report and making clear that the department intended to send the document to an FCO minister charged with affairs relating to the dependent territories, as well as the Finance Minister.[64] The working party paper's main stated purpose was to promote more understanding between departments, but also to 'brief those officials, particularly in the FCO, who encounter the problem for the first time'.[65] The impression in the immediate aftermath of the working party report is of a building head of steam. Littler – who is at the centre of most relevant corre-spondence – further notes that the FCO 'have come to recognise major UK revenue interests of a scale which overrides modest interests of remote depend-ent territories'.[66] Responding to the working party report, a D.A. Scott of the Dependent Territories General Department reinforces the impression of mounting interest in tax haven activities, writing that: 'We should not attempt to conceal from bankers or other interested parties the fact that we have engaged in a comprehensive review of the pros and cons of tax haven business in the British dependent territories'; 'the fact that we have discussed it inter-departmentally should serve as a warning to potential tax haven operators that they will not be able in future to play-off one territory against another'.[67]

Later, during the Parliamentary summer recess, a note was relayed stating that 'The Minister of State' (presumably attached to the Treasury, as the message is directed to Littler) had studied the working party report, and would be discussing the implications with the Finance Secretary, since it 'seems absurd that some of these territories should both exploit the tax system and receive aid . . . In principle, we should decide the total amount of help which we wish to give to them and trade off one kind of benefit against the other in order to achieve it'.[68] A note from the Finance Secretary later con-firms this line of reasoning, and explicitly states that the British government 'should consider using aid as a bargaining counter' where appropriate.[69] By the end of 1971, there was even discussion between departments of how UK legislation could be used to defeat that of territories like Cayman which was 'quite uncivilised' in its intention to undermine British revenue.[70] And yet, the very next year, the head of steam that was apparently building and about to force action against Britain's dependent territory tax havens dissipated completely.

In 1972, two events in particular altered the dynamic of attitudes towards tax havens in Whitehall. First, the sterling area was contracted and the Caribbean dependent territories were removed from exchange control considerations. As a result, the Treasury in particular lost relative interest in the activities of dependent territories as tax havens. From 1967–72, despite some personal misgivings from Treasury officials about tax havens undermining UK revenue whilst also claiming aid, the Department's over-riding priority was exchange control. With the contraction of the sterling area in 1972, the Treasury – like the Bank of England – largely appeared to lose interest. The second factor was UK preparation for acceding to the European Economic Community, in particular demanding broad tax harmonisation with EEC member states. As regards tax havens, the emphasis in Whitehall accordingly switched to territories within the European area – in particular to Gibraltar, which had expressed interest in turning itself into a tax haven. Focus is thus directed there, and also to the Channel Islands, with British concern that the EEC had an 'awkward habit' of quoting Gibraltar in the 'same breath' as Luxembourg.[71] (Indeed a striking 1975 correspondence can be found from then Foreign Secretary, and soon to be Prime Minister, James Callaghan, assuring officials in Bermuda that finalised British accession to the EEC would not impact negatively upon dependent territories acting as tax havens.[72]

Whilst the refocusing away from the Caribbean dependent territories and towards Europe seems primarily driven by sterling area contraction and EEC accession, there is, however, a further interesting factor to note. In 1972 many of the Whitehall figures who had established the informal working party on tax havens were replaced by a new set of civil servants who showed far less interest in the matter. In particular, Littler and Walker of the Treasury – key players in establishing the working party and mediating between the FCO, Revenue and Bank of England – are no longer to be found in the records.[73] Similarly O'Brien of the FCO, who had played a key role in the working party's creation and subsequent report, no longer features in the relevant correspondence. Instead two new figures in particular emerge: D.B. Andren of the FCO, and a Mr Pirie of the Treasury. In a 1974 handwritten note, Andren tells Pirie he made 'discouraging noises' about a possible meeting with the Revenue to discuss tax haven activities, and that he had discouraged any new review from being conducted.[74] To this Pirie replied that he agreed there was no need for any major review, as the contraction of the sterling area had 'greatly diminished the avoidance problem', but expressed doubts that the 1971 working party report succeeded in 'educating the FCO' about the scale and nature of tax haven activities, and hence wondered if a 'short note' might be produced to establish whether the problems highlighted in 1971 remained important.[75] Yet Andren replied that the FCO 'cannot accept there is a case for a further review', repeating that contraction of the sterling area had 'considerably narrowed the scope for tax avoidance'.[76]

Strangely, this blasé attitude at the Treasury, and even more the FCO, appears hard to square with other events taking place in the period and which are recorded in the Treasury's official files. For instance, in May 1974 a copy of the publication *Tax Haven Review* – apparently intended for bankers, lawyers and financial consultants – fell into the hands of a concerned citizen by the name of Mr Sidwell. (We know that *Tax Haven Review* was not intended for a wider audience, because the subscriber information promised that to 'maintain the confidentiality of this privately circulated newsletter, the full name of Tax Haven Review will not appear on the envelope'.) Sidwell promptly forwarded a copy to the Chancellor of the Exchequer himself, Dennis Healey, with a letter exclaiming that:

> [T]he Treasury probably have their eyes on such matters, but many feel that something could, and should, be done about these 'tax havens' that the wealthy can afford. It's a bit of an eye-opener for ordinary blokes to learn nowadays about such things. They have been highlighted by recent events.[77]

The 'recent events' Mr Sidwell alludes to almost certainly referred to the Lonhro scandal, which centred on corruption and tax avoidance activities in the Cayman Islands, and had generated a flurry of behind-the-scenes Whitehall activity as ministers were briefed and prepared for potentially difficult questions in the House relating to Britain's role in major tax haven activity.[78]

Concern was also growing in this period about the activities of the Channel Islands. In 1972 the Bank of England had expressed alarm – as usual centred on exchange control – that a thousand new companies had been established in Jersey and that the 'Channel Islands are aggressively selling their tax haven advantages'. As usual, the Bank's preference was to provide the territories with the requisite expertise to continue undertaking their activities, so long as they were conducted in a way favourable to UK exchange controls.[79] Yet by 1975 the Bank's enthusiasm for lending assistance to territories pursuing tax haven policies had attracted wider attention. The then Secretary of State for Industry Tony Benn wrote to Chancellor Denis Healey, relaying a clipping from the *Jersey Evening Post* sent by a Mr Dun, concerned constituent of Benn's.[80] Both Benn and Dun expressed alarm at reports that a 'tax conference' was held in Jersey, at which a certain 'Mr Gent of the Bank of England' spoke, 'giving advice on how to avoid paying UK taxes'. Dun in particular objected that Mr Gent 'suggests that the Bank of England will not be prepared to pass on information required by the Inland Revenue', and asked: 'does the UK Treasury have no control over the Bank of England in matters such as these – surely Bank employees should not be working against government policy? and just what sort of arrangements and deals are made at these events "behind the scenes"? – it really is just a bit too sordid to be true'.[81] Yet if Dun or Benn hoped the Treasury would respond with similar indignation they were to be disappointed. The department ignored the issue of Bank involvement, playing down the affair completely and not a little dismissively.[82]

The picture of events within Whitehall from 1974–75 is made even more confusing by the discovery that in late 1974 something of a U-turn was undertaken within the Treasury and FCO by the very figures who had previously been so dismissive of tax haven issues. Whilst Andren and Pirie were initially blasé, we later find them revising their position as 1974 draws to a close. In September of that year Pirie wrote Andren to say he had come across the earlier correspondence between Walker (of the Treasury) and Green (of the Revenue) regarding tax havens, and had grown concerned that the issue might still be very much alive, and that accordingly he was contacting the Revenue.[83] Strikingly, Andren – who a few months before had been so dismissive of any new review into tax haven activities – replied that he had now read the 1971 working party report. Furthermore, he had decided that upon reflection, following British accession to the EEC, the activities of the Channel Islands and Gibraltar made it necessary to consider *reconstituting* the FCO-Treasury-Revenue informal working party on tax havens.[84] However, the files available at the National Archives in Kew indicate that no such reconstitution took place. Accordingly, the 1971 report – intended as laying the groundwork for policy regarding dependent territory tax havens – passed unread into obscurity.

Conclusion

What to make of the above? It is difficult – and risky – to draw general conclusions from what consists of a relatively small amount of archival evidence. Yet a few observations and hypotheses may usefully be ventured. Firstly, it seems clear that tax haven activities had been developing for some time in the British Caribbean dependent territories before 1967, and that Britain had to some extent benefited from this insofar as it reduced the need for development aid to be paid out. But by 1967 the Revenue's growing concern about tax losses – and Treasury and Bank of England concerns about exchange control leakage – apparently made growing problems too big to ignore. However, the documents examined here indicate that it is precisely exchange control considerations that predominated; post-1972, interest in tax haven activities outside of the sterling area fell away dramatically. Simultaneously, it seems clear that a real dilemma was faced by the FCO – and the ODM – who had to ensure development for 'colonial pensioners' demanding to be allowed to pursue short-term gains via tax haven policies, yet which were likely to undermine the same British state keeping these territories afloat via development aid in the first place. Thus whilst it is difficult to be sure just from the sources examined here, it appears that prior to 1967 the FCO had been quite happy to allow tax haven activities to grow in British dependent territories and that this became a problem only when the revenue losses and exchange control issues became too great to ignore. Accordingly, a more general – though tentative – hypothesis might be advanced: that despite some concern about international pressures, the predominant attitude of the British state towards its affiliated tax havens in the late 1960s and early 1970s was to tolerate them insofar as they promoted development in otherwise economically hopeless dependent territories, which could be supplied with expertise so as to secure exchange controls and protect the balance of payments, and so long as revenue losses to the UK exchequer could be kept at tolerable – albeit high – levels. That is, that the growth of a network of tax havens in British dependent territories took place with the tacit – if often reluctant – acquiescence of the British state.

Yet this tentative hypothesis should be balanced by an alternative. One of the most striking aspects of the sources examined here is the extent to which records are characterised by confusion, inter-departmental wrangling, and conflicting priorities. The Revenue – perennially opposed to tax haven growth – lacked the clout of other departments, and its star waned after the Treasury lost interest after 1972. By contrast the relative importance of the Bank of England is striking. The Bank – not an official government department, and clearly acting autonomously despite its nationalised status – clearly possessed a great deal of information essential to both Revenue and Treasury purposes, and withheld it quite freely. Whilst certainly concerned about UK exchange control leakage, the Bank appears to have been positively comfortable with the growth of tax havens generally – and indeed by 1975 was apparently colluding openly on matters of tax avoidance with havens still in the sterling area. The hypothesis of tacit British acquiescence may thus need to be tempered with a countervailing view, which we can call the 'genie out of the bottle' account: that in the pre-1967 era tax haven expansion had quietly accelerated without the FCO – or Treasury, or Revenue – taking much notice. But by the late 1960s, real problems were beginning to emerge, and by the time these problems were recognised, bureaucratic wrangling and inter-departmental conflict, plus lack of access to information held by the Bank of England, meant that no concerted policy to bring British havens back under manageable control could be established. Instead, the growth had to be tolerated with measures put in place to try and mitigate its worst effects.

Which of these hypotheses – if either – turns out to be closer to the truth will require a great deal of further research and enquiry, though this chapter hopes to have made a worthwhile start.

Notes

1. <http://www.financialsecrecyindex.com> (accessed 20 March 2010).
2. Bank of England Archives, uncoded file marked 'Bahamas – Start Date 1934, Completion Date 1965'.
3. It is important to note that although tax 'avoidance' has now evolved to refer to specifically non-illegal tax planning activities, whilst tax 'evasion' denotes law-breaking, it is likely that in these archival documents the terminology is used a little more loosely with 'tax avoidance' being sometimes used to encompass activities which would now be more likely classed as 'evasion' – though sometimes the avoidance/evasion distinction is clearly appealed to as invoking a relatively strict dichotomy.
4. The National Archives (TNA), Public Record Office (PRO), T295/587, Inland Revenue correspondence, 18 October 1967.
5. TNA, PRO, T295/587, Treasury correspondence, 1 November 1967.
6. TNA, PRO, T295/587, second Treasury correspondence, 1 November 1967.
7. TNA, PRO, T295/587, Treasury correspondence, 13 November 1967.
8. TNA, PRO, T295/587, Treasury correspondence, 18 November 1967.
9. TNA, PRO, T295/587, Minutes of meeting, 14 December 1967.
10. TNA, PRO, T295/587, Treasury correspondence 29 April 1968.
11. TNA, PRO, T295/587, Correspondence from Bank of England, 8 May 1968.
12. TNA, PRO, T295/587, Treasury correspondence, 29 April 1968.
13. TNA, PRO, T295/587, Treasury correspondence, 17 June 1968.
14. TNA, PRO, T295/587, Working Party On Balance of Payments Aspects of Tax Question.
15. TNA, PRO, T295/587, Inland Revenue correspondence, 20 August 1968.
16. TNA, PRO, T295/587, Inland Revenue correspondence, 21 August 1968.
17. TNA, PRO, T295/587, Treasury correspondence, 6 September 1968.
18. That information being: 90 per cent of companies are in Switzerland; two-thirds make a profit; average repatriation of earnings to UK is 60 per cent; total net taxed earnings of all companies are in the region of £8/12m, of which £5/7m is repatriated.
19. TNA, PRO, T295/587, Bank of England correspondence, 27 September 1968.
20. TNA, PRO, T295/587, Bank of England correspondence, 27 September 1968.
21. TNA, PRO, T295/587, 'Caribbean Tax Havens: Note of a Meeting Held in Mr Littler's Room in the Treasury on Tuesday 10th December, 1968'.
22. TNA, PRO, T295/588, FCO correspondence, 24 January 1969.
23. TNA, PRO, T295/588, Treasury correspondence; apparent finalised version following draft of 6 March 1969.
24. TNA, PRO, T295/588, FCO correspondence, 18 March 1969.
25. This is one of relatively few references to the interests of other nation-states. Indeed, the relative disregard for the impact of British-affiliated tax havens on other countries – with the sometime exception of America and France – is a conspicuous feature of these records.

26. TNA, PRO, T295/588, 'Tax Havens and Tax Concessions in the Dependent Territories', 25 March 1969.
27. TNA, PRO, T295/588, 'Tax Havens and Tax Concessions – Note of a Meeting Held in the Foreign and Commonwealth Office on 25th March, 1969'.
28. Multiple documents to this effect are can be found throughout TNA, PRO, T295/588, as well as T295/892.
29. See especially TNA, PRO, T317/1452.
30. TNA, PRO, T295/588, Treasury correspondence, 20 March 1969.
31. TNA, PRO, T295/588, Treasury correspondence, 24 March 1969.
32. TNA, PRO, T295/588, FCO correspondence, 28 November 1969.
33. TNA, PRO, T295/588, Bank of England correspondence, 11 April 1969.
34. TNA, PRO, T295/588, Treasury correspondence, 14 April 1969; Treasury correspondence, 15 April 1969.
35. TNA, PRO, T295/588, Inland Revenue correspondence, 24 April 1969.
36. TNA, PRO, T295/588, ODM correspondence, 2 May 1969.
37. TNA, PRO, T295/588, Inland Revenue correspondence, 7 May 1969.
38. TNA, PRO, T295/588, Bank of England correspondence, 7 May 1969.
39. See TNA, PR0 295/588, Inland Revenue correspondence, 14 May 1969; Bank of England correspondence, 16 May 1969.
40. TNA, PRO, T295/588, Inland Revenue correspondence, 9 July 1969.
41. TNA, PRO, T295/588, 'Circular Dispatch: Agreements with Developers and Other Commercial Organisations – Guidance and General Principles'.
42. TNA, PRO, T317/1452, FCO correspondence, 8 January 1970.
43. TNA, PRO, T317/1452, 'Property Development in the Smaller Caribbean Dependencies – Note by the Foreign and Commonwealth Office'.
44. TNA, PRO, T317/1453, 'The Jakeway Report', paragraph 37.
45. Ibid.: 15.
46. Ibid.: appendix 2, p. 3.
47. Ibid.: 19.
48. Ibid.: 16.
49. Ibid.: 17.
50. Ibid.: 28.
51. Ibid.: 30.
52. Ibid.: appendix 2, p. 3.
53. TNA, PRO, T317/1452, FCO correspondence, 8 May 1970.
54. TNA, PRO, T317/1453, Treasury correspondence, 21 May 1970.
55. TNA, PRO, T317/1453, FCO correspondence, 13 June 1970.
56. The correspondence surrounding the working party report – in file TNA, PRO, T295/892 – makes clear that the end product is very much a compromise balancing the competing concerns of the Treasury (preoccupied with exchange control), the Revenue (prioritising revenue loss) and the FCO (concerned about the dependency and development of tax haven territories).
57. TNA, PRO, T295/892, 'British Dependent Territories and Tax Haven Business': 7.
58. Ibid.: 10.
59. Ibid.: 11.
60. Ibid.: 11.
61. Ibid.: 13.
62. TNA, PRO, T295/892, '"First Impressions of the Cayman Islands", the Governor of

the Cayman Islands to the Secretary of State for Foreign and Commonwealth Affairs, George Town, Cayman Islands, 26 January 1972', Diplomatic Report No. 216/72.

63. TNA, PRO, T295/892, 'British Dependent Territories and Tax Haven Business': 14–16.
64. TNA, PRO, T295/892, Treasury correspondence, 13 July 1971.
65. TNA, PRO, T295/892, Treasury correspondence, undated, signed by R.G. Littler.
66. TNA, PRO, T295/892, Treasury correspondence, 20 July 1971.
67. TNA, PRO, T295/892, FCO(?) correspondence, 22 July 1971.
68. TNA, PRO, T295/892, Treasury(?) correspondence, 3 August 1971.
69. TNA, PRO, T295/892, Treasury(?) correspondence, 9 September 1971.
70. TNA, PRO, T295/892, FCO correspondence, 4 October 1971.
71. TNA, PRO, T295/1013, FCO correspondence, 18 February 1972.
72. TNA, PRO, T328/1157, FCO(?) correspondence, 30 January 1975. This assurance seems to be based on a note from the Hague, which states that the dependent territories won't be covered by EEC agreements even if they are tax havens; see TNA, PRO, T328/1157, Hague telegram, 28 January 1975.
73. We know, however, from Cabinet records that both were advising Denis Healey during the 1974–76 sterling crises under the supervision of Douglas Wass, Permanent Secretary to HM Treasury, so we must assume they were promoted out of the Treasury's tax haven affairs into grander things.
74. TNA, PRO, T295/1013, FCO correspondence. No date given but assumed to be 1974 due to place in file and date of reply from Treasury (Treasury correspondence, 28 February 1974).
75. TNA, PRO, T295/1013, Treasury correspondence, 28 February 1974.
76. TNA, PRO, T295/1013, FCO correspondence, 18 April 1974.
77. TNA, PRO, T295/1013, Private correspondence, 23 May 1974.
78. Many documents to this effect – including internal notes, preparation for parliamentary questions, early day motions and so forth are held in file TNA, PRO, T295/1013.
79. TNA, PRO, T295/1013, Bank of England correspondence, 7 December 1972.
80. TNA, PRO, T328/1157, Benn to Healey correspondence, 3 June 1975.
81. TNA, PRO, T328/1157, private correspondence, 30 May 1975.
82. See TNA, PRO, T328/1157, Treasury correspondence, 20 October 1975 and previous drafts of this in same file.
83. TNA, PRO, T328/1157, Treasury correspondence, 2 September 1974.
84. TNA, PRO, T328/1157, FCO correspondence, 28 January 1975.

CHAPTER 6

Tax Treaties between Developed and Developing Countries

The Role of the OECD and UN Models

ALBERTO VEGA

Introduction

In order to prevent double taxation from taking place, tax treaties distribute the taxing rights of the country of residence of the taxpayer and the country where the income has its source. As developing countries are normally net capital importers from OECD member states, they usually prefer taxation at source. In contrast, net capital-exporting countries are more favourable to taxation in the country of residence of the taxpayer, since residents of developed countries are the ones who are more likely to obtain income from foreign sources.

The OECD Model Tax Convention, the first version of which was published in 1963, is a basic reference for the negotiation of tax treaties. However, developing countries were not satisfied with the emphasis it placed on the principle of taxation in the country of residence and requested the United Nations (UN) to deal with this issue. Consequently, the United Nations Model Double Taxation Convention between Developed and Developing Countries, which was more favourable to taxation in the country of source, was published in 1980 (United Nations 2001a).

Thirty years after the publication of the UN model, this study sets out to assess the impact that some of the UN model's provisions have had on the treaties in force. We will compare those tax treaties concluded between one developed and one developing country with those concluded between two OECD member States. As will be shown, not all the provisions of the UN model have had the same impact and, in fact, there are considerable differences from country to country.

Finally, two of the most relevant changes that have taken place in the context of the tax treaties concluded between developed and developing countries, will be addressed: the growing importance of some OECD non-member states as capital exporters and the gradual introduction of mechanisms to promote developing countries' participation in the law-making process of the OECD. In view of these changes, the future of the UN model may be called into question.

The Role of the OECD and UN Model Tax Treaties in Practice

This section will assess whether or not OECD member states follow different policies when they conclude tax treaties with developed rather than developing countries; in other words, whether with developed nations they tend to follow the OECD model while, with countries still developing, they observe the UN model.[1] In order to do this, we will highlight some of the main differences between the two models and analyse the OECD member states' tax treaty network to see which model is followed.

In general, it is important to remember that the UN model, which is based on the OECD model, represents a compromise between the principle of taxation in the country of residence of the taxpayer and the principle of taxation in the country where income has its source, and gives greater weight to the source principle than the OECD model (UN 2001a: Introduction, paragraph 17). However, several authors consider the UN model to be very close to the OECD model, and therefore contend that it does not fulfil the expectations of developing countries, which are generally net capital-importing countries.[2]

According to Figueroa (1992: 12), this similarity was due to the greater homogeneity of developed countries, while for the group of developing countries it was not so easy to defend their common interests given their general diversity as a group.[3] However, since the members of the Group of Experts who were in charge of preparing an alternative model had been invited because of their technical knowledge and were not representatives of their respective countries, Court (1992: 15) considers that it was normal that the experts from developing countries did not present a united front. Indeed, Surrey (1978: 6) considers that the absence of political blocs was something positive for the work of the experts.

In any case, although the UN model may not have completely satisfied the interests of developing countries, according to Kosters (2004: 4) these nations quickly embraced it, and after the collapse of the Eastern bloc many provisions from the UN model were also inserted into the treaties of former communist countries.

Differences between the Models

In order to study the impact the two models have had on the tax treaties in force, we will analyse the tax treaty network of those states that were OECD members at the beginning of 2010. Therefore, countries such as Chile, Estonia, Israel and Slovenia, which joined the OECD very recently, will not be considered as member states, since almost all their tax treaties were concluded when they were still non-members of this organisation. In particular, the analysis will consider those double tax treaties in force which were available in the Lexis Nexis database as of July 2010.

We will begin by looking at the following differences between the two models. First, we will analyse the definition of permanent establishment contained in Art. 5 of both models, in particular the period of time required for a building site or construction to qualify as a permanent establishment. The notion of permanent establishment is important because business profits are only taxable in the country of residence of the enterprise, unless it conducts business abroad through a permanent establishment. Therefore, countries which are net capital importers are interested in a wide definition of the concept of permanent establishment because this will increase their capacity to tax the income generated within their borders. In particular, according to the OECD model, constructions remaining for more than twelve months will qualify as a permanent establishment, while in the UN model this period is only six months. Therefore, it can be observed that the UN model broadens the notion of permanent establishment, which benefits the interests of developing countries.

Second, we will look at another difference in the definition of permanent establishment (Art. 5 of both models). The UN model states explicitly that the furnishing of services, including consultancy services, by an enterprise through employees or other personnel engaged by the enterprise for such a purpose, will be considered as a permanent establishment as long as such activities continue for a period or periods aggregating more than six months within any twelve-month period. Thus, the introduction of this provision also broadens the notion of permanent establishment and increases the cases in which income may be taxed in the country in which it had its source.

Third, we will analyse the UN model's definition of royalty (Art. 12.3). Although the definitions of the UN and OECD models are very similar, the UN model states explicitly that the term 'royalties' includes payments of any kind received as a consideration for the use of, or the right to use, any copyright of literary, artistic or scientific work including cinematograph films, *or films or tapes used for radio or television broadcasting*. According to the OECD model (Art. 12.1), royalties are only taxable in the country of residence, whereas according to the UN model (Art. 12.2), royalties may also be taxed in the country of source up to a maximum percentage of the gross amount of the royalties which is to be established through bilateral negotiations. If, however, these payments are not considered as royalties, they will be taxed in the country of residence of the taxpayer (unless they are considered as business profits obtained through a permanent establishment). Nevertheless, even without the explicit mention of the UN model, payments for the use of films for radio or television broadcasting may also be taxed as royalties because they are received for using a copyright of an artistic work.[4] In principle, it seems that taxpayers from developed countries receive more payments for the right to use films than taxpayers from developing countries. However, whether the inclusion of these payments in the category of royalties favours developed or developing countries depends on whether the country of source is also allowed to tax royalties up to a certain amount, according to Art. 12.2 of the UN model.[5] On all accounts, the mere fact of a treaty using the terminology of the UN model is evidence that this model was taken into account during the negotiations.

Finally, the chapter will examine the particularity introduced in Art. 21 of the UN model, which details the taxation of those types of income that cannot be included in any other type of income covered by the two models. In principle, both the OECD and UN models agree that these other types of income should be taxed in the country of residence of the taxpayer, unless the recipient conducts business through a permanent establishment, in which case this other income may be taxed in the country in which it was generated. However, the UN model includes an additional provision indicating that items of income not dealt with in the foregoing Articles of the UN model itself may also be taxed in the country of source. Therefore, even if both models determine that in general these other types of income should be taxed in the country of residence, the UN model also allows the country of source to tax them, which is in the interests of developing countries.

Impact of the OECD and UN Models in Practice

In the findings, a distinction is made between two groups of treaties: those concluded between two OECD member states and those involving one member and one non-member state. Consequently, treaties between two OECD non-member states will not be examined, as an analysis of OECD member states' treaties should be sufficient to ascertain whether or not the UN model has had an impact in practice, particularly for those treaties concluded between member and non-member states.

Other authors such as Wijnen and Magenta (1997) have previously analysed the influence of the UN model on the tax treaties in force. When presenting the results below, the findings of these authors will also be mentioned. However, some methodological differences should be noted. Wijnen and

Magenta's analysis comprises the 811 treaties signed between January 1980 and April 1997 and presents the number of treaties that follow each of the particularities of the UN model. Moreover, they also distinguish two groups of treaties: those concluded between OECD member states and those in which at least one of the parties was a non-member state. In this sense, it is important to note that they only consider as a member state those countries which had joined the OECD when the UN model was published (1980) (Wijnen and Magenta 1997: 574). Therefore, they do not include current members such as the Czech Republic, Hungary, Korea, Mexico, Poland or Slovakia, and consequently, the results below are not directly comparable, even though they show many similarities.[6]

Time Required for a Construction to Qualify as a Permanent Establishment

We have analysed the treaties concluded by the OECD member states and have presented our findings in the following two graphs. The first graph shows the average length of time (in months) required for a construction to be considered as a permanent establishment in the case of those treaties signed with other OECD member states. The second provides the equivalent information for treaties between OECD member states and non-members.

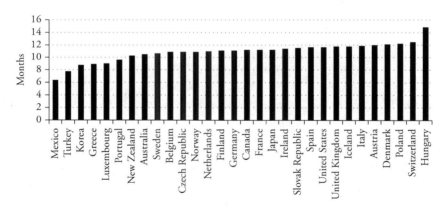

Figure 6.1 Average Number of Months Required for a Construction to Qualify as a Permanent Establishment in Tax Treaties with Other OECD Member States

As shown in the above figure, the length of time required by most OECD countries signing treaties with other member states ranges from ten to twelve months. Only a few countries require less time on average, notably Mexico, whose treaties are closer to the UN than to the OECD model. Other countries requiring a relatively short average time period are Turkey, Korea and Greece. It is not surprising that these countries have a relatively low level of development in the context of the OECD and tend to be net capital importers. In contrast, the only countries which on average require a time period equal to or longer than twelve months are Denmark, Poland, Switzerland and Hungary. In fact, certain OECD member states have included reservations to Art. 5.3 of the OECD model. For instance, Australia, Greece, Korea, Mexico, New Zealand, Portugal, the Slovak Republic and Turkey consider that any building site, construction or installation project existing for more than six months should be regarded as a permanent establishment (OECD 2010b: Commentary on Art. 5, paras 57 and 61).

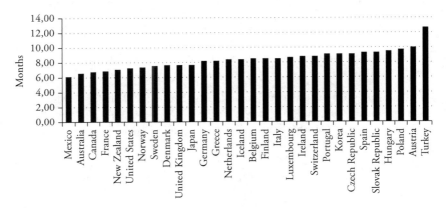

Figure 6.2 Average Number of Months Required for a Construction to Qualify as a Permanent Establishment in Tax Treaties with OECD Non-member States

With regard to treaties between OECD member and non-member states, it can be observed that constructions are on average considered as a permanent establishment after a shorter period of time, although there are some exceptions. There are eleven nations for which this period ranges from six to eight months, including Mexico, Australia and Canada. In most cases, tax treaties require a period of eight to ten months, with the main exception of Turkey, which on average requires more than twelve months. If we compare the time period a country requires for treaties with other OECD member states with the period required for treaties with non-OECD states, it can be observed that some countries follow a very similar policy with both types of countries, while others demonstrate considerable differences. For instance, the difference in the average length of time is less than one month for Korea, Mexico, Luxembourg, Portugal and Greece. However, in general most countries (notably Hungary, Denmark, Canada, France, the United States and the United Kingdom) require a longer time period for treaties with other OECD member states; although there are exceptions, as shown by the case of Turkey.[7]

Consequently, we can observe that the policies of Mexico and Turkey are completely different. Mexico is consistent, always requiring a short period of time, and thus favouring taxation in the country of source in its tax treaties both with other OECD member states (which favours a net capital importing country like Mexico) and with non-member countries (even though Mexico may be a net capital exporter to many developing countries). Turkey's tax treaties, on the other hand, require a short time if the other party is an OECD member state but considerably longer if they are not. It is therefore clear that Turkey does not always follow the recommendations of the UN or the OECD model. Rather, depending on its interests in each particular bilateral bargain, it agrees on shorter periods with more developed countries and longer ones with less developed nations, thus favouring taxation in the country of source in some cases and taxation in the country of residence of the taxpayer in others.

The analysis carried out by Wijnen and Magenta also evaluates the length of time required for constructions to qualify as permanent establishments. According to these authors, 513 treaties (63 per cent of the total studied) required a period of less than twelve months. Of these treaties, 484 (94 per cent) involved at least one OECD non-member, while only 29 (6 per cent) were ratified between member states (Wijnen and Magenta 1997: 575). Similarly, the empirical analysis Rixen and Schwarz (2008) conducted on the German tax treaty network shows that the more asymmetric the capital flow between two countries, the shorter the time period required for a construction to qualify as a permanent establishment. Moreover, other more general factors may affect the bilateral bargain, such as the strategic importance of certain countries.[8]

Services as a Permanent Establishment

In order to analyse the impact of this provision contained in Art. 5 of the UN model, we have calculated the percentage of OECD member-state treaties that include it. Again, a distinction is made between treaties solely involving two OECD member states and those signed between one member and one non-member state. Very few treaties between two OECD member states follow the UN model convention. The countries which mention that the furnishing of services may be encompassed in the notion of permanent establishment in a higher percentage of treaties are Portugal (12 per cent), Denmark (8 per cent) and the Czech Republic (8 per cent). Many countries, nonetheless, have not included this provision in any of their treaties with other OECD countries. On the other hand, the picture is very different when we observe those treaties signed by one OECD member and one non-member state, as shown in the following graph.

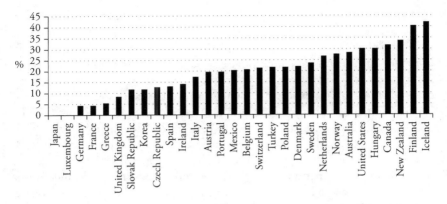

Figure 6.3 Percentage of Treaties with OECD Non-member States which Follow Art. 5.3(b) of the UN Model

It can be observed that the provision is more common in this second group of countries, although there are noticeable differences between states. In some countries, such as Germany, France, Greece and the United Kingdom, the percentage of treaties which follow the UN model for this is below 10 per cent; indeed, there are even countries (Japan and Luxembourg) that make no mention of this particularity of Art. 5 of the UN model in any treaties. However, most countries have included this provision in more than 20 per cent of their treaties and in the case of Canada, New Zealand, Finland and Iceland, this percentage is significantly higher. This aspect of the UN model was also analysed by Wijnen and Magenta, who found 221 treaties (27 per cent) that included the provision. Almost all the treaties they found (219) involved at least one OECD non-member state (Wijnen and Magenta 1997: 576).

Including Films or Tapes Used for Radio or Television Broadcasting in the Definition of Royalty

Another point we have analysed is the explicit mention in Art. 12.3 of the UN model that payments received for using films or tapes for radio or television broadcasting should be included in the term 'royalties'. Again, we have calculated the percentage of OECD member state treaties with this provision, and compared whether it is more frequent in treaties with member or non-member states. As can be observed in the following two graphs, this provision is present in a relatively high percentage of treaties between OECD members.

As shown in Figure 6.4, most countries follow Art. 12.3 of the UN model in more than 50 per cent of their treaties with other OECD countries. In fact,

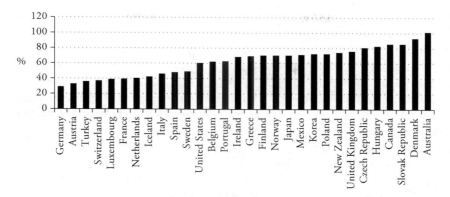

Figure 6.4 Percentage of Treaties with Other OECD Member States which Follow Art. 12.3 of the UN Model and Mention Films or Tapes Used for Radio or Television Broadcasting in the Definition of Royalty

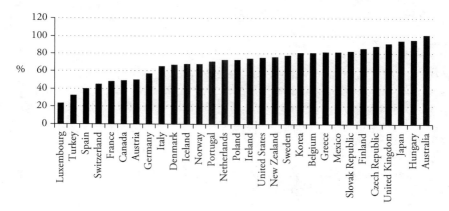

Figure 6.5 Percentage of Treaties with OECD Non-member States which Follow Art. 12.3 of the UN Model and Mention Films or Tapes Used for Radio or Television Broadcasting in the Definition of Royalty

Australia has included this provision in all of its treaties. This shows that OECD member states may deviate from the OECD model if they are more interested in applying certain provisions of the UN model. Figure 6.5 above shows that the percentage of treaties between OECD member and non-member states is even higher. Thus, when defining the concept of 'royalties', general practice is to observe the UN model and include a reference to film and tape broadcasting, as is done notably by the United Kingdom, Japan, Hungary and Australia.

Comparing the OECD member-state treaties that follow the UN model in the two above groups, we can observe that there are some countries (including Canada, Denmark, Luxembourg and Spain) which follow this aspect in a higher percentage of treaties with other OECD member states than with non-member states. In general, though, the percentage is higher in the group of treaties signed with non-member states, particularly for the Netherlands, Sweden, Germany, Iceland and Japan. The study by Wijnen and Magenta shows that 712 treaties (88 per cent of the total of their sample) adhered to this aspect of Art. 12.3 of the UN model. In particular, 610 treaties (86 per cent) involved at least one OECD non-member state, while only 102 treaties in their sample (14 per cent) were between two OECD member states (Wijnen and Magenta 1997: 581).

According to Kosters (2004: 10), the use of a broad definition of royalties (including the mention of payments for broadcasting films) should be seen in combination with the level of withholding taxes granted to the source state. Thus, the previous author notes that during the treaty negotiations between the Netherlands and developing countries, a broader definition of royalties was only accepted if the other party agreed to reduce the rate of taxation at source.

Taxation at Source for Other Types of Income

Finally, we examine whether or not the treaties signed by OECD members include the provision outlined in Art. 21.3 of the UN model, according to which items of income not covered by the other Articles of the convention may be taxed not only in the country of residence (which is the general principle followed both by the OECD and UN models) but also in the country of source.

Figures 6.6 and 6.7 show the percentage of treaties of OECD member states which follow this particularity of the UN model.

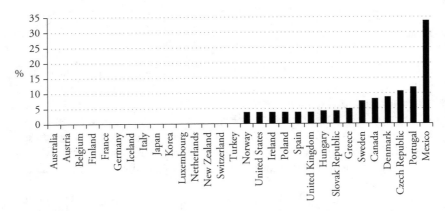

Figure 6.6 Percentage of Treaties with Other OECD Member States which Follow Art. 21.3 of the UN Model

Most countries have not ratified any treaties with other OECD member states in accordance with Art. 21.3 of the UN model. The few that have, with the exception of Mexico, only include it in a very small percentage of their treaties. It is also important to note that some countries have included reservations on this Article; indeed, countries such as Canada, Mexico, Portugal and the Slovak Republic state that they would wish to maintain the right to tax income arising from sources in their own country (OECD 2010b: Commentary on Art. 21, paragraph 13).

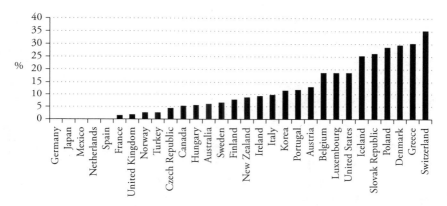

Figure 6.7 Percentage of Treaties with OECD Non-member States which Follow Art. 21.3 of the UN Model

In the case of the treaties signed with non-member states, more countries (including Denmark, Greece and Switzerland) have included this provision in a higher percentage of treaties, although there are also countries (such as Germany, Japan, the Netherlands, Mexico and Spain) which do not apply the UN model in any of their treaties. Although most countries follow the UN model for a higher percentage of treaties in the second group (treaties concluded with non-member states), there are some exceptions. For instance, Mexico, the Czech Republic and Spain follow the wording of the UN model in more treaties with other OECD countries than with developing countries. According to the study carried out by Wijnen and Magenta, 344 treaties (42 per cent of the total analysed) followed the UN model and mentioned the possibility of taxing in the country of source those items of income which cannot be included in other categories. Most of these treaties, 308 (90 per cent), included at least one OECD non-member state, while only 36 (10 per cent) were ratified by two OECD member states (Wijnen and Magenta 1997: 584).

Changes in the Context of Tax Treaties between Developed and Developing Countries

Economic Changes

Since the publication of the OECD model in 1963 and the UN model in 1980, there have been significant changes to the global economy which have also affected the degree of development of many countries and, consequently, their interests when concluding treaties. According to the OECD model, in order to eliminate double taxation, it is usually the source country that has to give up revenue. Logically, this was a serious disadvantage for developing countries, which were usually net capital importers.

Therefore, the UN model, as its title suggests, was specifically designed as a guide for tax treaties between developed and developing countries. Given that it is not easy to draw a line between developed and developing countries, it is sometimes assumed that, despite a few exceptions, OECD member states are developed and non-members are developing countries.[9] An economic classification such as that of the World Bank is, however, more accurate. This institution's main criterion for classifying economies is gross national income (GNI) per capita, according to which four groups (low, lower middle, upper middle and high income) are distinguished.[10] The group of low-income economies ($995 or less) includes mainly sub-Saharan countries. In the category of lower-middle-income economies ($996–$3,945) there are countries from South America (such as Bolivia, Ecuador and Honduras) and Asia (such as China, India, Indonesia, Sri Lanka and Thailand). In the group of upper-middle-income economies ($4,946–$12,195), we find countries such as Argentina, Brazil, Chile, Mexico, Russia and Turkey, some of which are OECD members. Finally, the group of high-income economies ($12,196 or more) includes most OECD member states, along with several oil-exporting countries (Bahrain, Brunei Darussalam, Kuwait, Oman, Qatar and Saudi Arabia).

This notwithstanding, when negotiating a tax treaty, the other party's level of development is less important than its relative position as a net capital importer or exporter. Thus, according to the data provided by the United Nations Conference on Trade and Development,[11] we can see that certain countries with a low GNI per capita have become important capital exporters. For instance, in 2008 China was the thirteenth largest capital exporting country, even though in 1980, when the UN model was published, its investments abroad were very limited. Similarly, other non-OECD countries such as India and Brazil have also become important capital exporters.

Therefore, developing countries such as China, Brazil and India are probably net capital exporters not only to many other developing countries, but also to some OECD member states. Thus, these countries will also be interested in following those provisions of the OECD model which favour the principle of taxation in the country of residence, even though traditionally they have preferred to give greater weight to taxation in the country of source. Such a change in China's tax treaty policy has been observed by authors such as Khoo (2007).

Participation of Developing Countries in the Work of the OECD

Since 1997, developing countries have had the opportunity to express their positions on the OECD Model Tax Convention. In the 2010 version of the model, thirty-one non-OECD economies expressed their positions disagreeing with the text of a certain Article or with the interpretations put forward in the Commentary (OECD 2010b: Introduction, paragraph 4–5). Some positions disagree with fundamental aspects of the model while others contest secondary points; however, no positions are legally binding. Nevertheless, China and Indonesia have expressly declared that they will not be bound by their positions stated in the OECD model in negotiations with other countries (OECD 2010b: Introduction, Para 5, fn 1).

If we analyse the number of positions that each non-member state has included on the Articles of the model and the Commentary thereon, as well as the reservations and observations expressed by OECD countries, we can observe the following results. On average, non-OECD economies have included 22.19 positions on Articles and 2.90 positions on the Commentary (25.09 positions in total). Some countries, like Israel,[12] Croatia and the Democratic Republic of Congo have included only a few positions, while others, such as Argentina, Bulgaria, Ukraine, Morocco, Vietnam, Thailand, Brazil and India have included more than thirty. By contrast, OECD members have included an average of only 9.28 reservations on the Articles and 1.88 observations on the Commentaries (11.16 reservations and observations in total). In this group of countries there are also considerable differences. Some nations such as Finland, Poland, Hungary, Japan and Luxembourg have included a very limited number of reservations and observations (Austria and Iceland did not include any reservations or observations at all in the 2010 version of the model), while others, such as Canada, Portugal, Chile, the United States, Greece and Mexico have made extensive use of this option. In fact, these last three countries are in disagreement with more Articles and Commentaries than many non-member countries.

Moreover, it is important to stress that the OECD has recently launched several initiatives to foster cooperation with non-member states and other international organisations. For instance, most jurisdictions typically known as tax havens (such as Andorra, the Bahamas, Gibraltar and Liechtenstein) are members of the Global Forum on Transparency and Exchange of Information for Tax Purposes. Furthermore, the Centre for Tax Policy and Administration has relations with many other countries and organises around sixty conferences

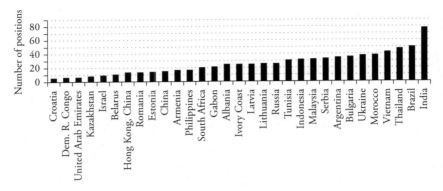

Figure 6.8 Number of OECD Non-member State Positions on the Articles of the Model and the Commentary Thereon

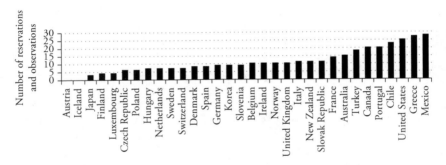

Figure 6.9 Number of Observations and Reservations by OECD Member States

a year so as to listen to non-OECD economies and promote an international consensus in the international tax area.[13] Nonetheless, Christians (2010b: 33–4) considers that the OECD law-making process is still excessively opaque and the use of soft governance methods has generated uncertainty over the legal status of certain instruments.

Another initiative developed by the OECD together with the International Monetary Fund and the World Bank is the International Tax Dialogue (ITD), which is a forum promoting greater coordination of these institutions in international tax matters, without the need to create a new institution. However, as Shelton (2004: 540) remarks, the absence of the UN in the ITD is noticeable. In this author's view, 'the UN is determined to proceed with at least the "upgrade" of its own tax work, without excluding the possibility of it establishing a global tax body' (Shelton 2004: 542). In other words, the Ad Hoc Group of Experts on International Co-operation in Tax Matters could be converted into an inter-governmental body (for instance, as a subsidiary body of the Economic and Social Council) or, further, a new international organisation could be created in this area, bringing all international tax matters together into one single body. The possibility of creating an International Tax Organisation which would develop international norms for tax policy and administration was included in the *Recommendations of the High-level Panel on Financing for Development* (UN 2001b), also known as the Zedillo Report. Although several authors have welcomed this proposal (see especially Tanzi 1999; Horner 2001; Whisenhunt 2002; Altman 2006; Sawyer 2009), the establishment of such an institution in the near future seems improbable given the reluctance of most countries. In any case, the evolution of the current institutions should also be taken into account when considering the role that the UN model should have in the future.

Summary and Conclusions

After analysing the tax treaty network of the OECD member states the following general conclusions can be drawn. Those treaties concluded between one OECD member and one non-member state generally follow the UN model more closely than those ratified by two member states. In particular, tax treaties with developing countries tend to include a broader definition of the concept of permanent establishment, which favours taxation in the country of source and benefits net capital importing countries. Thus, the length of time required for a construction to qualify as a permanent establishment is shorter in this type of treaty. Moreover, the provision in the UN model that the furnishing of services may be considered as a permanent establishment is to be found almost exclusively in tax treaties with developing countries and the wordings of Art. 12.3 and Art. 21.3 of the UN model are also more frequently found in this type of treaty.

We have also shown that on some occasions where tax treaties are signed between two OECD member states the UN model rather than the OECD model is followed. For instance, the average number of months that Mexico, Australia and Canada require to consider a construction as a permanent establishment is closer to the UN than the OECD model. Furthermore, the fact that Mexico follows the UN model for the taxation of other sources of income in more than 30 per cent of its tax treaties with other OECD members shows that, if necessary, an OECD member can deviate from the OECD model. In fact, we have also seen in the issue of the definition of the term 'royalties' that the inclusion of an explicit reference to payments for using films or tapes for radio or television broadcasting (following the UN model) is common practice not only in treaties between developed and developing countries, but also in those between two OECD members.

Moreover, the historical evolution of the main model tax treaties shows that the decision to publish an alternative model to the one established by the OECD was conceived at a time when the role of developing countries as capital exporters was very limited and it was in no way possible for them to participate in the drafting of the OECD model. However, this situation has now changed, since some developing countries, such as China, are among the largest capital exporters. Furthermore, since 1963, the OECD has significantly increased its membership to include countries such as Chile, the Czech Republic, Korea, Mexico, Slovakia and Slovenia and has launched several initiatives to take into account non-member states' opinions on tax matters. For instance, the possibility that both member and non-member states can show their disagreement with certain provisions of the OECD model (through reservations, observations or positions) should be seen as a very useful negotiation tool for new treaties between developed and developing countries. Thus, if non-member countries can already express their opinion on the model of this organisation directly within the OECD, we may wonder whether it is still necessary to update the UN model. Indeed, instead of having two separate models, it may not be an exaggeration to consider that countries actually have one model with several alternatives for some aspects.

Given that the OECD is clearly the leading institution in international tax matters,[14] it would probably be more in the interests of developing countries to strengthen their direct participation in this international organisation.[15] However, this does not mean that the work of the UN Committee of Experts on International Cooperation on Tax Matters has become completely redundant. OECD non-member states could, for instance, use this institution to coordinate their positions before attending OECD meetings. This could be particularly useful for least developed countries,[16] which usually lack the resources and technical expertise to participate in these types of international negotiations. Moreover, other OECD non-members with similar characteristics, such as oil-exporting countries and microstates (many of which are usually considered tax havens), may also discuss their particular needs in the UN before expressing their position on the OECD model. However, the specific ways in which the participation of developing countries in the UN and the OECD could be increased is a complex matter which should be the object of further research.

Notes

This chapter was prepared during a research trip to the Max Planck Institute for Intellectual Property, Competition and Tax Law (Munich). Financial support from the Spanish Ministry of Science and the European Social Fund is acknowledged (grant BES-2008-003252). This work is part of the activities of the Research Group in Tax Law (2009 SGR 886), financed by the Government of Catalonia.

1. As Rixen (2008) explains, the distributive conflict between two countries depends on the capital flows between them and, therefore, bilateral bargaining accommodates different conflicting distributive interests better than multilateral conventions.
2. In the opinion of Dagan (2000), tax treaties are not really necessary for the elimination of double taxation, since the same objective can be achieved through unilateral means. For this author, tax treaties may have other advantages in comparison to unilateral measures (such as reinforcement of investor certainty and assistance in tax enforcement), but also disadvantages, especially for developing countries, since their use tends to favour taxation in the country of residence of the taxpayer instead of taxation at source. Moreover, there are many other factors beyond the existence of conventions for the avoidance of double taxation which may promote foreign direct investments (FDI) in a country. For an analysis of the influence of tax treaties on FDI, see Davies (2004).
3. Furthermore, at the time of the negotiation of the UN model, developing countries had the disadvantage that their tax departments were clearly undertrained and understaffed (Irish 1974: 300).
4. In fact, even though Art. 12 of the OECD model does not mention payments for the use of films, the Commentary on Art. 12 states that rents for films are also treated as royalties, though it may be agreed through bilateral negotiations that these rents shall be treated as business profits and, consequently, shall be subject to the provisions of Art. 7 and 9 of the model (OECD 2010b: Commentary on Art. 12, paragraph 10).
5. For a general analysis of the convenience of the taxation of royalties by the country of source, see Brooks (2007).
6. Any reference to the OECD member states in the context of the work of Wijnen and Magenta should be understood in the restrictive sense with which these authors use this notion.
7. Countries which are net capital importers from Turkey may still be interested in concluding treaties with this country because, as Baistrocchi (2008: 367–72) explains, there is a prisoner's dilemma among developing countries which induces them to follow the OECD model for fear of driving FDI away to competing jurisdictions if all other conditions are equal.
8. According to Reese (1988), the content of the tax treaty negotiated during the 1980s between the United States and China responds to the strategic importance of China for the United States and therefore its provisions cannot be directly applied to other treaties with other developing countries.
9. For instance, this simplification is made by Wijnen and Magenta (1997).
10. For more details, see <http://data.worldbank.org/about/country-classifications> (accessed 12 August 2010).
11. For more details, see <http://www.unctad.org/Templates/Page.asp?intItemID=4979& lang=1> (accessed 12 August 2010).
12. Israel joined the OECD in September 2010, once the last version of the OECD model had already been published in July 2010. Similarly, Estonia has been a member state since December 2010.
13. According to the OECD, these relations with non-member states should ensure that OECD approaches and innovations reflect the reality of non-OECD economies' circumstances. For more details, see <http://www.oecd.org/dataoecd/25/62/44459895. pdf> (accessed 14 August 2010). However, Christians (2010a) points out that 'these conferences may be venues for greater participation in global tax dialogue, although to

date there is little evidence that developing country expertise is influencing the policies emerging from the OECD's work'.

14. As Christians (2010c: 31) explains, 'the United Nations is a potential rival, but its historical role in developing tax policy standards has been peripheral'.

15. Increasing the number of member states may also have its own disadvantages, especially if we take into account the importance of the consensus principle (Ault 2009: 763). In fact, after the creation of the United Nations, a Financial and Fiscal Commission was established by the Economic and Social Council. In principle, it was expected to continue the work of the Fiscal Committee of the League of Nations, but its broader membership, which included developing countries and the Soviet bloc, prevented the possibility of reaching a consensus (Picciotto 1992: 51). Consequently, the task of developing instruments for the prevention of double taxation was undertaken by an institution with a more homogeneous membership, the Organisation for European Economic Co-operation (OEEC), which later became the Organisation for Economic Co-operation and Development (OECD).

16. For more details about the notion of least developed country, see <http://www.unohrlls.org/en/ldc/related/62> (accessed 21 July 2010).

CHAPTER 7

Taxation and State Legitimacy in Kenya

ATTIYA WARIS

Introduction

There is hardly any other aspect of history . . . so decisive for the fate of the masses as that of public finances. Here one hears the pulse beat of nations at its clearest, here one stands at the source of all social misery. (Goldscheid 1962: 2)

One fundamental purpose for acknowledging basic rights is to prevent or eliminate the degree of vulnerability that leaves people at the mercy of others. (Chapman 1996: 37)

The spirit of a people, its cultural level, its social structure, the deeds its policy may prepare . . . is written in fiscal history. He who knows how to listen to its message here discerns the thunder of world history more clearly than anywhere else. (Schumpeter 1991: 101)

The honouring of basic rights is an active alliance with those who would otherwise be helpless against natural and social forces too strong for them. (Shue 1996: 33)

Taxpaying and non-taxpaying citizens in developing countries including Kenya, both in their individual capacities and as a society, perceive taxation as firstly a necessary burden or obligation to the state and secondly, as a remission that has no commensurate benefits or guarantees.[1] In the former element, the concept of 'necessary burden' has resulted in revenue collection disparities in developing countries as the relatively large size of the economy is not reflected in the proportionately small amount of tax revenue collected. There are numerous reasons for this, including but not limited to the societal perception of tax as a burden leading to both avoidance and evasion of tax. The effects of both domestic and global policies, which allow inputs of diverse actors as well as poor governance practices, fuel this perception.[2] The perception of governance practices extends societal perceptions towards the lack of accountability, transparency and responsibility of the state in its collection and use of fiscal resources in the eyes of citizens, taxpayers and society or the tax bargain. In the latter element, there is a distinctly slow and minimal improvement of human well-being in developing countries. Although developed countries were granted the right or power to levy tax, the 'no commensurate benefits or guarantees' was softened and the 'burden' alleviated by developing social welfare provisions that led to the improvement of the lives of citizens. This fiscal redistribution policy has not been undertaken, adopted or achieved in most developing countries.

Weber (1972: 67) argues that legitimacy arises out of the confidence of the ruled and this chapter will explore how one could extend it by arguing that fiscal legitimacy arises out of the confidence in the fiscal behaviour of the state and its handling of the fiscal resources placed in its trust. This chapter thus seeks to explore not only how to improve tax collection but also tax distribution in developing countries and Kenya specifically. As a result, the objective of this chapter is to explore the crisis of the legitimacy of the fiscal state in developing countries with specific reference to Kenya through an analysis of its Constituency Development Fund. A socio-legal approach following Schumpeter will be undertaken by extending his fiscal sociology as a methodology in both tax law and human rights law in an attempt to reflect society and societal needs in the collection and distribution of tax. Thus, the aphorisms set out together above are the links that this chapter will seek to draw together.

Mumford recently extended Schumpeter's methodology of fiscal sociology by arguing that it requires that taxation be recognised in terms of not only law and its interaction with society but also the racial, ethnic, historical, economic, political, ideological, and belief systems in which it exists (Mumford 2008: 219). Schumpeter also argued that states go through stages of historical development and stated that a social welfare state was a fundamental characteristic of the penultimate level of development: the fiscal state. The social welfare state and the guarantees it provides to society include the provision of goods and services that improve the well-being of individuals and groups within society. It has been extensively applied in developed countries worldwide but has not yet taken root effectively in developing countries. All these elements are referred to within this chapter.

Over the past fifty years, another model of the well-being of peoples has been developed: human rights. Human rights are defined as the basic moral guarantees that people in all countries and cultures have simply because they are people (Nickel 1987: 561–62). The argument posited will be that human rights principles, which set out 'benefits and guarantees' of individuals and society, can be interpreted as the element of well-being within Schumpeter's definition of fiscal sociology. His argument is thus extended to international human rights principles and explores whether these are a possible tool in solving the crisis of the developing fiscal state.

The focus of this chapter is on human rights law and has been chosen to test whether in fact it can be an alternative or additional guide to tax law and policy for the fiscal state to use in legitimising not only its continued existence but also its collection and distribution of tax resources in the eyes of society. This in turn will, on the one hand, enable analysis as to whether societal perception of taxation can change with the intention of removing or minimising the perception of 'burden' by providing 'benefits and guarantees' to society. The discussions following will attempt to unpack the objective set out above and explain how it will be pursued.

This chapter is divided into five main parts. The first section will consider the problem of whether taxation in Kenya can legitimise the continued existence of the state. Secondly, I will discuss Schumpeter and his theory of the fiscal state in order to situate the theoretical framework on which this chapter is based, utilising fiscal sociology and an historical approach. Thirdly, I will attempt to address the issue of fiscal legitimacy in the context of the developing state. Fourthly, I will discuss whether linking human rights and the right to development as a tax expenditure may assist in an increased legitimacy of the fiscal state. Finally the chapter will utilise all these diverse parts and begin to analyse whether the current Kenyan Constituency Development Fund (CDF) is achieving state building and fiscal legitimacy through development.

Fiscal Legitimacy in Developing African States: A Kenyan Context

Fiscal legitimacy and fiscal crisis are weights on either side of a balance. The pivot of the balance is society's confidence in the fiscal state. This confidence can be assessed in various ways and can be perceived through diverse characteristics in the evolving relationship between the state and society. Traditional areas of state activity included defence, foreign affairs, the administration of law and order and the protection of private property. However, there is a growing concern for economic and social welfare not only of the state as a whole but of individual citizens as well. Fiscal legitimacy can be described as an accountable, responsible and transparent fiscal system that is effective and efficient and just and fair. Movement away from this description is movement away from fiscal legitimacy and towards fiscal crisis.

Measuring the perception of citizens and the confidence they have in a fiscal state is a technical process. In addition, perceptions and confidence change with constantly changing fiscal laws and policy. The tax bargain involves the tax levied on the state and the expenditures undertaken by the state that society perceives as being justifiable and for their benefit. State expenditure is divided into recurrent and development expenditure. Recurrent expenditures are preconditions to the existence of the state, including the political and social roles of governance consisting of defence (both internal and external), foreign affairs, and administration of justice. Development expenditure on infrastructure, health and education and social security may be considered as investments to stimulate economic growth but will be considered necessary for a political regime to maintain societal loyalty and increase fiscal legitimacy (Heller 1974: 255). This chapter, while recognising the importance of gauging these perceptions, makes a first foray into the area. As a result, this first step and the measurement of citizens' perceptions and confidence levels will be addressed from the perspective of the fiscal laws and policies of the state of tax revenue and developmental expenditure.[3]

Legitimacy is a complex and multidisciplinary issue.[4] It has been explored mainly in political science with some limited forays by legal scholars. Weber argues that legitimacy arises out of the confidence of the ruled (Weber 1972: 267). As long as the ruled citizens continue to have confidence in and obey the state, it remains legitimate. Citizens, however, will only continue to obey as long as they believe in the fairness of the policies and laws being implemented. As a result, fiscal legitimacy is a reflection of the confidence society has in the state's performance in collecting and spending its tax revenue as expressed in accepted laws and polices. Fiscal legitimacy is but one small facet of legitimacy, which this chapter will seek to explore.

Fiscal legitimacy is critical to the existence of the post-colonial fiscal state as it is the source of its support, it assists in state building and it promotes sovereignty and independence by reducing reliance on foreign aid. This fiscal state has two roles to play in the maintenance and improvement of fiscal legitimacy: political and legal. Although government as a political actor assumes the responsibility of deciding what ends are to be pursued and what resources it is prepared to commit in dealing with problems, as a legal actor the state must then proceed to establish the mechanisms to further these ends (Nonet and Seznick 2000: 112). This chapter, while recognising the importance of political legitimacy, will limit itself to improvement of legitimacy from a legal perspective. It will proceed on this premise without seeking to replace politics with law. The enhancement of fiscal legitimacy will thus be discussed from the point of view of how to harness the law and policy-making process to create an optimum condition for increasing well-being and state development.

Good governance paves the way to fiscal legitimacy by building people's faith in the state and ensuring their acceptance of its laws and policies. Good governance has today become the centre of attention for many post-colonial fiscal states in the drive to improve efficiency and effectiveness through transparency, accountability and responsibility practices in order to be both just and fair. States can enhance fiscal legitimacy by: firstly, involving independent third parties in the auditing and evaluation of public policies to strengthen transparency and accountability; secondly, promoting better, fairer and more public spending; thirdly, broadening the tax base and making tax systems fairer and more balanced; and finally, reinforcing the capacity, authority and accountability of subnational government bodies. Fiscal legitimacy is not only an issue of capacity: in addition to strengthening administrative capabilities, societal participation and open and informed debate can result in more transparency. Independent actors with the capacity and the financial independence to carry out a critical evaluation of policies and proposed reforms can also add to the good governance and fiscal legitimacy.

A Summary of Kenyan Fiscal History

Fiscal sociology recognises that each state in the world has its own unique history. Schumpeter posited that in order to understand the 'thunder' of fiscal history of a state one must analyse its history (Schumpeter 1991: 101). What limited information there is on the pre-colonial period in Kenya identifies two types of governance.[5] One type of governance posited by Ochieng' is that in this era society was made up of a system of lodges, sectional relations and codes of justice which contributed to the corporate polity of their social groups and communities (Ochieng' 1985: 44). The second more complex type of governance, is characterised as an ethnic community that had a system where a payment in kind was made to a chief or ruler for the purposes of protection. This tax or tithe was payable in terms of the produce from the land or animals and security was provided through a system of warrior classes (Ocaya-Lakidi 1977: 137–39). At this stage many of these nations in Kenya were small and required little or no administration. Life was at subsistence level and mainly communal.

When the British landed on the East African coast and began their process of the colonisation of Kenya, fiscally the island states and the coastline of Kenya could be best described as having been tribute states of the Portuguese and Arabs. There were elements of tax states in the complexity of taxes levied and collected. However, there was no recorded redistribution of tax revenue. In the East African hinterland, the remainder of the ethnic communities or tribes continued to exist as they always had as a combination of pre-primitive and primitive states practising communal self-subsistence. It is this mixture of ethnic nations, communities and city-states with a diversity of complex, simple or non-existent fiscal policies that the British encountered when they began their occupation of East Africa.

During colonisation, areas of Kenya that subsequently resisted occupation, or were unaffected by either the real or actual control of subsequent colonial administrations, maintained some elements of these ways of life. The imperial and colonial state policy ensured that the link between tax expenditure and tax revenue was crystallised regarding only one part of the tax base, the Europeans. Belated and mixed attempts by colonial authorities towards the end of colonisation to try to link the benefits of taxation for the Africans and Asians were limited and largely unsuccessful. The results of attempts by certain parts of the African population to agitate for the link between the taxes paid and expenditure to improve well-being was also mixed.

Until the Second World War the few measures in the realm of social policy benefited Europeans almost exclusively (Fuchs 1985: 100–3). The result of colonisation on the services and infrastructure of the colonial state was such that there was a bias towards development in the areas where Europeans lived and the areas they needed to access for the purposes of farming and the transportation necessary (Acemoglu et al. 2001). The Asians and Africans lived in areas with little or no services and infrastructure.

In contrast, during and after the Second World War the vague concept of social welfare became a favoured means of expressing a new imperial commitment to colonial peoples (Lewis 2000: 147). The policy before the Second World war on public outlays and social development was scant and limited relative to other programmes (Subrahmanyam 2004: 4). Metropolitan forms of social engineering were now applied more vigorously to colonial issues. A new generation of professional experts entered the stage of colonial policy. Social welfare included: implanting rural social betterment by animating civil society against social collapse; devising urban remedies for the incapacitated and the destitute; correcting the deviant; and training Africans to be their own policemen.

However, allocations to improve the welfare of people remained racially divided both in collection of hut tax and in distribution for health, education and other social services. Development records show that in the years 1957–1962, less than 10 per cent of allocated revenue to social services was development expenditure whereas the bulk of expenditure was to maintain the provision of the existing services which were mainly for the Europeans (Subrahmanyam 2004: 4).

Not all citizens within the state had equal access to all the services, and one condition of the attainment of independence was maintaining the rights of those already granted benefits before independence in certain categories of social services such as pension benefits.[6] This provision was however, immediately withdrawn on the grounds of lack of resources for the rest of the population. Since the majority had never had access to any of these services in the past and in many cases were not aware of the existence of these benefits in the rural areas, the provision and subsequent withdrawal of these services did not register with the population as being the loss of a benefit directly related to the payment of taxes.

Upon independence, taxation was perceived as a force of oppression and domination. This chapter explores the Kenyan post-colonial fiscal state in order to establish whether this partial, fragile and tenuous link between tax revenue and expenditure was maintained and whether there has been progression towards fiscal legitimacy. The colonial period thus had two decisive legacies: economic underdevelopment and the policy inheritance (Fahnbulleh 2006: 46).

The attempts made to reverse the fiscal crisis can be divided into three main periods. Firstly, the immediate post-independence period was the era of President Kenyatta, whose leadership was characterised by strong authoritarian and single party rule with sporadic policy changes mainly as a reaction to changing economic circumstances both nationally, regionally and internationally and severely limited societal participation (1964–1980).

Secondly, the era of President Moi is divided into two. He initially continued authoritarian and single party rule but this was tempered by the realisation of the debt abyss into which the developing world was disappearing. Internationally there was the introduction of loan conditionalities that were then applied across the developing world without much reference to societal conditions and circumstances with the inclusion of the voice of creditors (1981–1992). Moi subsequently bowed to international pressure and reduced authoritarian rule, introduced multi-party politics and limited presidential terms. Fiscally the role of international actors grew and they controlled the policies implemented during this period (1993–2003).

Finally comes the election of Kenya's third President Mwai Kibaki, coupled with the realisation by international lending institutions that the imposed loan conditionalities were proving unsuccessful. Fiscal policies moved partially towards concentration on home-grown strategies for resource collection and distribution involving greater participation that ran and continue to run parallel to the reform policies applied since independence, under the direction of different members of the international community (2003 to date).

The first post-independence strategy was set out in Kenya's first planning document entitled 'African Socialism and its Application to Planning in Kenya' (Republic of Kenya 1965). Its main stated aim was to guarantee every citizen full and equal political rights as a firm basis for rapid economic growth. It was stated specifically that the economic approach of the government would be ensuring Africanisation of the economy, education, employment, welfare and public service but not jeopardising growth. Amongst other things, this planning document declared that the government would concentrate investment in places where it was likely to maximise returns, which would subsequently be redistributed to the rest of the country. This approach concentrated resources in the same places as the colonial state had done, at the expense of opening up the rest of the country. No attempt was made to engage society in participation in the redistribution of state resources. Instead the encouraging of self-help was coupled with voluntary assistance from charities, civil society and philanthropic individuals. The use of paternalistic attitudes, corruption, clientelism and limited redistribution led to the eventual failure to create or develop fiscal legitimacy. This policy has continued throughout Kenya's independence era and only began to change slightly in the current Kibaki era through the development of the Constituency Development Fund amongst other changes.

Defining Fiscal Sociology for Developing Countries using Human Rights

Schumpeter's fiscal sociology is best defined by Backhaus as the analysis of taxation and public finances undertaken by studying the 'lives of individuals, groups and societies'. It includes in it the unintended impact of taxation as well as regulation and has implications for almost every activity of government that somehow affects the private sector (Backhaus 2002: 73). Goldscheid defined fiscal sociology as the historical nature of the state at a point in time and its functional interdependence between finances and social development (Goldscheid, as cited in Musgrave 1992: 99). The space created by fiscal sociology to allow a multi-disciplinary discourse on fiscal relations between society and the developing state while allowing for diversity in state forms is thus where this chapter will situate itself. It will use the political, economic, legal, cultural, institutional and historical factors of a society to link in the state. It will also add the discourse of human rights as a measure of the complex social interactions. The lens through which this will be discussed will be the participation of society and citizens in the institutional processes of the fiscal state.

Human rights principles are the principles and policy consideration benchmarks that can be a measure of the effectiveness, efficiency and accountability, and responsibility of the state to society. Thus, human rights can create concrete provisions that are progressively enforceable and realisable. The widest possible interpretation of human rights claims, principles, policies, laws and values will be used in this chapter. The use of this extremely wide scope is firstly to attempt pragmatically to point out the potential breadth of human rights considerations that can be linked into taxation through fiscal sociology. Secondly, to assert normatively that human rights are appealing by virtue of the standards that they set and that there is a need to test their practical realisation. The need to see whether a state can be self-sustainable while providing for the society therein leads to the discussion and use of fiscal sociology not only at the overall theoretical level, but also at the more detailed level of discourse in developing countries, as is broken down into the macro and the micro levels of fiscal sociology.[7]

The substantiation of the possibility of adding on both the post-colonial state and human rights as a benchmark is made possible by several arguments. Firstly, that the typology of states inherently recognises the uniqueness of each state. Secondly, it also recognises the evolving meanings and allows for the contextualised analysis of terminology that benchmark the progression of states such as 'state' itself, 'well-being', 'administration', 'tax' and 'welfare'. Thirdly, Schumpeter also argued for the interconnection between the development of a state and the tax regime as long as the state could be distinguished from private interests. It will be argued that these developments as well as the inherent flexibility in the theory of fiscal sociology allows for not only the extension of fiscal sociology to apply to developing states but also to use human rights as a possible benchmarking alternative to the social welfare state.

Participation is the tool used in the application of this theory to analyse whether in fact a link can be made between human rights and taxation at a macro level. Schumpeter stated that economic analysis deals with the questions of how people behave at any given time, the economic effects of their behaviour. Economic sociology, he added, deals with the question of how people come to behave as they do. He then defined human behaviour as including actions, motives, propensities and social institutions relevant to economic behaviour (Schumpeter 1954: 19). This reference to human behaviour is what allows the discussion to then flow into the area of participation and participatory budgeting (PB) as an analysis of how budgeting decisions are made by society and thus allows one to consider if the behaviour of society can be tied into human rights.

In order to analyse the link in developing countries, like Kenya, between the issues of tax revenue and tax expenditure, this chapter looks at human rights through the lens of fiscal sociology. The inquiry requires a foray into how this connection or link can be made on the basis of history, societal needs and future regionalism in developing countries like Kenya, in the context of fiscal sociology. Fiscal sociology provides the methodology not only for developing policy proposals but also for analysing present policies in the case of the linkage an/or connection being made between revenue and tax expenditure and how the link can be used to finance and or strengthen the financing of human rights, development and the alleviation of poverty by increasing redistribution in order to reduce inequalities.

The Declaration of the Right to Development (DRD) sets out critical obligations in its articles:

States have the right and the duty to formulate appropriate national development policies that aim at the constant improvement of the well-being of the entire population and of all individuals, on the basis of their active, free and meaningful participation in development and in the fair distribution of the benefits resulting therefrom. (UN General Assembly 1986)

This entails three important basic principles, firstly the primary responsibility of states to apply policies aimed at improving the well-being of the population, secondly, that the human person is the central subject and should be the active participant, and finally that there should be distribution of benefits.

The DRD went one step further and placed the responsibility of the realisation of the right to development not only on individual states in consideration of their populations but also on states collectively for all peoples.

States have the duty to take steps, individually and collectively, to formulate international development policies with a view to facilitating the full realization of the right to development. (Ibid.: Article 4)

In 1995 the world embraced the significance of well-being and development for all. However, states have neither absorbed this right into their constitutions nor have they, with a few exceptions, declared this as a human right (United Nations 1995: Introduction). From the perspective of Schumpeter's typology of fiscal states, the fiscal state's levels of development achieved include provision of a diverse array of social welfare benefits to its citizens, whereby as a result the state perceives no additional rationale in adding a constitutional provision for an issue already well settled in state–society relations. However for the post-colonial fiscal state this need for the recognition of the developmental needs of its citizens is necessary in order to provide better guidelines for the resource uses of the state.

Measures have also been developed with which states can analyse their realisation of human rights. These include the use of approaches like Amartya Sen's 'capability' (Sen 2000), development indicator,[8] and the Millennium Development Goals,[9] which set benchmarks that allow for the realisation of human rights while taking into consideration the resource constraints that states face. In addition, global organizations that are formally or informally linked to other organizations, agencies, and governments around the world, such as the United Nations and the World Bank, view citizens' participation in claiming their rights and budgetary design practices as a crucial part of their responsibility to improve their well-being.[10] In addition, more recent endeavours have begun within the United Nations to analyse how fiscal policies and budgets can be converted in order to realise human rights (UN International Children's Fund 2007). Scholars are now beginning to recognise not only the importance of the link between tax and human rights: Alston et al in one footnote of his most recent edition has expressed the possibility of using Schumpeter's fiscal sociology to draw together the lines of this debate (Steiner, Alston and Goodman 2007: 305).

The right to participate in decision making has a basis in UN Human rights instruments,[11] and expert studies (see generally Ganji 1969; Ferrero 1983; United Nations 1985) as well as instruments in economics (United Nations General Assembly 1974) and development strategy.[12] Development is seen as being special/specific, such that strategies must be developed by the people themselves and adapted to meet local conditions and needs (United Nations 1990: 155–56). This makes participation the primary mechanism for identifying appropriate goals and criteria (ibid.: Paragraphs 150, 179). In this case, the right to development becomes not so much a right to improve material conditions, but the right to have a voice in and share control over the economic environment (Barsh 1991: 329) albeit within the limitation imposed by budgetary constraints and state legislative procedures.[13]

As stressed above, the state's duty is to formulate development policies on the basis of 'active, free and meaningful participation' (UN General Assembly 1986: Articles 1.1 and 8.2). This term is linked to the concepts of 'equality of opportunity in access to basic resources' and 'fair distribution of income' (ibid.: Article 8.1). Linking tax revenue to tax expenditure through human rights is best expressed here within the right to development and its link to its resource requirements. Participation is a tool that can be used to ensure accountability, responsibility and transparency as well as efficiency and effectiveness in the context of limited resources.

Within the developing country context, participation is seen to foster good governance. Proponents point to corruption, opaque resource allocation, the failure to deliver basic services and a power structure that does not allow non-elites an opportunity to have their voice heard. At an overall level, participation is said to promote transparency, increase social justice and help individuals become better citizens.

The challenging part of this project is to not only the attempt to bring together two seemingly unconnected fields of taxation and human rights at a theoretical level but to also attempt a practical application by analysing existing state systems using this approach. The specific focus chosen for the purposes of this chapter was the Constituency Development Fund in Kenya. The fund has several critical elements that are pertinent to this study. Firstly, there was the legal provision that specified direct allocation of tax revenue to tax expenditure, creating the link that this chapter proposes. Secondly, the revenue allocation was specified for development purposes leading to the development of the fiscal state. Thirdly, the allocation of tax revenue is to the smallest grass-root electoral area (constituency) which allows the highlighting of a microcosm of the state–society relationship. Fourthly, it specifies the use of local citizenry in the constituency to decide on their needs or requirements based on their priorities for the year, which had to be undertaken by people in the area, and allows for an analysis based on well-being and social welfare as posited by Schumpeter.

The CDF uses the term development but does not define it. This allowed not only for the use of the economic interpretation of development tying in with Schumpeter's arguments on tax development and state development but also allows space for inclusion of the right to development as well. These two terms together are the stands that begin to build up the link between taxation and human rights. The 'right to development' as it has developed through international law inherently requires a link to resources and this adds another strand to the tax/human rights link. Finally, the acceptability of the use of the right to development as a human right in the past thirty years is contextualised based on three grounds. Firstly, that this is the most modern and recent interpretation of a human right. Secondly, it was proposed by developing states, the subjects of this chapter. Finally, independently through different mechanisms, states are already making attempts to apply it, albeit indirectly.

Participation is a key issue in the discourse of Participatory Budgeting. Downs (1957: 29) credited Schumpeter with formulating the premise that politicians do not seek elections to offer programmes but vice versa. However, Musgrave asserts that Schumpeter himself argued for a stronger leadership, with the state acting as a rational instrument and not a villain, a theory that is not well fitted in developing country discourse (Musgrave 1992: 112). Thus, here too the issue of society will be extended further than foreseen by Schumpeter to include elements of direct democracy.

Although the specific focus of this study is Kenya and the variation over time of the choices that rulers made in the collection and distribution of tax, the aim of the chapter is to enquire into the tax policy choices and the results of their application. Although there is concern with reforms of tax systems, and some statistical data is provided, there is no attempt undertaken here to calculate the amount collected, lost or stolen. The main purpose is thus to locate whether the participatory process of citizens through the articulation of their needs in state budgeting processes can result in not only re-legitimising taxation but also realising human rights, while recognising the limitations of the system and this research.

Contextualising Fiscal Sociology

In post-colonial fiscal states in Africa citizens of all classes have sought to avoid paying taxes and state fees,[14] decreasing the state's extractive capacity. This has been compounded by the effects of both domestic and global policies, which allow fiscal and policy inputs of diverse actors, as well as poor governance practices including corruption, clientelism and patronage.[15] There is a distinctly slow and minimal improvement of human well-being in developing countries. Comprehensive fiscal redistribution has not been under-taken, adopted or achieved in most developing countries. As a result, civic indiscipline in some states has arisen, reducing fiscal legitimacy and increasing the fiscal crisis. If these states are to develop in addition to reducing their reliance on foreign aid, the trust and loyalty of citizens and society must be recovered. Laws and policies that reflect societal thought must be put into place and pursued in order to convince citizens of the state's ability and right to continue collecting revenues for the public good. The state will not succeed until citizens believe they are participating fully in public life and that their tax payments will not be lost to government corruption. This chapter thus seeks to explore not only how to improve tax collection but also tax distribu-tion in post-colonial fiscal states in Africa and Kenya specifically through the strengthening of the state–society relationship in order to alleviate poverty and achieve development.

Mumford (2001) posited that the legitimisation of tax could be seen through the culture of taxation prevalent in a society, the method of collec-tion, the ease as well as the societal response to the use of a state's resources and the forms that its redistribution takes.[16] Moore argues most recently that Schumpeter's fiscal sociology is extremely pertinent in the analysis of develop-ing states (see generally Moore and Rackner 2004). Thus, fiscal sociology has been expanded to include influences from both the socio-legal school and constitutional law influences on public finances (Mumford 2008: 219) but also to post-colonial states. This chapter will approach the analysis of tax law by following the conceptualisation of fiscal sociology in the tradition created by Goldscheid and Schumpeter and distilled by Mumford and Moore.

Schumpeter argued that the most important achievement of the fiscal state is the increased welfare of the state, no matter what type of state one is con-sidering. The arguments posited and analysed in this chapter are based on the assumption that post-colonial states are aiming to achieve the characteristics of the fiscal state, geared towards fiscal self-sufficiency and state-building resulting in increased fiscal legitimacy. More specifically, as this chapter will argue, they are attempting to develop the core concept within the fiscal state: improved welfare and societal well-being. The ensuing analysis will undertake a detailed analysis of the historical development of the Kenyan fiscal state with the final goal of improving well-being.

Meeting the Challenge to Fiscal Legitimacy through Well-being

Social welfare rests on the idea that the social provision of goods and services be treated as a right by all citizens, rather than an act of charity, a gift from some to others (see generally Kelley 2000), an idea that Schumpeter has adopted as being a constituent element of the ultimate level of the state: the fiscal state. The modern welfare state can be approached in many different ways, as an instrument of social control or betterment: as a part of a state or a stage in the development of capitalism; as a minimum safety net for those in need; as social insurance for the middle classes; or everything a government needs to do to improve the well-being of the people (see Carrier and Kendall 1986; Esping-Andersen 1990; Howard 1993). Social welfare objectives include, among others, direct spending for income security, housing, health care, education, employment and training, and social services. People see social welfare states as a guarantee for a minimum standard of living, protecting citizens from loss of income beyond their control, especially retirement, sickness, disability or unemployment. Thus, this includes public assistance and social insurance, serving both the poor and the middle class (see Pampel and Williamson 1989; Marmor, Mashaw and Harvey 1990). However, Scandinavian authors add a third dimension to the welfare state, which is ensuring that all citizens receive the standards available of a certain level of services without discrimination (see Briggs 1961). Wilensky has also stated that the 'essence of the welfare state is government-protected minimum standards of income, nutrition, health, housing and education assured to every citizen' (Wilensky 1975: 1).

The concept of social welfare is the main goal in Schumpeter's discourse of transition from the tax state to the fiscal state. This section will thus attempt to ascertain whether the fiscal policies geared towards social welfare can be also geared towards human rights, and thus whether there are similarities and parallels to be drawn between these concepts in order to apply fiscal policies in the achievement or realisation of human rights. There are several issues to be considered in drawing this parallel: they are the similarities and difference in firstly, the content of welfare and human rights; secondly, the obligations that both these concepts place on the state, and finally, the fiscal burden involved in their realisation.

Kenya and the Constituency Development Fund

The problems that the Kenyan fiscal state and society are grappling with have been discussed earlier with the intention that perhaps this current practice may provide a solution and, with a few amendments to the approach, provide further solutions not only to the legitimacy of the fiscal state but also the realisation of human rights. In addition to the need to achieve improved social welfare and legitimise the fiscal state, there is also the issue of accountability, corruption, clientelism, patronage and the 'big man' system in Kenyan politics. The ensuing discussion will not only analyse participatory budgeting (PB) in Kenya, as developed by the CDF, but will enquire into whether or not the issues set out above, all of which form part of the governance practices under the right to development, are being achieved or can be achieved if the

CDF process were to be undertaken or analysed within the context of human rights laws in order to improve fiscal legitimacy.[17]

The CDF is the first attempt ever made in Kenya to link tax revenue deliberately and concretely to tax expenditure. Through the CDF citizens are placed in the position of distributing resources which they are aware are sourced from themselves. This chapter will explain and evaluate the development of the CDF, and explore the question of whether human rights could be integrated into the discourse in the allocation of CDF resources.

Establishment of the Constituency Development Fund

The CDF Act came into existence in the wake of a new regime in 2004, a new push for decentralisation and the rejection by referendum of the draft Constitution. Thus, this legislation can be seen as a development stemming from the already ongoing national endeavour to decentralise the government's resource distribution and reroute its application directly to the grass-roots level. The reason for the introduction of this CDF Bill was that it was seen that grass-roots development did not seem to be very far-reaching. Before the CDF was implemented, MPs would go to public meetings, usually during the school holidays (as they were based in the urban centres) and ask the District Commissioner (who usually handled seven or more constituencies) to undertake work like building dispensaries and roads based on their constituents' requests. However, the DCs were perceived as not being very responsive to the needs highlighted by the MPs and they would not usually carry out MPs' requests, since their superiors were those in local government and they owed no duty or responsibility to the MP. This request cycle would continue until the next public meeting. As a result, MPs would use their personal money and money obtained voluntarily and forcibly from other sources to finance activity at constituency level in order to show or prove their effectiveness to their electorate. Hence, the proposed CDF would mean that the use of personal money to fund development, the patronage system of begging for infrastructure and trips to state house would no longer need to continue.[18]

Under the Constituency Development Fund (CDF) Act of 2004 (Republic of Kenya 2004), for the first time ever in Kenya, each constituency was allocated the functions and abilities to be considered a development unit with fiscal resources from tax revenue being channelled directly to it as a development area.[19] These resources are distributed by a Constituency Development Committee (CDC) made up of the elected representative (Member of Parliament) and a group of grass-roots representatives who are assumed to best understand the developmental needs of the constituency.

The CDF can be seen as a development stemming from the already ongoing national discourse and debate since before independence on whether to have a centralised or decentralised government. The CDF also aims to remedy the imbalance in local regional development brought about by partisan politics and clientelism. Its resources are specifically provided to assist only constituency-level development projects, particularly those aimed at combating poverty at the grass-roots. The CDF as expressed in the legislation is devoted to community-based projects, which ensures that the prospective benefits are available to a wide cross-section of the inhabitants of a particular constituency. However, the CDF is not to be used to support political bodies/ activities or personal award projects. The resources are allocated to the constituency based on requests for funding by any constituency members or institutions for development purposes. The legislation defines development purposes as: infrastructure, health and education, such as schools and clinics (Republic of Kenya 2004).

The CDF Act requires the government to set aside a proportion of not less than 2.5 per cent of its ordinary revenue for disbursement under the CDF programme. Three-quarters of this amount are divided equally between Kenya's 210 constituencies whilst the remaining quarter is divided based on a poverty index to cater for poorer constituencies.

Projects under the Act are required by the Act to be community-based, and it also specifies that all projects shall be 'development' projects (Republic of Kenya 2004: section 21). Thus the CDF funds projects that benefit the community at large, such as construction of schools and health centre buildings, water projects, roads, chiefs' offices, and police posts.[20] The training of CDF committee members can also be supported by CDF. After the 2007 Amendments, acknowledged benefits that have arisen from its application have included a reduction of corruption, increasing grass-roots development as well as direct attempts to alleviate the financial burden of MPs during campaigns and their terms in office by placing at their disposal government resources for use in their respective constituencies.[21]

The initial 2.5 per cent of the ordinary revenue collected by the government that was allocated to CDF was increased by parliament through the annual budget to 7.5 per cent in 2006 and 8.3 per cent in 2007, as seen in Table 7.1 below.

Table 7.1 Constituency Development Fund Allocations 2003–2008 in KES (Kenyan Shillings)

	Average amount per constituency	Total annual allocation/% of ordinary government revenue
2003/4	6,000,000	1.26 billion
2004/5	20,000,000	5.6 billion (2.5%)
2005/6	30,000,000	7.2 billion (2.5%)
2006/7	50,000,000	10.038 billion (3.5%)
2007/8	50,000,000	10.1 billion (tbc)

Source: CDF Secretariat

In actual figures the amount per constituency grew by a third until 2007 when a reduction in the total revenue resulted in the actual amount received per constituency remaining stable despite an increase in the revenue share of 0.8 per cent.

Legitimising Taxation through the CDF and its Challenges

Through the structure and provisions of the CDF, there is the possibility of connecting directly and thus bringing to the forefront the connection between the payment of taxation and its use for the good of the taxpayer. The current absence of the legitimacy of taxation is an issue addressed by the CDF at a microcosmic level through its direct distribution of a percentage of tax revenue for a fixed set of purposes which are intended to directly improve the lives of citizens at grass-root level. However, it also brings to light the difficulties and issues of concern at national level as the same problems that concern state distribution of the national budget are reflected at this level. These concerns impede and stunt the legitimisation process and must therefore be analysed in order to realise the problems that will follow the legitimisation of taxation as well as the achievement of human rights principles, as it would affect any other process of the application of taxation policy at all levels of the state apparatus.

This analysis does not mean that there have not been actions to remedy the abuse of the CDF process. There are several instances that cut across the themes below that show how the challenges posed by those abusing the process are being answered. However, in support of the checks and balances that can take place and are taking place through the legislative system in Kenya, seventeen former officials of the Sabioti CDF were summoned before the police in April of 2008 and asked to explain how the 100 million was spent from the CDF kitty, including the then MP of the area (Omonso 2008).

In a different situation, a CDF handover failed to take place when the outgoing MP Jackson Rono and his CDF Committee was asked to account for all projects and set out those that were complete and those that were ongoing in Eldama Ravine constituency by the incoming MP Joseph Ayabei.[22]

In Laikipia, the government ordered that investigations be carried out and that the relevant officials vacate their offices while the investigation was ongoing as to why money allocated to a water project was not used for the required project. The officials were also required to hand over the books of accounts (Ndirangu 2007). This stemmed from the report of a Sabioti CDF manager having gone missing and presumed murdered after he went to make a location check of fifty ongoing projects and found that none of them existed, after which he compiled a report and sent it to the National CDF Management Committee (Omonso and Ng'etich 2008).

Chweya (2006) argues that the CDF does not fit perfectly in any of the models of decentralization. The CDF has been established through an Act of Parliament, but it is not managed through an elected council as is the case of local authorities. The managers who constitute the CDC are largely appointees of the MPs. Prior to the establishment of the fund, most MPs struggled to please their constituents using their own funds. This contributed to widespread corruption and abuse of public resources. The availability of the fund, therefore, has relieved MPs of the pressure of resource generation to sustain patron–client relationships. However, it has created new challenges for engaging people in development, and being accountable and open to criticism.

In early 2009, in response to growing concerns about the low utilisation of completed facilities, weak capacity in identifying projects, low use of available technical capacity in implementing projects, poor management, few large-scale projects, lack of adequate financial controls, allegations of interference, corruption and embezzlement, a CDF Review Task force was created and is currently holding public hearings nationwide (CDF Secretariat 2009). The analysis of this chapter may provide ideas for consideration by this task force. The resulting themes include the purposes for which the CDF was created and which have emerged during its existence. They are in order of importance: development and poverty alleviation; corruption and clientelism; participation; accountability, responsibility and transparency; mismanagement of state resources and finally decentralisation and the constitutionality of the CDF process. All these themes apart from the first will be discussed in this section. The theme of development and poverty alleviation will be discussed separately in the next sub-section and in more detail for the purpose of linking it to human rights and for a more detailed analysis.

Corruption and Clientelism

Corruption and clientelism were very evident at the commencement of the CDF process in 2004 but have since been reduced and controlled through legislative amendments that have improved oversight. However, there remains a continual problem with both corruption and clientelism that is evidenced by different facets of the CDF process both in project implementation and in the flow of funds.

In the process of the implementation of projects, there has been noted collusion between key members of the tender committee and contractors. In some cases government officials may also be part of the collusion. Not only are genuine suppliers locked out of the tender process, but the same two or three corruptible contractors may be repeatedly given work. This includes not only ghost contractors but also contractors with a history of shoddy work. Quotations and specifications for projects may be exaggerated; faulty or substandard buildings are approved by corrupt government officials. In addition there is also the possibility of collusion with fake Project Committees (PCs) where CDCs may collude with family members, political allies and acquaintances to set up PCs for dubious projects. These PCs then manage the project but divert most of the funds for personal gain.

Many MPs have been accused of directing the majority of funds to a few locations/divisions based on voter patterns in the constituency. This is a very common occurrence and especially where a constituency has no long-term plan for development and where information about funded projects is not shared with communities.

A few committees actually illegally amend fund accounts so that the records reflect development while on the ground no projects or project committees exist. Others keep two set of books. This is fraud and is a criminal offence. Other CDCs attempt to avoid lengthy procurement regulations by funding projects for small amounts such as KES 100,000 over three years or more. This means the PC cannot meaningfully make good use of the money and this increases the chances of fraud and misallocation.

Some CDF officials have taken advantage of projects funded by other funding bodies such as other devolved funds like LATF (Local Authority Transfer Fund), as well as other international and local donors, and instead abscond with the money designated for that project. This has actually resulted in the creation of the position of fund managers and requirements in the CDF Amendment Act 2007 that all CDF projects should have a sign/billboard displaying project information including the total amount allocated, the identity of the contractor/engineers and the CDF project reference number.

As a result a critical issue remains concerning oversight of the MP and the CDC. There is thus the need to consider whether to redefine the role of MP and limit his/her powers over the fund. One possibility is to ensure that the MP remains as an ex-officio patron of an independent, locally elected CDC. Currently, instead of reducing the element of the 'big man' in Kenyan politics, the problem of clientelism/patronage has instead been reinforced. Making the CDCs independent of the MP would not only remedy this but also overcome the constitutional objection based on the separation of powers principle. His/her role should be to facilitate strategic, long-term development planning, arbitrate when there are wrangles and conflicts, and oversee and ensure the prudent use of funds. No MP and family members or business associates should be allowed to benefit directly from the fund.

Organisations such as the Kenya Anticorruption Commission, the National Management Committee (NMC), Public Procurement Appeals and Review Board and other agencies of redress should be compelled to act swiftly and decisively in cases of corruption: failure to do so should be actionable. The CDF Act should be improved to seal loopholes, and CDF record-keeping and reporting strengthened, standardised and enforced.

Participation

The CDCs under the first Kibaki regime, and their selection, resulted in controversy, with MPs accused of appointing their relatives, cronies and yes-men for reasons of patronage and the desire for pliant management (Nyaga 2008). There is a resulting need for the CDCs to be locally elected/nominated. A mechanism needs to be devised whereby CDCs can be elected or nominated through local means to ensure they represent the public and their interests. Measures also need to be adopted to protect committee members from political interference, to limit the length of committee membership and to allow removal from office in cases of abuse.

Public participation should be protected by making it mandatory that all CDF processes, especially procurement, are open to meaningful public involvement. The CDF Act should recognise the right of all members of the public to participate in a CDF. This can be achieved by ensuring the CDC is elected or nominated by the public. The CDC and PCs should be compelled to report back to the public and to respond swiftly to their complaints and concerns, all CDF documents should be available to the public and officers who withhold information should be penalised. Greater awareness should be maintained so that the public understands CDF systems and processes including the record-keeping structures. All projects should originate at grass-roots level; if not, they should receive grass-roots endorsement. Representatives of the PCs should attend important CDC meetings such as the project-selection and tendering meetings, and all meetings where financial decisions are made. All meetings should be public.

In addition, participation seems to be only skin deep, without any actual open and public participation, as has been undertaken in both Brazil and India. The aim still seems predominantly for the organised institutions/ committees to benefit with one project at a time. Ordinary citizens who may for instance require low-cost housing to be built have not managed to access these funds as is the case in Brazil.

Accountability, Responsibility and Transparency

The speed with which the CDF Act 2004 was implemented and the speed with which the 2007 amendments of the CDF Act were enacted has meant that roles have needed clarification and accountability structures strengthened. From its inception there have been numerous issues relating to the lack of accountability, transparency and responsibility.

The roles and responsibilities of CDF officers should be clarified to ensure that at each stage liability is specific and clear. At present the CDF committees take decisions under collective responsibility allowing unscrupulous individuals to manipulate this ambiguity. Some MPs tend to dominate all aspects of

CDF operations, such that no decision can be made or payment made without the MP's approval. In these situations the CDC has no say in the running of the fund and the MP usually works closely with two or three officials, keeping the rest in the dark. Officials who raise questions or criticisms are likely not to be notified of meetings, and are likely to be dropped from the CDC. In such cases the CDC is not transparent, record keeping is likely to be poor, and information to the public not forthcoming. Such CDCs tend to operate with a lot of secrecy and with minimum involvement of the public. Certain contractors are likely to be favoured, and genuine proposals are likely to be ignored in favour of those that favour the MP in one way or other. CDC members are likely to include illiterate and non-technical people who cannot understand the MP's tricks and his 'kitchen cabinet' who are likely to be the coordinator, treasurer, chairman and secretary. These very people are also likely to be on the tender committee.

The CDF Act charges government with the implementation of the CDF. It does not clarify the aspects of implementation. In practice the district development officers (DDOs) and other district officers (DOs) have responsibilities without authority and are easily coerced into approving the expenditures of powerful politicians. Conversely government technical departments give technical expertise to the CDF through invisible and non-formalised means: BQs, certificates of completion and so forth are seldom officially signed, allowing technical officers to escape liability. The DDO should be empowered to demand compliance and conversely liable when complicit in the abuse of funds.

The independence of the NMC was called to question in 2008 and it was replaced by an independent Board, a definitely positive move, geared towards improved participation and oversight. However, the need to strengthen the Board's powers remains in order to punish errant CDF officials who flout CDF regulations and guidelines. The independence of the Board needs to be safeguarded by securing its budgets, functions and powers through statutory means and de-linking it sufficiently from central government. Legal provisions have been made to improve accountability from the Board through regular, relevant and comprehensive reports including expenditure reports, the setting of high performance standards where the Board is accountable to the CDC through regular, institutionalised reporting, establishment of rapid response times to public requests and complaints, and reconstitution of its structure. However, this can be further strengthened by extending CDF accountability to concerned citizens and the public in general.

Some CDCs receive project funds and fail to release these to the PC. This was especially common with earlier CDF disbursements, but as the press, civil society organisations (CSOs) (Machuhi 2009) and the public (Kwamboka 2009a, b) have become more vigilant it is hoped that fewer CDCs will be susceptible to misuse. Some CDCs set up parallel accounts where, in collusion with officials at the district office, they siphon off the money into a separate account to avoid close scrutiny. This is fraud and a criminal offence.

The CDF Act and guidelines do not protect the role of the labourer. CDF should emphasise the need to pay all labour contracted under a CDF at the government rate. There is a need to review the law to ensure that CDF projects favour labour-intensive means as a way of guaranteeing local labour attractive wages. The present guidelines also do not emphasise the keeping of labour rolls. Strict standards should be set for all committees and contractors undertaking CDF projects to maintain up-to-date labour rolls. Labour payments should be witnessed by members of the PC/CDC to ensure money intended for labour is not siphoned off.

Mismanagement of State Fiscal Resources

Mapesa and Kibua (2006) have also argued that the management of the fund has a potential to introduce the politics of reward and punishment at the local level. Areas which do not support the MP and members of the committee may be excluded from benefiting from the fund. Additionally the funding of projects can be used for manipulation by communities, especially during campaigns for national and civic elections. Further, the fund provides MPs with the opportunity for stifling free, fair and competitive elections, since they have exclusive control over the key local resource for development. In the case of the latter, not all civic leaders are members of the CDC, and indeed, those that belong to the committee can potentially exploit their membership for their own selfish interests.

Decentralisation and the Constitutionality of the CDF

The Act gives very wide discretion and an exclusivist role to MPs. Given the extra-constitutional nature of the role of MPs in the operation of the CDF, one can only conclude that the predominant role assigned to MPs was inspired by political considerations rather than legal or other necessities. By giving too many powers to MPs over the operation of the CDF, and by insisting on implementation of the projects through the departments of Government in the District, the Act negates the principles of devolution, which it seeks to establish through section 3. Among other reasons, MPs, who are the key players in the operation of the CDF, are part of the national government and it cannot therefore be said the Act transfers decision making and implementation to local level.

The CDCs are not expected to answer to the Controller and Auditor General in questions on expenditure. The CDF Act thus infringes the principle of accountability, which is the hallmark of a truly democratic system of government provided for under our Constitution. The scenario presented by the Act, whereby the legislator makes a law (in this case the CDF Act), participates in implementing the law through the CDC and the DPC, and then accounts for the expenditure to Parliament (in this case to himself) throws democratic accountability overboard. It undermines the concepts of constitutionalism and good governance.

Linking Taxation Using Human Rights within the CDF

Good governance, development and poverty alleviation in the improvement of the general well-being of citizens of a state are all critical elements in the achievement of human rights principles and policies and have been discussed in the preceding sections. The development of Kenya to the point of the creation and development of devolved funding has additionally culminated in the need to address the concern of people in the achievement of a progressively higher standard of living, welfare, dignity and well-being. This can possibly be seen through the CDF as a microcosm of the question posed by this chapter, the use of human rights policy and principles as a possible link to join the collection of tax revenue to the distribution of tax expenditure.

The intention of the CDF Act remains a laudable principle. Section 3 states that:

> The provisions of this Act shall apply, as more specifically provided for in the Act, and shall ensure that a specific portion of the national annual budget is devoted to the constituencies for purposes of development and in particular in the fight against poverty at the constituency level.

Section 21 of the CDF Act adds that projects under the Act shall be community-based. What therefore is a development project? Whether it was a fundamental omission or not on the part of the draftsmen to fail to define the word 'development' under the Act, defining a development project would have been an arduous task. However, the draftsmen could have provided criteria for identifying a project as a development project. It is not sufficient for the Act to outlaw the use of CDF funds for political and religious bodies and activities. It can be argued that, by failing to define and enlighten constituents on the concept of development that the government had in mind, the CDF Act has paved the way for an eclectic and unstructured expenditure of taxpayers' money in the name of development.

In addition, the CDF Act does not appreciate human development, particularly human resource development, as a prioritised development project. This is demonstrable from the fact that the funding of education of constituents by way of bursaries is severely restricted by section 25(2), where an education bursary scheme is not to exceed 15 per cent of the total funds allocated to the constituency in any financial year. This is a narrow and myopic approach to the concept of development, since human resource development, i.e., progressive acquisition of skills and knowledge, is indispensable to the attainment of other aspects of development, whatever the meaning of the term. In Brazil, and in Porto Alegre specifically, currently, one theme is decided upon annually and the theme for 2009 is housing (Baiocchi 2001). The fixing of the proportion of allocation in Kenya adds rigidity to the distribution pattern and leaves out the addressing of the real needs of constituents.

Although the amendment to the Act does provide more guidance, it still maintains the allocations as set out above, with no definition of the term development. There is no provision in the Act that would exclude the reading of the right to development into the Act and it is on this basis that this chapter analyses the use of tax revenue for the purposes of development and shall thus read into the text of the Act and its application the human right to development, which is a human right.

A Key Element of the Right to Development: Participation

Participation is one of the core elements of the right to development. The CDF Act uses the terms grass-roots and participation extensively. However, the CDF cycle set out above shows clearly that despite this, the system is very much top-down and centre-out in its implementation process. The various committees of the CDF both at the national level and at the constituency level are faced by two major challenges: its legitimacy and whether it has the technical capacity required to administer the fund. Both these challenges tie into the issue of participation.

The composition of the CDC raises certain issues. First, the Act does not set out any minimum professional qualifications for persons appointed to the committees. The only criteria the MPs are called upon to consider are honesty and integrity, literacy of the appointee, knowledge and experience of the nominees and the importance of reflecting political, gender and ethnic diversity. The guidelines already referred to do not reflect a true representation of constituencies. For example, the Act only provides for one slot for young people in the membership of the CDC. Since young people are the majority of the Kenyan population, it is undemocratic to limit them to one slot since they are also limited in their areas of interest which is most likely education. This in itself would probably qualify as a constitutional challenge to the CDF Act, because it negates the requirements and principles of democratic government.

Furthermore, no institutionalised mechanism exists for the community to nominate individuals to the CDFC who are representative of their interests. Instead, under both the current Act and the amendments, the constitution of the CDC is left entirely to the will of the MP. The community is therefore vulnerable to the prejudices the MP may hold on a partisan, ethnic or class basis.

Incumbent MPs may take advantage of the low level of civic knowledge and use the projects to entrench themselves in local constituency politics. This will make it increasingly difficult for new political aspirants to achieve political office, especially if the local people are misled to associate the CDF funds with the incumbent MP. The ultimate casualty in this scenario will be democracy.

Assuming that this capacity is now going to be endemic to every CDC, it would be practical to put in place systems that would ensure that persons nominated to the CDC are representative of the constituency in order to capitalise on the benefits of participatory democracy, which would raise the capacity of the committee to function efficiently. Consequently, decisions arrived at by the said committee would be both technically sound and more acceptable to the community, perhaps by full and open participation at all levels of the process.

The challenges facing the management of the fund, which are not related to the Act, can be backstopped by an enlightened and participative citizenry. The publication of CDF issues through the media, and sensitisation of communities by civil society organizations have begun bearing fruit. In a number of constituencies, citizens have begun questioning the management of a CDC and blowing the whistle. Mombasa District provides a good example where sensitisation of communities is bearing fruits. Community-based action groups supported by civil society organisations, are checking on the management of the fund. Beside empowering the community through civic education, project committee members also need to be trained and their selection should be based on predetermined qualifications, to be spelt out in the amended CDF Act.

In sum, the following can help improve the management of CDF: firstly, promote awareness and participation through civic education; secondly, institutionalise capacity building; thirdly, uphold professionalism in the constitution of committees; fourthly, enhance coordination and consolidate efforts among stakeholders; fifthly, formulate and implement a national monitoring and evaluation framework; finally, amend the CDF Act.

Achievement of Human Rights and the Right to Development

There is no concrete reference made anywhere in the CDF legislation or structure to imply that the state considered human rights principles in the creation of the CDF. My interviews yielded comments criticising the process of linkage to certain issues such as: Firstly, the failure effectively to link the CDF process and procedure to the people as taxpayers and thus by extension the failure by citizens to perceive that it was their tax money being used for their development.[23] Secondly, that the list of demands being made of the CDF currently make no connection to the human rights or tax contribution of the citizenry.[24]

Although the representative of the Centre for Governance and Development, K. Masime, agreed that the CDF definitely linked taxation to economic, social and cultural rights, he tempered his comment with what he perceived to be a low understanding of the people generally that the CDF actually involved development and thus no understanding at all that it included issues of human rights. However, he felt that the CDF was doing an extremely good job as regards economic rights. He criticised the CDF from a human rights perspective by stating that it failed to provide for sustainable development, as the Act allows only for capital but not recurrent expenditure for development projects: there was no provision for the funding of personnel for staffing the structures built through the CDF projects.[25]

Nevertheless, one aspect is of note. The issue of using human rights as a guide to budgetary policy remains a novel one at the level of both application and theory. However, what is more important in this case is whether one can perceive the possible achievement of human rights principles and policies through the process and procedure of the CDF. This can be set out as follows: the right to education is being consistently and continually fulfilled by the increase in the number of education bursaries granted and schools being built. The right to health is being improved by the construction of more hospitals and clinics. The right to water is being fulfilled by the building of boreholes and wells and the provision of water pipes, even if communal, to areas where the people had no access to water. The right to work is being fulfilled by requiring that the work undertaken in developing a constituency be locally sourced.

Thus the progressive realisation of socioeconomic rights is taking place, and as the Clerk to the National Assembly pointed out quite rightly, as concerns the human right to development, the perception of the people was moving forward quite swiftly as 'forty to fifty years ago people did not know that they had the right to choose what they wanted'.[26]

Conclusion: Achieving Fiscal Legitimacy and State Building in Kenya through Human Rights

Those who describe rights as absolutes make it impossible to ask important factual questions. Who decides at what level to fund which cluster of basic rights and for whom? How fair, as well as how prudent, is our current system of allocating scarce resources among competing rights, including constitutional rights? Who exactly is empowered to make such decisions about allocation? Attention to the costs of rights leads us not only into problems of budgetary calculations, as a consequence, but also into basic philosophical issues of distributive justice and democratic accountability. Indeed it leads to the philosophical dilemma, what is the relationship between democracy and justice, between principles of collective decision making, applicable to all important choices, and norms of fairness that we consider valid regardless of deliberative decisions or majority will? (Holmes and Sunstein 1999: 131). The CDF's objectives include firstly, to fund projects with immediate social and economic impact in order to uplift the lives of the people; secondly, to alleviate poverty; and finally to promote development and in particular the fight against poverty at the constituency level.

The CDF is thus a hybrid of de-concentration and devolution, and reflects the contradictions that exist in the power relations between the centre and the periphery. Kenya has a history of centralization of power and resources around the centre, and especially the President. The CDF has particularly moved the power base from the centre to the local level. However, the power it grants is centred on MPs as 'Big Man' and, it can be argued, is reinforcing a coveted power-base at the local level. While it is still too early to make conclusions, there are signs of MPs beginning to build fiefdoms within their constituencies using the fund. Prior to the establishment of the fund, many MPs had very little to do with their constituencies after elections. They had no funds for development and no offices for operations. The norm for constituents was hanging around MPs' homes and following them into public places, including bars, hotels and *harambee* functions. This norm was not informed by development issues but rather by client–patron relationships, which was detrimental to constituency development but beneficial to the patrons and their clients (see Oxhorn, Tulchin and Selee 2004).

Most of the above justifications for the fund assume that, once it is established at the local level, the above challenges are solved. This is not the case, and so far, experience with the fund shows that there can be unfairness and lack of transparency at the local level. It is common knowledge that, at the local level, there are several divisions based on sub-ethnic, regional, class and patron–client relationships. These factors have to be managed at the local level. Secondly, cases of misappropriation and inability to spend the budgeted amount have been experienced in many constituencies and indeed were the cause of the public outcry. Thirdly, cases of either ghost or poorly implemented projects have been noted. Fourthly, the issue of equal distribution of budget allocation, without taking into consideration issues like level of development, area size, and resource-endowment of constituencies may not realize the equal allocation, as expected.

The CDF is a noble initiative and has brought many benefits to communities around the country. However, the CDF has some major flaws which if not rectified will undermine the impact of the fund. It would be an error to dispose of the entire CDF initiative on the basis of these emerging issues. It is possible to resolve these shortcomings through a widely consultative process where the input from stakeholders is taken into account and integrated into an amended Act. It is prudent to ensure that the legislation governing the CDF is watertight enough to withstand a thorough critique and the rigours of implementation.

To summarise this conclusion and perhaps the form and content of this research as a whole, this chapter ends with the words of Goldscheid that it commenced with:

> There is hardly any other aspect of history . . . so decisive for the fate of the masses as that of public finances. Here one hears the pulse beat of nations at its clearest, here one stands at the source of all social misery. (Goldscheid 1962: 2)

Notes

1. See Bratton, Mattes and Gyimah-Boadi (2005: 142) for examples of citizens' perceptions of evasion and avoidance of tax.
2. The Kenyan government since 1997 had not released audited accounts and a recent government statement stated that all audited accounts would be released by July 2005 but this has not been done to date. See Kenya National Audit Office (2009). The last published report is the 2006–7 report 'The Report of the Controller and Auditor General Together with the Appropriation Accounts Other Public Accounts and the Accounts of the Funds of 2006–2007' (2006–7).
3. Availability of updated fiscal statistical data in developing countries is limited. In addition, the originality of the approach of this thesis also meant that there has been no analysis undertaken using the proposed approach that could provide a viable picture of the status of tax and human rights in Kenya. As a result, interviews were conducted to fill in gaps in information and literature that was factual as well as perceptions based, which would not be reflected in statistics. In addition, due to the absence of freedom of information legislation, in Kenya access to legislative and statistical data is limited. A search of various sources to pinpoint fiscal data on Kenya showed that information that exists is limited and hard to find. Kenya National Archive data from the commencement of British colonisation to independence is sporadic as a colonial office fire is said to have destroyed many of the records, resulting in the use of mainly secondary data and some primary data in the form of a few reports in this thesis. There are also limited fiscal and other records available for the years 1963–1970 but no reason could be ascertained for this state of affairs in Kenya. Data is available for 1970–2007 but is interrupted. In addition, it is limited by the absence of a published Hansard and law reports since 1980. Publication re-commenced in 2005 and currently there is a project to publish the past missing volumes of these publications. However, at the time this research was conducted in 2007 access to both was still impossible. However, in 2009 certain Hansard publications and Law reports have been periodically released and withdrawn on the official government website. In addition, the most recent Welfare Monitoring Survey is for 1997; the last time a

population census was taken was in 1999; the last Integrated Labour Force Survey (ILFS) available is of 1998/1999 while the most recent poverty line statistics available at the Kenya Bureau of Statistics are for 2005 and the most recent Kenya Integrated Household Budget Survey (KIHBS) is for 2005/2006. Statistical analysis was also further limited due to the absence of data locally and this translates into inaccurate analysis undertaken both locally and internationally for example by the international reports such as the WB and IMF 2009 reports on Kenya which officially utilise all these as well as specifically 2004 data.

4. See generally McAuslan and McEldowney (1985) for a discussion on legitimacy from a legal perspective, and Connolly (1984) for a discussion on political and social legitimacy.

5. Roberts (1986: 662) states that there is almost no knowledge from either written sources or archaeological findings between the 5th and 10th centuries. A detailed study can be found in MacLean (2005).

6. Republic of Kenya. The Constitution of the Republic of Kenya ((1988) 1992) Chapter VIII provided that social security was only available to all colonial administrators and civil servants working in government and a limited section of Asian civil service personnel.

7. Group of Experts on the UN Programme on Public Administration and Finance (1997) paragraph 12.

8. This is a measure of progress of nations developed allowing for cross-country comparative context. However, despite a large amount of growing literature on this issue, it has been focussed mainly on the distributional or equity aspect of development without recognition of changes at the source base. However, equity without efficiency is not sustainable over time. There is thus the need to look into the optimal use not only of distribution but also collection of resources. The need to integrate efficiency into the index is a case of attempting to integrate welfare and production economics. See generally Arcelus, Sharma and Srinivasan (2005).

9. The Millennium Development Goals are the current global and quantified targets for addressing extreme poverty in its many dimensions – income poverty, hunger, disease, lack of adequate shelter and exclusion – while promoting gender equality, education, and environmental sustainability. They are also basic human rights – the rights of each person on the planet to health, education, shelter, and security as pledged in the Universal Declaration of Human Rights and expounded by the UN Millennium Declaration Project 2005. See generally Schmidt-Traub (2009) for the most recent discussion on how to achieve the MDGs.

10. There is now an entire World Bank department dedicated to participation and citizen engagement Basok and Ilcan (2006);World Bank (2009).

11. United Nations General Assembly. International Covenant on Civil and Political Rights (1966) article 25 (rights to elect representatives and take part in the conduct of civil affairs); United Nations General Assembly. Declaration on Social Progress and Development (1969), seeking active participation of all members of society, individually or through associations, in defining and in achieving the common goals of development, and article 15 (effective participation in a democratic system).

12. United Nations. Declaration of Principles and Programme of Action of the World Employment Conference (1976) (participation of the people in making decisions which affect them through organisations of their own choice); United Nations. Report of the World Conference on Agrarian Reform and Rural Development (UN Doc.

A/54/485) (1979) (participation is a basic human right and (is) also essential for realignment of political power in favour of disadvantaged groups).

13. See generally Fukuda-Parr, Lawson-Remer and Randolph (2008) for the most recent method developed for measuring progressive realisation of human rights.

14. See Bratton, Mattes and Gyimah-Boadi (2005: 142) for examples of citizens' perceptions of evasion and avoidance of tax.

15. The Kenyan government since 1997 has not released audited accounts and a government statement stated that all audited accounts would be released by July 2005 but this has not been done to date. See Kenya National Audit Office (2009). The last published report is the 2006–7 report The Report of the Controller and Auditor General Together with the Appropriation Accounts Other Public Accounts and the Accounts of the Funds of 2006–2007 (2006–7).

16. Current analysis includes tax revolts in Japan on one hand and support for the welfare state in Finland on the other. See Mumford (2001).

17. The following section draws on interviews carried out in Kenya in 2007 with officials and members of the public, including the following people: Creck Buyonge, Cru Gikonyo, Muriuki Karue, K. Masime, G. Masinde, Mohamed, Onesmus Mutungi, Nixon Nyaga, Owino Opondo, and Fred Oundo.

18. Miriuke Karue, interview with Attiya Waris, 2007.

19. In Kenya the constituency is the unit of political and electoral representation of which there are 210 in the country. Each constituency is further subdivided into locations for local administrative purposes. A district is a grouping of 4–6 constituencies and before the implementation of CDF in 2003 the district was considered the unit of local development.

20. At the constituency level, the CDF Act specified at the constituency level that up to a maximum of 3 per cent of the total annual allocation may be used on office running expenses, 5 per cent shall be set aside for emergency while not more than 10 per cent shall be allocated to the education bursary scheme annually.

21. From interviews with the people noted above.

22. Summary of this story available at: <http://www.marsgroupkenya.org/multimedia/cache/cache_c21f969b5f03d33d43e04f8f136e7682_e9db7c06a31177cb72c586429a9d3fbf?StoryID=299450>.

23. G. Masinde, interview with Attiya Waris, 2007.

24. Fred Oundo, interview with Attiya Waris, 2007.

25. K. Masime, interview with Attiya Waris, 2007.

26. M. Mohamed, interview with Attiya Waris, 2007.

CHAPTER 8

The Role of Inter-company Transfers of Intangible Assets in Tax Avoidance Practices in Nigeria

OLATUNDE JULIUS OTUSANYA

Introduction

Nations have traditionally used their tax systems as a means of exerting power, as well as a means of raising revenue. However, the ability to govern business through the taxation system faces challenges (Killian 2008). Nationally-centred tax systems are increasingly ineffective at governing mobile capital (Sikka and Hampton 2005; Killian 2008; Sikka 2008a). The mobility of capital has been aided by accounting technologies which emphasise private property rights and the appropriation of economic surpluses.

'Intangible assets', such as patents and trademarks, are increasingly seen as the key to competitive success and as the drivers of corporate profit (Dischinger & Riedel 2008).[1] Some of the recent literature has argued that, in searching for competitive advantages, most multinational companies adopt aggressive global strategic tax planning which can sometimes result in 'abusive tax avoidance' (Sikka and Willmott 2010: 342). A major 'abusive tax avoidance' practice involves the use of inter-company transfers of intangible assets (intellectual property) and transfer pricing within a group structure which allow multinational companies (MNCs) to shift income from higher-tax to lower-tax countries in order to avoid taxes and increase profits (Dischinger and Riedel 2008; Gravelle 2009; Overresch 2009; Sikka and Willmott 2010). The avoidance of taxes results in a loss of tax revenue which can undermine government legitimacy and hinder economic and social development (Cobham 2005; Richardson 2006; Sikka 2008a; Otusanya 2010; Sikka and Willmott 2010). The availability of taxation revenues are crucial to any attempt by the state to redistribute wealth, alleviate poverty and provide a range of public goods, such as education, health and other services. However, taxation is viewed by MNCs as just one of the costs to be minimised (Christensen and Kapoor 2004; Sikka 2008a); one such strategy to cut costs is to reduce or avoid the payment of tax (Sikka and Hampton 2005).

Governments lose vast sums of money as a result of tax evasion and avoidance strategies. Thus, for example, in the UK, despite spending vast amounts on tax collection, law enforcement and economic surveillance, the UK Treasury has estimated that the UK loses between £97 billion and £150 billion of tax revenue (approximately 8–12 per cent of GDP) each year as a result of tax avoidance and tax evasion (see Sikka and Hampton 2005; Sikka 2008a). It has been estimated that the US may be losing tax revenues of around $345 billion each year (see Senator Carl Levin Report 2007). Assets held offshore beyond the reach of effective taxation equal about one-third of total global assets (Tax Justice Network 2007). The offshore holdings of the World's highest net worth individuals amount to $11.5 trillion, with a conservative annual cost in terms of lost tax revenue to the governments of the World of at least $255 billion a year (Tax Justice Network 2007). It has been estimated that every year between $500 and $800 billion leaves Southern countries due to criminal activities, corruption, and tax evasion and tax avoidance practices (Baker 2005).

Tax avoidance is not just the prerogative of developed economies. It is also encountered in developing countries and involves huge sums of revenue. As a result of these 'informal' economic activities,[2] it has been estimated that developing countries are losing more than $385 billion in revenue annually as a result of tax avoidance and tax evasion (Cobham 2005),[3] while paying £100 million (approx. $190 million) a day in debt repayments alone to richer countries (Oxfam 2004). African countries have been estimated to be losing up to 50 per cent of tax revenue due to corruption (AAPG 2006). It has been reported that poorer countries are losing annually an estimated $500 billion (£270 billion) in revenue (Christian Aid 2005).[4] The amount lost each year due to the use of offshore banks, trust and companies which dwarfs most countries' annual overseas aid budget.[5]

The globalisation of commerce has facilitated the movement of intangible assets, such as patents, trademarks and copyrights, to other parts of the world. Tax avoidance has been pervasive in the domestic context, but the intensification of globalisation has resulted in the adoption of more complex practices. As a consequence MNCs can shop around for favourable tax regimes in order to avoid paying taxes. Offshore tax havens providing secrecy and low regulation have been identified as key vehicles for facilitating tax avoidance (Palan 2003; Tax Justice Network 2006 and Christian Aid 2005).[6] The US Senate Sub-Committee on Investigations (2008) stated that the United States loses an estimated $100 billion in tax revenue annually due to offshore tax abuses.

The practice of using intangible assets or intellectual property rights to avoid taxes and to shift capital is a well-established phenomenon but the impact of this practice on developing countries is relatively small. However, although there is a body of literature which has documented the use by MNCs of various tax avoidance schemes and strategies (see, e.g., Sikka 2008a; Otusanya 2010; Sikka and Willmott 2010), there has been little research conducted on how MNCs devise strategies relating to intangible assets and intellectual property in order to avoid taxes and to shift capital in developing countries, in particular in Nigeria.

This chapter is divided as follows. The following section examines the literature on the use of various tax schemes and strategies adopted by MNCs (including those relating to intangible assets) to avoid the payment of taxes. The next section considers corporate drives for increased profits and competitive advantages within the framework of global capitalism. I then provide a brief survey of the sociopolitical and economic environment of Nigeria in order to help the reader understand role of MNCs in the Nigerian context. The next section provides evidence to show that, despite laws and regulations imposing tax on non-resident companies, MNCs continue to engage in the tax strategy of shifting profits and to challenge local taxation law. Finally I discuss the significance of tax avoidance and its implications for economic and social development in developing countries.

A Review of the Literature

Governments in developing countries have faced challenges as to how to deal with the revenue leakages resulting from the extensive use of a variety of tax avoidance schemes by the economic elite and by MNCs (see Sikka 2003, 2005, 2008a; Bakre 2006a, b; Gravelle 2009). Tax avoidance is a global problem. It involves the abusive exploitation of gaps and loopholes in domestic and international tax laws which allows MNCs to shift profits from country to country, often to or via tax havens, with the intention of reducing the tax they pay on some or all of their profits.

Tax avoidance is a practice adopted in both developing and developed countries (see Szeflet 2000; Sikka 2008a; Sikka and Willmott 2010). It is an issue of major economic and political significance in many countries across the globe, including a number of developed Western states (Robinson 1998). It is not limited merely to developing countries. According to a report by the Nigerian Internal Revenue Service (IRS), 80 per cent of the tax gap is due to 'under-reporting' by corporations, which demonstrates that MNCs are largely responsible for the tax gap reported yearly. A number of studies have also reported cases where MNCs have deprived the state treasury of enormous sums of tax revenue (see Brittain-Catlin 2005; Bakre 2007; Otusanya 2010).

MNCs also pay much less tax on their profits in relative terms than smaller companies, and the difference is what enables them to pay for the onshore premium.

Several studies have shown that MNCs sometimes engage in inter-company transactions in order to shift profits from high tax to low tax locations (Grubert and Mutti 1991; Hince and Rice 1994; Grubert 2003). It has been shown that governments and tax authorities have become increasingly concerned about the location of value-driving intangibles in low-tax countries because it diminishes the MNCs corporate tax base in their countries (Mutti and Grubert 2007; Dischinger and Riedel 2008; Gravelle 2009). Mutti and Grubert (2007) examined the use of hybrid structures and cost-sharing agreements as tax-planning strategies by MNCs. They argued that these strategies were encouraged by the US adoption of 'check-the-box' regulations which resulted in inter-subsidiary payment between affiliates incorporated in one foreign country and their branches operating in another foreign country becoming invisible to the IRS (Mutti and Grubert 2007). Grubert (2003) noted that industrial intangibles linked to research and development represent the major source of income shifted from high- to low-tax countries. Thus, for example, Vodafone's intangible properties are held by an Irish subsidiary, and Shell's central brand management is located at a Swiss affiliate from where it charges royalties to operating subsidiaries worldwide (Dischinger and Riedel 2008).

It has been reported that corporations and the economic elite have remained powerful in a number of advanced democracies in their use of developing countries for their own capitalistic interests (Murphy 2009a, b). Sikka and Hampton (2005) have argued that large firms roam the world in search of attractive locations, and in the process acquire more power than the governments that host them. It is Western nations which seem to be the promoters of this phenomenon in developing societies (AAPPG 2006; Christian Aid 2008).[7] As Christian Aid (2006: 1) has noted, more money flows from Sub-Saharan Africa to the UK than vice versa:

> Despite good intentions and billions of pounds worth of aid and debt relief to Sub-Saharan Africa, more money flowed out of poor African coffers into Britain in 2005 than the other way round. More than £27 billion from sub-Saharan Africa flowed in the opposite direction towards the UK.

The evidence shows that those responsible for the flow of money from Sub-Saharan Africa in 2005 were large corporations and rich individuals who took £22 billion in profits and capital flight from Sub-Saharan Africa and that this money sits in UK banks (AAPPG 2006). This figure included debt repayments of over £1 billion from Nigeria and other African countries to the UK,

£17 billion of capital flight from the region, and over £4 billion worth of profits made by UK companies in Africa and remitted back to the UK (Christian Aid 2006). AAPPG (2006: 14), quoting Raymond Baker in oral evidence before it, noted:

> We have been putting some $25 billion a year of foreign aid in Africa in the most recent years. Compare that with my estimate of the money that goes illegally out of Africa and ultimately into Western coffers, $100–200 billion. In other words, for every $1 of foreign aid that we are generously handing out across the top of the table, we are taking back some $4–8 in dirty money under the table.

As evidence shows from the AAPPG Report (2006), individuals and institutions in both Africa and the UK have been implicated in this huge outflow of funds from Africa. The activities of Western-based MNCs were responsible for most of the losses as a result of transfer pricing and illegal transactions (AAPPG 2006; Christian Aid 2008; Greenpeace 2008). Western countries provide infrastructures which facilitate tax avoidance in developing countries. Corporations, especially MNCs, are mainly responsible for the outflow of funds from Africa as they are able to make use of a sophisticated network of notional companies in tax havens in order to hide billions of dollars of profit from the revenue authorities (Kapoor 2005; Martens 2007). For example, in 2006, Venezuela's tax agency billed the local unit of British oil company, Royal Dutch Shell, for the sum of $17.7 million (€13.5 million) for allegedly under-paying taxes in 2005. The tax agency argued that it billed the company after reviewing its 'transfer pricing', or the revenues and costs it reported at its home office and Venezuelan branches during 2005 and discovering the under-payment of taxes.[8] Martens (2007) has argued that, in cases where governments have not granted tax exemptions or where they carry out other forms of tax dumping, transnational corporations often use alternative methods to avoid tax payment. According to Martens (2007: 16), this is done 'by manipulating prices in internal transaction ("transfer pricing") or by shifting receivables and payables within an enterprise in order to generate profits in countries where the tax conditions are more favourable'.

Although it has been argued that the losses that public funds incur due to false transfer pricing are unknown, some studies have estimated that falsely declared import and export prices have resulted in annual tax losses of $53 billion in the USA alone (see Pak and Zdanowicz 2002). A study by Sikka and Haslam (2006) on transfer pricing and its role in tax avoidance and capital flight has shown how MNCs use transfer pricing to shuffle profits from developed and developing countries in order to avoid paying taxes on these taxable profits. It has been estimated that $200–$280 billion leaves developing and transitional countries annually due to the use of transfer pricing (AAPPG

2006, quoting Baker 2005). A recent study by Sikka and Willmott (2010) provides examples of transfer pricing practices in both emerging and developed economies, but argues that the bourgeoning corporate social responsibility literature is largely silent on the role of transfer pricing in tax avoidance and flight capital practices. Their study has drawn attention to the 'dark side' of transfer pricing by examining its role in relation to struggles over the distribution of economic surplus (Sikka and Willmott 2010).

According to the Organisation for Economic Co-operation and Development (OECD), well over half of world trade comprises transfer pricing within corporations. Thus corporations use transfer pricing to alter prices within the corporation as a global whole in order to gain the best tax advantages. In the 1980s and early 1990s, MNCs (such as Chevron, Exxon, Mobil and Texaco) were caught using transfer pricing to put profits beyond the reach of the US tax authorities (Brittain-Catlin 2005). This led to the largest-ever tax case brought by the US government, and the Internal Revenue Service (IRS) claimed that the oil giants owed $6.5 billion in taxes that should have been paid as the companies properly marked up sales to their foreign affiliates. Chevron and Mobil were reported to have settled out of court, but Exxon and Texaco litigated and were eventually successful in winning their cases in 1997. The role of MNCs in tax avoidance was also evident in the AAPPG Report (2006: 51) which states that:

> Sphynx UK and Sphynx Bermuda were used by Congolese officials to divert the proceeds of oil sales in order to conceal them from official government figures so they could avoid paying the government's private debts and to skim off profit by mispricing the oil sales.

It has been argued that tax havens and offshore financial centres (OFCs) have contributed to the mobility of capital, and a body of literature has revealed that these tax jurisdictions are the 'engine' of the tax avoidance industry (Sikka 2005; US General Accountability Office 2005; US Senate Sub-Committee on Investigations 2006; Picciotto 2007; Sikka and Willmott 2010). Tax havens and OFCs have been described as being responsible for affecting economic and social development (Cobham 2005), creating poverty (Oxfam 2000; Bakre 2006a, b), and for having considerable negative implications for the poor and the poorer nations of the South (Oxfam 2000; Tax Justice Network 2005; Christian Aid 2005, 2008).

Although tax havens and OFCs are important features of globalisation, they play a considerable part in tax evasion and avoidance practices (Gravelle 2009).[9] Such practices flourish within such jurisdictions because financial activities are separated from the major regulatory units (individual states) by geography and/or by legislation (Hampton 1994; Oxfam 2000). Tax havens and OFCs are regions which are relatively small geographically, with relatively small populations, and which lack natural resources, have no strong army and which are diplomatically weak (see Sikka 2008b).[10] In order to survive, they offer shelter to international capital through bank secrecy,[11] confidentiality, little (or no) regulation, and low (or no) tax (Oxfam 2000; Palan 2003; Tax Justice Network 2005).[12]

Whereas Tanzi (2000) has stated that it is uncertain exactly how, and to what extent, globalisation and the mobility of capital have affected tax revenues, other writers have argued that tax administrators and policy makers face a considerable challenge in curbing their effects. There is evidence to show that the operation of tax havens and OFCs and the global expansion of MNCs have been the 'mainstay' behind tax avoidance in the world and are one off the consequences of globalisation.[13] As Christian Aid (2005: 10) has stated: 'Tax havens have allowed multinational companies [and] rich individuals to keep their wealth away from the prying eyes of national tax authorities'.

Globalisation and Pursuit of Profits

The review of the literature (above) showed that tax avoidance has been aided by the intensification of globalisation, as MNCs seek to roam the world in order to maximise their profits and economic gain (Bakre 2007; Sikka 2008a, b). This pursuit of corporate profits is facilitated by the role played by both local and infrastructures offered by tax havens and offshore financial centres (OFCs) (Palan 2002; Sikka 2003, 2008a, b). This section considers globalisation as the theoretical framework for understanding the structures which facilitate the mobility of MNCs and their pursuit of profit.[14]

Globalisation has produced a multiplicity of linkages and interconnections associated with the growing mobility of goods, services, commodities, information, people and communication across national frontiers (Harvey 1989; Giddens 1990; Tomlinson 1996). Sikka (2008b) has argued that such developments are shaped by the interplay between corporate power, globalisation and the state. This interplay can be used to create financial opportunities and economic gains which are beneficial not only to MNCs but to the economic elite.

As part of the competitive process for international capital, the power of MNCs is also strengthened, as nation-states, in order to stimulate their own domestic economies, offer numerous subsidies and tax incentives for the purpose of attracting investment (Strange 1996). Such competition creates opportunities for MNCs to devise tax strategies to take advantage of tax differentials and to play off one nation-state against another. Some of these structures allow a variety of actors to build secrecy missions and corporate structures that cannot easily be penetrated, and to evade and avoid taxes

(Hampton 1996; Palan 2003; Tax Justice Network 2005; Dasai et al. 2006; Sikka 2008b). This has been accomplished through financial engineering, novel corporate structures (Mitchell and Sikka 2005), cartels, tax avoidance (Bakre 2006a, 2007; AAPPG 2006; Sikka 2008a), and transfer pricing (Sikka and Willmott 2010). As a result, the drive of developing countries to generate revenue in their own domestic economies is constantly restricted by the use of various tax strategies (such as tax evasion and avoidance) by MNCs and the economic elite (Willmott and Sikka 1997; Sikka 2008a).

Globalisation is considered to be the most advanced phase of capitalism (Lenin 1939).[15] Corporations, particularly MNCs, are key vehicles of globalised capitalism. Although MNCs are governed by law and contracts, in their search for higher profits they show little allegiance to any particular nation, community or locality (Bakan 2004). The mobility of MNCs is shaped by changes in contemporary capitalism whereby corporate performance and values are driven by higher earnings. Stimulated by profitability, intense competition and pressure to increase earnings, capitalist enterprises constantly seek new ways of increasing profits. Thus, although tax revenues are crucial to any attempt by the state to redistribute wealth, alleviate poverty and provide a variety of public services (such as health and education), corporations often regard tax avoidance practice merely as another way of cutting cost rather than as a practice which can undermine the development of a just and fair society (Sikka 2008a). One way in which corporations can cut 'costs' is by reducing or avoiding their tax obligations. For instance, holding and developing intangibles outside the host country can produce significant tax savings for corporations. In other words, by holding intangible property (such as patents and copyrights) in a favourable tax jurisdiction, this enables MNCs to avoid tax on this property in the host country. Such transfers and locations can be used to craft tax benefits for MNCs through their affiliates (Altshuler and Grubert 2005; Mutti and Grubert 2007). The scale, power and complexity of globalisation poses challenges to the taxation of corporate income and profits, as MNCs have become more mobile, and foreign companies have either set up business in new jurisdictions or operate joint venture or contract agreement with local companies. Such international tax strategies and schemes are also being increasingly shaped by the emergence of microstates (known as tax havens) which makes it feasible for corporations to devise corporate structures, contracts and agreements which are financially beneficial for shifting profits between subsidiaries and intermediaries.[16]

Thus, globalisation has played a key role in facilitating the mobility of finance and in shaping a complex web of interaction and relationships involving nation-states, MNCs, and elite (see Hampton 1996). This process is facilitated by states which offer shelter to finance and to 'footloose' capital. These microstates use their sovereign legislative power to enact 'light' regulations and to have low-tax or no-tax regimes in order to persuade companies to establish structures which boost their profits by avoiding or evading the payment of taxes (Mitchell et al. 2002; Palan 2002). Thus, 'footloose' capital seeks out locations that offer political and economic stability, secrecy, confidentiality; and the same locations can also be used for illicit activities (such as tax evasion and tax avoidance). OFCs and tax havens therefore have an integral and central part to play in tax evasion and tax avoidance practices of MNCs (see Hampton 1996). However, while OFCs and tax havens may substantially benefit MNCs and the economic elite, they are detrimental to the economic development of developing countries.

Increasing globalisation inevitably raises the issue of whether it is morally or legally acceptable for corporate profits to be move to defined geographical locations in order to avoid the payment of taxes. Hence, the notion of cost, revenue, deemed profits are highly contestable and open to competing interpretations, which demonstrates that there is gap in taxation of international non-resident entities. Nation-states have sought to counter some of the flexibilities available to corporations by the adoption of deemed profits to regulate the taxation of non-resident companies. While countries with considerable administrative resources could do more to challenge the anti-social tax practices of MNCs, many developing countries are poorly equipped to do so, and their tax authorities have relatively little power to scrutinise the complex structures and practices devised by MNCs.

The Economic and Political Context of Nigeria

Nigeria is located in West Africa, in the eastern corner of the Gulf of Guinea, an arm of the Atlantic Ocean. Lying between 4 and 14 degrees north and 3 and 14 degrees east, it covers an area of about 924,000 square kilometres. It is the second largest country in Africa and has a population of about 145 million (US Senate Sub-Committee on Investigations 2010). Nigeria has an abundance of natural and human resources. The major economic resources of the country include agricultural produce (cocoa, kola nuts, rubber, timber, palm oil and kernel, etc.) and natural resources (petroleum, iron, coal, salt, clay and limestone etc.) (see Falola and Heaton 2008). For a considerable time, agriculture dominated the Nigerian economy, but since the 1970s the export of crude oil has accounted for about 90 per cent of Nigeria's foreign earnings, making the economy extremely dependent upon this single source (Uzoigwe 2004; Falola and Heaton 2008). Nigeria is now the sixth largest producer of crude oil in the world (Uzoigwe 2004; NNPC 2008).[17] Since independence in 1960, Nigeria has been ruled mainly by military regimes with some democratic interludes. Thus, stable and accountable democratic institutions have never really been established.

Taxation is one of the sources of income of the Nigerian government which is used to finance public utilities and enable the government to carry out its other social responsibilities. Nigeria practices fiscal federalism in which the fiscal responsibility of government is based on a three-tiered tax structure divided between the federal, state and local government. Issues of taxation of incomes, profits and capital gains as it affect companies are clearly the exclusive preserve of the federal government.[18] The Nigerian Federal Inland Revenue Service (FIRS) was created in 1943. It was carved from the erstwhile Inland Revenue Department that covered what was then anglophone West Africa (including Ghana, Gambia, and Sierra Leone) during the colonial era. In 1958, the Board of Inland Revenue was established under the Income Tax Ordinance of 1958.[19] The name later changed in 1961 when the Federal Board of Inland Revenue (FBIR) was established under Section 4 of the Companies Income Tax Act (CITA) No. 22 of 1961. In 1993, through the Finance (Miscellaneous Taxation Provision) Act No. 3 1993, FIRS was established as the operating arm of the FBIR. In 2007 the FIRS Act 2007 granted autonomy to the Federal Inland Revenue Service in respect of the administration of company income tax, petroleum profits tax, capital gains tax and value added tax.

The Companies Income Tax Act Cap 60 LFN 1990 regulates the taxation of companies (other than those engaged in petroleum operation) throughout Nigeria. The Petroleum Profits Tax Act 2007 imposes tax on petroleum companies at the rate of 85 per cent after various deductions are allowed.[20] In 1993, the Value Added Tax Decree (now the VAT Act) abolished the 1968 Sales Tax Decree of 1986, establishing VAT with a standard rate of 5 per cent chargeable on most goods and services (except those exempted by the Act). The education tax at the rate of 2 per cent is payable by all resident companies.

For the administration of the above taxes, the Nigerian Companies Income Tax Act 2004 uses the concept of a 'fixed base' rather than 'residence'. Thus, any company that has a fixed base or a non-residence company operating through a fixed base or permanent establishment as defined in a tax treaty is subject to the Nigerian tax regime. Therefore, Nigerian companies are taxed on worldwide income, while companies registered in foreign jurisdictions with a fixed base or permanent establishment are taxed only on Nigerian-source income. Other payments, such as dividend, interest, royalties, management consulting fees and fees for technical services and commissions, are subject to withholding tax at rate of 10 per cent for corporate recipients. These withholding taxes are final for non-resident recipients.

Although tax evasion and tax avoidance are not hermetically sealed social practices, they are often targeted by law. There are twelve Nigerian tax statutes on different aspects of taxation and its administration (Federal Republic of Nigeria 1999; CITN 2002) (see Table 8.1). The tax laws contain provisions dealing with sanctions and penalties and the powers of tax regulators (the

Table 8.1 Tax-related Legislation in Nigeria, 1990–2007

Year	Tax Related Legislation	Chapter/ Decree
1990*	(a) Capital Gains Tax Act	43
	(b) Companies Income Tax Act	60
	(c) Petroleum Profit Tax Act	354
	(d) Sales Tax Act	399
	(e) Stamp Duties Act	411
	(f) Customs and Excise Management Act	84
	(g) Industrial Development (Income Tax Relief) Act	179
1993	(a) Education Tax Decree	7
	(b) Value Added Tax Decree	102
	(c) Personal Income Tax Decree	104
1996	Finance (Miscellaneous Taxation Provisions) Decree	30, 31 & 32
2007	Federal Inland Revenue Service (Establishment) Act	

Note: There were a number of Acts promulgated prior to 1990, but most of these were revised in 1990

Source: Extracted from Laws of the Federation of Nigeria. Available at http://www.nigeria-law.org/LFNMainPage.htm (accessed 21 March 2008)

Revenue Boards) to enforce tax payments and impose sanctions on errant taxpayers.

Table 8.1 shows that the Nigerian tax system has a wide range of taxation statutes. These statutes lay down regulations for tax administrations and for preventive measures to check the incidence of tax evasion and tax avoidance (Abdulrazaq 1993). The tax system has two distinct categories of anti-avoidance provisions for combating tax avoidance (Chartered Institute of Taxation of Nigeria [CITN] 2002).[21] As Abdulrazaq (2002: 675) notes:

The first form of legislation is usually effected by the enactment of specific provisions, to prevent known tax avoidance devices. The second form which legislation against avoidance may take, constitutes an attempt to prevent avoidance in general. This is done by the enactment of a general anti-avoidance provision, which vests the Revenue Authority to disregard all transactions entered into for the purposes of avoiding tax.

For example, there is no specific anti-avoidance legislation for transfer pricing, capitalisation, but transactions are required to be conducted at arm's length. In common with other tax jurisdictions, the adoption and application of both specific and general anti-avoidance rules has been problematic in Nigeria. In the 1990s a number of tax Acts were revised to make avoidance difficult. In principle, a variety of penalties and criminal sanctions could have been imposed in connection with tax evasion;[22] however, they were considered to be inadequate and ineffective (Abdulrazaq 1993; Fasoto 2005).[23] As Abdulrazaq (1993: 38) observed:

These sanctions however seem not to be adequate and moreover the tax administration is weak. These aspects of the tax administration would seem, therefore, to account for the lack of adequate usage of the various sanctions at the disposal of the tax authorities.

In Nigeria, the federal inland revenue service and states internal revenue service or a relevant tax authority is authorised under the law to sue, and recover in a court of competent jurisdiction, tax charged against taxable persons, but which remains unpaid at the expiration of a given notice period issued for the demand of such payments. It has been argued that tax appeals are an important component of a tax administration system. Thus the Nigerian tax system offers a multi-layered objection and appeal process which compels the complainant to go through an appeals process before gaining access to the regular court system.[24] The judicial powers of the federation of Nigeria are vested in the various courts in the country (see Section 6 and Section 36 of Federal Republic of Nigeria Constitution 1999).[25]

One of the major factors shaping the post-independence sociopolitical and economic development of Nigeria has been its integration into the world capitalist system (Babawale 2006). Nigeria has not only been an exporter of slaves, but during the colonial period (1900–1960) it exported agricultural produce and raw materials. However, with it now being one of the word's largest exporters of crude oil, Nigeria has gained the attention of MNCs. This suggests that in respect of its location in the global system, Nigeria remains primarily extractionist and its situation is aptly captured and characterised as a rentier state by local private capitalists and MNCs (Osaghae 1998). As Graf (1988: 219) observes:

> [. . .] is that it serves the link between production and distribution. For this reason, particularly all aspects of exploration, production and marketing in Nigeria are dominated by international capital, typically in the form of the MNCs.[26]

According to Babawale (2006) the role played by MNCs in the Nigerian political economy has received increasing attention and MNCs have been implicated in anti-social tax practices. As Akinsanya (1986: 218) observed:

> MNCs have been depriving or have underdeveloped Nigeria, through clandestine devices like transfer pricing, over invoicing of imports, under-invoicing of exports and over-pricing of technology.

As a consequence, between 1970 and 2001, exports were under-invoiced to the tune of $21 billion, while the over-invoicing of imports was about $2.4 billion, resulting in a total trade mis-invoicing of about $18.7 billion

(Lawanson 2007: 31). It has been reported that Nigeria lost an estimated £502 million (N105.4 billion) in tax revenues between 2005 and 2007 to the UK, the EU and Ireland as a result of trade mispricing (Christian Aid 2009).

It has been argued that Nigeria is one of the few countries that has consistently benefited from foreign direct investment (FDI) (Ayanwale 2007). In the 1970s, foreign investment played a major role in the Nigerian economy and until 1972 much of the non-agricultural sector was controlled by foreign-owned trading companies which had a monopoly on the distribution of imported goods. Between 1963 and 1972 an average of 65 per cent of the total capital was in foreign hands, of which the federal and regional governments held 22 per cent and Nigerians held only 10 per cent (Osaghae 1998; Jerome and Ogunkola 2004). Evidence has shown that Nigeria's share of FDI inflow to Africa averaged around 10 per cent, from 24.19 per cent in 1990 to a low level of 5.88 per cent in 2001, up to 11.65 per cent in 2002 (Ayanwale 2007: 9). The flow of FDI into Nigeria from transnational corporations (TNCs) ranged from $588 million in 1990 to $1.2 billion in 2003 (Ayanwale 2007: 9) and $1.9 billion in 2004 (Falola and Heaton 2008: 236). Despite the huge inflow of FDI, there has been a huge outflow of capital from Nigeria. Thus, as Lawanson (2007: 13) has noted:

> Between 1970 and 1979, an annual average of about $455 million flew out of Nigeria. In the succeeding decade of 1980 to 1989, the capital flight phenomenon assumed a more serious dimension, as it increased by more than fivefold on the annual average to around $2.4 billion. But between 1990 and 2001, however, the annual average of capital flight from Nigeria declined by 20 per cent to between $1.9 billion and $2 billion.

Evidence shows that almost 60 per cent of the FDI inflow into Nigeria went into the extractive (oil) industry through the Memorandum of Understanding (MOU)[27] and the Joint Venture (JV) with oil MNCs through its agency, the Nigerian National Petroleum Corporation (NNPC).[28] The economic policies of attracting FDI created opportunities for anti-social practices by the economic elite who benefited from private deals with MNCs in oil sector, as well as in other sectors.

It has been argued that, although MNCs may claim to be socially responsible organisations, they are nevertheless capitalist organisations whose success is measured by increases in profits and high capital returns (Sikka 2008a). As a result of this corporate ideology, MNCs may be susceptible to anti-social practices in their drive for higher returns. In the last few years, there have been reported cases in Nigeria of unethical tax practices by corporate bodies, particularly by MNCs, using international structures (see Bakre 2007; Tax Justice Network 2006). For instance, an audit exercise conducted in 2005 by the Nigerian Federal Inland Revenue Service (FIRS) implicated some

MNCs in the oil and gas industry in Nigeria in illicit tax schemes; and $77.97 million and N42.68 million was recovered in unpaid tax revenues from five multinational oil companies (MOCs) as follows:

> Halliburton Group paid $6,686,308 and N136,970,372, Agip Oil Co. $57,797,805, Philip Oil Co. Ltd paid $13,022,453, Tecnit Cimimontubi Nig. Ltd paid $646,204 and Eagle Transport Ltd N5,711,459 at the same time Chevron was still been investigated for tax evasion.[29]

These huge tax revenue recoveries drew public attention to the role of MNCs in draining the revenue base of the Nigerian State. In 2003, an indigenous consulting firm also claimed that the activities of MNCs in the oil and gas sector of Nigeria had for a long time been opaque and closed to non-initiates and that MNCs had been involved in evading and under-paying taxes to the Nigerian government.[30]

Case Studies

This section explores some cases of tax avoidance practice in Nigeria in order to show how some MNCs are involved in tax avoidance practices.

The intensification of the global market and the inherent corporate power of MNCs is highly evident in their strategies of avoiding taxes. The transfer of intangible assets and intellectual property among MNC's affiliates and related transfer pricing issues are not new phenomena. However, what is interesting is the use of intangible assets to shift taxable income abroad and the corporate clout to challenge the enabling law in the host country to claim non-liability to some taxes in developing countries. Such schemes enable a group of companies to shift taxable profits through royalties and technical fees paid by their affiliates in developing countries to tax havens, thereby avoiding the host country's taxation. This section provides evidence of how MNCs and their affiliates in Nigeria have used the transfer of such property to evade tax payments.

Cadbury Nigeria Plc and Cadbury Schweppes Overseas Limited

This case involved Cadbury Nigeria Plc (CNP) (a public limited company engaged in the manufacturing and sales of beverages, chocolate and cocoa-related products) and its parent company, Cadbury Schweppes Overseas Limited (CSOL), based in the UK. The company has 40,000 employees and business operations in 200 countries. CSOL owns 50.02 per cent of CNP and 49.98 per cent is owned by a highly diversified spread of Nigerian individual and institutional shareholders. Its global revenue stood at £5.38 billion in

2008 (Cadbury 2008 Annual Report and Accounts). CNP has four Nigerians as members of the Board, namely the Chairman of the Board, one executive director, and two non-executive directors.

In common with other tax jurisdictions, Nigeria raises tax revenues by levying value added tax (VAT) on the supply of goods and services.[31] In essence, the vendor of such services charges VAT at the rate of 5 per cent on the contract value. In this way the local subsidiary acts as a tax collector and the sum collected is remitted to the tax authority. In the above context, this case demonstrates how Cadbury Schweppes Overseas Ltd (CSOL) used the transfer of intellectual property through Cadbury Nigeria Plc (CNP), its affiliate in Nigeria, to avoid VAT payable on such inter-company transfers.

On 15 October 1980 CNP entered into an agreement with CSOL to grant it 'certain rights in relation to recipes, processes, know-how and trade-marks'; and the property of CSOL was entitled to payment of royalties at 2 per cent of annual sales and technical fees at the same rate. This suggests that CSOL had an elaborate organisational structure for developing recipes, processes, know-how and trade-marks. The centre operated as a profit centre to sell its products and technical property. The scheme was executed through an agreement between CSOL and its other subsidiaries, including CNP. In this agreement, paragraph 7(a), inter alia, stated thus:

> In consideration of the undertaking contained therein, the Nigerian company will pay to overseas an annual royalty of 2 per cent (or such higher rates as may be agreed between the parties) of the net sales value of the Nigerian company in respect of any financial year as endorsed by its officially appointed auditors such fees to be paid subject (to obtaining any statutory consents) as soon as reasonably possible after publication of its annual report for the relevant year.[32]

On the basis of the terms of this agreement between CNP and CSOL, federal inland revenue service (FIRS) discovered that the Nigerian affiliate had paid (between 1995 and 2003) N2,696,345,264 ($21.57 million) to CSOL as technical service fees and royalties. On 28 October 2004 FIRS took action against CNP to recover what was claimed to be 'Value Added Tax' (VAT)[33] in the sum of N122,253,622 ($978,029) and accrued interest and penalties of N4,024,330 ($32,195) on technical and royalty payments between 1994 and 2002. By 19 May 2005 the amount of VAT and penalties payable was further reviewed by FIRS (as more data was available), claiming the aggregate sum of N249,121,726 ($1.99 million) comprised of VAT of N134,817,258 ($1.08 million) and interest of N114,304,468 ($914,436). The thrust of FIRS' claim as encapsulated in paragraph 7 and 8 of the amended Statement of Claim was:

That the services being provided by Cadbury Schweppes Overseas Limited (CSOL) and consumed by CNP is categorised as imported services which are VATable services under the VAT Act No. 102 of 1993 as amended.[34] Furthermore, by virtue of the CNP consuming the services and the parent company receiving royalties and payment in respect of the services thereof, CSOL has become a taxable person liable to render and pay to FIRS a true and accurate monthly return of all taxable goods and services supplied or rendered by it and as an agent for FIRS for collection of taxes arising from the agreement dated 24 November 1999 between CNP and CSOL in accordance with VAT Act and FIRS circular No. 9701.[35]

FIRS further claimed that the consumption of the overseas technical services and know-how by CNP had in fact added value to CNP's products. It could be conceptualised as the management's strategy to create integrated corporate structures to provide a range of services to their subsidiaries and affiliated companies. CSOL claimed ownership of the recipes, know-how and trade-mark; and all the affiliated companies had to pay a royalty for their use. As the services rendered and the supply of know-how were of valuable consideration, CNP was liable to VAT in as much as the goods and services consumed were expressly listed in Schedule 1 to the VAT Act as exempted. However, CNP contended that:

CSOL does not carry on business in Nigeria and therefore the royalty and technical services fees payments made to it are not subject to VAT deduction. It contended furthermore that while VAT is payable on goods and services supplied, exploitation of trade marks (royalty) is neither goods nor services within the meaning of VAT Act and therefore not VATable. That the Best of Judgement and penalties as well as interest thereon were not based on an accurate figure of payment of royalties and technical fees paid to CSOL and are manifestly excessive, incorrect and unreliable. CNP also claimed that the FIRS assessment was not based on the information supplied by the company as evidenced by various invoices and the Auditors but erroneously based on wrong considerations and as well the assessments were arbitrary and vindictive.[36]

One of the main planks of CNP's defence was that CSOL did not carry on business in Nigeria and therefore the royalty and technical services fees payments made to it were not subject to VAT deduction.[37] In the light of this contention, a defence witness testified that:

The Overseas Company (CSOL) does not have any business relationship with any other company apart from CNP and that it has no physical presence in Nigeria.[38]

Contrary to the defence witness's submission, it was argued that, whether a company is carrying on business will depend on the facts of each case. Paragraph 4 of the agreement further stated that:

> Overseas shall advise and disclose to the Nigerian Company from time to time such of the following technical information and know-how as the Nigerian Company may reasonably request to enable the Nigerian Company to manufacture the products in Nigeria, namely: formula, recipes and processes in relation to the products (including any improvements thereto coming to the knowledge of Overseas) and technical information and know-how on the methods of and apparatus and techniques for manufacturing the products.[39]

CNP wished to use the non-residence rule to defend their position, but Section 8(b) of the VAT Act 1993 recognised a non-resident company's activities as VATable in Nigeria, which led to the rejection of CNP's objection of Best of Judgment (BOJ). The contradictions and contentions relating to VATable services and liability of a non-resident company in Nigeria were later cleared, as the Tribunal ruled that:

> We hold that the Overseas Company (CSOL) carried on business within Nigeria within the ambit of the Value Added Tax Act. We also hold that the payment for royalty and technical services in this case are for the supply of goods and services and are VATable.[40]

Accordingly, FIRS was entitled to judgment for Value Added Tax against CNP in the sum of N134,817,258.00 ($1.08 million) and interest in the sum of N114,304,468.00 ($914,436). Thus the total indebtedness of CNP was N249,121,726 ($1.99 million) and the rate of interest on the judgment debt was 6 per cent per annum until it had been completely liquidated.[41]

This case has shown how technical fees and royalties can be used as a tax avoidance strategy for moving taxable profits from subsidiaries to the parent company in tax havens under the pretence that the company is a non-resident company. The next case shows how a multinational oil company located in a tax haven used a cost arrangement with an affiliate in Nigeria to transfer taxable profits out of the country. It shows how MNCs can use their non-resident status as a condition for claiming non-liability to pay tax in Nigeria.

Shell Petroleum International Mattschappij B.V

Shell Petroleum International Mattschappij B.V (SPIM) is a multinational oil company (MOC) incorporated in the Netherlands. Its shares are held by Shell

Petroleum N. V., also incorporated in the Netherlands.[42] Through its global network, SPIM's activities consist of rendering technical and managerial services to over forty companies in the Royal Shell Group operating in the oil and gas industry throughout the world. The Group's 2007 income increased to $31.93 billion from that of $26.31 billion in 2006. The offices and laboratories from which the services are provided are also located in the Netherlands, a tax haven. Shell Nigeria has four subsidiary companies and, in addition, has a 25.6 per cent shareholding in Nigeria Liquefied Natural Gas (NLNG). It has more than 5,315 employees in its workforce of which approximately 95 per cent are Nigerians. Shell Nigeria has three Nigerians on its Board and the country chair.[43]

The Shell Group, through its Nigerian affiliate, Shell Petroleum Development Company of Nigeria (SPDC),[44] had a special sharing arrangement with another affiliate, SPIM, in which services and expenditure were charged to the Group's company account on a cost basis in such a way that SPIM was left with no profit. This suggests that the Shell Group designed this scheme to enable SPIM to render technical and management services to its subsidiaries in return for massive charges. However, it could, on the other hand, be seen as a tax strategy to book profit outside Nigeria, in other words in tax havens. To minimise taxes, SPIM registered in a favourable tax jurisdiction (in this case, the Netherlands) claiming ownership of technical and management services. Since the whole Shell Group relied on such services, all companies, including the Nigerian affiliate, SPDC, had to pay royalties for its use.

When the Nigerian Federal Inland Revenue Service (FIRS) noticed this scheme, it served SPIM a notice of assessment in 1989 claiming 40 per cent of the yearly payments made by SPDC between 1981 and 1988 to compel SPIM to pay tax on the income derived in Nigeria. Upon service of this notice, SPIM resisted the charges by applying the argument of non-residence status to claim non-liability to tax in Nigeria. It claimed that:

> The company is not liable to income tax in Nigeria on the basis that the services rendered by it to SDPC were performed outside Nigeria and that the payment received in return contained no profit element. (Nigerian Revenue Law Report 1998–99: 64)

The SPIM action led to a series of meetings between SPIM and FIRS both in Nigeria and at The Hague. Through these meetings SPIM proposed a settlement through a letter from its solicitors that:

> 7½ per cent of the payment to it by SPDC be used as its deemed profits which will be assessed to tax at the prevailing rate 'for five years starting from 1991'. (Ibid.)

However, FIRS agreed to adopt the proposed deemed profit only 'up to and including the 1993 year of assessment'. The tax implication of the above proposal by SPIM was that the company would be paying corporate tax at the prevailing tax rate of 40 per cent on only 3 per cent of its turnover on its Nigerian operation. The justification for this alternative structure was that the tax authorities would find it difficult to ascertain the real profits that most foreign companies earned in Nigeria, hence deemed profit basis was intro-duced. Despite the clear provision of the law, SPIM challenged the Nigerian State's power to assess it for tax and the power of the revenue authority to effect changes in the tax rules by appealing to the Body of Appeal Commissioners. The major contentions in this case were:

> The nature of taxation, the power of the tax authority to assess a foreign company on deemed income, on the principle of and satisfaction, the limit of the power of a tax authority to withdraw a concession, whether the attempt to withdraw the concession is justifiable in the instance case, the liability of a foreign company to Nigerian income tax and the meaning of 'place of business'. (Ibid.: 65–68)

On the basis of these contentions, two witnesses gave evidence to the Appeal Commissioners. Mr F.J.K. Korver (Head of the Accounting and Finance Unit of SPIM's Exploration and Production Division), who was the first witness, testified and claimed that within the Royal Dutch Shell Group there was a distinction between operating companies and service companies to which SPIM belonged. The role of the service companies was to collect, develop and disseminate know-how experience of the operating company around the world; and the service they rendered was charged on an at cost basis, which meant that there was no profit or mark-up on the cost of services. Mr Korver, before the Appeal Commissioners, claimed, inter alia, that:

> The fact that we do not make profits on the service rendered, made us believe that we should not be liable to tax in Nigeria and we expected the agreement that was made between SPIM and FIRS would also be respected. (Ibid.: 73)

He argued further that SPIM carried out services which were similar to those carried out in Nigeria and in the Netherlands, and that the same cost-sharing method was used to pay tax in the Netherlands. According to Mr Korver:

> The tax paid in the Netherlands is exclusively paid on cost sharing activities which consist of interest income, examples of the income from overdue payment and bank accounts. (Ibid.)

Mr Korver further agreed that the agreement between the two companies provided that SPIM would not only render technical services to SPDC but would render managerial services and undertake purchases of materials for the latter.[45] SPIM sent staff to Nigeria to collect data and discuss assistance and, on such visits, it used the office of SPDC.

Contrary to Mr Korver's evidence, the second witness, Mr Arowomole (a Deputy Director of FIRS), claimed that the business of SPIM was technical and management services, and that the company derived its income from those services in Nigeria where the rate of income tax, in respect of such services, was (under Section 8 of the Companies Income Tax Act 1990) 10 per cent. He testified further that:

> Any income that accrued in Nigeria or derived from Nigeria or brought into Nigeria or received in Nigeria was chargeable to Nigerian Income Tax whether the service was performed outside Nigeria or not. (Ibid.: 74)

The Body of Appeal Commissioners (BAC) held that:

> We have observed that SPIM had all along been adopting tax evasion practices. In one breath, it had consistently maintained that it was not liable to tax in Nigeria because it had no fixed base for carrying on business in Nigeria and that the services it rendered are rendered in its office at The Hague. Above all, the services rendered by SPIM were rendered on a cost sharing basis which involves no mark-up for profits to SPIM. So that it had no profits and did not render Annual Tax Returns, a compromise has to be made to make it pay tax. In another breath, it was the same SPIM which proposed the compromise of $7^1/_2$ per cent of Annual Turnover as SPIM deemed profit for tax purposes and prevailed upon FIRS to enter into the 6 February 1992 agreement (see Exhibit H). The evidence of Mr Korver (as contained in Exhibits G, H, and R) confirm our findings that the SPIM had been carrying on business in Nigeria using SPDC's office. (Ibid.: 75)

Subsequent to the above findings, the BAC ruled in favour of FIRS that:

> The provisions of the amended Decree override the agreement between the parties. Hence, the amendment to the assessment subsists. SPIM was liable to Nigerian tax for the services it was carrying out in Nigeria and most importantly the special payment put together by it was nothing more than a scheme to avoid payment of tax in Nigeria. (Ibid.: 64)

Being dissatisfied with the BAC's decision, SPIM appealed to the Federal High Court on the following grounds:

Firstly, the company (SPIM) is not liable to income tax in Nigeria on the basis that the services rendered by it to SPDC were performed outside Nigeria and the payment received in return contained no profit element. Secondly, the agreement between it and FIRS subsists, notwithstanding the new Section 26(1) (b) of CITA 1993 as accord and satisfaction. (Ibid.: 64)

FIRS, on its part, argued that SPIM was liable to pay 10 per cent tax on its turnover and that there was an element of profit in the cost recovery system being practised by SPIM.[46] Therefore, SPIM was liable to pay Nigerian tax whether or not the service for which the income was earned was performed in Nigeria. After the High Court had carefully studied the various cases and decisions of the BAC, the Judge held that:

> I cannot see the basis for the argument as to whether SPIM was liable or not to pay tax in Nigeria for the business they did and which they earned living from. SPIM did not deny, in fact, they affirmed that they were rendered services. They also agreed that they were paid fees for those services. By those two admitted facts, they themselves became liable to pay tax in Nigeria. (Nigerian Revenue Law Report 1998–99: 81–82)

In addition, SPIM admitted that they used the available office of SPDC whenever they were in Nigeria to render services. The Judge further emphasised that the place of their business in Nigeria need not be owned by them, or rented by them, or that the use of the place be given to them gratis.[47] Thus the Judge agreed with the findings of the BAC that 'SPIM were liable to Nigerian tax for the services they were carrying out in Nigeria, services for which they were being paid'; and that 'the payments received in Nigeria were put together with other payments from other parts of the World was nothing more than a scheme to avoid payment of tax'. Hence, the appeal on the increment for the 1993 year of assessment from $7^1/_2$ to 10 per cent was allowed, while the appeal that SPIM was not liable to tax in Nigeria was dismissed (ibid.).

The implication of this case was that SPIM's special sharing arrangement had deprived the Nigerian State of considerable tax revenues for the period of eight years (1981–88) to which the assessment related. FIRS was therefore able to recover £20.09 million which SPIM claimed had already been withheld from payments to SPIM by SPDC who had paid the same over to FIRS. Allowing SPIM to appeal to the change in rate from $7^1/_2$ per cent to 10 per cent of deemed profit further reduced the tax revenue on $44.75 million revenue made by SPDC to SPIM in 1992.

The above cases demonstrate the adoption of various exploitation schemes by MNCs and local companies in their continuous drive for profit. They show how strategies can be devised to move taxable funds from a developing country to a home country in order to avoid paying tax. This is made possible with the connivance of local directors in the affiliates in exploiting local business and institutional structures to deprive a developing country (in this case, Nigeria) of the revenue needed for social and economic development.

Summary and Discussion

This chapter seeks to contribute to emerging discourses by focusing on the role of multinational corporations (MNCs) in tax avoidance in developing countries through inter-company transfers of intangible assets. This chapter has shown how transfers of intangible assets (such as recipes, know-how, trade-marks and technical and management services) can provide a means of shifting profits in order to avoid the payment of taxes, strategies which undermine the governing system and also the quality of life of citizens. Substantial transfers of intangible assets from developing countries have been facilitated by the ability of MNCs to create hybrid entities in their affiliates abroad and to reach favourable cost-sharing agreements with these affiliates (Mutti and Grubert 2007). The chapter argues that transfers of intangible assets are driven by incentives to save taxes (through the relocation of profitable intangible assets to tax havens) and to optimise profit-shifting strategies. Thus, MNCs may manipulate their intangibles to shift taxable profits between high-tax production subsidiaries to other subsidiaries in low-tax countries.

There is evidence to show that corporations (local or MNC) are major actors and that they have been implicated in various tax avoidance schemes in order to hide their revenue from the tax authorities. The activities of MNCs are facilitated by secrecy structures shaped by globalisation, weak institutional structures and weak regulation, and by capitalist and capital accumulation drives by companies. Thus, as a result of globalisation and the liberalisation of the markets, MNCs have adopted a variety of tax strategies by using the enabling structures in offshore financial centres and tax havens; strategies which have been facilitated by creative roles played by corporate managers. The emergence of offshore financial centres and tax havens poses new challenges to nation states. The secrecy and confidentiality structure in some seventy jurisdictions (tax havens) around the world is central to the activities of MNCs in tax avoidance (US Senate Sub-Committee on Investigations 2005, 2008; Tax Justice Network 2005). As a consequence of their activities, hundreds of billions of dollars are stashed away out of the reach of tax authorities (Romonet 1997; US Senate Sub-Committee on Investigations 2008).

Furthermore, managers in corporations with global structures have been able to construct transactions and design schemes to move taxable funds from local affiliates to their parent company located in jurisdictions which permit the avoidance of regulations, and which allow secrecy and confidentiality to disguise inter-company agreements. Such tax schemes employed by the MNCs, local partners and managers have contributed negatively to the Nigerian economy.

The two case studies (of Cadbury Nigeria Plc and Cadbury Schweppes Overseas Limited; and Shell Petroleum International Mattschappij B.V) have provided examples of the schemes which MNCs can devise to reduce their tax liabilities. The cases demonstrated the use of intangible assets as a tax avoidance scheme as a result of the parent company being located in a tax haven. They show how globalisation and also weak institutional structures in Nigeria and abroad have permitted such practices by MNCs not only in the oil and gas sectors but in other sectors of the Nigerian economy. Despite the fact that companies (such as those in the case studies) have been implicated for tax avoidance practices, the Nigerian state also needs companies to invest in Nigeria in order to stimulate the economy and to generate the tax revenues needed for its economic and social development. As a result, the Nigerian state still continues to encourage and attract foreign direct investment through tax incentives and concessions. While developing countries need to continue to secure economic and political development through foreign direct investment (FDI), MNCs sometimes have more resources and power than the elected government. Thus, it has been argued that, although international trade has the capacity to provide increased investment, employment and economic development, it can also impoverish societies through tax avoidance and capital flight (Sikka and Willmott 2010). Governments in developing countries have therefore found themselves to be in a contradictory position of having to promote international investment while at the same time promoting the fair distribution of wealth and the maintenance of social order. However, the evidence in this chapter has shown that large sums of Nigerian government revenue have been undermined through tax avoidance practices of some MNCs which, while enriching the few, have impoverished many citizens in Nigeria.

Taxation is widely regarded as an essential component of a fair and compassionate society. However, it has been argued that the tax base in most developing countries has been severely eroded by tax avoidance practices (Alm, Bahl and Murray 1991). Low tax yields in poorer regions of the world limit the domestically generated resources available to governments for essential public services, such as healthcare, housing and education. Tax avoidance practices in developing countries have drained tax revenues; and reductions in tax payments have increased the income gap, harmed competition, undermined free trade and entrenched poverty (Baker 1999). This flight of capital has been up to ten times the $78 billion that developing countries were receiving in aid.[48] It has been found that developing countries lose at least $200 billion annually because of their inability to tax multinational enterprises and wealthy individuals (Tax Justice Network 2006).

This chapter has suggested that, if the loopholes in the tax laws are not closed, then the rule of law and the effective administration of tax will not be strengthened in Nigeria, and that, as a result, it may continue to lose billions of dollars to the activities of MNCs and their affiliates. Although Nigeria and other developing countries continue to drive their economy through foreign direct investment, they should take care to ensure that they do not lose their economic power to MNCs, and they should also remember that they have obligations and responsibilities to their own electorates, not just to local and international capitalists. This is because the anti-social tax practices of some MNCs pose serious challenges to the development of a stable and mature democracy in developing countries.

The study of tax avoidance offers rich possibilities for interdisciplinary research (see Bakre 2007; Sikka 2008a, b), as it provides a window for studying some of the problems facing the world today. This practice raises major questions about the assumed social responsibility and ethics of MNCs, but such issues have attracted little attention in the corporate social responsibility literature (see Sikka and Hampton 2005). Although MNCs have embraced the idea of corporate social responsibility in order to show their commitment to national and local economies, they have still been involved in condoning and perpetuating anti-social tax practices. Thus, companies have boosted their profits by engaging in strategies to avoid the payment of tax and in order to gain competitive advantages. To understand how anti-social tax practices are perpetrated, further research could be conducted by examining micro-practices (such as accounting technology and transfer-pricing schemes) which are often used by MNCs to advance their economic and financial best interests in developing countries.

Notes

1. The International Accounting Standard No. 38 defines an intangible asset as a identifiable non-monetary asset without physical substance (see para 38).
2. A number of terms are used to refer to this phenomenon, such as 'informal economy', 'underground economy', 'shadow economy', and 'anti-social practices'. These terms are used interchangeably by different authors to refer to a broad range of activities including, *inter alia*, activities relating to the labour market, tax evasion, tax avoidance, financial corruption, breaches of government regulation, and other criminal acts. The phrase 'anti-social practices' is used in this study.
3. From these estimates the shadow economy has $285 billion, with offshore asset-holding and corporate profit-shifting contributing $50 billion each.
4. From a report titled 'The Shirts off their Back: How Tax Policies Fleece the Poor,' available at <http://www.christian-aid.org.uk/indepth/509tax/> (accessed 14 January 2006).

5. *Accountancy Age*, 13 September 2005.
6. Offshore tax havens are regions which are relatively small geographically, and which offer shelter to international capital through bank secrecy and confidentiality, and little (or no) regulation and low (or no) tax (Palan 2003).
7. See also *The Democrat's Diary*, 11 July 2005.
8. The Venezuelan tax authority often scrutinizes transfer pricing among MNCs, which are able to take advantage of the global economy to move profits to a country with lower or no taxes (*International Herald Tribune*, 24 November 2006, available at <http://www.iht.com/articles/ap/2006/11/24/business/LA_FIN_Venezuela_Oil_Shell.php> (accessed 1 December 2006)).
9. Tax havens are countries that have enacted tax legislation especially designed to attract the formation of branches and subsidiaries of parent companies based in heavily taxed industrial nations.
10. Of the existing 72 tax havens, 47 are from the developed countries in Europe, America and the Caribbean, and 39 of these tax havens are British dependencies or protectorates (Tax Justice Network 2005).
11. Banking secrecy and trust services provided by globalised financial institutions operating offshore provide a secure cover for laundering the proceeds of political corruption, fraud, embezzlement, illicit arms trading and the drug trade (Tax Justice Network 2006).
12. There are different techniques for tax avoidance, amongst which are offshore banking licenses, captive insurance companies, offshore corporations or International Business Corporations (IBCs) special purpose vehicles and segregated account companies (Palan 2003: 41–5).
13. Walters (2001) argued that globalisation is a social process in which the constraints of geography on economic, political, social and cultural arrangements recede, and in which people become increasingly aware that they are receding and in which people act accordingly.
14. Globalisation has been defined as the intensification of worldwide social relations which link distant localities in such a way that local happenings are shaped by events occurring many miles away and *vice versa* (Giddens 1990: 64).
15. Lenin argued that the growth of 'finance Capitalism' and industry in the Western countries had created 'an enormous superabundance of capital which could not be invested profitably at home. Therefore, it needed to move out and subordinate non-industrial countries to sustain its own growth' (quoting from Loomba 1998).
16. A number of these states are not very powerful and are often lacking in the natural, human, military or diplomatic resources needed to create successful economies, and use their sovereignty to offer shelter to finance, footloose money and capital.
17. Development of Nigeria's oil industry available online from the official website of NNPC at <http://www.nnpcgroup.com/development.htm> (accessed 9 January 2009).
18. Federal government has responsibility of administering companies income tax, petroleum profit tax, value added tax and capital gains tax.
19. History of FIRS, available at <http://www.firs.gov.ng/About-Us/History-of-FIRS.aspx> (accessed 19 July 2010).
20. Income for petroleum profits tax purposes refers to the value of oil and related substances extracted, except gas, plus any other income of the company.
21. The Nigerian General Anti-Avoidance Provision, as contained in s.17 of the Personal Income Tax Act of 1993 (PITA 1993) with corresponding provisions in §18 of the

Companies Income Tax Act 1990 (CITA 1990), §21 of Capital Gains Tax Act 1990 (CGTA 1990) and §26 of the Petroleum Profit Tax Act 1959, as amended.

22. See: ss.86-89 Personal Income Tax Act 1993; ss.71-78 Companies Income Tax Act 1990; §§6-7 Education Tax Act, 1993; §§48-58 Petroleum Profit Tax Act 1959 as amended; and §§21-33 Value Added Tax Act, 1993 (CITN 2002).

23. See §96 Personal Income Tax Act 1993. §66 Companies Income Tax Act 1990 provides that the Revenue Board has power to sell off the defaulting taxpayer's goods or chattels, bonds or securities as well as his premises so that the amount owed can be recovered (CITN 2002).

24. *The Punch*, 14 February 2010.

25. §36 provides for a fair hearing before 'a court or other tribunal established by law and constituted in such a manner as to secure its independence and impartiality'.

26. Groups such as Elder Dempster dominate the shipping industry, while UAC, UTC, John Holt and others control commerce (distributional and manufacturing). Shell, Mobil and Total dominate the oil sector, Cappa, Dumex, Brunelli, Julius Berger the construction sector, and ITT the telephone and the telegraph sector.

27. The Memorandum of Understanding (MOU) with oil producers guaranteed them at least $2.30 per barrel after all Government taxes and royalties had been deducted (US Department of Commerce 1993).

28. Since the 1970s Oil exports accounted for 90 per cent of the total exports in Nigeria and contributed to about 70 per cent of GDP (Akanni 2007: 10).

29. *This Day*, 16 August 2005.

30. *Zero Tolerance*, July 2006.

31. There are number of exemptions as contained in s.3 of the Value Added Tax Act 1993 (*e.g.* basic foods items; baby products, books and educational materials; all medical and pharmaceutical products; medical services; services rendered by community banks, people banks and mortgage institutions; plays and performances conducted by educational institutions as part of learning; and all exported services) (CITN 2002: 561–2).

32. Court Judgment, Suit NO. VTBR/W/5/2004; Nigerian Tax Note, July, 2006.

33. VAT is consumption tax administered in Nigeria on all consumable goods and services which are not specifically exempted from tax (as contained in the Value Added Tax Act 1993, as amended).

34. VATable is a term which denotes that goods and services are subject to Value Added Tax in Nigeria.

35. Court Judgment, Suit No. VTBR/W/5/2004; Nigerian Tax Note, July 2006.

36. Court Judgement, Suit No. VTBR/W/5/2004; Nigerian Tax Note, July 2006.

37. See para. 4 of the Amended Statement of Defence.

38. Court Judgement, Suit No. VTBR/W/5/2004.

39. Court Judgment, Suit No. VTBR/W/5/2004.

40. Court Judgment, Suit No. VTBR/W/5/2004; Nigerian Tax Note, July 2006.

41. Court Judgment, Suit No. VTBR/W/5/2004; Nigerian Tax Note, July 2006. The judgment was duly signed by Hon. Justice S. A. Ajayi (Chairman), and Mr Kayode Sofola, Prof. J.S. Odama, Chief O. Olapade and Alhaji S. A. Barau (as members).

42. Shell is the sixth largest oil multinational company in the world by turnover, after Exxon and the four state-owned companies. The Royal Dutch/Shell group comprises over 2,000 companies in more than 100 countries. It is the most profitable oil company in the world and the second largest in the private sector. Shell is the

tenth largest corporation in the world (Corporate Watch, available at <http://archive.corporatewatch.org/publications/shell.html#2> (accessed 7 October 2008)).

43. Shell Nigeria has Basil Omiyi as the country chair, and Mutiu Sunmonu, Chike Onyejekwe and Bayo Opadere as Managing Directors (Company Webpage).

44. Shell Petroleum Development Company of Nigeria (SPDC) is a member of the Shell Group whose diverse activities contribute to the economies of over 140 countries. Shell is by far the largest foreign oil company in Nigeria, accounting for 50 per cent of Nigeria's oil production; and Nigeria generates roughly 12 per cent of Shell's oil production world-wide (Corporate Watch, available at <http://archive.corporatewatch.org/publications/shell.html#2> (accessed 7 October 2008); <http://www.shell.com.home/content/nigeria/about_shell/who_we_are/structure/structure.html> (accessed 7 October 2008)).

45. The technical services to be rendered included the sale of geological and service data, the acquisition of service data, topographical surveys, petroleum engineering studies, draining field development, construction abandonment and a full range of production activities including maintenance of service data.

46. Section 51(a) of PPTA 1958, as amended, states that any person who – (a) being a member of the Board charged with the due administration of this Act or any assistant employed in connection with the assessment and collection of tax who – demand, withhold, renders a false return or defrauds any person, embezzles any money shall be guilty of an offence and be liable to a fine or to imprisonment (CITN 2002: 480–81).

47. The place of their business means any identifiable place. It might be an hotel they were staying in which is in Nigeria once they are carrying on their business in such location. It is a place they are using at a given time (p. 82).

48. It has been stated that the much publicised G8 deals of 2007 would deliver $1 billion in debt cancellation and $25 billion in aid flows mostly to Sub-Saharan Africa. But this is dwarfed by the $50 billion the region would lose in capital flight (Kapoor 2005).

CHAPTER 9

Gender, Poverty and Taxation

An Overview of a Multi-country Study of Gender and Taxation

CAREN GROWN AND IMRAAN VALODIA

Introduction

Through gender budget initiatives (see Budlender 2000), gender activists have successfully raised the imperative for considering gender issues in public finance. There is little doubt that gender budgeting is now a well entrenched tool in a number of countries, and that at least some governments do systematically consider gender issues in expenditure programmes (ibid.). The other side of government budgeting, the revenue side, has received very little attention from analysts and activists concerned about the gender impacts of government policies. Drawing on a three-year, eight-country study this chapter outlines why gender activists should be concerned about the revenue side of the budget, shares some of the research findings of the study, and highlights some policy issues. The project investigated gender bias in taxation systems in eight countries: South Africa, Ghana, Uganda, Mexico, Argentina, India, Morocco and the United Kingdom – countries at different levels of development, with different histories of development, and in different regions of the world. Research teams within each country compiled a quantitative and qualitative picture of the gender dimensions of tax policies and tax reforms. We draw extensively in this chapter on various papers written for the project.[1]

Countries everywhere are struggling with increased budget deficits, sluggish growth and widespread economic insecurity brought on by the global economic downturn. Taxes provide the essential resources to address these problems, enabling governments to invest in public spending and private incentives both to stimulate growth and mitigate the impact of economic globalisation. Because taxes are the main source of recurrent revenue directly under government control, tax policy is at the heart of the debate about what services government should provide and who should pay for them, including the share paid by men and women as workers, employers and consumers. As tax systems have evolved over the post-war period, most countries have introduced reforms designed to broaden the base of personal income taxes and reduce the highest marginal rates on individuals and corporations. Trade tariffs, formerly a major proportion of tax revenues in developing countries, have been all but eliminated. Revenue losses have been made up by greater reliance on indirect taxes, especially consumption taxes. The most common of these is the value-added tax (VAT), which is broad-based, easy to collect and difficult to evade. Some form of VAT has been adopted by more than 125 countries. Today, indirect taxes make up about two-thirds of tax revenue in low-income countries, compared to about one-third in high-income countries.

As countries look for ways to increase revenue productivity, they need to be mindful of mobilising development resources in ways that do not place undue burdens on the poor and marginalised. Since women are particularly vulnerable to poverty, especially during economic downturns, attention focusing on the way in which countries are attempting to increase domestic revenues, and the impact of this on poor women, is urgently needed.

In each country, researchers examined the system of personal income taxes and considered whether there was any gender bias. The personal income tax legislation was applied to certain household typologies to assess the taxes that each household paid. The researchers used national consumption expenditure surveys to assess the impacts of indirect taxes on different types of gendered households. The conclusions were that, although reforms had addressed much of the explicit discrimination in personal income taxes, the taxation of income from jointly owned assets remained an area of discrimination. Furthermore, the manner in which the tax system related to existing gendered social relations gives rise to a number of implicit biases in the tax system. For example, in South Africa, because women are under-represented in secure employment with pension benefits, men benefit disproportionately from tax incentives related to pension provision. Somewhat against expectations, VAT did not place an unduly heavy burden on women. This is primarily because VAT systems in all of the countries studied zero-rated basic food items, which are disproportionately consumed by females. Because men consumed a disproportionate amount of certain goods, such as alcohol and tobacco, that attracted excise taxes, males paid a disproportionate share of excise taxes. Fuel taxes were found to be progressive – these taxes were mainly paid by high-income households and did not place an undue burden on women.

Conceptual Approach and Methodology

Janet Stotsky (1997) provides a very useful framework for assessing the gender implications of tax policies. She distinguishes between two types of gender biases in taxation – explicit and implicit bias. An explicit bias occurs when specific provisions in the tax legislation intentionally treat men and women differently. For example, in systems where income taxes are separately levied on individual members of a household, the tax system has to allocate tax allowances and deductions – such as allowances for dependents – which apply to the individual members of the household. In Morocco, based on a typical male breadwinner model of the household, the tax system allocates these allowances to men, thereby reducing men's tax burden compared to that of women. Thus, the tax system is explicitly treating males and females differently, and is explicitly biased against women. An implicit bias, on the other hand, occurs not because the system is specifically treating males and females differently, but because of the manner in which tax legislation interacts with gendered social relations, norms, and economic behaviour. For example, because of social relations and norms which impose on women a heavier burden for care, they tend to deploy larger proportions of their income on basic consumption goods such as food, and clothing. Taxes such as VAT, which impose a tax on the consumption of goods and services, may have the effect of placing a heavier burden on women. Thus, VAT is likely to be implicitly biased against women.

There is much that is useful in Stotsky's framework, but it has some important limitations, since it is based on the idea that bias stems from treating men and women differently and therefore that a non-biased system would treat them the same. Yet, in order to achieve substantive equality, different groups in society may require different treatment. As Diane Elson points out, different treatment is not necessarily biased treatment. Elson (2006) develops the implications of the Convention for the Elimination of All Forms of Discrimination Against Women (CEDAW) for tax systems. CEDAW allows for different treatment when that treatment is aimed at overcoming discrimination. Although there is no specific mention in CEDAW of taxation, CEDAW implies that women must be treated as equal to men in tax laws: as individual, autonomous citizens, rather than as dependents of men. CEDAW also implies that the impact of tax laws (in terms of tax burden/incidence and incentives for particular kinds of behaviour) should promote substantive, and not merely formal, equality between women and men, including egalitarian family relations. Thus, one could argue that CEDAW requires that taxation systems should seek to transform the traditional gendered roles in society. The project adopted this wider perspective offered by CEDAW.

The main methodological challenge faced by the project was dealing with the lack of adequate data on gender and taxation. In many cases it was difficult to locate data on income taxes disaggregated to reflect gender, and the researchers had to use other data, such as employment, to assess how income taxes may have different gendered outcomes. The incidence studies of indirect taxes used data drawn from income and expenditure surveys. But these surveys report on incomes and expenditures for households. Gender, the primary concern for the project, is an individual characteristic (not a household characteristic). We therefore had to find a means of 'getting at' individuals inside the household – that is, a way of attributing household income and expenditure to different members of the household, with gender being the key issue of interest.

The literature identifies two solutions to this problem, one at the individual level and one at the household level. Unfortunately, neither of these approaches is adequate from a gender perspective. The individual-level approach is to use equivalence scales to divide household consumption among members of the household. Equivalence scales are fairly random and 'allocate' consumption on the basis of 'need' – more consumption is allocated to certain household members. For example, the OECD equivalence scale assigns a value of 1 to the first household member, 0.7 to each additional adult and of 0.5 to each child. Since, in a nuclear family, the male member is likely to be defined as the first household member, these equivalence scales have clear gender biases. Moreover, while related, individual expenditure may diverge considerably from individual consumption and using equivalence scales may lead to misleading results.

By contrast, the second approach does not focus on individuals inside the household but instead splits households by their 'head', in other words, identifies households as being either male- or female-headed. In most of the developing countries that we are concerned with 'household headship' is a very imprecise concept and says nothing about the realities of power or decision making. The concept is also bound within what might be considered to be a sexist view of the household. More practically, very early in the project we realised that the statistical agencies in the countries that we studied defined the headship in very different and country-specific ways, thus undermining the scope for cross-country analysis (see Budlender 2003 for an elaboration of the problems with the concept of headship).

We attempted to go beyond headship by exploiting other variables in the household data – specifically household sex composition and adult employment – to get at a more 'engendered' household typology. In the first instance, our analysis distinguishes between households with a greater number of adult females against households with either a greater number of adult males or an equal number of adult males and females. Our hypothesis here is that households with more adult females than adult males may have different patterns of expenditure compared to households with more adult males or equal numbers of females and males, and therefore will have a different pattern of tax incidence.

In the second instance, we use the concept of employment as a proxy for bargaining power in the household. We distinguish between female-breadwinner households, male-breadwinner households, dual-income households and households with no income, and hypothesise that employment and, therefore, income allows women to exert greater control over household expenditure. Thus, in households where women earn a large proportion of the income they may be able to exert more control over the household's budget and skew the household's consumption toward more 'female goods'. If the VAT system places a heavy tax on such goods, these households would bear a higher incidence of the tax.

Relatedly, a further methodological innovation was to explore whether different expenditure items could be classified as either male goods or female goods. In all of the countries studied, expenditure patterns are indeed 'engendered'. For instance, across all countries, female-type households tend to expend more of their income on 'basic goods' such as food, while male-type households tend to spend a larger fraction of their income on luxury goods such as alcohol and tobacco. We examined tax incidence of specific commodities to learn which household types bear a larger or smaller share.

After identifying tax incidence by household type and by commodity, we conducted a number of policy experiments to assess the impact of changes in VAT and excise tax rates in order to ascertain the degree to which the various country tax systems could be rendered more gender sensitive. For example, in India, which does not zero-rate any food items, we assessed the impact of zero-rating an extended basket of basic consumption goods such as is presently the case in South Africa. The Uganda team simulated the impact of zero-rating salt, a basic consumption commodity and one that may be considered to be an important input in food storage activity and therefore the time use of women. Our findings, summarised in the following section, suggest that there may be some policy space for such gender-sensitive reform of the tax system.

Most important, household level data cannot be used to address *intra-household* gender differences. Individual level data will need to be collected to identify intra-household patterns of expenditure and tax incidence. Unfortunately, we did not have access to such data. It may well be that the intra-household tax issues are very important for a comprehensive assessment of the gender issues in taxes. Male members of the household may be able to shift the burden of taxes on 'male goods' such as alcohol and tobacco onto female members. Our analysis is therefore limited by the fact that we were unable to explore these intra-household issues.

Why Tax Policies Matter for Gender and Poverty Analysis

There is, of course, a direct relationship between taxation and government expenditure. Without access to sufficient revenues, governments are unable to fund expenditure programmes, which are critical for addressing gender equity. Taxes are the principal form of government's unencumbered revenues. As highlighted by Bahl and Bird (2008), governments' failure to mobilise sufficient revenue constrains their ability to provide and improve public services. Countries that are unable to raise sufficient revenues are likely to under-provide social services thereby increasing the burden of care and social provision done by women (see Elson 2006). One way to get a sense of the ability of government to fund expenditure is to examine the tax/Gross Domestic Product (GDP) ratio – a simple yet powerful indicator of the extent to which government is able to harness resources to fund social expenditure. In general, as countries develop the tax/GDP ratio tends to increase. South Africa's tax/GDP ratio is approximately 28 per cent, which compares very favourably to other countries studied in this project. These ranged from 9–15 per cent in Mexico, Uganda and India, to 20 per cent in Ghana and Morocco, to 27 per cent in Argentina, and finally to 36 per cent in the UK. In general, those countries with a higher tax/GDP ratio tended to devote more resources to social expenditure.

In most countries, tax systems and tax policies have undergone substantial reforms. This has resulted in significant changes to the structure of taxation. One of the key changes has been a reduction in income tax rates for both individuals and corporations. Trade liberalisation has significantly reduced taxes on international trade as tariff levels have decreased. This fall in revenue has been compensated for by increased revenues from indirect taxes – primarily sales taxes and VAT. Many developing countries have introduced VAT. In general, low-income countries now rely heavily on indirect taxes, with indirect taxes making up approximately two-thirds of tax revenues (Bahl and Bird 2008). As argued above, women tend to spend large proportions of their income on basic consumption goods. Unless VAT systems are carefully designed to zero-rate basic consumption goods, it can have the effect of significantly reducing the purchasing power of poor women.

Tax policies have always been concerned about equity. The 'ability to pay' – that those that earn more should pay a larger proportion of their income in taxes – is a well established principle in tax policies. Using tax policy to redistribute income and improve economic equality was, until the rise of neoliberalism, a common objective of governments. In addition to these standard concerns with income groups and other kinds of social stratification, the distributional impacts of tax policies between men and women need to be carefully evaluated. Policy makers need to be aware of the extent to which tax policies, such as the tax treatment of income derived from jointly owned assets, reinforce or break down gender inequalities.

Tax policy makers also need to consider the impact of taxation policies and tax reforms on both paid and unpaid work, and the interdependence between these two sectors of the economy. Thus, where tax policies, such as on income taxes, impact on labour supply incentives and encourage or discourage shifts into paid work, policy makers should consider the consequences for unpaid labour, and the gender distribution of such unpaid work. Where tax policy may impact on unpaid work, for example through VAT on products used in providing care, policy makers need to be aware of the possible impacts in paid work (for example, by reducing the time that women have to offer their labour in the paid economy). Evaluating the impact of tax policies on both paid and unpaid work will often involve evaluating both financial and time costs and benefits.

It is also important to be aware of the impact of tax policies both between households and within households. Thus, in addition to concerns about the race, spatial or income profile of households, the impact of tax policies on different types of households – dual earner households, single-parent households, multiple-generation households, pensioners, female-breadwinner households, same-sex partnership households, among others – needs to be carefully assessed. For example, policy makers need to be aware of how systems of individual filing of income taxes impacts on the total taxes paid by these different household formations. Policy makers need also to consider how tax policies impact on women and men within these households and the degree to which gender inequalities within the household are improved or reinforced by taxation policy. Thus, for example, not only should policy makers be aware that increasing VAT on children's clothing may reduce the disposable income of women more than it does of men, but such action may also have the effect of reinforcing existing power inequalities within the household.

Tax policies affect people differently over their life cycle. This is an important gender issue because women, more so than men, take on many different roles and live in different situations and households over their lives. Tax policies need to take account of these transitions in roles and households. For example, in many developed countries, women tend to participate extensively in paid employment before they have children (Nelson 1996). The presence of children reduces women's labour supply. This is less so for men. Unless tax policies take account of this transition and the associated gender differences, taxes can have the effect of reinforcing gender inequalities and gendered social norms. An example of this is that a women's poverty in retirement can be caused by the (unequal) tax treatment of her husband's deceased estate which, combined with her care responsibilities in her previous households, may result in inadequate provision for her future. It is therefore important that tax policies take a life-time perspective on the impact of taxation.

Main Findings and Policy Implications

Vertical and Horizontal Equity in Personal Income Tax (PIT)

The study examined the impact of PIT on different household types according to vertical and horizontal equity (Table 9.1). Each country's PIT rates were applied to individual income, which was then summed for each household. When households were grouped at half the median income, the median income, and twice the median income, the analysis showed that most countries achieved a modest degree of progressivity in their personal income tax systems. Horizontal equity was examined for three household types: 1) one male earner with two dependent children and a financially dependent wife; 2) a single parent (either male or female) who is employed with two dependent children; and 3) a dual-earner married couple with two children.

Table 9.1 PIT Incidence across Household Types at Different Income Levels

	Single parent with children and no other adult	Female breadwinner: A female earner, one dependent man and children	Male breadwinner: A male earner, one dependent woman and children	Couple with children: Dual earners
2 x Median Household Income	Argentina[1], Ghana[2], India[3], Morocco, South Africa, Uganda, UK	South Africa, Uganda, UK	India, South Africa, Uganda, UK	
Median Household Income	Ghana[2], India[3], Morocco, Uganda, UK	Uganda, UK	India, Uganda, UK	
½ Median Household Income	Morocco, UK	UK	UK	

Notes: When a country is listed more than once in a row, this means that the incidence of PIT falls most heavily on the household category indicated in the column.
[1] Self-employed single parent households with children bear the largest burden in Argentina.
[2] Single-parent households with children bear the highest incidence in Ghana.
[3] Single-parent households bear more tax than female-breadwinner or dual-earner households in India only if the single parent is a man.

Tax systems were generally horizontally inequitable across household types. Male-breadwinner households with a single earner, a financially dependent spouse and two dependent children typically pay a higher share of their income in tax than do dual-earner households with two dependent children in Argentina, Ghana, India, South Africa, Uganda and the UK but there were interesting variations.[2] In Morocco, dual-earner households where the woman's income is higher than the man's pay more tax than those households where the man earns the higher income, because tax reductions for dependants are available only to men. In Ghana, single-parent households bear a heavier tax burden than do both dual-earner and male-breadwinner households: they cannot claim tax relief for a financially dependent spouse unlike the other household types.

The finding that dual-earner households face the lowest PIT incidence could be viewed as transformative since it does not create a disincentive for women to join the labour market or reinforce existing unequal gender roles. However, the finding that single-parent households with children bear a larger PIT burden than do male-breadwinner households with children and a dependent spouse is a matter for concern. Single parents – who in many countries are more likely to be women – have to play the dual roles of breadwinner and caregiver and doing so has costs, not least for care of children.

Incidence of Indirect Taxes on Women and Men

Since indirect taxes have become an increasingly important revenue base for developing countries, as noted earlier, the study also examined the incidence of VAT, excise duties and fuel levies for different households. Tax incidence is the percentage of total income or expenditure that is paid in taxes for consumption – either for specific consumption items or in total. In developing countries especially, consumption expenditure rather than income is often used as the base, as the data is generally more reliable and it arguably provides a better measure of household well-being.

Given the lack of studies on the gender impact of indirect taxes, the methodology the project adopted is worth describing in some detail. Ideally, to conduct a gendered incidence analysis, data are needed on individual expenditure. But since such data do not exist in most countries, researchers classified households into two 'gender type' categories.[3] First, based on gender norms that produce gender-specific expenditure patterns, households were classified by sex composition – distinguishing those with a greater number of adult females from those with a greater number of adult males and those with an equal number of male and female adults. Second, as a proxy for household bargaining power, households were categorised based on the employment status of the adults, assuming that employment (and the income it yields) allows women to exert greater control over household expenditure. This category distinguishes among female-breadwinner households (with no employed males), male-breadwinner households (with no employed females), dual-earner households and households with no employed adults.

Indirect taxes are widely perceived to be less progressive than direct taxes, since low-income households spend a larger proportion of their income to fulfill basic needs than do high-income households. The country studies showed that, in contrast to perceived wisdom, overall indirect tax incidence falls most heavily on households in the richest quintiles in Uganda, Mexico and Morocco; on households in the middle quintiles in South Africa and the UK; and on both the richest and poorest households in Ghana. In Argentina overall indirect tax incidence is proportional. In only one country, India, do households in the lowest quintile have the higher indirect tax incidence (see Table 9.2).[4]

Table 9.2 Greatest Incidence of Each Type of Tax by Income Quintile

Incidence falls most heavily on:	Total indirect taxes	VAT	Excises	Fuel tax
Quintile 5	Ghana[1], Mexico, Uganda, Morocco	Mexico, Morocco, Uganda, UK		Argentina, Ghana, India, Morocco, South Africa, Uganda
Quintile 3–4	South Africa, UK	South Africa	Argentina, Morocco, South Africa	
Quintiles 1–2	Ghana[1], India	India	Ghana, India, Mexico, UK	Mexico[4], UK
Proportional	Argentina[2]	Argentina[3], Ghana	Uganda	

Notes:
[1] Indirect taxes are U-shaped, falling on the lowest and highest quintiles.
[2] Indirect taxes are slightly progressive.
[3] VAT is slightly regressive.
[4] Fuel tax was a subsidy and lower quintiles received less subsidy than higher quintiles.

More complex patterns emerge when taking gendered household structure into account. The project found that male-breadwinner households bear the heaviest burden of total indirect taxes in four of the eight countries, largely owing to these households' greater consumption of goods that are subject to excise duties or fuel levies (see Table 9.3). Households with no employed adults bear the heaviest overall indirect tax incidence and the heaviest incidence of excise duties only in the UK while female-headed households bear the highest incidence of indirect taxes only in India.

Given that female-type households are generally clustered in lower income brackets, and that many countries use zero-rating and exemptions to VAT in order to protect households in lower income brackets, it follows that male-type households generally bear a higher incidence of indirect taxes. The tax incidence is also higher on male-type households because these households typically consume more goods subject to excise and fuel duties than do female-type households.

Table 9.3 Incidence of Indirect Taxes by Household Type

By headship (comparing male-headed versus female-headed)

Incidence falls most heavily on:	Total indirect taxes	VAT	Excises	Fuel tax
Male-headed households	Argentina, Ghana, Mexico, Morocco, South Africa, Uganda, UK	Argentina, Ghana, Mexico, South Africa, Uganda, UK	Argentina, Ghana India, Mexico, Morocco, South Africa, Uganda, UK[1]	Argentina, Ghana, India, Morocco, UK, South Africa, Uganda
Female-headed households	India	India, Morocco	UK[1]	Mexico

By employment status (comparing male-breadwinner, female-breadwinner, dual-earner, none-employed)

Male-breadwinner households	Argentina[2], Ghana, Mexico, South Africa, Uganda	Argentina[2], Ghana, Mexico, South Africa, Uganda	Argentina, Ghana, Mexico, Morocco[2], South Africa, Uganda	Ghana[2], Uganda, Morocco[2]
Female-breadwinner households				Mexico
Dual-earner households	Argentina[2], Morocco	Argentina[2], Mexico, Morocco, UK	Morocco[2]	Argentina, Ghana[2], Morocco[2], South Africa, UK
None-employed	UK		UK	

By household sex composition (comparing male-dominated, female-dominated and equal numbers)

Male-majority households	Argentina, Ghana, India, Mexico, Morocco, South Africa, Uganda, UK	Argentina, Ghana, India, Mexico[3], South Africa, Uganda	Argentina, Ghana, India, Mexico, Morocco, South Africa, Uganda, UK	Argentina, Ghana[3], India, Uganda, UK
Female-majority households				Mexico
Equal-number households		Mexico[3], UK		Ghana[3], South Africa
Proportional		Morocco		Morocco

Notes: In Mexico, fuel tax was a subsidy and therefore the cells indicate which household type received less subsidy.

[1] The differences in incidence for female-headed and male-headed households are not statistically significant.

[2] The differences in incidence between male-breadwinner and dual earners are not statistically significant.

[3] The differences in incidence between male-majority and equal number households are not statistically significant.

It should be added that evaluating tax incidence on the basis of income rather than expenditure would likely produce less equitable results, in terms of both gender and income. In the one country studied for which income data were available, Mexico, the incidence analysis based on income found that households in which most income is earned by women have a higher indirect tax incidence than households where men earn most income. Incidence is lowest in households where men and women earn similar incomes.

All countries further disaggregated the incidence of indirect taxes for each household employment category by quintile. Total indirect tax incidence falls most heavily on the richest male-breadwinner or dual-earner households in Argentina, Morocco and Uganda, while it falls on middle quintile dual-earner households in South Africa and non-employed households in the UK. The highest incidence of excise duties generally falls on male-breadwinner or dual-earner households in the middle quintiles in most countries.[5] The incidence of fuel taxes is generally progressive with regard to both income and gender.

Importantly, the existence of children in the household has an impact on the incidence of indirect taxes. Generally, incidence falls more heavily on households without children. An exception is VAT in Morocco, where households with children bear a larger incidence of VAT. Finer differences emerge when the analysis is disaggregated by quintiles. Poorer households with children bear a greater incidence of VAT relative to equally poor households without children in Ghana, Mexico and Uganda. In South Africa, female-breadwinner and non-employed households with children in the middle quintiles bear a higher VAT and fuel levy tax incidence than do female-breadwinner and non-employed households without children in the same quintiles.

Because of gender-specific expenditure patterns, the tax incidence for specific commodities brings out the gender-differentiated results far more starkly than the results by type of tax. Female-breadwinner households bear a larger tax incidence on food relative to male-breadwinner households in most countries, except Argentina and Uganda. Households in the poorest or middle-income households bear the greatest food tax incidence in India, Mexico and UK, while in South Africa the poorest non-employed households – which are mostly female headed – bear the highest tax incidence on food. By contrast, the incidence of tax on medical expenditure falls on the richest female-majority households in Argentina, Mexico and Morocco, and the richest equal-number households in India and South Africa. The incidence of children's clothing varies by country. The poorest male-breadwinner households in Argentina and the poorest dual-earner households in Mexico and Uganda bear the highest tax incidence on children's clothing, but the poorest female-breadwinner households in Ghana and Uganda bear the highest tax incidence on children's clothing.

For some goods, the analysis by household sex composition (as opposed to employment status) makes the gender differences more apparent.[6] The incidence of tax on utilities (water, gas and electricity) falls on the bottom or middle quintiles for most countries, except in India, Uganda and South Africa where it falls on the richest households, but fails to benefit the poor who cannot afford these anyway. And in all countries, the tax incidence of utilities falls most heavily on female-majority households, owing to their importance for women's traditional roles. These items have significant time-saving consequences for women, despite their higher monetary cost.

The patterns of tax incidence on alcohol and tobacco are not surprising given the gendered patterns of expenditure on these items. Male-breadwinner households by and large bear the highest incidence of tax on both alcohol and tobacco expenditures in all countries in the study, although tax incidence of these goods also falls on dual-earner households in India, the UK, Argentina and Morocco, and non-employed households in Argentina, Ghana, Mexico and the UK.

What explains the largely positive nature of these findings? Several countries in the study, including South Africa, Ghana, Mexico, Uganda and the UK, zero-rate or have reduced rates on basic necessities. The authors simulated an increase in the VAT on these items to see the effect it would have. In South Africa, introducing a 14 per cent VAT rate on basic food and paraffin had the largest negative impact on the poor and female-type households. In the UK, removing the zero rate on basic food increased incidence disproportionately among poorer households and those with no employed adults. In Mexico, a rise in the tax rate from 0 to 15 per cent on basic and non-basic food disproportionately affected poorer households but it had no impact on any of the gendered household types. Collectively, these simulations suggest that specific and targeted measures are important for ensuring that the burden of VAT is not borne disproportionately by poor women.

In other countries, the authors undertook a variety of simulations to see if more gender equity could be introduced into the system. In these simulations Argentina, India and Morocco reduce or zero-rate key basic food basket items. Ghana completely removes the VAT on children's clothes and footwear and halves kerosene tax rates. Uganda removes the VAT on salt and halves the tax on paraffin.

The results show it is possible to reform VAT and excises in ways that promote gender equality and maintain revenue neutrality. In Morocco, reducing VAT on tea, coffee and edible oils lowered the tax incidence for poorer female- and male-breadwinner and non-employed households. In Ghana, reducing the tax incidence on children's goods benefited poorer female-breadwinner and female-dominated households more than their male-household counterparts. In Uganda, the zero rating of salt and paraffin benefited poor and male-headed households without significantly impacting on total revenue. In Ghana, halving the tax on kerosene benefited poorer households more than richer households but had no additional impact across different household types.

Because reforms that reduce or zero-rate commodities entail revenue losses, researchers tried various scenarios to offset these. Accordingly, Argentina increases tax on luxury items (cars, boats, electronics), tobacco and wine; the UK increases taxes on fuel for private transport; Ghana, India and Morocco increase tax rates on tobacco; Morocco increases rates on all recreational goods; and Ghana increases rates on alcohol and communications. In most cases, the reduction of taxes on food, children's clothing and household fuel, when coupled with measures to increase tax on luxury items, tobacco and alcohol, turned out to be revenue-neutral. Exceptions were the UK and Morocco simulations, which resulted in a revenue loss in the former and an increase in the latter.

As expected, an increase in tax on tobacco and alcohol also increased incidence for male type households, except in the UK where a tax hike on tobacco increased the incidence for poorer female-breadwinner and non-employed households, which include many single-mother households.

It is important, however, to be cautious about increasing taxes on alcohol and tobacco. Such a move could have negative effects beyond increasing the incidence of these taxes on the poor. Increasing taxes on tobacco could induce a shift to cheaper and inferior tobacco products with negative effects on health. There could also be a potential negative gender impact from increasing taxes on both alcohol and tobacco if men reduce their contributions to women's household allowances as a result of the price increases on these goods.

Conclusion

The findings generated by the research project outlined here suggest a rich agenda for the gender considerations of tax policy. In many countries, the tax system continues explicitly to discriminate against women. This is especially so in areas such as the taxation of joint income. The results for indirect taxes are very encouraging and show that well-designed tax policies can go some way to alleviating the burden on poor women. For many developing countries trying to increase their tax/GDP ratio, VAT is an attractive form of taxation – it is relatively easy to collect, relatively easy to administer and it is difficult for taxpayers to evade. A number of commentators have expressed concern about the burden that VAT may place on those with low incomes, in particular women. The findings suggest that it is possible to design VAT in a manner that addresses these concerns, and that even low-income countries such as Uganda can administer VAT with a limited number of items zero-rated.

The fact that so many people fall below the tax threshold in low-income countries indicates that such countries are likely to continue to rely on indirect taxes as a primary revenue source, making it important to understand that there is much that can be done to make these taxes more equitable, both for poor households and for women. Ultimately, however, the challenge for all countries is to increase employment and livelihoods for the broad base of the population, so that more and more people can be drawn into the personal income tax net. It must be added that taxes on personal income are not the sole source of direct taxes. In focusing on domestic resource mobilisation, governments should consider a range of other direct taxes, including taxes on dividends and corporate income, and land and property taxes – all of which have gender-specific impacts.

There is much that countries can do to make personal income tax systems more gender-equitable. First, they can shift away from joint filing systems, which act as a disincentive for women to work because their income is generally taxed at the highest marginal rate of their spouse, towards individual filing systems which do not have this problem. Second, they can review the tax codes and take steps to eliminate explicit gender biases. Finally, they can examine the structure of deductions, exemptions, and allowances to ensure they do not contain implicit biases.

As noted above, zero rating of basic necessities in value-added taxes can facilitate greater income and gender equity in indirect tax incidence. While exemptions and zero rating are discouraged in the policy literature because they are deemed to narrow the VAT base and result in revenue losses, the findings of this project suggest that it is possible, even in low-income countries, to administer VAT systems with at least some zero rating of basic consumption goods. Moreover, the results suggest that there may be ways to compensate for any losses resulting from zero rating in a manner that promotes gender equity in taxation.

There are a number of issues that this project did not explore which warrant future examination. First is the gendered impact of local government revenues, which tend to rely heavily on property and land taxes as well as consumption taxes. Second is the issue of taxation in the informal economy. While most of the tax literature is concerned mainly with the inability of the tax authorities to reach those operating in the informal economy, there are some grounds for concern about how those operating in the informal economy may be affected by the tax system. Third is the need to look at both the revenue and expenditure sides of the budget in order to evaluate the gendered impact of social policy instruments. Supplementing the analysis with other types of taxes and incorporating assessments on the expenditure side will provide a more complete picture of the gender equality issues associated with public finance.

Taxation is part of a political process within countries, revealing insights into the legitimacy of the state and the power of different interest groups, in the private sector and in civil society. However, tax policy is shaped not only by state institutions and competing interests, but also by prevailing ideology. The current policy consensus is that tax policies should focus on raising revenue in a manner that broadens the tax base, simplifies collection and promotes compliance, thereby generating resources that can potentially fund expenditure on public services and safety nets to address poverty and hardship. Equity goals, however, should not be abandoned but in fact broadened to include gender. This should move beyond conventional notions of vertical and horizontal equity to a tax framework based on promoting substantive gender equality, as reflected in CEDAW. For tax policy makers this implies considering how taxes reinforce or challenge current gender and social inequalities and designing tax instruments so that such inequalities are overcome.

Notes

1. An edited volume drawing on the projects findings edited by Caren Grown and Imraan Valodia has been published by Routledge (Grown and Valodia 2010). Various country reports are available at <http://sds.ukzn.ac.za/default.php?7,12,85,4,0>. We draw extensively in this chapter on the research material generated in the various country studies, and we are indebted to the authors of these country studies.
2. In the UK, the existence of the Child Tax Credit and Working Tax Credit reduces the total tax burden on both single-earner and dual-earner households, more so for the latter.
3. The typical approach is to divide households into those headed by males and those headed by females. However, the definition of household head differs from country to country, which makes cross-country comparison impossible.
4. Most countries studied zero rate or exempt some goods and services, especially those consumed by poor households. For example, education and public sector medical services are exempt in South Africa, the UK, Uganda and Ghana; some basic foods have reduced rates in Argentina, are zero rated in Uganda, Mexico, the UK and South Africa, and are exempt in India and Morocco. Exports are zero rated in Argentina, India, Mexico, South Africa and the UK.
5. The UK is an exception, where excise tax incidence falls on the poorest dual-earner and non-employed households.
6. These results are reported in the country case studies, online at <http://www.american.edu/cas/faculty/cgrown.cfm> and <http://sds.ukzn.ac.za/default.php?7,12,85,4,0>.

PART III

Recasting Taxation Policy: Principles and Their International Implications

CHAPTER 10

Equity, Efficiency and Progressive Taxation

Paolo Ermano

Introduction

Generally, the literature on taxation focuses on the inverse relation between tax schedules and the effects on labour markets and savings. The main result is that the lower the progressivity of the tax schedule, the higher the positive effect on labour markets and on savings markets. This result derives from the assumption that taxes distort market incentives. According to Meltzer and Richard (1981), the size of the government, seen as a share of income redistributed, is determined by the deviation between mean and median income, but the degree of tax distortion that affects the labour market depends on the extent of redistribution: more unequal societies face stronger redistributive policy imperatives with detrimental effects on efficiency and growth. Even if such theories have found little empirical support, they have produced effective results: among all OECD countries, tax schedules have flattened over recent decades and the Gini coefficient has risen even if the size of government has increased (Atkinson and Piketty 2007; OECD 2009b).

Contrary to these theoretical findings, this chapter would like to investigate the reasons behind the reintroduction of a strong progressive tax schedule characterised by a high top marginal tax rate. This investigation will consider from a theoretical point of view the connections between individual ability, economic freedom and market competition.

There are two reasons for this approach: first, it allows us to link economic taxation with economic freedom – by considering not just the economic incentives of who currently displays a high level of productivity, as is usual in neoclassical economics, but also by considering who is currently unable to be an efficient worker for want of a reference market; second, it shifts the attention from the problem of economic growth to the problem of *democratic* growth: it is exactly on the behalf of this sphere of human progress that the policy maker should focus more closely on who is deemed to be less efficient than required by market standards.[1]

The Context

To understand the line of reasoning of this study, it is appropriate to start with an empirical consideration: over recent decades wage inequality has increased significantly in different OECD countries (Erikson and Janatti 1997; Smeeding 2002; Atkinson 2003; OECD 2008b). Several explanations, ranging from economic liberalisation to market globalisation and to a sharp growth in the innovation rate, have been advanced to justify this spread. In particular, standard economic theory suggests that a higher degree of openness plus a positive innovation rate have increased the return to education, thus modifying the wage distribution in favour of highly specialised workers in what is commonly known as 'skill-biased technological change' (Atkinson 2003; OECD 2009b).

Beside labour market explanations, two other phenomena can account for this increase in inequality: in OECD countries the size of government has generally increased and top marginal tax schedules have been flattened in accordance with optimal tax theory (Rodrik 1997; Mankiw et al. 2009).

From an economic perspective, the idea that every state has to provide institutional frameworks to foster economic growth can explain the growing size of governments in the developed world: the state must intervene to correct market imperfections. In a classic work by North and Wallis the increasing importance of government functions for sustaining economic activity is described in terms of institutional economics: every transaction has some hidden costs (externalities) that experience a partial internalisation through several institutional frameworks provided by the state (North and Wallis 1982). Following their argument, sustained economic growth needs the help of complex institutional structures and these can be provided only by the state: to put it simply, increasing growth implies increasing complexity, hence more institutional structures are needed (Beinhocker 2006).

This neoinstitutional approach is mirrored, in essence, in the neoclassical debate over the relationship between government size and economic development: the expansion of markets determines economic development but introduces more complexity. On this topic, considerable research has produced conflicting results, but the most accepted and empirically tested hypothesis concerns what is commonly labelled the state's compensatory role. The argument follows: since economies that have experienced high rates of economic growth also have a high degree of market openness, they need to develop larger welfare states as a response to the volatility caused by economic openness (Cameron 1978; Rodrik 1997).[2] Government expenditure is considered essential to mitigate the negative effects produced by economic growth and globalisation. This hypothesis finds a partial confirmation in the share of revenues that are used for public social expenditure in OECD countries, rising from 16 per cent in 1980 to 21 per cent in 2005 (Adema and Ladaique 2009). In a different context, Bergh and Karlsson have interpreted this hypothesis in the spirit of neoclassical analysis by advancing the idea that big governments serve to promote economic freedom and globalisation, and thus foster economic growth (Bergh and Karlsson 2010). The two perspectives suggest a radically different interpretation: in the first, made famous by Rodrik, government enlargement is a byproduct of economic growth; in the second, government enlargement is one of the most important determinants of economic growth.

Depending on the perspective chosen we can describe a different economic world, but one feature is common to both explanations: the expansion of government and of the welfare state is necessarily financed by taxation. An examination of the data indicates that governments of advanced economies are mainly financed by taxes levied on personal incomes: according to OECD data, in 2005 personal income tax plus social security contribution amount to nearly 50 per cent of the total tax revenue (OECD 2008b) but over recent decades the tax schedules in these countries have been reduced in favour of top incomes, shifting the burden of financing government policies to lower incomes (Mankiw et al. 2009). This is in line with some exponents of economic theory. From Hayek to the highly influential work of Mirrlees, neoclassical economists have advocated modifications of the tax schedule in favour of wealthier sections of society, suggesting that individuals with high ability should pay relatively less tax in order not to dissipate the economic incentive to work and to produce wealth (Hayek 1960; Mirrlees 1971). In short, the logical argument is that high income, as a proxy for ability, implies or signals necessarily high ability.

Of course, many variables determine the quality of welfare state policies, not just the marginal tax rate; however the volume of resources collected remains important. Hence two important economic principles follow: firstly, less able individuals, i.e., individuals with lower income, pay taxes that are mainly used to develop institutional frameworks favouring economic activities capitalised by those marked as the most able individuals, believing that this would be the most efficient way to increase total wealth and, as a by-product, their income; secondly, resources used for welfare policy are collected from those who are generally the direct beneficiaries of these policies. Apart from the equality issue, this would not be a problem for an economic system experiencing continuous growth, since at every step the volume of resources gathered increases and the number of potential beneficiaries is likely to fall. But when negative shocks hit the pace of economic development, this market-base redistributive scheme led to conflicts between classes of workers because the most able could reveal themselves to be incapable of protecting the system from negative shocks, notwithstanding the benefits that society has granted them (as the recent sub-prime crisis has shown with the example of banks and their well-paid employees and employers); secondly, inasmuch as the shock is unavoidable, the economic system needs additional resources both to recover and to refine its institutions; these resources should be collected from those who still have them; finally, the number of potential beneficiaries of welfare policy might increase so much that the current flow of public resources becomes inadequate.

Tax Schedule Following a Neoclassical Framework

To better understand the implications of linking income and ability it is important to remember that neoclassical economics contends that there should be no limits to the income that an individual can obtain in return for his contribution to the production of total wealth.

If we assume that the only source of income is the wage, then every individual should receive a wage equal to the value of his marginal productivity that amounts to his marginal productivity multiplied by the price of the product sold. In this framework two elements determine the individual wage: the first, marginal productivity, is directly determined by individual ability and effort, once controlled for firms' organisation and technology; the second, the price of the product, depends on market conditions: the same individual performance can lead to different wages depending on the value that the market gives to the products sold in terms of utility, pleasure, happiness and so on.[3]

Therefore, there are conditions that lead to a higher or lower income that can be controlled neither by the firm nor by the workers. To some extent the structure of the market influences wages (Tse 2002). If we widen the focus to macroeconomic dynamics, even the substitution rate in the labour market plays an important role in wage bargaining: the lower the supply of a certain skill, the higher would be the price that a firm has to pay to obtain that skill. Potentially, the value of certain skills can jump markedly, conferring an extraordinary skill premium on those that possess them.

This framework has three implications:

- Firstly, most economists think that wages are linked to the current effort deployed; however, similar level of effort can lead to a different wage. Individuals with the same investment in terms of years of education and the same working effort can have two different wages: in fact, markets and the degree of specialisations alter marginal values of identical efforts and this could be deemed unacceptable from the social point of view even when it results from fair market competition between goods and firms (Manso Palazuel 2006). For example, in western countries a physician on average gets a lower wage than a CEO independent of their educational investments and/or efforts (O'Leary and Sloane 2005).

- Secondly, fads and fashion modify skill premiums by changing the prices of products, situations where the link between the investment in human capital and its return is radically severed. Moreover, faster innovation rates create conditions for a continuous modification of skill premiums due to technological change; it is true that this eventuality will raise the premiums from investment in education, but in case of excessively rapid innovation processes, the obsolescence rate of education might increase too much, making this investment less valuable.

- The latter observation forces us to consider insights from contract theory: some individuals have higher bargaining power in terms of contingent market dynamics, a power that can create a rent in case of institutional persistency or path dependency since contracts are usually not easily or often renegotiated. Thus, luck can play a relevant role in determining the wage of an individual (Lazear and Shaw 2007; Lefranc et al. 2009). For example, in many European countries football players enjoy a higher wage than other sportsmen due to the well-known 'superstar effect'; other professional athletes, even in popular sports like hockey or basketball, receive wages that are not just determined by a linear function of their abilities, their human capital (Rosen 1981; Lucifora and Simmons 2003). Or, sadly, how fortunate is the white man compared to a black woman in the US (Darity and Mason 1998) or a man compared to a woman across the European Union (Gradin et al. 2006), both phenomena that lead, more or less unintentionally, to an unfair and unequal path-dependence process in wage distribution (Pierson 2000).

So, if markets are not perfect, in the sense that they are not able to convey the necessary information to individuals and agents do not have the instruments to respond rapidly and rationally to every bit of information obtained from market interactions, a link between income and taxes will lead to unequal results: the extension of this link to take in the problem of the welfare state produces an inflexible society unable to guarantee the variety that is a precondition for all innovation processes.

Tax and Freedom

As elaborated in the previous section, the markets' volatility loosens the connection between tax levy and skills; but reducing yields to who is accidentally judged as less skilled can produce unfair and potentially dangerous outcomes, especially in environments characterised by several sectors and several institutional frameworks. But there are other and probably more subtle reasons that can be advanced to propose a more progressive tax schedule: some of them are closely related to the problem of freedom.

To demonstrate the point, insights from institutional economics would be useful. Firstly, not all goods are subject to economic transactions. This could be quite a truism since not everything is the object of market transactions. Some goods cannot be exchanged since there are legal agreements that limit these types of bargaining (for example, inalienable rights); for other goods there are no valuable reasons to exchange them (for example, clean air, or participation in a public debate); some other goods have characteristics that cannot be fully exploited for market purposes due to our limited technological development (for example, energy markets present several examples of this kind). There are even other cases where the introduction of an economic value could reduce or even destroy the internal (and sometimes the external) motivations that drive someone to pursue certain goals (Frey and Jegen 2001; Ostrom 2005): volunteering provides an interesting example of this. There are goods that have to be transformed to become valuable but cannot be mechanically placed on a production line: this is typical, for example, of art creation. Finally, there are useful specialisations or important knowledge that might be achieved for the general well-being that hardly have an economic value, forcing some specialists to find an occupation where they necessarily display lower productivity levels with respect to their specialisation. Should they pay the same marginal tax rate as those who have an absolute preference for that job? Both these individuals face the same conditions, display the same effort, but reach different results: if the former obtains the same result as the latter we must consider him more able since he does something that he did not choose as first option. Thus, if there were reasons for giving high rewards for choosing a job in the high-value sectors, there might be more reasons for imposing higher taxation on them as a compensation for individuals that have made different choices. By using a financial analogy, we can say that it could be safer to differentiate our social investment in the highest number of sectors to secure high rewards from the (unforeseeable) future stream of resources.

Secondly, there are activities that yield revenues from markets in which the entire set of costs are not perfectly reckoned: for example firms that operate in sectors in which it is impossible (or not feasible) to calculate the amount of negative externalities produced, or firms that operate at a lower cost thanks to some positive externalities that are not added as costs in their balance sheets. This kind of rent allows these firms to pay relatively higher wages and instruments to protect their rents (Stigler 1971).

Thirdly, Mirrlees' framework is static and the most famous dynamic extension made by Roberts reaches only very specific results (Roberts 1984). But the time dimension is crucial to understand the role of faulty specialisations in terms of the cost that the economic system will bear when certain specialisations are no longer valuable due to, for example, technological progress. Possible reasons advanced to explain a wrong specialisation choice are: (1) it is an individual fault; (2) it is a mismatch regarding economic incentives due to imperfect markets; (3) it is, in Hayek's terms, an 'unintended consequence' of some kind of shock (Hayek 1945). Only the first causes are directly linked to an individual's choice making him responsible for his mistake. But in the other two cases the system itself yields to unrewarding investments, imposing a redistribution policy to cope with such situations.

Taxes and Efficiency

From the empirical point of view, the main arguments against an excessive taxation are twofold: the first concerns the connections between taxes and growth and the second concerns individual freedom.[4]

The former argument has been highly debated in the literature since the conclusions depends strongly on which kind of taxes are considered, the pattern followed to modify the tax schedule and how these resources are spent (Johansson et al. 2008; OECD 2008b). Generally speaking, the main channels through which taxation harms economic growth are deemed to be the following (Engen and Skinner 1996):

1. High tax rates can discourage investments;
2. Tax policy can discourage productivity growth, in particular R&D activities;
3. High tax rates reduce wealth accumulation;
4. Taxes may reduce labour supply growth, by discouraging labour force participation, by distorting occupational choice or the acquisition of education and skills;
5. Heavy taxation on labour supply can alter the efficient use of human capital by dissuading workers from employment in sectors with high social productivity but a heavy tax burden.

It is well established in neoclassical models that a high tax rate negatively affects private investments mainly through the crowing-out effect, even if there are some distinctions that have to be made between the effect of different tax policies. However, nothing is said about the effect of public investments since the latter depends on the policy followed by each government: for example, the highest rate of economic growth in the US during the last century had been reached during the Second World War, when taxes were high and public (not private) investment consistent. For sure, investments in education, labour training and infrastructure have a positive effect on future economic growth (Cullison 1993; Belloc and Vertova 2004).

Similar conclusions can be drawn when R&D expenditures are considered (Thomson 2009). But also in this case, several studies have found a positive statistically significant relation between R&D expenditure and government support.[5] It must be pointed out that lower corporate tax rates encourage foreign investments, but the same can be said about government support to foreign company investment: the magnitude of these two effects is difficult to measure in comparative terms since, as before, not only the tax rate itself but also the schedule is determinant.

Regarding wealth accumulation, Piketty (2003) shows that a positive threshold exists above which any capital income tax rate will eliminate, in an inter-generational model, any possibility of wealth accumulation without affecting the total capital stock in the economy: this kind of policy would sustain inter-generational mobility. It is interesting to note that personal income can have an important role in economic growth in states lacking developed financial markets whereas, as in OECD countries, individual income should not have any relevance in determining the possibility of being able to raise enough capital for any kind of activity or investment. Furthermore, once the capital stock is preserved, how it is distributed depends on norms that can vary from one state to one another: what matters is the overall process of accumulation.

The same can be said about the supply of labour: several examples exist in which a higher tax rate did not discourage the labour supply (we have both substitution and income effects), whereas usually it affects labour demand: lower taxes bring down labour costs and firms respond by increasing labour demand (OECD 2008b). But, once again, as Nickell underlines, the final outcome of every fiscal policy depends also on the social security system, that is, how resources are spent (Nickell 2004).[6]

Education and human capital accumulation represent a delicate topic. From one side the theory suggests that progressive employee tax rates lessen the incentive to acquire a higher level of human capital through education: this seems to be particularly true in the tertiary sector (OECD 2008b). However, an unequal society in itself has a detrimental effect on the incentives to attain higher level of education when this inequality is the result of some institutional friction. Even the nature of education, that is, public or private, can produce different results (Checchi 2001). But there is an important point that has to be made clear: those variables produce different outcomes depending on the overall development of the society investigated: less developed countries are more sensitive to public investment in education than to labour tax rates (Fernandez and Rogerson 1996).

In the end, the direction through which income taxes can influence economic growth is not clearly established.

The second main argument against high taxes relates to the political dimension. Advocates of libertarian theory assert that there are no reasons to force people to pay too many taxes on the basis of three arguments: first, the state is not entitled to impose taxes above the minimum requirement needed to provide basic services, as external defence, law enforcement and (eventually) health care (see Nozick 1974 among others); second, since markets work better than the state in allocating resources, a society would be better off reducing the volume of resources expended by the government; and third, from the economic perspective, more productive people by themselves create wealth that contributes to increase the welfare of the entire population, therefore by levying high taxes on them they can be forced to reduce their contribution to the overall population (Hayek 1960). This view implies that the lower your ability in contributing to economic growth the higher should be your contribution to what is commonly labelled the least efficient economic sector, the public sector. Therefore, since the fewer, better trained and skilled members of the society contribute by assumption relatively less to the accumulation of pooled resources, they will have fewer incentives to improve the quality of public intervention and the more numerous and less able members of society would seek to reduce their taxes instead of increasing the quality of public expenditure.[7] In this way, the lower quality of public allocation of resources becomes a truism. But it is due to public intervention through its institutions that the market system works properly, which means, it is properly these 'less efficient' mechanisms that determine the extent of economic liberty against possible threats: thus, by reducing the capacity of the public apparatus' freedom faces a threat.

A Progressive Allocation of Resources

As has been shown, strong objections can be advanced against the recipe of a flat tax schedule. A more progressive tax rate would not solve all the problems listed above, but it would produce the following effects:

- It works as an automatic stabilizing mechanism against economic fluctuations, leaving resources to the subjects that need them more.[8]
- It increases the amount of resources to be spent during period of crisis.
- Higher proceeds allow the government to invest in sectors that sustain the production of social capital that, in the medium and long run, reduces the cost of running the economic system and enhances economic performance.
- Since the greater beneficiaries of public intervention on the economic systems are the richer, because they make greater use of the economic institutions, a more progressive tax schedule is a fair intervention in the

economy that allows government to develop better institutions and infrastructures.

Different proposals can be advanced to enhance the extent of economic redistribution between individuals, like the minimum or maximum wage. According to us, the less distressed procedure would be a tax system with a strong progressive schedule similar to the tax system applied, for example, in the US between the Second World War and the 1965 tax-rate cuts, the first of several tax-rate cuts which ended in 2003 with the top marginal rate set at 33 per cent. Tax brackets should be calibrated according to wealth distribution to prevent the spread between the top decile and the bottom decile of the population stretching above a certain ratio, a procedure adopted in many cooperative firms. Such decisions clearly involve the ethical sphere or, with Rawls, 'the Sense of Justice' (Rawls 1971).[9]

However, the current economic crisis has shown how politics might be in trouble in proposing a modification of the tax schedule to favour the less able members of society: even if important economic and social reasons support strong progressive taxation, shifting the tax burden onto the wealthy is being strongly resisted everywhere. Recent examples of this resistance include the pictures of President Obama depicted against the background of the communist hammer and sickle during the campaign over the new health care policy; the same denigrating campaign against financial reforms in the US; more recently, the difficulties in finalising the Basel III agreement; the letter posted by President Sarkozy and Prime Minister Brown in the Wall Street Journal advocating higher taxes for bankers (Brown and Sarkozy 2009).

Nevertheless, more strictly economic considerations can be advanced to support this policy. Firstly, there would be less wage competition between citizens of the same community, thus increasing social capital in terms of higher trust. In fact, according to many empirical studies on trust, inequality reduces the extent of trust along individuals, increasing institutional costs to secure transactions (Fiscer and Torgler 2006; Ostrom 2005).

Secondly, greater fairness through redistributive mechanisms implies higher resources to be managed by the state that can adjust welfare policies in a more flexible way, and, by the same token, higher disposable revenues for the government would help to accumulate resources to arrange policies against economic crisis (probably without issuing public debt) thereby stabilising the business cycle, as suggested by Musgrave (1959).

Thirdly, higher levels of income inequality depress political participation (Solt 2008). But the efficiency of the government expenditure is linked with the extent of political participation via the control of resources allocation. This can be achieved if a larger number of groups are entitled to obtain whichever kinds of rent on the gathered resources (Olson 1982).

Fourthly, it would eventually be possible to provide all individuals with a minimum income, especially to those who produce goods that cannot be exchanged in the market place but yield positive externalities for society: for example, individuals that spend their time with children or with the elderly or taking care of the environment; in general it would be easy with a minimum income to pursue intellectual and artistic activities or contribute to the enhancement of social capital in a given community (Levin-Waldam 2003).

And all these benefits reduce the cost of running the economic systems.

Conclusion

This chapter has sought to examine the reasons behind the imposition of a higher progressive tax rate. By analysing the standard assumptions of neoclassical economics on income taxes and their implications, it has been shown that there are deficiencies in the links between taxes and growth and between taxes and freedom. In particular, by referring to the labour market, standard economics models can be seen to be of limited value, mainly because markets are incomplete and the time dimension plays an important role in determining our investment in education. Furthermore we have also suggested that the usual objections to high tax rates – that they limit growth and reduce freedom – can be called into question: the empirical evidence in support of the statement 'lower taxes imply higher growth' is highly contentious and there is no direct correlation between the extent of economic freedom and the tax burden.

To sum up, a stronger progressive tax rate might: (1) increase the volume of resources to be spent during a period of crisis or economic shocks; (2) allow the government to invest in sectors that are crucial from a social and cultural point of view but that are not subject to commercial markets; (3) sustain economic growth due to the higher proceeds used to develop better institutions and infrastructures; (4) automatically stabilise economic fluctuations.

The research agenda opened by this analysis is extensive. Firstly, what conditions and variables have to be used to determine a progressive tax schedule? Optimal tax theory uses very specific assumptions to derive its results; however other assumptions have to be proposed to advance a different approach to tax theory. Maybe the problem is the opportunity of using the word 'optimal' for purposes that do not belong merely to the economic sphere. Secondly, a proposal for a stronger progressive tax schedule entails a change in the way we conceive the role of public expenditure. Almost all OECD countries are characterised by a flattened tax schedule mainly because the public sector is considered inefficient: this is not necessarily true once we acknowledge the eminent role of the public sector in maintaining the conditions that allow the market to work properly, as suggested by institutional economists. Thirdly, tax competition on a global scale can undermine the positive feedback between the public and the private sector already mentioned. Are international institutions able to prevent such competition? How could they achieve this? These questions surely deserve further investigation.

Notes

1. To some extent, this consideration was indirectly advanced by Wicksell who proposes unanimity, or qualified unanimity, as a budgetary decision criterion to guarantee collective involvement and to reduce the extent of coerciveness, even if Wicksell's intention was to limit the power of the majority over the minority (Buchanan 1954).
2. Varian in a seminal contribution analyses the role of taxation and redistribution policies as a form of social insurance (Varian 1980).
3. These propositions do not work for CEOs: in a recent paper Bertrand and Mullainathan (2000) show that CEOs' pay reacts to shocks outside of CEOs' control, such as oil price shocks, which suggests that this standard model, where compensation equals marginal productivity, is a little ingenuous.
4. Some authors see in the need for insurance against exogenous shocks the origin of redistributive policies and therefore the reason for taxation (e.g., Varian 1980). Following this line of reasoning, the higher the probability of encountering an exogenous shock, the more effective and extensive should be a redistribution policy: so, more volatile economies should be characterised by higher tax rates and less volatile economies by lower rates. But volatility is reduced through different channels, most of them institutional and, as North and Wallis (1982) suggest, those channels are supplied by the use of common resources, collected through taxes.
5. On the impact of public R&D expenditure on business R&D: Guellec and Van Pottelsberghe de la Potterie 2003; Atkinson 2007.
6. See also Pissarides 1998.
7. On the other side a public choice scholar would reply that interest groups will prefer a government that manages a higher volume of resources, but as far as there is a public commitment toward strong progressive taxation there could be more groups fighting for the cake. On interest groups and public resources: Olson 1982.
8. This proposal is in line with the idea of using a precautionary approach instead of a maximisation approach. To understand the use of this precautionary approach in the economic field see Arrow and Fisher 1974; Henry 1974.
9. During the great bubonic plague epidemic called Black Death, many priests increased the price of their services for two reasons: the reduction in the supply of clergy (more or less 25,000 deaths) and the increasing demand for their 'specialisation'. To oppose this immoral behaviour of the clergy, the Archbishop of Canterbury issued the first general ecclesiastical mandate on clerical stipends to set a sort of maximum wage in form of maximum tariff in exchange of priests' services in order to save the honour of the Church and to respect God's Commandments. Unfortunately, many bishops ignored this and the following provisions (Putnam 1915).

CHAPTER 11

Comprehensive Lifetime Taxation of International Citizens

A Solution to Tax Avoidance, Tax Competition, and Tax Unfairness

DOUGLAS BAMFORD

Introduction

In this chapter I present a proposal for a different way to organise international taxation. This is a holistic response, whereby the focus is placed on the comprehensive income of individuals rather than numerous disjointed taxes. The system proposes to determine the tax rate for individuals based on their *proportional economic allegiance* to different states and the tax rates they would face within each state. It would then share the tax collected for the individual out to states according to both their allegiance and the level of taxation in those states. This would require the creation of a World Tax Organisation to administer the information and payments required. I primarily present the proposal as a solution to the problem of international tax competition and avoidance, as this fits in with some of the themes of this book and recent political developments.[1] The argument here is that a proposal such as this is increasingly in the interest of the majority of states and their citizens. However, as I will make clear towards the end of the chapter, there are many other advantages to this proposal. The proposal seeks to resolve or reduce three issues: tax competition, tax avoidance and unfairness. However, the proposal also respects the constraints placed on any international tax regime; to allow states to set their own tax rates, and to enable an efficient world economy.

I will begin with an explanation of the problems of tax competition and avoidance, and the idea of a comprehensive tax base as a response to the latter.

The past sixty years have seen great technological advances and economic growth. In that time, the global economy has become much more integrated, led by multinational corporations, with the greater efficiencies this brings (Tanzi 1999: 173). Globalisation has brought negative consequences as well, such as tax competition and avoidance. Tax competition drives down tax rates, which reduces the ability of governments to raise revenues. Individuals with interests in multiple countries can also cross borders in order to avoid taxation, as well as benefitting from tax competition. Both of these problems leave governments and electorates with fewer resources, and increasingly less power over taxation (Avi-Yonah 2000: 1578, 1597–603). Tax competition and avoidance are therefore increasing problems for 'onshore' states and their electorates, and one which the proposal outlined below seeks to counteract. Just as finance has been turbocharged and globalised by computer technology, an international tax regime can utilise technology to counteract these problems (Musgrave 2006: 182). This proposal is only possible given developments in IT, and challenges the assumption that political and economic institutions should remain largely the same while the world around them changes.

Tax Competition and Tax Avoidance

In this section I will highlight two problems of international taxation in the modern world, tax competition and tax avoidance. Improvements in technology have driven financial globalisation, as resource ownership effectively appears on a computer screen, and huge transfers can be made on a global scale instantly. This results in increasing instances of tax competition and avoidance.

Governments are always competing to secure investment, and need to make conditions within their country as attractive as possible for investors and multinational corporations. One well-recognised form of competition between countries is based on taxation; a country will be more attractive to a firm if they have a lower tax rate. Furthermore, countries need to make sure that taxes are the same for their own citizens as they are for foreign investors, and for their citizens should they invest abroad. Tax havens usually begin the competition process by offering lower tax rates, and major economies have to respond to this. All of these pressures lead to a race to the bottom, whereby countries have to lower their tax rates on capital income. Vito Tanzi sums up the consequence of tax competition as being that the 'world tax base will thus become one of the "commons" to be exploited' (Tanzi 1999: 183).

Some people think that tax competition is a good thing (see, for example, Fleming, Peroni and Shay 2001: 342). It would reduce the ability of states to maximise their revenue and size, and therefore their ability to become over-powerful 'leviathans'. The limited resources states would have as a result of lower taxation might mean that they have to cut down on wasteful and inefficient activities due to their limited resources. Others simply believe in the libertarian ideology that taxation and state activities are wrong.[2] Another suggestion is that individuals should be able to choose the state which matches their own preferred levels of taxation and services (Kaufman 1998: 182; Avi-Yonah 2000: 1625–31).[3] The proposal outlined here allows states to choose their own tax rates, and therefore retains a degree of tax competition. However, it also includes counterbalances to this race to the bottom. This is important since most accept that there are major disadvantages to tax competition. The loss of revenue to states will mean that they either have to cut back services (Tanzi 1999: 180)[4] and any redistributive programmes, and/or raise revenue from more regressive forms of taxation (Avi-Yonah 2000: 1616–25; Fleming, Peroni and Shay 2001: 343).

So while there may be reasons for states not to raise taxes to the maximum level, tax competition is often harmful, particularly to the worst off who would (certainly in an ideal world) benefit most from government spending. This has led Avi-Yonah to attempt to distinguish between beneficial and harmful tax competition (2000: 1628). Developing this point, I would suggest that harmful tax competition occurs where countries are effectively forced by global competition to set tax rates at a lower rate than they would if each state were to set tax rates in isolation. It is possible to say that such a situation would violate the background conditions of justice.[5] We can thus compare the tax rates that states would set either as a result of a democratic process, or according to a theory of distributive justice (cf. Rawls 1999a or Dworkin 2000: chapter 2). The international taxation proposal outlined below has features that counterbalance tax competition, without requiring the imposition of global tax rates.

Benefitting from tax competition is effectively a form of (perfectly legal) tax avoidance on the part of those who pay less than they would in the absence of tax competition. Some people will gain and others will be worse off when compared to this hypothetical baseline. In this way there is also a moral role for holistic international tax proposals such as the one presented here; they show how tax competition allows some individuals to engage in a form of what I will refer to as moral tax avoidance; tax avoidance compared to the hypothetical baseline of how much tax the individual would have paid.[6]

It is very difficult to get a definition of tax avoidance, particularly since we cannot expect people to organise their affairs so as to maximise their exposure to tax. A definition which insisted upon maximisation would be ridiculous; it would seem to imply that we should engage in smoking and drinking as leisure activities if there are high 'sin' taxes on these activities. At the opposite extreme, if tax avoidance is defined from the perspective of actual tax law, then it would almost cease to exist, since there would only be evasion. One sensible

242 | Douglas Bamford

approach would be to say that tax avoidance is legal within the letter of the law, but not within the spirit. It would then be up to the legislature, judiciary or enforcement authority to close any loopholes and crack down on any abuse.[7] However, while this issue of unintended legality is a necessary requirement, it is not sufficient as it does not specify which types of act are avoidance acts. I would supplement it by adding the further requirement that avoidance activity takes the form it does to increase gain where the gain is only available due to distortionary tax laws and rates. This then includes scope for the form of moral tax avoidance above.

Where the lawmakers have been limited in their powers as a result of international tax competition, we could attempt to include this in our understanding of avoidance as well. Tax laws have to take account of international competition, and thus we could say that those who benefit from such laws are engaged in a form of tax avoidance, albeit an unquestionably legal one. However, one practical sense in which the issues of international tax competition and avoidance are linked is where labour income is effectively shifted to capital income, which will have a much lower rate as a result of tax competition. The authorities could try to ensure that this re-characterisation, or shifting, of category is shut down. However, this is very difficult to achieve while the tax authorities distinguish capital from labour income, as it is easy to pay workers in tax-efficient pension entitlements or shares that appear later as capital gains. One solution to this avoidance activity is to move to a comprehensive tax base, which has also been proposed as a general response to tax avoidance. The move to a comprehensive tax base, which focuses on individuals, is therefore a way to respond to the problems of tax avoidance and tax competition, and I will discuss this next.

The Comprehensive Tax Base

The current consensus on taxation is to have broad-based, low-rate taxation. This means that the authorities put low taxes on lots of different activities and transactions, for example income, consumption, corporate profits, land and certain forms of transaction. The broad-base approach is generally favoured as it is considered more feasible, although the feasibility constraints lead to the disregarding of many forms of personal income. An alternative approach is a comprehensive base with a focus on persons.[8] Unlike broad-based taxes, these taxes can be tailored to the circumstances of the individual. This is preferable because it means that the tax the individual pays can more easily correlate to an idea of distributive justice, whatever approach to distributive justice is taken.[9] Furthermore, while it is possible to attempt progressive taxation with broad-based taxes, this can only be achieved on an incidental basis, whereas comprehensive taxes can much better sort individuals according to their personal circumstances before determining appropriate tax rates.[10]

A second reason to prefer comprehensive taxation is that it should reduce the scope for tax avoidance. Individuals would no longer be able to re-characterise their income into different forms so as to thereby reduce tax liability. For example, individuals would not be able to set themselves up as self-employed businesses in order to pay themselves in 'dividends' rather than salary. As Boris Bittker (1967) pointed out, the move to a comprehensive tax base does not in itself answer all questions of categorisation. There will be all sorts of business expenses, for example, that could be counted as income or not, where counting them as income may make business activities more difficult and ignoring them may result in a (particularly distortionary and inefficient) form of tax avoidance. It is simply impossible to remove all boundaries between taxable and non-taxable activities. As such, the rules on business expenses and other forms of potential avoidance activities would have to be well defined and amended wherever new forms of abuse are discovered. However, since under comprehensive taxation the tax rate would be personal to the individual, there would be no benefit from shifting income from one form to another. This would thereby shut down most forms of income re-characterisation, such as that from personal to business taxation. Comprehensive taxes are superior to broad-based taxation because they reduce the scope for tax avoidance, as well as being amenable to attempts at distributive fairness.

A comprehensive personal tax would obviously replace many existing taxes such as income taxes, estate or accession taxes, and capital gains taxes. A comprehensive income tax should also replace corporation tax, assuming that the income received by individuals on their corporate investments would be taxed when received. This is what undermines the move to re-characterise income into a different category, something which is more likely where international tax competition drives down tax rates on some forms of income. Not all taxes would have to be replaced; some could remain, such as VAT and certainly Pigovian or 'sin' taxes.

Another feature of comprehensive taxes is that they lend themselves to a lifetime view of individual circumstances. If we wish to focus on individuals, then it may make sense to look at their entire economic lives rather than the particular periods therein.[11] This can be done through the use of a lifetime averaging system, such as that proposed by William Vickrey (Vickrey 1972, 1994). A lifetime approach is not strictly necessary for the proposal below, but it would be advisable for several reasons. Firstly, it would assist in the fight against avoidance as people would not be able to artificially move their income across accounting periods in order to reduce their tax liability. It would also avoid economic distortions due to threshold effects,[12] as well as being fairer to those with more volatile income (cf. Vickrey 1972: 165–66). Most important of all, the proposal below looks back at past allegiance, and this makes most sense if combined with a focus on total lifetime income. As such, I will assume a lifetime comprehensive tax for the remainder of this chapter.

In a single state setting, a comprehensive tax base is relatively straightforward. However, in a real-world multi-state setting it becomes much more complicated. An individual's income (or consumption) will occur in multiple jurisdictions, and this raises questions about how much tax they should pay on which income and where the revenue should go. If it were left up to the citizens, they could use their international status to split their income, enabling them to avoid comprehensive taxation according to their total income. My solution is to split individuals into 'national' and 'international' economic citizens, where international citizens are those with personal and economic relationships with more than one country.[13] States would calculate the income and tax liabilities of their national economic citizens themselves. However, states would calculate the local income for international citizens, and possibly collect it, but would share the information and income with the other countries with which the individual in question has economic ties. This would ensure that all citizens are judged for tax purposes on their global personal income.

I have said that comprehensive personal taxes are superior, but several comprehensive tax bases have been proposed. The classic view of comprehensive income is the accretion view, as provided by Simons in developing work by Schanz and Haig (hence the moniker SHS income) (Goode 1977). Simons (1938: 50) defines income as the value of consumption expenditure plus any increase in wealth during a given period.[14] A second approach would be a variant of the comprehensive income approach (Bamford 2010), with the focus on resources that are newly available for consumption. This has the advantage that there is no need to account for capital gains on property or investments until they are realised. Furthermore, when individuals invest through a financial institution, the investment is ignored for the purpose of income taxation until the individual receives more than the inflation-indexed value of their total investments. Anything received above the amount of wealth they have previously invested will then count as income. This results in an income definition that is part-way to a consumption definition.

Indeed, a third comprehensive personal tax would be one that focused on the market value of items consumed by the individual (e.g., the proposals by Seidman 1997; McCaffery 2002). The downside of such taxes is that they do not measure the economic power that individuals obtain. One consequence is that they would enable individuals to amass huge fortunes, and to pass them between generations, potentially leading to huge class differences.[15] As such, in the remainder of this work, I will assume a comprehensive income approach, though the proposal outlined below could be adjusted to work with consumption taxes. Whichever comprehensive tax base was introduced, it would need to be on an international scale; introducing it in one jurisdiction would have many unwanted economic consequences.[16]

International Taxation: Cooperation, Competition or Holistic Responses

I have said that national comprehensive taxes are complicated in an international setting, and this is the issue to which the proposal below responds. Before presenting it, however, it is worth considering some of the literature on international taxation. In this section I will argue that a multilateral holistic approach is preferable to the current bilateral approach. Bilateral tax cooperation is the common response to tax competition.[17] This is where countries agree over which country gets to tax which income, be it on the basis of the individual's *residence* (or citizenship),[18] or the *source* country of the income (cf., e.g., Musgrave 2006: 168).

The bilateral cooperative approach is sensible in the face of tax competition, but it is less than ideal. The problem with the bilateral approach is that the cooperation is between one country and another, which leads to imbalances. Tax havens do not have to make these agreements, and where they do so they will minimise their obligations. They will tend to avoid any limitations on their ability to set low tax rates, and to require the sharing of information on foreign citizens. Secondly, in bilateral agreements the more powerful country may have more say over which model treaty to use, and at which points to deviate from the model (see for example Alberto Vega's chapter in this volume). As such, the outcomes of treaties may reflect the relative strength of the bargaining nations rather than any idea of fairness between the taxpayers and service recipients of the countries involved. Furthermore, the focus of even the model treaties is generally to improve economic efficiency rather than to bring about any notion of inter-individual or inter-nation fairness (Fleming, Peroni and Shay 2001: 338). Indeed, this problem of unfairness between citizens and between nations is an additional problem with the current international taxation field which the proposal outlined below seeks to resolve.

This alternative response to tax competition has been referred to as a holistic solution (Bird and Mintz 2003: 423), and it is an avowedly global and multilateral one. This approach is to introduce some form of world tax organisation, as suggested by Tanzi (1999), which would coordinate the taxation of international citizens.[19] This organisation could be combined with an organisation that sets and withholds international taxes in order to provide international goods (cf. Schratzenstaller's chapter in this volume) and/or with the current World Trade Organisation to create a WTTO. Bird and Mintz suggest that this might be a utopian suggestion, and unworkable without an international tax police. Their argument is that states would have no interest in collecting taxes for another state. However, if the collecting country were to receive a share then of course they would have an interest in collecting and declaring revenues, even though they would have to share them. I think the proposal I outline below therefore gets around this problem, and I will discuss this issue further below.

Some argue that the existing cooperative approach is sufficient, but I think that a holistic solution is preferable in order to stem the problems of international inequity, tax avoidance and competition. For one thing, a holistic system should be fairer as it allows the apportionment of income between different countries according to a formula, rather than according to who finds it easier to withhold the tax. Indeed, I would go further and suggest that the cooperative approach cannot have fairness inbuilt.[20] It is also superior because it provides more scope for providing incentives to join and punishments to states which eschew tax cooperation. Tax havens often have nothing to benefit from tax cooperation, and since they often drive capital taxation competition there would need to be a more global response. However, this response would have to be such as to treat all states in a reasonable manner, not one that simply cracks down on and punishes states with lower tax rates. By allowing, but counterbalancing, tax competition the proposal meets this requirement. I will postpone discussion of fairness issues until the end of this chapter.

Proportional Economic Allegiance

I have so far discussed the global comprehensive taxation of international individuals as a possible response to tax competition and avoidance (actual and moral). However, current tax agreements work within a broad-based tax structure. As such, international tax agreements generally specify which state can tax which form of income, between for example the 'source' and 'resident' country. However, I find this very unsatisfactory. Source, residence and citizenship are not as simple as they may appear. An individual may receive investment returns from a company headquartered in one country, but with operations in many countries. Some people have multiple residences and citizenships, for family or business reasons. Furthermore, it is not only capital that can cross borders, individuals also do so.

The existing literature greatly oversimplifies along the dimension of time, while the proportional allegiance approach I propose can take account of these complexities. International citizens will move between countries, having different countries of residence at different times. Past residences will have had a formative influence on the development of the individual, and so should be taken account of in the allocation of tax revenues. The proposal below utilises the idea of economic allegiance, the advantage of which is that past allegiances are readily amenable to this approach. By focussing on 'proportional economic allegiance', the revenue sharing proposal I outline below is designed to take account of multiple allegiances and past residences.

The notion of economic allegiance or affiliation is not new. It was introduced as a way to deal with the complex issue of international equity. This notion was discussed in the early part of the twentieth century by Georg von Schanz and also by a committee of economists on behalf of the League of Nations (Harris 1996: 276–78; Kaufman 1998: 194–201). The aim of the League of Nations committee was:

> to derive an elaborate schema of tax classification and to apply a concept of 'economic allegiance' allowing for (*a*) the location of production or source of income, (*b*) the location at which the final product is used or the income is received, (*c*) the location of the legal machinery by which property rights are enforced, and (*d*) the domicile of the property owner. Ideally, different types of taxes would be imposed on the situs of wealth or of source of income as split up among various locations according to each of these four factors. (Musgrave and Musgrave 1972: 65)

This approach based on economic allegiance is useful as a composite of residence, citizenship and source principles. This approach has always been dismissed as unfeasible. However, while it may have been unfeasible in the 1920s, I suggest that modern IT and communications technology renders feasible this more ideal approach.

I will not aim in this chapter to specify the ideal formula of allegiance, though I will offer some rough principles and suggestions. One way to divide the factors that determine economic allegiance is into personal and economic concerns. Personal factors would be the country of birth (and perhaps even of parents' birth), citizenship(s), location of education, and the amount of time spent living in various countries. Economic factors would be the location in which individuals earned labour income, and the locations of investments. Account could also be made of the amount of time the individual has spent working in different countries, represented by hour-credits (see Bamford forthcoming).

It is important to explain the factors used to determine economic allegiance. As an example of the proportional allegiance approach, consider Jackie, whose allegiances are split equally into thirds between countries A, B and C. Jackie may have grown up in country A, where she is a citizen. She has spent thirty years in country B where she runs a business which mostly operates in and gains profits from country C. The personal factors count towards countries A and B, with more influence for country A, while the economic factors are split between countries B and C, with more influence for country

C. In this simplified example, we can see why Jackie's allegiance is split evenly between the three countries.

This is relatively simple if investment locations are taken to be the location of incorporation. However, to focus on the head office seems unfair in the case of multinational corporations, which operate in multiple countries. As such, it may be necessary to split the investment individuals make in multinational corporations according to some formula recognising the division of investment, sales, and profits by that corporation. Musgrave and Musgrave suggest that this could be adequately covered by accounting for operation costs between the countries (Musgrave and Musgrave 1972: 81–83). Where companies have subsidiaries, these would be traced down from the parent company such that the holdings of the parent company are apportioned between various countries (this could be calculated once or twice in a year) (Musgrave and Musgrave 1972: 76–77). This tracing is very difficult to do in any precise way, as explained by Musgrave (2006: 176), but a tracing approach is preferable even if imperfect. Even if it is not economically perfect, it would be reasonable enough to do.[21] The downside of tracing and attributing downstream investments to investors in this more accurate way is that most investors would then need to be classified as international citizens. If more individuals count as international citizens, a World Tax Organisation would become more difficult and expensive to administer.

I have said that there should be some formula, but said nothing about the weightings of the inputs. It is not necessary to state exact portions, and no doubt this should be determined by a suitably fair international procedure. However, one suggestion I make is that economic factors should be given more weight over personal considerations depending on the income of the individual in question. So for example, there could be bands for people with different income levels. Perhaps those with relatively low lifetime incomes should have a 50/50 split between economic and personal factors; those with medium incomes have a 60/40 split; while those with very high incomes should have a 75/25 split. It would also be possible to further weight returns to economic income between gift, labour and investment income. This idea of proportional economic allegiance will be utilised in the proposal for calculating the tax rate for international citizens, and how this revenue is shared between countries. I will now describe the international taxation proposal which utilises this idea of proportional economic allegiance.

International Revenue Collection and Sharing

I will now outline the proposal for the collection and sharing of the tax revenue from the comprehensive income of international citizens. I distinguish two questions, which correspond to two stages of the procedure: what rate of tax should each individual citizen pay on their total income? And, how is this total apportioned between countries? Some of the answers to these questions are left intentionally open, and in some cases I highlight different possibilities. Important elements are the creation of shares representing the allegiance between the particular citizen and the various countries, and the corresponding weightings. I will describe in the following section how this might work in practice, and what roles a World Tax Organisation could take on or delegate to countries.

Different countries have different tax rates, representing local views about economic justice, as well as for reasons of economic efficiency. Fortunately, the system proposed does not require a world-wide tax rate on the comprehensive income of international citizens.[22] Nor is it necessary for countries to set different tax rates for international and national citizens. Each country would simply report its tax rates for home citizens to the world tax organisation. This information can be used to determine the tax rate that international citizens would have paid had they earned their total global income but with allegiance solely to each respective country.[23] The tax rate for a particular international citizen is linked to a) her economic allegiance to the various countries, and b) the tax rate between those countries. The tax rate for the global income of the individual is calculated based upon the mean tax rate for this individual in each of these countries, weighted according to her allegiance to these countries.

Take the example of Jackie from the previous section, whose allegiances are split equally into thirds between countries A, B and C. The tax rate in countries A and B is high (she would pay, say, 50 per cent), while country C has a lower tax rate (say, 32 per cent). As such, Jackie would pay a 44 per cent rate. Her tax rate is closer to 50 per cent than 32 per cent because she has a greater allegiance (two-thirds) to the higher tax countries. This is relatively straightforward even in more realistically complicated cases, since the calculation can be undertaken automatically by computer. Applying the formula will determine the tax rate for the individual in question, and that in turn will determine how much they should pay in total tax.[24]

The second question is where this total should go. The allocation of tax revenue would again utilise the proportional economic allegiance. The individual's total tax would be split between states according to the degree of allegiance that they have with the individual in question. However, that is only the first stage in calculating the distribution of tax revenue for each individual. There is an important additional weighting element, relating back to the tax rates mentioned above. As such, countries who would have imposed a higher tax rate on the individual in question would get proportionally more of the revenue than countries with lower taxes. This feature acts as a brake on race-to-the-bottom tax competition, by rewarding the countries with higher tax rates. Setting the power of this weighting will involve a trade off between the good and bad elements of tax competition. However, there should be little reason to worry about this resulting in overly high tax rates; states would not set their rates too high as it would repel economic activity. Returning to the example of Jackie from above, she paid 44 per cent of her total global income in tax. This would be split equally between countries A, B, and C if they had the same tax rates. However, the distribution of revenue is weighted away from low-tax countries and towards high-tax ones. As a result, because state C has lower taxes it may only receive 24 per cent of Jackie's tax payment, while countries A and B receive 38 per cent.

An optional feature would be to add an additional weighting factor, which would take account of the level of economic development of the countries involved. This would serve as a form of international redistribution, perhaps acting as a more formal and secure form of aid transfer between nations (cf. Musgrave and Musgrave 1972: 74–75; Avi-Yonah 2000: 1649). This may be politically unpopular in wealthy countries, and be considered by some to be unfair. Some would think that the richer countries owe nothing to members of poorer countries, while others take the opposite view that they owe a lot.[25] As the proposal here only applies to international citizens, this would exclude national citizens, revenues from national citizens would not be utilised for redistribution, and some would feel there should be a more all-inclusive approach. Furthermore, this additional weighting factor may not be necessary, on the assumption that poorer countries will apply their tax rates at lower levels of earnings, thus putting them in a strong position in the weightings. Having explained the nature of the calculations, the input factors and weightings involved, I will now explain how it might work.

How It Could Work

In the previous section I mentioned the role of a International Tax Organisation (which I will refer to as the ITO in the remainder of this chapter), which would be necessary in order to administer a tax on international citizens.[26] While such an organisation would be necessary for the tax-sharing proposal, there are several possible ways in which such an organisation could work. The more centralized approach would be for this ITO to perform all tax calculations and payments. A centralised organisation could deal directly with the individual, though it would arrange withholding and policing through the various national tax authorities.

A more decentralised approach would be for the ITO to be information gathering and sharing, with each international citizen having a designated lead country which would undertake the administration of their account in light of the information collected. In this case, the ITO would still operate a database of all international citizens, coordinate investigations into whether citizens should be relabelled as international taxpayers, make available each individual's withholding rates for national tax authorities, deal with taxpayer complaints, perform audits on national tax authorities, and act as a clearing house for payments between countries. The choice between these two options is a political one, and both seem, prima facie, acceptable to me.

An important decision which would need to be made is the location in which tax should be paid or withheld. The jurisdiction which should withhold the tax from individuals should be determined largely on the basis of simplicity in terms of payment, withholding and collecting the tax. Most of the time, this will be the source country for the income. In the case of gifts, it should perhaps be the residence and citizenship of the gift-giver (to avoid the incentive for gift-receivers to use a third-party country solely for the purposes of tax reduction). There would need to be strict rules, applied throughout all countries, as to which type of income is collected by which jurisdiction. Hopefully such rules should reduce cases of double-taxation. However, citizens would be able to make a case to the ITO should they pay tax on the same income in two countries.

As I mentioned in the introduction, modern information technology makes the otherwise utopian ITO proposal feasible. A state's computer system can communicate tax and income information instantaneously to an ITO and this information can then be shared with other states throughout the world. It would be necessary for the states to tag the information as to the source of each recorded amount of income. So as well as the date of receipt and amount, the withholding state would have to inform the ITO of the originating location of the income, any tax withheld and perhaps the type of income (labour, investment return, or gift).

Implementation

The ITO would only be feasible if the vast majority of powerful states desired it. Some states may feel that they do very well out of the current system, and may assert their sovereign right not to sign up to such an agreement. Membership of the ITO scheme would therefore need to be insisted upon as a condition of engagement in the global economic system. This would provide incentive for all states to join, once a tipping point of economic development is reached. Those joining the ITO would need to sign covenants about appropriate government spending,[27] human rights, financial and political transparency, and agree to allow audits and inspections by the ITO. Countries who fail to meet these requirements could have their international citizen tax revenue withheld and they could also face sanctions.

Resistance to any comprehensive global income plan will come from the very wealthy (inevitably an extremely powerful group), and also from tax havens. Many tax havens have a history of offering banking secrecy (Avi-Yonah 2000: 1584, 1668–89), and this too would be incompatible with comprehensive international income; there would have to be international transparency about ownership and such information would have to be shared with the ITO. All wealth would have to be attributed to individuals, and the receipt of new wealth by international citizens would have to be made known to the ITO. Wealthy individuals and tax havens would try to undermine moves to create a comprehensive income taxation system, and would try to circumvent it if it were introduced. However, if there was a strong enough movement to jump the numerous hurdles in order to establish such an ITO then the states involved would be willing and able to propose strong sanctions on countries that did not agree to share information on individuals. Since tax havens are always parasitic, they would have much to lose if they cut themselves off from the wider economy.

It is easy to dismiss the idea of an ITO, particularly because states would have to give up a certain amount of sovereignty over taxation, something which they are generally reluctant to do. However, the existence of numerous tax treaties shows that states are aware that they have to make agreements with others. Furthermore, as I have said, the existence of tax competition actually makes this sovereignty largely useless. States have the formal power to set their tax rates, but they are severely limited in their ability to raise taxes. An important feature of the tax calculation I have proposed is that it does not restrict states in the setting of tax rates. As such, states would not need to give up the right to determine their own tax rates when signing up to this scheme. Furthermore, there is no creation of a global state or leviathan to challenge the states. States would need to agree to use the same tax bases, and some may lose some business or taxation revenue. However, these losses are minor when compared to the gains on offer.

Indeed, it is quite plausible (and almost guaranteed in most cases) that states would have *more* power over tax rates on their citizens and international citizens under the ITO proposal. Paradoxically, giving up formal power to keep all the revenues they can get may in fact increase their actual power. In addition, states would very likely increase their revenue, since they would no longer lose revenue to tax avoidance. An international comprehensive tax base should greatly reduce the scope for avoidance, for reasons I will explain in detail in the section after the next. States would also cease to suffer as much from revenue loss from tax competition, due to the counterbalancing weighting. If wealth and asset ownership continues to be moved to tax havens, with an international elite increasingly holding a substantial amount of resources offshore then it will be in the interest of states to cooperate in a more thoroughgoing way to regain some power. The majority of their citizens should support such moves if their government resources continue to be eroded in the absence of global agreement.

Nevertheless, if a global agreement were not forthcoming, what might be the prospects for regional implementation (Musgrave 2006: 182)? Some tax harmonisation proposals are led by regional trade areas, so as to avoid distortions within the region. As such, are there any prospects that the EU or NAFTA could move to a comprehensive tax base? The problem with this is that the region would then have trouble assessing and taxing international citizens with interests outside the region. Furthermore, investors may move their investments outside the region in order to hide their comprehensive personal returns, which could result in a lot of capital flight. A region would have to have agreements with the other countries of the world to attempt to uncover the relevant income information. This seems an unlikely prospect in the absence of an international multilateral agreement and organisation. Nevertheless, it is worth mentioning the possibility that in advance of global implementation the system could begin with multiple regional implementations. This might make the move to global implementation smoother, assuming that the regions made sure that their systems were entirely compatible from the outset.

Challenges

I will now briefly discuss the practical problems facing this proposal. The first is how to pay for the ITO. Two options immediately present themselves. One is to levy a tiny percentage of all transfer payments between countries. A second would be to have a set annual budget, to which states would contribute in proportion to their size of their economy. The ITO could then deduct this amount from the revenue transfers to each state. Running an international bureaucracy would be difficult, as it would be very important that it should provide information very quickly, but it would be difficult to incentivise the staff to work quickly enough. Further problems would arise because of language and currency issues. The ITO may have to operate regional offices which would have access to information and be able to provide individuals and the central ITO with information as required. Regarding currency, the ITO would presumably have to set currency exchange prices, and convert all transfers into one currency so as to allow calculations in just one currency. The choice and application of currency trading prices would then be potentially contentious, and would need to be determined in as obviously neutral a fashion as possible.

Another set of problems arise from the collection of tax. The first problem would be that states could collude with international citizens in order to hide income. This would benefit the individual, but does not seem to offer states much benefit as they would be reducing their own tax revenues as a result. The only reason a country would do this would be to attract investors or consumers, and the ITO could attempt to uncover such activity.[28] A related problem is that states may be disinclined to uncover income and collect tax on international citizens. 'No country's tax administration seems likely to give high priority to enforcing another country's taxes', as Bird and Mintz (2003: 423) put it. However, they write with the assumption that all the revenues raised will leave the country, which is not the case under this proposal. Given that the country involved must gain revenue from the increase in income on their soil, there is plenty of incentive for them to uncover such income. A final problem on this score would be that developing countries may not have the resources to investigate the income for international citizens. One way around this would be to have local ITO offices which would undertake such investigations in tandem with local authorities in countries where local tax offices lack expertise and resources. This would have the further advantage that it should help in the fight against corruption, since international tax haven secrecy facilitates the concealment and laundering of corrupt money (as detailed in Shaxson 2011).

A more theoretical concern with an international comprehensive approach is whether it is logically possible to attribute comprehensive income to a particular jurisdiction. Ault and Bradley (1990) argue that the focus on the income for the individual seems to come at the expense of any particular definition of income source which could be attributed to a particular state. They write:

> Large changes in wealth occur continually by virtue of changes that have no locational aspect. Examples are the discovery of a new drug formula or new consumer good. Even more significant are simple changes in expectations and beliefs about the future, which can result in large changes in asset values. Attaching locations to these phenomena inevitably involves arbitrary line drawing, with its attendant controversy. (Ault and Bradley 1990: 230–31)

It may be necessary to give up the pretence to attribute all of an individual's income in exact proportion between activities within different jurisdictions. In a globalised world this would be impossible, just as it is impossible to say how much of an individual's income is due to their activity rather than that of others (Rawls 1999b: 79). Nevertheless, for the purposes of taxation, the formula of apportionment need only be *adequate and acceptable* for the purpose of sharing international tax income (see also Kaufman 1998: 175).

Revenue Sharing and Tax Avoidance

I said above that it is difficult to find a suitable definition of tax avoidance. Some forms will be perfectly acceptable (such as investing in a tax-favourable pension), some are clearly against the spirit of the law (re-characterising income by paying it in a different form or in another jurisdiction). In this chapter I also propose a third category of tax avoidance, at least from a moral point of view. This is to compare the tax that individuals pay in the current world, with race-to-the-bottom tax competition and tax haven secrecy, with the tax that which individuals would pay under a fairer scheme such as the proposal above.

A move towards a comprehensive tax base would reduce the possibility of the problem of shifting income in order to avoid taxation. Given that the taxation is applied on global lifetime income, tax rates apply irrespective of the form, time and place in which the income arrives. It is worth noting that this move is not a solution to all problems. For one thing, it might result in a greater amount of tax evasion, as some forms of income are difficult to capture, such as perquisites. Sharing information on the consumption and property ownership of international citizens, and comparing this with income figures, may enable the authorities to uncover the severe cases of abuse.

Second, any tax-favourable categories (such as pensions) will encourage tax avoidance through re-characterisation of income (Cooper 1985: 660–63, 694–701). Tax-favourable categories would therefore need to be strictly limited and internationally compatible. However, as there would not be a distinction between different forms of income there would be no advantage to the re-characterisation of income from one form to another. International citizens may attempt to move their income to lower tax jurisdictions, but this will have limited effect, since it will still take some account of the source of the earnings and the past history of the individual in question.

Third, as mentioned above, there will always be difficult cases, particularly with regard to business expenses. As such, there would need to be international agreements and standards about what does and does not count as income, with provision for dynamic rule changes to cope with new forms of abuse. This might mean that there should be a maximum amount of expenses which an individual can claim from their employer for travel or accommodation. Each country may have a different maximum cost based upon the average cost of accommodation in the country. International standards of this type should be sufficient to stop most of the forms of abuse that would trouble us.

I would like to point out a further use for the current proposal. The beneficiaries of what I have referred to as moral tax avoidance (rather than legal) clearly benefit financially from tax competition, or from the use of tax havens. I suggest that we can use the international citizen tax proposal above as a moral heuristic, to provide a baseline from which to determine whether individuals are engaging, morally if not legally, in a form of unacceptable tax avoidance. We would then be able to say that a particular wealthy individual benefits to the tune of x thousands of pounds a year as a result of their activities. One obvious criticism of this point is that we have no way of knowing what the tax rates would be if the proposal were enacted. However, it is possible to make certain assumptions. The first is that rates would be higher than they are under the influence of tax competition. The second is that high-earning individuals would not pay very low tax rates on their global personal income, as many no doubt currently do. To determine tax rates that individuals would pay would require numerous assumptions, but we could pick out certain individuals with large comprehensive incomes, and who pay very little tax, and say that they are in fact avoiding tax as a result of an unduly favourable tax environment. We may not be able to give a precise amount by which an individual benefits, but we can generate a minimum amount by which they benefit.

Further Considerations and Advantages of the System

Three prominent principles arise in the context of international tax agreements, and these principles apply to holistic multilateral approaches as much as they do to bilateral forms of international taxation cooperation. The first two are related, so I will consider them together. The first is the need to avoid double taxation, which is where individuals with economic interests in two countries pay tax on the same income twice. This does not treat the individual fairly, as they pay more tax than their fellows in either country. Furthermore, it leads to violation of the second principle, efficiency, because the prospect of double taxation would affect investment choices. As indicated, the second principle is that states need to work together on taxation to avoid creating inefficiencies. Tax discrepancies could distort investment choices, resulting in a less efficient allocation of global capital. As such, the principle of efficiency requires a degree of international capital neutrality, whereby investors face similar tax rates whether they invest at home or abroad (Capital Export Neutrality) (Musgrave and Musgrave 1972: 69; Harris 1996: 449; Musgrave 2006: 170–71; Avi-Yonah 2000: 1604–11).[29]

The comprehensive approach I have outlined is intended to ensure that all of an individual's income is taxed, but only once, thus meeting the first principle of having no double taxation. Capital neutrality is effectively secured since the tax rate applies to the individual rather than the investment. This does potentially give individuals some incentive to try to focus their investments on lower rate countries. However, doing so will often affect their income in such a way as to make it unattractive. As I have said, states would still have the ability to set their own tax rates on their domestic citizens, and altering their rates to attract foreign citizens will affect the income received from all of those individuals who have any economic or personal allegiance to their state. However, the system automatically ensures efficiency and so there is no need for states to make any further tax agreements in the name of efficiency.

The third principle, equity, is more controversial. The work of Peggy and Richard Musgrave has highlighted the distinction between inter-individual and inter-nation equity (Musgrave and Musgrave 1972; Musgrave 2002).[30] The former is the Aristotelian requirement that like be treated as like, in this case that an individual A in one country is treated the same as a relevantly identical individual B in another country, and not like some relevantly different individual C. Richard Musgrave has distinguished this into two types of cases, horizontal and vertical equity, which is to imagine an ideal where individuals are placed on a ladder and to ensure that in the real world everyone is on the correct rung when compared to any given other (Aristotle 1976: book five; Musgrave 1959: 160).[31] This issue of fairness of course relates to that of distributional justice, about which there is much disagreement (Rawls 1971, 1999a, 2001; Nozick 1974; Dworkin 2000; Cohen 1989). Even ignoring these disagreements, the issue of fairness becomes more complicated on an international level. One ready conclusion is that all individuals should pay tax once on each source of income, but certainly not twice (i.e., to avoid double taxation). However, ensuring this would not be the end of the story. There is also the issue of equity or fairness between nations (and hence taxpayers and service recipients).[32] If individuals do not pay the tax twice, it means that one state may obtain an inequitable slice of the tax revenue from that individual. Unfortunately, discussions about international taxation usually seem to proceed on the assumption that what is at stake is the right to tax a particular base, where this right implies the right to keep all of the revenue in question.[33] Indeed, the bilateral cooperation literature, understandably, views the issue from the perspective of one particular country signing a tax treaty. This means that the wider question of equity between the taxpayers and service recipients of different states does not take centre stage. When taking a holistic approach, however, it is possible to attempt to determine rules for sharing revenue in a fair manner. The ability to have a fair apportionment of revenues is a further advantage of the revenue-sharing scheme.

Much of the literature has referred to equity issues, to ensure that individuals and states are treated appropriately vis-à-vis one another. The above proposal meets these requirements very well. As states would have more power to change their tax rates, there would be more equity between home citizens since they would be able to decide the most appropriate tax rates according to distributive justice and through the democratic process. For international citizens, it is less immediately clear with whom they should be on an equitable relationship – they share relationships with single-nation citizens who are in different countries and hence do not have a single point of comparison. By proportioning tax rates according to allegiance, international individuals are placed on a suitably equitable level with the various individuals in the several countries with which they have an allegiance. This also applies between the contributions to tax and the recipients of services, where those sharing a degree of allegiance will potentially have a share of the gains and costs of government programmes. The revenue sharing means that equity between states is built in to the system. Tax revenues are apportioned between states, where the weighting ensures that account is taken of the extent to which the rates within the country have influenced the tax rate for the individual in question.

One final point I would like to make is that the proposal would also mitigate the problem of brain drain. It does so because it takes account of past residence, and not just current residence. Brain drain occurs where talented and skilled individuals leave poorer countries for richer countries where they can earn more money. This effect essentially means that poor countries are subsidising rich countries. The upbringing and training of such individuals is paid for by the poor country, but the rich country gets the benefit. The proposal ensures that some of the tax revenues for international migrants will be shared with their past countries.

Conclusion

I have outlined a proposal for a comprehensive tax on international individuals, whereby the revenue would be shared according to a formula of proportional economic allegiance. This would remove the options for tax avoidance available in the current global economic environment. Furthermore, the use of tax rate weightings would discourage damaging tax competition, by providing a strong incentive to set higher rates.

The idea of global tax administration has been dismissed on two grounds. One is that it would not be feasible, while the other is that states would not agree to it. The problems of administrative feasibility are overcome due to developments in information technology that allow instantaneous global information sharing and tax calculations. This means that proposals for proportional revenue sharing – dismissed by the League of Nations committee in the 1920s – are now administratively feasible, and I have sketched out how these would work. I have argued that the problem of gaining agreement is less weighty than it used to be given that states have less incentive to retain their formal sovereignty. States are losing control over their ability to tax international citizens, while the resulting tax competition also causes them to lower taxes on domestic citizens. As such, ceding power to an international organisation could paradoxically give states more power to set tax rates. Since the proposal outlined does not require a global tax rate, it would give electorates more choice over taxation matters.

Implementing the proposal for an ITO with revenue sharing would have many other advantages. It would increase fairness, as it would put nationally based and internationally based citizens on a similar footing. It would also increase fairness between countries, who currently rely on the negotiation of treaties (or not) with the spoils mostly going to the country with the power to withhold the tax. The proposal should also enable states to increase tax rates without any ensuing efficiency loss. The move to a comprehensive tax base should greatly reduce the scope for tax avoidance, albeit at the expense of greater potential for evasion. The proposal therefore deals with the problems of tax competition and avoidance, and the ensuing revenue loss, outlined at the beginning. A further point is that even in the absence of the implementation of the global scheme, we can use the *idea* of such a scheme as a baseline against which to determine an additional (moral) form of tax avoidance. This gives us a position from which to judge the tax payments of those who benefit from tax-haven-based tax avoidance and evasion.

Notes

1. The rise in state indebtedness and government budget cuts in light of the recent banking crisis has shone a light on tax avoidance. The development of organisations such as UK Uncut, and the increased profile of the Tax Justice Network, bear this out. Nicholas Shaxson's recent popular journalistic book on the subject of tax havens (Shaxson 2011) is a sign of increasing interest in these issues, albeit from a very low base.

2. For example organisations like the CATO institute, perhaps influenced by (Hayek 1960; Friedman 1962; Nozick 1974). The former two are consequentialist libertarians, which is an unattractive political philosophy combined with questionable empirical assumptions. The philosophical libertarianism of Nozick is more coherent, but I find it unconvincing for reasons such as those found in (Nagel 1975; Cohen 1995: 229–44; Freeman 2001; Dworkin 2000: 110–12, 1983).

3. I am very sceptical about this position, since this would involve self-selection bias. Those who do not need government services (the wealthy) are those who have the power to move to lower tax jurisdictions and thus reduce their taxation, while those with greater need will generally have little or no ability to choose a society with higher taxes and services.

4. Some have questioned whether this process really does threaten the welfare-state in advanced countries, utilising statistics that show no collapse in tax revenues during the first thirty or so years of globalised corporations (Swank 2002: 252–57; Hobson 2003). This of course does not include the effects of tax competition and avoidance on less developed countries, and the shift to a greater tax burden from the super-rich to everyone else in more developed countries (Swank 2002: 256–57 n14). Furthermore, the analysis also pre-dates the fall-out from the on-going financial crises of recent years, the boom of which no doubt increased tax revenues.

5. Such argument, with its policy implications, is made in (Dietsch and Rixen 2012), applying the arguments of (Ronzoni 2009).

6. This notion of moral tax avoidance is no doubt contentious. However, I think some who would reject the terminology may be able to find something acceptable in the

underlying thought, though disagree with this form of expression. Possible bases for such a position would be that people 'are not to gain from the cooperative efforts of others without doing our fair share' (Rawls 1999a: 301), that people have responsibility to those in their community (Miller 2001), or that people should contribute an appropriate amount to their community (White 2003: Ch 3)

7. For a summary of the options available to states, see Evans (2009).

8. Though this is confused where we consider the case of families, which are a valid tax base, but not individual persons.

9. See for example Rawls 1999a; Dworkin 2000; Cohen 2008.

10. For more on progressive taxation see for example Musgrave (2002) and Paolo Ermano's chapter in this volume.

11. For recent discussion on this issue see Schlunk (2006); Zelenak (2009).

12. By threshold effects I mean that an otherwise arbitrary threshold (i.e., a tax year), will produce an incentive to take an action that the individual would not have otherwise had any reason to make (Vickrey 1972: 165).

13. This would include spending a portion of time in a country, though not including a short holiday or business trip.

14. With a lifetime taxation approach, the Simons view effectively becomes a consumption tax with gifts to others counted as a form of consumption, similar in form to the one proposed by (Andrews 1974).

15. For a review of the recent discussions and relevant empirical data on this issue, see Auerbach (2009:147–65); also Bird and Mintz (2003: 422–23).

16. For an argument about this from the consumption tax angle see Musgrave (2000).

17. Led since the 1960s by Peggy Musgrave (see for example Musgrave 2006: 173–78).

18. Nancy Kaufman counts citizenship as a further base, though it is rarely used and usually associated with the United States (Kaufman 1998: 148, 189–94). The problem with the utilisation of a citizenship tax base is that tax competition would be accompanied by citizenship competition. The wealthy and powerful could shop around and remove themselves from obligations to those with which they previously had an economic relationship. Poorer countries will tend to lose out as their citizenship is less valuable. A global citizenship-based tax would do nothing to improve inter-individual and inter-nation fairness and nor would it counteract problems such as brain drain.

19. The requirement for a supranational body to deal with tax issues is also discussed in Avi-Yonah (2000: 1676).

20. More powerful states could attempt to bring fairness about, though it would be complicated given the number of treaties it would involve. However, even such an attempt would probably be undermined by tax-haven states.

21. One question that may arise at this point is whether the same principle should be applied for labour income. That is, should the workers for a multinational company have their income apportioned according to the nationality of its investors and consumers? There is a case to say this should be done, but I do not think it is as important as it is in the case of investment returns. After all, a company can change its headquarters relatively easily as a response to taxes, but decisions about the location of employees are much more likely to be based on straightforward economic motivations.

22. There would need to be a broadly common approach to defining income, otherwise people would attempt to realise different kinds of income in different jurisdictions.

23. This is straightforward where the countries take a lifetime approach to taxation. However, if the states have an annual approach to taxation it is still possible to calculate

what they would have paid on their income for each year had they earned it solely within the country in question, and then calculate the total tax paid over the course of the years as a percentage of lifetime income.

24. Excluding any other taxes and charges, such as Pigovian 'sin' taxes.

25. For a sample of the extensive debate on global justice in political philosophy, see (Rawls 1999b; Nagel 2005; Julius 2006; Caney 2006; Ronzoni 2009; Brown 2009). This debate is about the justice relations that hold between individuals across borders. Since this proposal focuses on international citizens, who themselves have cross-border relationships, it is entirely compatible with position that direct distributive justice relations stop at the border (a view held by Nationalist, Rawlsian, or Nagelian inspired thinkers). If the more cosmopolitan position is taken, then redistributing tax revenues on international citizens only may or may not provide adequate means to achieve full international justice, though this proposal would no doubt be an improvement on the status quo from this perspective.

26. An international tax organisation is mentioned by Tanzi (1999: 181–85), who also suggests it could administer a Tobin tax, possibly to provide revenue for global goods, and seek to limit tax competition. My proposal limits tax competition through the use of tax rate weightings in the allocation of revenue. The possible future necessity for a global tax organisation is mentioned in Avi-Yonah (2000: 1675–76); Musgrave (2006: 182).

27. Such as limits on the proportion of budget that can be spent on military activities in order to avoid wasteful arms proliferation.

28. For example by comparing the economic activity within the country and its trade balance with the reported income for international citizens.

29. An alternative is that foreign investors should be attracted by making sure that they pay the same tax that they would if they invested at home (Capital Import Neutrality).

30. I find equity based arguments inadequate in terms of justice, for reasons outlined in (Murphy and Nagel 2002: Ch 2).

31. For the relation to international equity see also Kaufman (1998: 156–63, 167–82).

32. For an overview of the Musgraves' contributions see Brooks (2009: 473–80).

33. If the resident country has a higher tax rate than the source country, they may tax the foreign income while allowing a deduction or tax credit for the tax paid abroad to avoid double taxation. In this case, the source country still takes on the right to tax all of the income, although the resident country takes the additional tax required to raise the individual's tax rate to the domestic tax level.

CHAPTER 12

Tax Justice through Country-by-Country Reporting

An Analysis of the Idea's Political Journey

DRIES LESAGE AND YUSUF KAÇAR

Introduction

This chapter analyses the political journey of the idea of 'country-by-country reporting' as a new financial reporting standard for multinational corporations (MNCs). Proponents believe that financial reporting on a country-by-country basis, among other things, will enhance MNCs' compliance with tax laws, thus furthering tax justice. Given the huge interests at stake, the journey the idea has made through the institutions thus far is quite remarkable and successful. It started with an idea of few committed and specialised individuals in the United Kingdom (UK). Now, it is seriously discussed at a high level within international forums such as the European Union (EU), the Organisation for Economic Cooperation and Development (OECD), the International Monetary Fund (IMF) and the World Bank. However, fully fledged country-by-country reporting on a mandatory basis has not been adopted yet by any international organisation or national government.

The chapter will try to explain the idea's relative success thus far, as well as the obstacles it continues to meet. In due course, it will point to certain political mechanisms that propel its progress, but at the same time risk containing and isolating it from the mainstream of policy making with regard to financial reporting and taxation of MNCs. A third objective of the chapter is to reflect on prospects. In general, we hope that this explorative case study can be a contribution to the study of the creation of international norms and the roles of transnational advocacy networks. There will also be connections to political questions such as the compartmentalisation between issue-areas and their concomitant bureaucracies and international regimes, as well as the significance of crisis for change in the international political economy.

The chapter will proceed as follows. In the first section the concept of country-by-country will be introduced. Next, arguments of advocates and opponents are presented. Subsequently, we provide an analysis of the idea's political journey until now. Then we move on to an analysis of facilitating factors and obstacles. We conclude with some reflections on prospects and ways to move forward this campaign which we find worth endorsing from a normative point of view.

What is Country-by-Country Reporting?

Country-by-country reporting is meant to be a new financial reporting duty for MNCs. In their annual public financial statements, companies would have to report, by country, the following items: the company names under which the group operates; sales, purchases and financial costs, split between third parties and intra-group transactions; labour costs and employee numbers; pre-tax profit; several details about assets; several details about taxes (paid and due) and other payments to the government (Murphy 2009a, b). The level of detail on each item or the possible addition of other items is open for discussion. Correct compliance with this new reporting duty – as is the case with the existing ones as well – is enhanced by the fact that firms' accountants and auditors are supposed to deliver correct data and that fraud in this matter is susceptible to prosecution.

It is important to note that this chapter focuses on the above described comprehensive form of country-by-country reporting, i.e., reporting of taxes and other payments to the government, but also the underlying economic data (sales, purchases, financial costs, profits, etc.) that lead to these tax duties. These additional data are necessary to assess more accurately whether and to what degree the amount of taxes paid corresponds to a reasonable application of the tax laws and to economic reality. This form should not be confused with the more minimalist notion of mere 'publish what you pay' reporting requirements, which only comprise taxes and other payments to the government. Moreover, we focus on a country-by-country standard for *all* sectors. This notion of country-by-country reporting (with all relevant data and for all sectors) will throughout this chapter be referred to as the 'maximalist' form of country-by-country reporting.

Under current international and national financial reporting standards, multinational groups are not obliged to report per country. MNCs are merely supposed to provide a rudimentary form of 'segment reporting', i.e., reporting on the basis of product divisions within the group ('food', 'cosmetics', etc.) and/or region ('Europe', 'North America', etc.). Each country can operate its own financial reporting standards. However, more than one hundred countries require or permit the International Financial Reporting Standards (IFRS) of the International Accounting Standards Board (IASB), the main international regulatory body in this field. Since 2005, the IASB IFRSs are obligatory for the consolidated financial statements of EU companies which are listed in the EU's stock markets. The United States (US), though, has its own standards, issued by its Financial Accounting Standards Board (FASB). However, a convergence effort is underway. Proponents of country-by-country reporting would like to amend the existing standards. One concrete avenue is to amend the IASB's 'IFRS 8', which deals with segment reporting; thus it would easily find its way into many national regulations as well. This does not exclude, however, that action is also taken directly vis-à-vis national governments, including the US, and the EU. In addition, country-by-country requirements can also be imposed outside the framework of IFRS.

Arguments for and against Country-by-Country Reporting

Pro: Financial Transparency and Tax Justice

The basic idea is that country-by-country data would entail an interesting dynamic by exposing MNCs' financial strategies to more intense public scrutiny. Several constituencies would benefit from it. For the financial markets – for whom financial statements are basically meant, according to the private sector – data by country provide insight into a multinational group's country-specific investment risks. It is, for example, useful to know whether the company has significant activities in politically unstable countries. By extension, presence in certain countries can also be susceptible to reputational risks (e.g., by getting involved in corruption or tax scandals).

Local communities, civil society and media, in their turn, might be interested in MNCs' contributions to the public treasury. In some cases it will become clear that certain companies pay conspicuously few taxes. In others, when informed about the payments to the government that have actually been made, people may ask questions about the spending of that money (e.g., has it been spent in the public interest or disappeared into the pockets of a kleptocratic elite?). In still other cases, country-by-country reporting can help to hold the government to account with regard to its corporate taxation policies. Some countries apply, for example, quite generous special tax schemes for companies, operate an opaque 'ruling' regime that allows MNEs and tax authorities to strike deals on complex tax issues in advance, and/or have poor enforcement mechanisms. Through country-by-country reporting the budgetary impact of such policies would become more visible to the public (as well as to other governments).

Other potential beneficiaries are tax authorities. Country-by-country data would disclose part of the international tax planning strategies of multinationals. Imagine an MNC with high levels of production, sales and employees, but very low profits in a particular jurisdiction. At the same time, for its subsidiaries in tax havens it reports huge profits, little employment and almost no taxes paid. Together with data on intra-firm trade and financial costs, this information could be indicative of aggressive tax planning strategies and transfer price manipulation (i.e. setting prices for cross-border trade within the multinational group in an artificial way in order to allow profits to be shifted to a low-tax jurisdiction). These indications would then warrant further inquiry.

In March 2011 we interviewed by telephone, on the condition of anonymity, three Belgian and three Turkish senior tax officials, charged with the taxation of MNCs. These interviews served a merely explorative purpose, without any further methodological pretentions. We asked them a) whether and how country-by-country disclosure as a new financial reporting standard could provide value-added for the national tax authorities, b) whether public financial statements of MNCs are frequently used for taxation purposes, and c) whether they had ever heard of this proposal. The answers showed a remarkable level of agreement. The response to the first question was markedly positive in all cases. Both countries already apply sophisticated instruments to control transfer price manipulation, e.g. through documentation requirements for MNCs with regard to transfer pricing information. This documentation can be inspected in case of suspicion. Yet tax officials say that financial reporting by country would be helpful in order to discover certain patterns that would justify deeper investigation. Such reporting would also provide a better picture of the economic reality of the multinational group, including holding structures. In certain cases it can be interesting to get additional data on the economic substance of overseas subsidiaries with which important volumes of intra-firm trade have taken place. To sum up, country-by-country could effectively provide information that is very difficult or even impossible to obtain by other means. Furthermore, a mandatory requirement to publish information on intra-firm trade and other elements by country is an extra safeguard for the accuracy of tax statements. As to the second question, the use of public financial statements for taxation matters is not a common practice in the tax administrations, although specialised services use them in specific circumstances. We believe country-by-country reporting could increase this usage. Concerning the third question, none of our six interviewees had ever heard of this campaign, which indicates that its support base has considerable growth potential.

Finally, through country-by-country reporting, governments, international organisations and economists will have more possibilities to monitor certain trends, on the basis of which statistics (e.g., on intra-firm trade) and tax policy making can be improved (Murphy 2009b: 16). In sum, more transparency as such will not bring about a larger tax contribution from MNCs, but it is likely to engender multiple pressures and self-discipline.

Contra: Compliance Costs, Competition and Confidentiality Concerns

Opponents claim that country-by-country reporting will entail huge compliance costs. In their structure and operations MNCs do not always follow a country-wise logic. Therefore, this new reporting duty would increase accounting and auditing costs. Then there is the question as to whether the benefits outweigh the costs and disadvantages. First, the financial markets are said to be little, if at all, interested in information by country. Many people in the private sector and the accounting industry uphold the idea that financial reports are exclusively aimed at the capital providers and not at other stakeholders. Second, there are competitiveness issues involved. A recurring argument is that it would not be a good idea if European companies incurred higher costs and other major inconveniences because of country-by-country reporting, while competitors from, for example, the BRIC countries are exempted. Third, spokespeople from the business sector express confidentiality concerns. In certain cases, financial information by country implies disclosing business secrets. It reveals the financial health of operations in a particular country. It is also argued that particular host governments strongly dislike and (by contract) even forbid the disclosure of payments to the government, for example, in the case of extractive industries. Such reporting could jeopardise assets and future investment opportunities. Fourth, the private sector fears that financial information by country will be taken out of context, oversimplified and misinterpreted by the public and NGOs, which could unduly harm companies. Fifth, it is claimed that tax authorities have already enough instruments at their disposal to calculate the tax duties of MNCs (see, e.g., Business Europe 2010; Confederation of British Industry 2010; Mouvement des Entreprises de France 2010; PricewaterhouseCoopers 2010a; IASB 2010; Bundesverband der Deutschen Industrie 2011).

The Idea's Journey
Civil Society

The comprehensive notion of country-by-country reporting was first put forward by the British chartered accountant Richard Murphy in a 2003 paper (Murphy 2003). Murphy is director of Tax Research LLP and co-founder of the Tax Justice Network (TJN), a UK-based global civil society network of organisations and individuals. Not much later, through the work of TJN, it was picked up by other organisations, including well-known development charities such as Oxfam, Christian Aid, Action Aid, CCFD Terre Solidaire, as well as network organisations such as Eurodad (see their respective websites). Now, country-by-country reporting has become a priority in the campaigns and lobbying of these organisations. This trend is part of the growing awareness within civil society about the relationship between taxation and development. TJN, the most specialised organisation in this field, has played a crucial role in this evolution. Yet although sensitivity to tax issues is becoming mainstream within the global anti-poverty movement, only a minority of organisations explicitly focus on it.

The concept of country-by-country reporting has received support from another, very powerful strand of civil society activity, notably the debate about the financial contributions of the extractive industries (oil, gas and mining) to the authorities of developing countries. These concerns were crystallised in the international Publish What You Pay coalition (PWYP) from 2002 onwards. The London-based PWYP has now more than six hundred member organisations across the world. The coalition 'aims to require full transparency in the payment, receipt and management of natural resource revenues; public disclosure of extractive contracts; and civil society participation in the monitoring of revenue expenditures'. Although its agenda is broader than that, at the heart of the PWYP campaign has always been the mandatory disclosure by companies of their payments 'to governments in taxes, fees, royalties, bonuses and other financial transactions for every country of operation'. PWYP considers national and international accounting standards as an important instrument to achieve this (van Oranje and Parham 2009: 28). In 2006 PWYP was at the forefront of a campaign to lobby the IASB to adopt a provision on country-by-country reporting in its indicative international accounting standards. The occasion was an IASB public consultation with a view to the development of a new standard with regard to segment reporting (IFRS 8). Founding members of the PWYP campaign, notably Global Witness, Save the Children, Care, Cafod, Transparency International and Open Society Institute, cooperated with TJN's Richard Murphy to submit an elaborate proposal on country-by-country reporting. According to van Oranje and Parham 'never before had the IASB been lobbied so extensively by civil society' (2009: 81). Interestingly, the submission was based on a maximalist conception of country-by-country reporting; it was intended for all sectors and would require not only disclosure of payments to the government, but also the underlying base data (turnover, profits, etc.) (Global Witness et al. 2005). Even though the focus of PWYP is on the extractive industries and reporting of payments to governments, it continues to be supportive to the maximalist approach. In its 2010 submission in response to a public consultation of the European Commission, it states: 'Our submission focuses on the extractives sector since this is the area of competence of the Publish What You Pay network. However, it should be noted that we believe the rationale for Country-by-Country reporting requirements is equally applicable to all other sectors' (PWYP 2010).

Still another entry point to country-by-country reporting is the concern about illicit financial flows. This category not only comprises criminal and corrupt money, but also tax fraud, including trade mis-pricing and mis-invoicing by MNCs. A key civil society player in this field is Global Financial Integrity (GFI), based in Washington DC. GFI strongly endorses the maximalist version of country-by-country reporting (GFI 2009). In late 2008, GFI was chosen to host the Task Force on Financial Integrity and Economic Development. The Task Force is an offspring of the Leading Group on Innovative Financing of Development.[1] The Leading Group, headquartered in Paris, is a multi-stakeholder partnership consisting of sixty-three member states, a number of multilateral organisations (such as the UN, IMF, World Bank and OECD), non-governmental organisations and the Gates Foundation. It is also known for its work on the air ticket levy, research and debate on a financial transaction tax, and alternative financing mechanisms for medical drugs. The Task Force resulted from a working group within the Leading Group on illicit financial flows led by Norway, in which organisations such as GFI and TJN were actively involved. Now, the Washington-based Task Force comprises the following organisations: Christian Aid, Eurodad, GFI, Global Witness, TJN, Tax Research LLP, Transparency International and the secretariat of the Leading Group.[2] Given this composition, it is no surprise that the Task Force has put forward the maximalist version of country-by-country reporting as one of its priorities. As such, the Task Force provides an additional platform for the global lobbying campaign. In June 2009, it published a comprehensive and authoritative report on the matter (Murphy 2009b). Finally, growing interest for the idea is evident within the labour movement. The UK's Trade Union Congress (TUC) (2010) and the German Deutscher Gewerkschaftsbund (DGB) (2010) are strongly in favour of a maximalist form of country-by-country reporting.

In sum, the idea of country-by-country reporting has mainly been propelled by civil society organisations. This happened basically from four different angles: 1) a general concern about tax justice in advanced and developing countries alike (TJN and trade unions); 2) taxation as a domestic resource for development finance (the development NGOs); 3) having the extractive industries contribute their fair share to the public revenues of developing countries (the PWYP campaign and related groups); and 4) illicit financial flows (GFI and Task Force on Financial Integrity and Economic Development). In all four sectors, TJN as the most specialised player has always been strongly involved, especially when it came to putting forward country-by-country reporting as a new international financial reporting standard.

National Authorities

One of the biggest successes of the country-by-country movement thus far is new legislation in the United States. A 'publish what you pay' provision was adopted in the famous July 2010 Dodd–Frank Wall Street Reform and Consumer Protection Act,[3] which came about in response to the global financial crisis. The act was preceded by two years of public hearings. It must be clear, however, that this act is not about a maximalist approach to country-by-country reporting. It only requires oil, gas and mine companies to publish what they pay to the US and foreign governments. Yet it can be considered as a landmark achievement, as the US is one of the first countries – and immediately a great power – enacting country-by-country legislation. In a separate statement, the White House said:

> This provision is an essential new tool in promoting transparency in the oil and mineral sectors. This legislation will immediately shed light on billions in payments between multinational corporations and governments, giving citizens the information they need to monitor companies and to hold governments accountable . . . The challenge for us now is to make this a global standard. The United States is committed to working with other countries to ensure the implementation of similar disclosure requirements in other financial markets and will make this a priority in the year ahead. (White House 2010)

At the time of writing, the US Securities and Exchange Commission (SEC) is drafting the modalities for implementation. In May 2010, the Hong Kong Stock Exchange had already adopted similar rules.[4]

Shortly after the release of the June 2009 report of the Task Force on Financial Integrity and Economic Development, the UK's Financial Secretary to the Treasury, Stephen Timms (Labour), announced a proposal of country-by-country reporting at an international gathering of finance ministers in Berlin. This meeting took place on 22–23 June 2009. This was a conference of ministers and senior officials of nineteen OECD countries to assess progress with regard to the implementation of the OECD standard on transparency and exchange of information in tax matters. After the meeting, Timms was said to have 'received strong support from a number of countries including Norway, Sweden, Belgium and Korea' (Mathiason 2009). The ministerial gathering in Berlin was a follow-up meeting to the October 2008 meeting of this ad hoc group, which was convened on the initiative of the French Minister for the Budget, Eric Woerth, and the German Minister of Finance, Peer Steinbrück. These meetings received informal support from the OECD secretariat, of which the presence of OECD top officials and featuring on the OECD website are indications. The official conclusions of the Berlin meeting, though, did not mention the idea of country-by-country reporting.[5] Britain was soon joined by France, at least for mere consideration of the idea. In a declaration concerning global governance and a follow-up to the G20, issued after the thirtieth France–UK summit in Evian on 6 July 2009, the French President Nicolas Sarkozy and British Prime Minister Gordon Brown stated: 'We also call on the OECD to look at country by country reporting and the benefits of this for tax transparency and reducing tax avoidance'.[6] In late 2009, the French government introduced a requirement for banks to report in an annex to their annual financial reports the names of their branches and subsidiaries in tax havens and some other data,[7] however none of the other data as promoted under the maximalist version of country-by-country reporting are required.

With the advent of the new coalition government of Conservatives and Liberal Democrats in the UK, the momentum for full country-by-country reporting faded somewhat. However, before the elections, Vince Cable, Liberal Democrat and now Business Secretary in the government of David Cameron, wrote: 'New accounting standards are also needed to force multi-national companies to declare publicly the profits they make, and the taxes they pay, in every country in which they operate. That way anomalies would be quickly spotted' (Cable 2009). However, at this point there are no signs that Liberal Democrats are pushing for a maximalist form of financial reporting by country. In March 2011, Caroline Lucas of the Green Party introduced the first bill on country-by-country reporting in the UK House of Commons, and in early 2011, new momentum for 'publish what you pay' provisions for the extractive industries reemerged. In a letter in response to an open letter from Bono, President Sarkozy announced that he would call upon the European Commission to draft EU legislation in this sense (Sarkozy 2011). The idea was soon backed by the UK (Stewart 2011), Germany (MacNamara and Thompson 2011) and European institutions (see below).

Finally, national regulatory bodies, such as the French and British official accounting standard setters, are open to the idea of full country-by-country reporting, but question whether financial statements and the IFRS context are the right place to provide this kind of information. If policy makers want to push this through, they suggest other publication channels (Accounting Standards Board 2010; Autorité des Normes Comptables 2010).

European Union (EU)

Maximalist and minimalist versions are gradually gaining ground within EU institutions. In various contexts, the European Parliament has adopted resolutions in favour of country-by-country reporting. In response to a Commission draft regulation on IFRS 8 (segment reporting), it made a case for country-by-country reporting in general, and explicitly requested a mandatory provision for extractive industries (European Parliament 2007). In a 2008 resolution with regard to the follow-up to the UN Monterrey Conference of 2002 on financing for development, the European Parliament called on 'the Commission to ask the International Accounting Standards Board (IASB) to include among these international accounting standards a country-by-country reporting requirement on the activities of multinational companies *in all sectors*' (European Parliament 2008, our italics). Ever since, the European Parliament continued to grasp each opportunity to adopt the language of country-by-country reporting. In a 2010 resolution on promoting good governance in tax matters, it stressed 'the need to revise current international accounting standards with the aim of increasing transparency [and called] in this regard for a requirement for the disclosure in companies' annual accounts, on a country-by-country basis, of accounting information relating to tax havens' (European Parliament 2010a). In another 2010 resolution, this time on the effects of the global financial and economic crisis on developing countries and on development cooperation, it asked the Commission to report 'how country-by-country reporting on profits and taxes paid can become a rule for transnational companies in the EU'. It continued by noting:

> that half of all illicit financial flows out of developing countries are related to the mis-pricing of trade and [reinforced] its call for a new, binding, global financial agreement which forces transnational corporations, including their various subsidiaries, automatically to disclose profits made and taxes paid, on a country-by-country basis, so as to ensure transparency about sales, profits and taxes in every jurisdiction where they are located. (European Parliament 2010b)

In yet another 2010 resolution, on the Millennium Development Goals, it called 'on all the Member States actively to crack down on tax havens, tax evasion and illicit financial flows, within the G20 and UN framework, and to promote greater transparency, including systematic disclosure of profits made and taxes paid and a country-by-country reporting system to enable developing countries to keep their own resources for their development' (European Parliament 2010c).

Further momentum built up in the first half of 2011. In a resolution on cooperating with developing countries on promoting good governance in tax matters, the European Parliament explicitly called upon the Commission to integrate a comprehensive form of country-by-country reporting for all MNCs in its reform of accounting directives and to propose the same to the IASB. The Commission was requested to report on these efforts within the next six months. The Parliament further sent messages to the UN, G20, OECD and IASB in this regard (European Parliament 2011). In sum, what we see here is a persistent majority in the European Parliament calling for a maximalist version of country-by-country reporting. This parliamentary momentum, though, cannot be translated into binding EU legislation automatically. Under current EU rules, the IASB should first adopt this change in its IFRSs and subsequently the EU institutions should endorse it. Of course, the EU can make proposals to the IASB. Another possibility, though, is that the EU decides to adopt a country-by-country reporting requirement outside this framework.

The European Commission, for its part, has not yet explicitly endorsed the maximalist country-by-country approach. However, it is showing more openness to the idea. In April 2010 the European Commission released a communication to the Parliament, Council and Economic and Social Committee on tax and development. In that communication the Commission signalled growing interest in the concept of country-by-country reporting, and endorsed the ongoing work of the IASB and OECD in this field (European Commission 2010f). Meanwhile, civil society organisations are attempting to insert the maximalist country-by-country standard into the ongoing revision of the EU's directive 'on the harmonisation of transparency requirements in relation to information about issuers whose securities are admitted to trading on a regulated market' (Tax Research LLP and Tax Justice Network 2010). According to Eurodad, the Commission also plans to revise the EU directives on annual and consolidated accounts (the so-called Fourth and Seventh Directive), another opportunity to influence the agenda (Molina and Romero 2011). This entry point is a way to circumvent the IASB, as these directives deal with more foundational aspects than the concrete IFRSs. In the framework of these efforts, in late 2010 the European Commission for the first time held a public consultation explicitly and exclusively on financial reporting on a country-by-country basis by MNCs.[8] This was probably in response to growing interest among member states and in the European Parliament. The consultation generated a number of interesting comments from business and the accounting industry (along with civil society and regulators) to which we refer elsewhere in the text. Legislative proposals from the Commission are expected later in 2011.

On 14 June 2010 the EU Council of Foreign Affairs – in its configuration of development ministers – welcomed the communication of the European Commission. In its conclusions it paid special attention to country-by-country reporting. Just like the Commission, it encouraged the OECD and IASB to continue their work. Importantly, unlike the Commission, the ministers also encouraged the IASB to look beyond the extractive sector (Council of the European Union 2010). These remarks did not imply an explicit endorsement of the maximalist approach yet.

In contrast, a major development at Council level was the conclusions of the Competitiveness Council of 10 March 2011, inviting 'the Commission to come forward with initiatives, in consultation with Member States and relevant stakeholders, on the disclosure of financial information by companies working in the extractive industry, including the possible adoption of a country-by-country reporting requirement [and] International Financial Reporting Standards (IFRS) for the extractive industry' (Council of the European Union 2011). What we have here is a political endorsement by the EU ministers of a European version of the US Dodd–Frank Act, which makes its adoption at EU level very realistic. Momentum had already been built up through the support of the British, French and German governments for an initiative for the extractive industry. It is unclear yet whether this EU legislation will require the reporting of more data than payments to the government. The EU Internal Market Commissioner, Michel Barnier, has already indicated that in the upcoming Commission proposal only payments to governments will be covered (like Dodd–Frank), and that country-by-country reporting will be required instead of the more detailed project-by-project approach (Tait 2011).

Organisation for Economic Cooperation and Development (OECD)

In January 2010, the Committee on Fiscal Affairs (CFA) and the Development Assistance Committee (DAC) of the OECD decided to set up an informal Task Force on Tax and Development.[9] The Task Force includes representatives from all stakeholders, notably the OECD, emerging and developing countries, international organisations, civil society and business. Interestingly, these stakeholders can decide jointly on the course to follow. The group is to feed the work of the DAC and CFA and their respective administrative departments. This initiative forms part of the interest the OECD has already been displaying for a few years with regard to the development dimension of taxation, and more precisely globalisation-related issues such as international tax evasion and tax havens. About the same time as the launch of the OECD Task Force, the OECD secretariat published a paper on domestic resource mobilisation, taxation and development. Having referred to the request from the July 2009 France–UK Summit, the paper discussed the pros and cons of country-by-country reporting without taking position (OECD 2010c). The conclusions of the May 2010 OECD Council meeting at ministerial level 'acknowledge the urgent need for progress in the field of tax and development', but do not mention country-by-country reporting.[10] In May 2010, at its first meeting, the OECD Task Force on Tax and Development created three subgroups, with one charged with a study of country-by-country reporting. This sub-group is due to develop a 'scoping paper' for the next Task Force meeting in 2011. The Task Force has opted to consider country-by-country reporting in the framework of the non-binding OECD Guidelines for Multinational Enterprises, governed by the OECD Investment Committee.[11] An earlier idea of exploring country-by-country reporting in the framework of the OECD Principles of Corporate Governance (OECD 2010c: 31) seems not to have been retained. Thus, at the time of writing, the OECD has not yet endorsed country-by-country reporting – far from it. If the OECD comes to adopt it, this will likely occur within the framework of the non-binding guidelines for multinationals. In that case, it would apply to all multinationals in North and South, be it under a non-binding instrument.

International Accounting Standards Board (IASB)

The IASB – the central player at international level in this field – is unlikely to move on country-by-country reporting in the near future. After the civil society campaign on IFRS 8 (segment reporting) in 2006, it did not adopt a country-by-country standard. However, in a discussion paper with a view to a possible revision of IFRS 6 (extractive industries), it explicitly considered the proposal of the PWYP campaign. Under this proposal, data by country should be disclosed on payments to the government, reserve volumes, production volumes, production revenues, costs, as well as the names and locations of each key subsidiary and property – a comprehensive form of country-by-country reporting. The paper, which was drafted by a team consisting of staff members from the standard-setting bodies of Australia, Canada, Norway and South Africa, contains the results of a consultation with an advisory panel, consisting of representatives from the extractive industry, auditors, users (financial investors) and regulators (no civil society).[12] After its release, the discussion paper was made subject to a public consultation. The authors stick to the view that financial statements are intended for capital providers and not for the broader society. Partly based on this perspective, they reject the proposal to report data other than payments to the government on a country-by-country basis. With regard to such payments, they conclude that further study is required to assess whether a mandatory standard is justifiable on cost-benefit grounds (IASB 2010). In 2011 the IASB will decide how to proceed with the idea of reviewing IFRS 6. For the time being, there are no indications that the IASB is considering comprehensive country-by-country reporting for all sectors or is seeking to stimulate a debate about it.

International Financial Institutions and G20

In its reaction to the IASB Discussion Paper on Extractive Industries, the World Bank warmly supports the comprehensive PWYP proposals. The Bank also criticises the IASB's too narrow scope with regard to the societal relevance of IFRSs (World Bank 2010). As to the IMF, an important March 2011 paper on revenue mobilisation in developing countries – prepared for the Executive Board – mentions the idea of country-by-country reporting. It rightly states that the aims of the idea are dual: 'to promote accountability of governments for the revenues they raise; and to promote public transparency in the taxes paid by enterprises, permitting, it is hoped, the policing of transfer pricing abuses'. Along with some sceptical remarks about its value-added, it concludes by saying that further study and discussion are needed (IMF 2011: 43–44).

At the time of writing, country-by-country reporting is not yet on the official agenda of the G20. However, the G20 has already engaged in debates on international accounting standards. At its June 2010 Toronto summit, it urged the acceleration of the convergence process between the IASB and FASB. It also called upon the IASB to improve its involvement with 'stakeholders', without specifying which ones exactly (G20 2010: Paragraphs 30–31). In fact, this could also imply being more responsive to that part of civil society demanding country-by-country reporting. In February 2011, the UK Chancellor of the Exchequer George Osborne, echoing a proposal by the French President Nicolas Sarkozy, reportedly spoke out in favour of a 'publish what you pay' standard for the extractive industry at a meeting of G20 finance ministers in Paris (Stewart 2011). A reference to the US and European moves or even more in this regard is likely to appear in the conclusions of the November 2011 G20 summit in Cannes, also given the fact that commodity markets are prominently on the agenda there.

Media

A few international media outlets, such as *The Guardian*, cover the debate on country-by-country reporting systematically. *The Guardian* does so in a supportive way. For a few years, the *Financial Times* (FT) has also started following it. Sympathy also seems to be growing. In a remarkable editorial piece, the newspaper holds governments responsible for corporate tax avoidance. The FT strongly supports the adoption of Dodd–Frank-like legislation in the EU for the extractive industries. The text does not go into details about what form of country-by-country reporting would be desirable. But it is clear that the FT believes in the merits of country-by-country reporting, also beyond the extractive industries in developing countries:

> Civil society groups think such reporting will unveil tax avoidance undermining developing countries' tax revenues. In fact, the greater impact may be to expose the scandalous tax treatment of multinationals in the rich world. Current practice turns corporate tax largely into a voluntary gesture by the well-run multinational, whose methods of choice for locating income in lower-taxed jurisdictions are intragroup financial links and transfer pricing of intangibles such as intellectual property. As finance and intangibles grow in importance, so will the slipperiness of the corporate tax base. (Financial Times Editorial 2010)

This quote is another indication of MNCs' tax practices coming under increasing pressure.

Private Sector

Information about how the private sector thinks about country-by-country reporting can be derived from responses of employers' federations and accounting industry representatives to the IASB's and European Commission's public consultations. The business sector itself utterly rejects the idea (see, e.g., Business Europe 2010; Confederation of British Industry 2010; Mouvement des Entreprises de France 2010; Bundesverband der Deutschen Industrie 2011). The accounting and auditing industry, for its part, is equally negative across the board, at least for the time being. It usually refers to the same set of counter-arguments. However, this industry is in a different position than the rest of the private sector. In fact, heavier reporting requirements for MNCs would generate more business for them. But as good defenders of their clients, no big accounting firm is going to advocate country-by-country reporting – very much to the contrary.

However, if we take for example the December 2010 answer of Deloitte to the public consultation of the European Commission, we find a more nuanced view. The letter comes from a spokesman 'on behalf of European Economic Area member firms of Deloitte Touche Tohmatsu Limited'. Overall, Deloitte's approach is clearly sceptical and negative. The firm recalls that, according to the IASB, financial reports are intended for capital providers, and strongly doubts whether the costs will outweigh the benefits. But it acknowledges the 'increasing request from governments and NGOs' and encourages the European Commission 'to investigate the most appropriate way to respond to the demand for such increased transparency'. Notwithstanding all its reservations, it suggests that, if policy makers were to proceed with it, country-by-country information could be 'located either in a section of the annual financial report outside the financial statements or as part of a completely separate report'. Questioning whether the European Commission should play the leading role in taking forward this project, Deloitte recommends that it liaise with the IASB and national standard-setters on the need for country-by-country reporting, and also suggests than the planned post-implementation review of IFRS 8 (segment reporting) might be a good occasion to have this debate. Anyway, it would be good that the IASB comes up with an appropriate framework for MNCs that would like to provide this information voluntarily, so that MNCs have a standardised format that results in 'information that corresponds to the objectives sought by the various stakeholders. It would also render the information more useful by increasing comparability between those entities that decide to present this information' (Deloitte 2010). Despite all the caveats in the text, it is hard to read this as outright and unambiguous rejection.

Explanations for the Relative Success Thus Far

All in all, we can say that over this period of about eight years the maximalist notion of country-by-country reporting has made considerable progress. It is seriously on the table of the EU, OECD, IMF and World Bank. This is even more so for the 'publish what you pay' approach for the extractive industries, which has been translated into law in the US, while legislative activity in the EU is underway. To discuss the explanatory factors, we will make a distinction between the ideational and institutional sphere. Drawing from neo-Gramscian thought (Bieler and Morton 2004), we believe that the latter two are possible sites for social change, which can also affect material relations in the end.

Ideas

As was already mentioned above, the movement for country-by-country reporting is built on four different strands: 1) the generalist tax justice movement, 2) the development community's growing interest in the tax–development nexus, 3) the concerns about the ethics and social contributions of the extractive industry, and 4) the fight against illicit financial flows. It is interesting to see the concurrence of these four strands on a maximalist version of country-by-country reporting. Although there is a diversity in the focus and priorities linked to the functional missions of the respective organisations, there are no serious division or de-solidarisation between them with regard to country-by-country reporting. This is demonstrated by the various instances of close cooperation between organisations across the four movements and the repeated support for the full option. This way, the diversity of entry points to the debate is turning out to be a great strength.

All four currents have been spurred by societal developments over the last decade, such as the growing visibility of the dark sides of globalisation (illicit financial flows, tax havens), the project of the Millennium Development Goals and the UN process 'Financing for Development', the eruption of a series of highly mediatised tax scandals (often involving tax havens such as Liechtenstein and Switzerland), and of course the 2007–2009 global financial crisis. Extractive industries, big banks and other MNCs have come under increasing scrutiny and pressure to be transparent with regard to their financial operations and to pay their fair share in taxes. Another strength of the country-by-country movement is that it builds on the public call for greater transparency of powerful entities such as multinationals. This is a theme that can bind people together across the political spectrum. Transparency in financial and tax matters and policies against tax fraud – the lenses through which this campaign is basically framed – are, for example, not necessarily incompatible with neoliberal approaches. Certainly, certain neoliberal forces will oppose it, as they want to avoid an uncontrollable debate about the tax burden on multinational capital or prioritise private capital's right to keep secrets. But they will have a relatively hard time explaining what is wrong with powerful economic players being more transparent. Finally, the widespread controversy about extractive industries in developing countries forms a rather simple and effective frame to illustrate the usefulness of this project. Recently, large banks have joined the league of highly criticised multinationals (Task Force on Financial Integrity and Economic Development et al. 2010). From there, it is hard to argue why other MNCs should not be subject to the country-by-country standard.

Institutions

The movement is also helped by institutional elements. A major entry point has been the emerging interest in tax and development in the UN, OECD, EU and Leading Group, which in its turn is largely a result of the UN Financing for Development process and the first conference on this in Monterrey in 2002 (Lesage et al. 2010). This case shows the enormous importance of UN processes like this, even though they are often criticised because of a lack of immediate and substantial results. Another institutional factor is the recurrent IASB reviews of its IFRSs with concomitant public consultations. These are not geared towards a country-by-country agenda, but help to generate public attention for the campaign. This will again be the case for a future review of IFRS 8 (segment reporting). The same holds for reviews and consultations on accounting standards in the EU.

Finally, although a strong case is to be made for an international rule on country-by-country reporting (because of the geographical scope and the level playing field this would create), preferably through the IASB, national states possess ample discretion with regard to financial reporting standards, as illustrated by the US Dodd–Frank Act. This implies that reaching international consensus, which is very hard to achieve, is not necessary to obtain substantial results on the ground. The situation within the EU is more complicated given the EU's competencies, the internal market and the strong pressures on member states not to deviate radically from EU standards. In accounting, there is a global move to international convergence, not divergence (see below).

Analysis of the Obstacles Ahead

Ideas

As indicated above, opponents are developing their counter-arguments, and there will be an audience for that, including in politics. In particular, competitiveness and confidentiality arguments are not likely to fall on deaf ears. The following quote from the Confederation of British Industry (CBI), drawn from its response to the public consultation of the European Commission, is quite representative of the tone of most business submissions:

> Country-by-country reporting by multi-national companies may be a popular lobbying issue amongst some NGOs, but it is the information needs of their shareholders and investors that are most relevant. It is far from clear what role there is for the EU in this debate. Rather any additional prescriptive reporting requirements imposed by the EU on EU multinationals is liable to place them at a major competitive disadvantage to their non-EU global peers, and harm the prospects for EU growth and jobs, already under great stress. (CBI 2010)

Yet such arguments could not stop the Dodd–Frank Act; there are political limits to the portrayal of transparency as a competitive disadvantage. But we have to wait and see how the debate unfolds in the months and years ahead.

A second problematic evolution is what we would call a triple tendency of insulating and restricting rather than mainstreaming a maximalist version of country-by-country reporting. First, there is clear inclination to restrict the idea to the extractive industries. A powerful partner in the movement, the PWYP campaign, is indeed exclusively focusing on the extractive industries, while not opposing a broader application of the rule. Keeping the message focused is a deliberate choice of PWYP (van Oranje and Parham 2009: 65–66). The IASB has opened the discussion on the PWYP proposals with regard to the extractive industries, but not on the rest of the economy (IASB 2010). The US Dodd–Frank Act only deals with oil, gas and mining companies. The high-level support for country-by-country reporting in the EU (Sarkozy, Osborne, Competitiveness Council of EU ministers, European Commission) is equally getting geared towards these sectors only. Secondly, mere 'publish what you pay' provisions are gaining more traction than full country-by-country reporting, which also includes underlying base data such as turnover, profits and costs. Here we can again cite Dodd–Frank and the upcoming EU initiative, as well as private sector initiatives such as the 'Total Tax Contribution Framework' of PricewaterhouseCoopers (2010b). Thirdly, a significant part of the momentum at the official level is still situated within the sphere of development policy making (EU ministers of development, the OECD Task Force on Tax and Development), while in order to be successful, the maximalist approach should move up to economy and finance ministers, and for the EU, the decision-making bodies involving the internal market. Hence, there is a danger that, under pressure from business interests, Western governments will limit themselves to a minimalist approach in which the extractive industry is singled out as scapegoat, while leaving the rest of big business off the hook. Furthermore, a limited success can somewhat disempower the movement, as part of it could be satisfied with what has already been achieved.

A third issue complicating this campaign is the fact that country-by-country reporting and transparency *as such* will not automatically lead to more tax justice. Other and much more substantive measures relating to corporate taxation, maybe partly inspired by country-by-country data, will be necessary. It needs some explanation to convince people of the powerful social dynamics that these new financial statements will engender. For civil society organisations and trade unions that have to make priorities in their campaigns and lobbying, this might be a problem. It is not insurmountable, though (see below).

Institutions

The key international institution, the IASB, is a citadel hard to capture. It is a private body, to which governments have de facto delegated international regulatory power. Even the EU has decided that it will apply the IASB's international financial reporting standards (see, e.g., Chiapello and Medjad 2009). The power of the IASB is enhanced by the increasing international momentum for global convergence and even harmonisation around the IASB's IFRS system. This is also the direction the G20 has set. Even the US is coming under increasing pressure to join the IASB regime (Bruce 2008; Jones 2011; Jones and Fontanella-Khan 2011). In this context, the political appetite for national and even regional initiatives that differ from the global framework is likely to decrease. As the US and non-Western countries such as Japan, China, Russia, India, Korea and Brazil more and more converge towards, or even completely adopt, the IFRS system, the IASB-led accounting regime becomes less and less a European-centred affair, which also reduces the power of the Europeans within the IASB. This implies that growing support for country-by-country reporting in the EU will not easily translate into new IASB policy. The IASB is likely to argue that a country-by-country standard is also conditional upon support in the major emerging economies. To our knowledge, there are no indications that the BRIC countries are interested in country-by-country reporting. Reaching consensus will be quite difficult at the global level. This fundamental point should further be explored and discussed, but it seems recommendable to campaign for the introduction of a country-by-country standard outside the IFRS framework as well. In this regard the OECD is an interesting venue, as the power balance for country-by-country reporting is more favourable there (see above).

Another institutional issue is the ongoing bureaucratic compartmentalisation of policies. Both at the national and the international/EU level, there is little interaction between the world of accounting standard-setting and the world of taxation. The taxation policy makers do not have the tradition of interfering with accounting and financial reporting, and are not invited to do so either. Moreover, the far-reaching privatisation of accounting standard-setting further insulates this sector from public debate and politics.

Concluding Remarks

Despite the progress and the achievements, the struggle for full country-by-country reporting is still in an initial phase. Big business is gradually becoming aware of the campaign. Its reactions are negative and often aggressive. A considerable part of the political and regulatory elite is likely to be responsive to its arguments, while institutionally it is not self-evident that a global country-by-country reporting standard should be established or that nation states should adopt this norm in the absence of an international or even global regulatory framework. Further successes will require more societal and political support nationally and internationally. In this last section, we will discuss a few variables that might be critical for the future of the campaign.

A first observation is that the campaign possesses huge growth potential. Several civil society organisations are already on board, but this number is increasing, with more countries involved. More active participation from trade unions, in turn, could help to mainstream the debate beyond the development focus. What is more, under the current fiscal crisis in Europe and elsewhere, MNCs are increasingly vulnerable to criticism with regard to the abuse of tax havens and other ways of tax avoidance and evasion. At the same time, governments are under severe pressure to sustain their budgets, which might enhance their interest in an instrument like country-by-country reporting. In this context, it would be interesting to establish a bridge between tax policy and accounting regulation. As we indicated above, interviews with senior tax officials taught us that country-by-country reporting would assist them in a more accurate taxation of MNCs. But they also revealed that even senior tax officials have never heard about the campaign. If better informed, through formal and informal channels, tax administrations could encourage policy makers to consider country-by-country reporting. Besides, civil society and press can continue to publicise anomalies in the taxation of MNCs and tax haven abuse. In this sense, the mediatised actions of a new group like Uncut in the UK are examples that can be replicated worldwide (Boxell 2011). It can also be useful to have in each country a network organisation of tax activism groups (such as Attac), trade unions, development NGOs, parliamentarians and other partners to coordinate research and lobbying. An example is the Belgian Financial Actie Netwerk – Réseau pour la Justice Fiscale. Such networks can play a crucial role in bringing country-by-country reporting on the national agenda.

Notes

1. See <http://www.leadinggroup.org/rubrique20.html> (accessed 5 May 2011).
2. See <http://www.financialtaskforce.org> (accessed 5 May 2011).

3. <http://frwebgate.access.gpo.gov/cgi-bin/getdoc.cgi?dbname=111_cong_bills&docid=f:h4173enr.txt.pdf> (accessed 5 May 2011).
4. <http://www.hkex.com.hk/eng/rulesreg/listrules/mbrulesup/Documents/mb96_miner.pdf> (accessed 5 May 2011).
5. <http://www.oecd.org/dataoecd/51/38/43140770.pdf> (accessed 5 May 2011). Several reports available on the internet wrongly labelled the Berlin meeting a 'G20 meeting'.
6. <http://www.ambafrance-uk.org/30th-France-United-Kingdom-Summit.html> (accessed 5 May 2011).
7. Journal Officiel du 7 octobre 2009. See <http://www.legifrance.gouv.fr/affichTexte.do?cidTexte=JORFTEXT000021118925&fastPos=2&fastReqId=338270788&categorieLien=cid&oldAction=rechTexte> (accessed 5 May 2011).
8. <http://ec.europa.eu/internal_market/consultations/2010/financial-reporting_en.htm> (accessed 5 May 2011).
9. <http://www.oecd.org/dataoecd/7/36/44493096.pdf> (accessed 5 May 2011).
10. <http://www.oecd.org/officialdocuments/displaydocumentpdf/?cote=c/min(2010)6/final&doclanguage=en> (accessed 5 May 2011).
11. <http://www.oecd.org/document/51/0,3343,en_2649_33749_45240563_1_1_1_1,00.html> (accessed 5 May 2011).
12. <http://www.ifrs.org/NR/rdonlyres/FE7FBB8D-2F2B-44EE-B5B1-1C1D626E4289/0/ExtractiveActivitiesAdvisoryPanelmembers.pdf> (accessed 5 May 2011).

Chapter 13

International Taxes – Why, What and How?

Margit Schratzenstaller

Introduction

The international integration of national economies is progressing rapidly. At the same time, the provision and financing of international public goods is increasingly becoming an issue due to the emergence and growing acuteness of global long-term challenges like climate change or global imbalances and inequality.[1] These developments are the background for a growing discussion about the introduction of international taxes, which has been intensified by the current financial and economic crisis. Up to now, this debate has been held almost exclusively on a political level, while within academia the subject has not attracted much attention yet. This policy-oriented chapter aims to summarise the current state of the political discussion on international taxes and to provide a theoretical basis for it. After defining and clarifying the concept of international taxes, the chapter presents the most important theoretical arguments and considerations in their favour. It then establishes a catalogue of criteria for identifying tax bases and activities which appear to be particularly suited to be taxed on an international basis. The chapter also provides an overview of the most important suggestions for international taxes brought forward in the ongoing political discussion and their rationale, and we try to identify relevant economic effects of these taxes. The chapter closes with some reflections on the open questions and potential problems which have to be considered when contemplating the introduction of international taxes.

International Taxes: Some Basics

'Mainstream' public finance has only recently discovered international public goods as an area of academic interest and is still largely ignoring international taxes.[2] Most interestingly this neglect holds true also for the recent relevant 'off mainstream' scientific work on international aspects of public finance.[3] Up to now, the few economists dealing with international taxes have concentrated on selected ones. The so-called 'Tobin Tax' on currency transactions advocated by James Tobin in 1972 (Tobin 1978), the first academic proposal for an international tax, for example, inspired an academic debate about the proposed tax itself,[4] but not about the pros and cons of international taxes in general.

In the international/supranational political debate, international taxes have been discussed as a revenue source to finance international purposes for over a decade now. There are two strands of this debate. Firstly, international – or rather European – taxes have been repeatedly advocated by the European Commission since the end of the 1990s as alternative financing sources for the EU budget, which currently is primarily and increasingly based on budget-financed national contributions (Schratzenstaller and Berghuber 2007). Accordingly, EU taxes would be used to finance European public goods. Secondly, international taxes have been propagated in the context of development assistance for quite a while, more recently also as a policy instrument to fight climate change and to regulate financial markets. Initially NGOs were the driving force of this debate. Meanwhile, however, options for international taxes are also being considered by supranational organisations and groups of countries, under the heading 'innovative finance'[5] or 'innovative financial mechanisms'[6] respectively, or similar designations. Although the most prominent proposals for an international tax – the currency transaction tax (so-called Tobin Tax) and its modified and extended version, the general financial transaction tax – have played an important role in both debates, these have been conducted more or less independently of each other up to now. In this respect it is important to note one crucial difference between both debates, namely the 'additionality' of international taxes as innovative financial sources versus the 'revenue neutrality' of European taxes: International taxes as innovative financial sources in principle are intended to raise additional revenues for the funding of international concerns and public goods. In contrast, European taxes are seen as revenue-neutral in the sense that they replace national contributions to the EU budget and thus allow member states to reduce other taxes accordingly.

Generally, international taxes have the following characteristics:

• They are internationally agreed and organised (by a group of countries or worldwide).

- Besides their revenue-raising potential, international taxes are expected to have additional benefits (a so-called 'double dividend'), i.e., positive effects for societies and economies as a whole, by addressing economic, social or environmental imbalances. Sandmo (2003) even talks about a 'triple dividend' for the special case of global environmental taxes: positive environmental effects, lower efficiency loss of financing public expenditures if revenues replace more distortionary taxes (e.g., on labour), and additional resources for world development.
- The revenues from international taxes do not flow into national budgets, but are collected and allocated by supranational institutions/organisations to finance international public goods.

In principle, international taxes could be newly introduced at the national or the supranational level, or they could emerge from the assignment of existing national taxes to the supranational level. The latter variant is sometimes seen as an alternative to the harmonisation of taxes levied on the national level within a group of countries. A crucial feature of international taxes is that revenues are dedicated to finance international concerns. The internationally coordinated introduction of a specific tax, whose tax base and rate are harmonised completely or to a certain degree but whose proceeds go into national budgets, cannot therefore strictly speaking be labelled an international tax.

International taxes are inextricably linked to the concept of international public goods, which was made prominent by the United Nations (Kaul, Grunberg and Stern 1999). Public goods display two central properties: (some degree of) non-excludability and non-rivalrous consumption. Non-rivalry implies that consumption of the good by one consumer does not reduce the quantity available to the other potential consumers. Non-excludability means that, e.g., for technical reasons, no potential consumer can be excluded from consumption. These properties cause free-riding behaviour, i.e., the unwillingness of beneficiaries to pay for the provision of the public good and the impossibility to charge a price for its use.

International public goods are associated with cross-country spill-overs, i.e., their benefits are not limited to a certain region (local public goods) or country (national public goods).[7] Examples given by Stiglitz (2006) are: international economic stability, international security, the global environment, international humanitarian assistance and knowledge. Sandler (2001a) mentions activities involving the environment, security, financial stability, scientific discovery, health care, infrastructure, poverty reduction, culture preservation and research and development as important international public goods. In the European Union international public goods have played a large role – as European public goods – since its existence (Tabellini 2003). Recently they have been gaining in importance also outside the European Union as global economic, social and environmental imbalances increase.

Due to their main characteristics (non-excludability and non-rivalry in consumption), public goods are typically under-supplied. This problem is aggravated in the case of international public goods, as only part of their benefits can be internalised by the nation providing them due to the aforementioned international spillovers. This leads to additional free-riding problems which are the more serious as national sovereignty precludes the option to force countries to contribute to the provision of the international public good (Boucher and Bramoullé 2010). Moreover, a single country faces prohibitive costs of providing the international public good due to its sheer size. Therefore some coordination mechanism among the nations affected by an international public good is needed which includes not only its provision, but also requires innovative financing sources. However, the relevant publications on international public goods and mechanisms to finance their provision issued one decade ago are rather sceptical about the political acceptance as well as the administrative/technical feasibility of the collection of international taxes so that they are not treated in detail.

As Sandler (2001a, b), for example, carefully elaborates, the appropriate financing source depends on the nature of the respective global (similarly international) public good (see Table 13.1). The financing options are determined by the degree of excludability from the benefits of the international public good and the degree of rivalry in relation to its benefits as well as by the aggregation technique, i.e., the way aggregate provision of the international public good is determined by contributions. In principle, there are three ways to finance international public goods: charges levied by supranational organisations, voluntary contributions (including transfers between countries, with development aid as the most prominent example), and international taxes.

In the case of pure public goods, which are characterised by complete non-excludability of benefiting individuals and regions/states and by the complete absence of rivalry (e.g., curbing global warming), no direct compulsory user charges or national contributions can be levied, and sufficient voluntary contributions are unlikely, so that according to Sandler (2001a, b) international taxes remain the only financing alternative. This holds in principle also for impure international public goods with some rivalry but no exclusion. However, as the author states, as there is no international public finance system to collect international taxes, a supranational structure is needed through which some kind of collective action is organised – i.e., through which the international public good is provided and which charges member states based on their ability to pay to finance the collective provision of the international public good.

Roughly at the same time the European Commission launched its first contributions to the incipient international debate on how to raise the

Table 13.1 Financing Possibilities for Five Types of Global Public Goods

Type of public good	Examples	Financing possibilities	Remarks
Pure public	– Curbing global warming – Conducting basic research – Limiting spread of disease – Augmenting ozone shield	Must rely on global scheme based on either a benefit principle or an ability-to-pay-charge. Financing coordinated by either a supranational organization or some international taxation arrangement. A leader nation might provide financing if it gets enough benefits.	Neutrality is a concern: collective contributions may crowd out voluntary contributions. Partial cooperation brings free riding, so that an enforcement mechanism is needed.
Impurely public with some rivalry but no exclusion	– Managing ocean fisheries – Controlling pests – Curbing organized crime – Alleviating acid rain	Must rely on a supranational organization or an international taxation arrangement. Rivalry may motivate more independent behaviour than purely public goods do.	More private incentives to contribute. Rivalry lessens concerns.
Impurely public with some exclusion	– Missile defence system – Disaster relief aid – Extension services – Information dissemination	Exclusion promotes voluntary financing and club-like structures. An entrepreneurial or leader nation may come forward to market the good.	Exclusion is not complete, so arrangements may remain suboptimal.
Club good	– Transnational parks – Remote-sensing services – Canals, waterways	Charge each use according to the crowding that results and exclude non-payers. Toll per use is equal to marginal crowding costs so as to internalise the congestion externality. Tolls paid on total visits reflect differences in tastes; nations pay more if they visit more often.	Can result in an efficient outcome. Limited transaction costs. Full financing depends on scale economies, the form of congestion functions, and other considerations.
Joint products	– Poverty alleviation – Tropical forests – Peacekeeping – Defence	As nation-specific private benefits and club goods benefits become more prevalent among joint products, markets and club arrangements can be used to finance the good more efficiently. As the share of private benefits increases, payments can be increasingly based on benefits received.	Ratio of excludable to total benefits is the essential consideration. As ratio approaches unity, markets and clubs work perfectly.

Source: Sandler (2001b)

financial means required to finance the United Nations' Millennium Development Goals, explicitly drawing on international taxes as one potential revenue source and reviewing different options (in particular a kerosene tax, a flight ticket tax, a carbon tax and a currency/financial transaction tax) in considerable detail (European Commission 2004, 2005). The European Commission's most recent document 'Innovative Financing at a Global Level' (European Commission 2010c) is based on these two earlier documents. It should be noted here, however, that the European Commission is not very consistent in its recent contributions on potential international taxes. Thus a Commission Staff Working Document prepared shortly after the aforementioned document, entitled 'Financial Sector Taxation' (European Commission 2010d), indicates the central policy objectives of intensifying the use of financial sector taxes – among them a general financial transaction tax – namely: their potential role as regulatory instruments to correct for negative externalities of financial sector activities including excessive risk taking; as instruments to ensure an adequate financial contribution from the financial sector, which was very profitable in the two decades preceding the current financial and economic crisis, to public revenues in general and in particular to cover the budgetary costs of the crisis; and as revenue instruments to contribute to the consolidation of public budgets. While the issue at which level such taxes can be introduced – G20 versus EU – is explicitly addressed, no connection is made to the debate on financing options for international purposes; in this regard the scope of this second more recent document published by the European Commission is limited to identifying additional revenue sources for national budgets.

Why International Taxes – and Which Ones?

General Economic Rationale for International Taxes

A central theoretical public finance rationale for international taxes is based on the principle of fiscal equivalence formulated by Olson (1969) for federal states. According to this principle the financing and the provision of a public good should be assigned to the same jurisdictional level. The users of public goods should be responsible for their financing. At least for pure international public goods whose benefits accrue to a group of or to all countries worldwide, this implies that taxes to finance their provision should be assigned to the supranational level, as assigning these taxes to the national level would imply the danger of free-riding: the countries benefiting from an international public good would not contribute to its financing, i.e., they would not collect the required tax revenues, because they cannot be excluded from the benefits of the international public good. An internationally coordinated approach to innovative financing sources in general and to international taxes in particular is required to achieve a fair burden-sharing between the countries involved in the containment of negative externalities or the provision of international public goods. Moreover, innovative financing sources resting on internationally mobile bases cannot be effectively introduced without international cooperation because otherwise the respective tax base would be relocated to a non-taxing jurisdiction to avoid/evade the tax, which may entail negative consequences for growth and employment in the taxing country. Finally, an internationally coordinated approach may also be required to create a level playing field and to avoid competitive disadvantages (European Commission 2010c).

Properties of Good International Taxes

Two groups of criteria and principles are relevant when evaluating the suitability of individual taxes as international taxes: first, specific criteria and principles mostly derived from tax assignment theory; second, general criteria and principles always to be taken into account, irrespective of assignment considerations, when assessing individual taxes from an economic point of view.[8] The weight assigned to each criterion cannot be determined by economic considerations but is a political decision.

Specific Criteria and Principles Characterising Good International Taxes

To answer the question of which taxes should be assigned to the supranational level, one can refer to the criteria and principles fleshed out in the traditional fiscal federalism literature concerning the optimal assignment of taxes in countries within multi-tier governments.[9] Under the changed conditions of extensive and growing international integration, these criteria and principles can to a large degree be applied to a group of countries (in an extreme case, to all countries worldwide) assembled within a supranational institution. Generally, the following criteria may serve to evaluate the suitability of individual taxes as international taxes:[10]

International Mobility of the Tax Base

Taxes on internationally mobile tax bases which are exposed to the danger of erosion by international tax competition or which cannot be enforced at all at national level, because they would induce the relocation of the tax base or the tax subject to a non-taxing jurisdiction, lend themselves as international taxes. If such taxes are Pigouvian taxes, i.e., if they aim to internalise negative externalities, e.g., environmental damage caused by certain consumption and/or production activities, their unilateral introduction at national level run the risk of being inefficiently low and thus unable to secure the internalisation of negative externalities fully: if the tax does not cover at least the most important countries where tax subjects could migrate or shift their tax base to avoid taxation, undertaxation of the negative externality would result in the negative externality being at best insufficiently corrected, at worst not at all.

Existence of Cross-border Negative Externalities

Taxation of tax bases/activities with cross-border negative externalities[11] at the national level would result in an inefficiently low tax rate, as only domestic, but not cross-border, externalities would be considered when determining the tax rate.

Degree of Short-term Stability of Revenues

Taxes whose proceeds display a low degree of short-term volatility and are therefore a reliable financing source independent of cyclical fluctuations are good international taxes. This is important because supranational institutions/organisations financing international public goods by international taxes as a rule do not have the possibility to debt-finance expenditure in case of tax revenue shortfalls.

Degree of Long-term Revenue Elasticity

Taxes with high long-term elasticity are good international taxes, because they help to secure the financing of international public goods also in the long run; this is important because the financing needs for international concerns are likely to increase in the long run.

Fairness between Countries (Cross-nation Equity)

The tighter the link between the tax base (and therefore tax payments) and national income in the countries involved, the better a tax is suited as an international tax, as this secures a high degree of equity concerning the gross tax burden at national level. Hereby equity or fairness between countries can imply proportionality as well as cross-country progressivity.

Impact on National Competitiveness

Taxes which could have a negative impact on the competitiveness of individual countries, if implemented unilaterally, are good international taxes, as their multilateral introduction helps to create a level playing field.

Link to International Policy Concerns

Taxes which – as regulatory instruments – specifically address international policy concerns (e.g., climate change, instabilities in the financial sector) seem particularly suited to finance political expenditures in these policy fields, as such a link may strengthen political support and acceptance of the implementation of these taxes by taxpayers.

General Criteria for Evaluating Taxes from an Economic Perspective

Besides these specific criteria for assessing the suitability of specific taxes as international taxes, of course the conventional criteria should be applied to evaluate individual taxes from an economic perspective: i.e., effects on market efficiency and effects on equity and income distribution. Additionally, legal and administrative effects are to be considered.[12]

Effects on Market Efficiency

Does a specific tax distort decisions of private agents on investment in physical or human capital, on labour supply, etc., in otherwise efficient markets and thus lead to inefficiencies, or can a given tax contribute to the correction of market failures and thus improve efficiency? In this respect Pigouvian taxes aimed at internalising negative externalities (particularly environmental taxes) or taxes on activities with potentially harmful individual effects (gambling, consumption of tobacco and alcohol) are of specific importance.

Effects on Equity and Income Distribution

Does a specific tax reduce or aggravate existing inequalities in the distribution of income or wealth on an individual? (Progressive) taxes on personal income and wealth are equitable taxes, whereas consumption taxes display regressive effects, i.e., are associated with an over-proportionate burden for lower income groups.

Effects on Growth

Is a specific tax relatively neutral with respect to growth and employment, or does it significantly hamper growth? With respect to growth-sensitivity, property taxes as well as consumption and environmental taxes are to be preferred over taxes on personal and business income (Johannson et al. 2008; OECD 2010d).

Legal and Administrative Aspects

Does a specific tax comply with existing legal provisions (e.g., in the EU, to the Treaty provisions concerning the Single Market)? Is it administratively complex?

The Debate about European Taxes

In the EU the debate about the introduction of international or EU taxes is not new (Schratzenstaller and Berghuber 2007). Since the end of the 1990s, the European Commission produced three critical assessments of the current system of its own resources (European Commission 1998, 2004, 2010e). In these reports the European Commission considered the pros and cons of several reform strategies and alternative financing sources. One alternative, which was favoured by the European Commission in its earlier reports and is advocated again in its most recent one, is the assignment of one or more dedicated EU taxes to the EU, to (partially) replace existing revenue sources. As candidates for EU taxes, the European Commission has repeatedly mentioned a carbon dioxide or energy tax, VAT, excise duties (tobacco, alcohol, mineral oil), a financial transaction tax, taxes on transport and telecommunication services, corporation tax and a tax on the ECB's gains from seigniorage.

This short list of potential EU taxes shows that the EU tax could in principle take different forms:[13]

- A uniform surcharge could be levied by the EU on a given tax base, while the tax base and national tax rates would be determined by the member states (e.g., surcharge on VAT).
- The revenues of a tax newly introduced or already existing in all member states could be redirected from national budgets to the EU, while member states retain the right to set tax base and rate.
- A hitherto national tax could be assigned to the EU, which would amount to a complete harmonisation of the respective tax (e.g., corporate income tax), and the EU would be given the right to set tax base and rate.
- A new tax could be introduced, with the EU deciding on tax base and rate. This option has the advantage that no existing tax rate and base would have to be harmonised, and that no revenues would have to be redirected away from national budgets.

These different options would imply differing degrees of tax autonomy for the EU. While the option to levy surcharges on taxes remaining within the national tax sovereignty of member states as well as redirecting revenues from taxes remaining at the discretion of member states would give the EU the right to decide about the use of the tax revenues only, an EU tax would imply legislative powers in tax matters for the EU.

In any case, all options considered here would mean that some degree of revenue autonomy would be conferred on the EU, which currently does not have its own taxes at its disposal, nor is it allowed to incur debt.[14] The EU is therefore primarily dependent on contributions by EU member states (their own resources based on the national VAT base and on gross national income) to finance its expenditures, as its traditional own resources (agricultural tariffs, sugar customs duties, general tariffs), initially the main financing source of the EU budget, have been reduced to a rather small share of overall EU revenues. The negotiations about the last few EU financial frameworks (which usually cover a seven year period) and particularly about the current one (for the period 2007 to 2013) were seriously protracted by the acrimonious arguments between member states about their 'net contributor positions'. Specifically, the decreasing willingness of the so-called net contributors, whose contributions to finance EU expenditures exceed their direct monetary returns from the EU budget, to pay their shares suggests the need for fundamental reforms to the current system of self-generated resources. Otherwise it can be expected that the already suboptimal EU supply of European public goods – i.e., the support of R&D or cross-border transport infrastructure – is aggravated further. Already the current financial framework foresees declining expenditure in relation to GDP, compared to its predecessor, instead of an increasing or at least constant budget volume to meet the growing tasks and the future challenges which were already apparent before the current financial and economic crisis.

Abstaining from the use of taxes with double dividends also implies that the potential of certain taxes – which cannot be levied at national level for the reasons considered above – as policy instruments to improve market efficiency, for example, remains unused. Thus EU-wide implementation would enable the use of specific Pigovian taxes whose implementation requires a multilateral approach.

Moreover, the current system of self-generated resources is characterised by a high degree of complexity and a lack of transparency. It consists of several financing sources: traditional self-generated resources, gross national income (GNI)-based and VAT-based resources. Particularly the calculation of VAT-based self-generated resources for the individual member states is a rather complicated exercise.[15] Also the so-called UK rebate, granted since 1984 to the UK, considerably adds to the complexity of the system.

Of course, under the given institutional conditions, current self-generated resources could only partly be replaced by EU taxes. First, as the EU is not allowed to incur debt, at least one subsidiary revenue source is needed to cover potential revenue shortfalls of the EU tax. Second, exclusive tax financing of the EU budget would require a far deeper political integration of EU member states compared to the status quo.

The Debate about 'Innovative Finance'

This second strand in the policy debate about international taxes was inspired to a large degree by the so-called Landau Report commissioned by the French President Jacques Chirac and issued in 2004 (Groupe de travail sur les nouvelles contributions financières internationales 2004). The aim of the working group which compiled the report was to identify innovative financial sources to combat global poverty and inequality in order to achieve the so-called Millennium Development Goals. Accordingly innovative financial sources should be stable, predictable and reliable in the long run. They should also be rather automatic in the sense that they are not granted temporarily over short time spans only then to be renegotiated regularly. International taxes would lend themselves to become such a financing source. Also in this context different forms of international taxes are discussed:

- providing internationally coordinated tax incentives in the donor countries to increase voluntary contributions for development purposes;
- levying surcharges on existing taxes;
- implementing new international taxes, either on internationally mobile tax bases which cannot be taxed unilaterally or on global common goods/ cross-border negative externalities.

The aforementioned Commission Staff Working Papers issued by the European Commission (2005, 2010c) on innovative finance also examine, besides other instruments, international taxes as one potential innovative revenue source, widening the rather narrow focus of the Landau Report which concentrates on innovative financial mechanisms in the context of development policy. Also against the background of the causes and consequences of the current financial and economic crisis and regarding long-term global challenges, the European Commission in its most recent document identifies three areas in which international taxes might play an important role not only to raise revenues, but also as regulatory instruments helping to correct market imperfections in the future:

- The financial sector: here the focus is on international taxes which ensure an adequate contribution from the financial sector to the costs of the current and potential future crisis and are levied on leverage or risk-taking by financial intermediaries.
- Climate change: here internationally coordinated taxes – particularly carbon taxes – might help to finance policies to stop climate change.
- Development: here internationally coordinated tax incentives might contribute to raising additional private funds.

The question of how to use the additional revenues according to the European Commission is outside the scope of the report. While these innovative financial instruments are intended to raise additional funds to enable effective policies to cope with fundamental long-term challenges, the European Commission discusses EU taxes not as additional, but rather as alternative financing sources to replace existing ones within an altogether revenue-neutral approach.

The OECD maintains an altogether rather reserved position in the supranational political discussion about international taxes: in a policy brief, international taxes (environmental taxes, a currency transaction tax and an arms sales tax) are evaluated rather superficially as potential financing sources for the Millennium Development Goals, but rejected in principle as their implementation would take too much time to generate sufficient revenues in due time to effectively support those goals (Reisen 2004).

International Taxes in Practice

As mentioned above, the first few publications on potential financing sources for international public goods deal rather superficially with international taxes as one possible revenue source. In the volume edited by Gerrard, Ferroni and Mody (2001), *Global Public Policies and Programs: Implications for Financing and Evaluation*, featuring the proceedings from a World Bank Workshop, the three contributions addressing aspects of financing the provision of international public goods either neglect or completely ignore international taxes (Sandler 2001b; Barrett 2001) or just touch on them cursorily: Cooper (2001) very briefly mentions the Tobin Tax and elaborates on a carbon tax in slightly more detail, drawing the conclusion, however, that channelling its potential revenues into the financing of international public goods instead of national budgets would never be approved by national governments, thus rendering this financing alternative obviously unworthy of further attention.

Only in subsequent years did international taxes receive more attention as a potential financing mechanism for international public goods, and in addition to the 'notorious' proposal of a tax on financial transactions, further potential bases for international taxes were explored in more detail. In particular, environment-related taxes are increasingly propagated as international taxes, as they promise a double dividend by combining a – partly considerable – revenue potential with the reduction of negative (environmental) externalities. In particular, the focus of the recent documents issued by the European Commission are on taxes on kerosene, flight tickets and carbon emissions and will therefore be treated in more detail in this chapter.

Table 13.2 gives an overview over the most recent proposals for a general financial transaction tax, a kerosene tax, a flight ticket tax and a carbon tax.

This overview also gives an indication of the potential or – should the tax already exist somewhere – actual revenues. It goes without saying that it is difficult enough to estimate the revenue implications of reforms of already existing taxes; but it is even more challenging to estimate the revenue potential of taxes yet to be introduced, because revenue estimates cannot rely on past experience and empirical data on the tax elasticity of the tax base and the reactions of the potential taxpayers; this requires even more assumptions compared to revenue estimates for variations in already existing taxes. By far the largest revenues can be expected from a general financial transaction tax.

Table 13.2 Recent Proposals for International Taxes

Tax	Tax rate and base	Potential or actual revenues (source)
General financial transaction tax	0.01 per cent on all financial transactions between professional traders	in 2007 up to €94 billion in Europe up to €211 billion worldwide (estimate by Schulmeister, Schratzenstaller and Picek 2008)
Kerosene tax	EU minimum tax rate for diesel	€6 to 7 billion EU (estimate by European Commission 2005)
Flight ticket tax	country-specific progressive scales based on destination and class	in 2008 €170 million contributions to UNITAID, inter alia, from France (actual revenues, European Commission 2010c) from 2012 on €90 million p.a. in Austria (estimate by Austrian Ministry of Finance) from 2011 on €1 billion p.a. in Germany (estimate by German Ministry of Finance) from 2011/12 on £2.9 billion p.a. in the UK (estimate by HM Treasury)
Carbon tax	€12 / tonne CO_2 in Denmark €108 / tonne CO_2 in Sweden €20 / tonne CO_2 in Finland	in 2007, 0.3 per cent of GDP in Denmark 0.81 per cent of GDP in Sweden 0.29 per cent of GDP in Finland (actual revenues, European Commission 2010c)

Sources: European Commission (2010c), Schratzenstaller and Berghuber (2007), Schulmeister, Schratzenstaller and Picek (2008)

In Table 13.3, these potential international taxes are evaluated in a first, naturally rather superficial attempt. All taxes considered are levied on tax bases with negative cross-border externalities: highly speculative financial transactions, which are addressed by a general financial transaction tax, may cause particular instabilities in the respective national financial market which may spill over onto other countries; the negative environmental impact of air traffic, targeted by a kerosene tax and a flight ticket tax aim, is not limited to individual countries; and climate change – targeted by a carbon tax – is a global concern.

Table 13.3 Evaluation of Potential International Taxes

Tax	Negative cross-border externalities	Mobile tax base	Low short-term volatility	High long-term revenue elasticity	Fairness between countries	Negative impact on national competitiveness	Link to international policy concerns
General FTT	yes	yes	no	yes	?	yes	yes
Kerosene tax	yes	yes	no	yes	yes	yes	yes
Airline ticket tax	yes	no	no	yes	yes	yes	yes
Carbon tax	yes	?	yes	yes	no	yes	yes

Source: own analysis

The general financial transaction tax, the kerosene tax and the carbon tax all affect tax bases which are at least in part highly mobile: derivative and currency transactions forming a considerable part of the tax base on which a general financial transaction tax is targeted are very mobile and can be expected to migrate to low-tax or zero-tax jurisdictions to a considerable degree; internationally active airlines will cover their kerosene demand in zero-taxed jurisdictions as far as technically possible to minimise kerosene tax payments; and in particular the energy-intensive industry will probably be rather prone to migration to zero-tax jurisdictions to avoid a carbon tax.

While revenues from a general financial tax, a kerosene tax and a flight ticket tax can be expected to be rather volatile in the short-run, carbon tax revenues should be less cyclically sensitive and thus be less exposed to short-term fluctuations. All tax bases in question should be characterised by considerable long-term revenue elasticity, at least based on their rather dynamic development in the past.

An equitable national distribution of the tax burden should be given for the kerosene tax and the flight ticket tax, as the extent of air traffic should be positively related to a country's national income. The opposite may be assumed for the carbon tax, as poorer countries can be expected to spend a larger share of their national income on energy. The cross-country distributionary effect of the general financial transaction tax remains an open question due to the extreme regional concentration of financial transactions and the lack of data on the regional distribution of the users of national financial centres.

Finally, all taxes under consideration here may be expected to exert a negative influence on national competitiveness when implemented unilaterally, and there is a strong link between these taxes and the international policy concerns they would be used to finance (containment of climate change, stabilisation of the international financial system).

To sum up, there is not – and obviously cannot be – 'the' ideal candidate for an international tax. Based on the evaluation criteria applied here, the kerosene tax appears to be the most suitable candidate, followed by a general financial transaction tax. Two out of seven criteria are not fulfilled by the flight ticket tax, among them the criterion of a highly mobile tax base, which may be the reason why a flight ticket tax was introduced at national level by several EU countries recently without fearing the relocation of airlines to airports in non-taxing countries: in the UK in 1994, in France in 2006, and in Germany and Austria from 2011 on.[16] Here, France is the only country using receipts from its so-called 'solidarity tax' on flight tickets for international purposes:[17] instead of contributing to budget consolidation, as in Germany and Austria, the French flight ticket tax serves to finance health programmes in developing countries via UNITAID. Also a carbon tax, whose tax base should partially at least be rather mobile (energy-intensive industries), is levied in several EU countries. The Scandinavian countries levy carbon taxes at very different rates. Ireland and Greece have just introduced a carbon tax as one element of their budget consolidation packages.

Of course, the consideration here of the suitability of currently debated candidates for international taxes can only be of a very preliminary and ad hoc nature. Further in-depth empirical analyses are needed to substantiate and quantify this qualitative assessment. Furthermore, as pointed out already, it depends on the prevailing political priorities as to how each evaluation criterion is weighted. With regard to the options studied here, it is interesting to note that these fare rather similarly under the evaluation criteria applied.

Table 13.4 summarises the most important (economic) effects of the international taxes discussed in this chapter, taking into account effects on market efficiency as well as on equity and income distribution, and administrative and legal aspects. All taxes considered here may at least to some degree be deemed to contribute to the correction of market failures (instabilities on financial markets,[18] environmental damage), whereby their effectiveness differs (an air ticket tax is less effective than a kerosene tax). Whereas the effects of a general financial transaction tax on income distribution appears as yet unclear and requires further in-depth analysis, both taxes on air transport should be progressive, and carbon taxes can be expected to have a regressive effect. Open legal questions are an issue for a general financial transaction tax and carbon taxes.

In addition, all taxes under scrutiny here can be expected to be relatively growth-friendly based on recent empirical findings from the OECD (OECD

Table 13.4 (Economic) Effects of Potential International Taxes

Tax	Effects on market efficiency	Effects on equity and income distribution	Administrative and legal aspects
General financial transaction tax	Depending on the tax rate, the volume of trading would be reduced. **A very low tax rate can be expected to significantly reduce highly speculative short-term transactions with potentially destabilising effects without negatively affecting the price finding mechanism and thus the allocative efficiency of financial markets. The likelihood of circumvention should be limited with a very low tax rate and the introduction of the tax by a core group of countries.**	Distribution effects are unclear. They depend on the possibility of financial intermediaries passing on the costs to their clients (in particular those initiating the transaction) and the relative distribution of financial transactions.	Open legal questions especially with respect to taxation of currency transactions. Legal concerns on the compatibility of such a levy with the free movement of capital and payments between member states and between member states and third countries under article 63 of the Treaty of the Functioning of the European Union (TFEU) as well as regarding WTO compatibility; the tax would discriminate against all transactions involving countries with different currencies compared to those within one country and within the Eurozone.
Kerosene tax	Incentives for using least-cost abatement opportunities. Some reduction of demand for air travel. Global approach necessary because of international nature of this sector's services and risks of carbon leakage. Reduction of distortion of competition between transport modes. The 'polluter pays principle' is applied in a sector where CO_2-emissions have significantly increased in recent years. Distortion of competition between EU and third country carriers	**Progressive effects likely as air travel demand increases with income.**	**Low administrative costs.** Amendments of hundreds of bilateral Air Service Agreements necessary to permit the taxation of all carriers on intra-EU routes.

Table 13.4 (continued)

Tax	Effects on market efficiency	Effects on equity and income distribution	Administrative and legal aspects
	on routes which benefit from an exemption. Low cost carriers and charters more affected than traditional ones.		
Airline ticket tax	**No incentives for using least-cost abatement opportunities.** Less efficient than the kerosene tax for internalising the externalities of aviation. Limited reduction of demand for air travel and therefore limited environmental effectiveness. Reduction of distortion of competition between transportation modes.	**Progressive effects likely as air travel demand increases with income.**	**Low administrative costs.**
Carbon tax	Like other carbon pricing mechanisms, it provides incentives for using least-cost abatement opportunities. Risk of distortive effects in the Single Market by an uncoordinated approach in EU countries.	Like other carbon pricing mechanisms, it may require accompanying social expenditure to address social hardships as low-income groups spend a higher share of their income on transport and energy.	Carbon border tax: Practical and legal concerns (WTO compatibility) and administrative costs as well as risks of trade conflicts and retaliatory measures.

Source: Based on European Commission (2005, 2010c); in bold letters: own amendments

2010d). This is a generally desirable property of taxes attracting increasing attention recently within the theory and practice of public finance ('quality of public finances'). Concerning potential EU taxes to replace national contributions to the EU budget within a revenue-neutral reform of the system of self-generated resources, the implementation of the options outlined here would help to make national tax systems more growth-friendly by enabling cuts in more distorting national taxes. In the same vein one could argue in favour of these potential international taxes as additional financing sources for international concerns, as their use would help avoid exploiting potentially more distortionary financing instruments.

Potential Problems Associated with the Introduction of International Taxes

In the debate about international taxes a number of potential problems and objections are raised. Some are of a more practical nature, while others address more fundamental aspects.

Global versus Regional Taxes

First of all there is the discussion as to whether international taxes have to be implemented globally, or whether a regional approach – i.e., implementation by a group of countries – is sufficient and feasible without the fear of a significant loss of competitiveness vis-à-vis non-taxing countries or regions and the resulting relocation of the tax base. Also the regulatory potential of certain international taxes may be eroded when introduced in a group of countries only. Therefore for some international taxes the necessity of finding mechanisms to prevent tax evasion arises. For example, carbon taxes which are not implemented worldwide may be associated with risks of carbon leakage. In this case some kind of carbon border tax could be a solution (European Commission 2010c).

The issue 'global versus regional' has been broached rather intensely also in the recent debate about the option of an EU-wide introduction of a general financial transaction tax. In general many EU countries are sceptical as to whether a general financial transaction tax can be effectively introduced in the EU only, without the participation of important trading locations outside the EU. This issue has an economic and a political dimension. Concerning the economic dimension, further empirical analyses are required to determine whether and to what extent the tax bases and tax subjects in question react to international differences in tax rates. While the tax sensitivity of foreign direct investment and multinational enterprises with respect to cross-country corporate tax rate differentials is the subject of numerous empirical studies (mostly with the result that the tax elasticity of investment and multinationals, respectively, is deemed high),[19] there are only a few studies exploring empirically the influence of tax rate differentials on the location of foreign direct investment and multinationals (interestingly, mostly with the result that there is no significant relationship).[20]

The political dimension is quite pointedly captured by the following statement made by the European Commission (2010c: 5): 'Actions by the EU alone would be less effective but could be considered, particularly if there are good reasons to expect that an EU role of global leadership would be followed by other key countries'. A similar reasoning can be found in the Landau Report, which expects that the introduction of international taxes by a core group of countries may trigger a process in which the acceptance of international taxes increases. Such a process could be initiated within a two-stage approach by the introduction of a 'light version' of a specific international tax (i.e., a financial transaction tax with a very low tax rate levied on specific financial transactions only which could be taxed rather easily) in a first step, which would allow a core group of countries to collect experiences which could be shared with further countries and might convince these to follow suit (Schulmeister, Schratzenstaller and Picek 2008).

Earmarking the Revenues of International Taxes

Linking international taxes to the provision of international public goods, as is done throughout this chapter as well as in the political debate, implies earmarking their revenues. Earmarking the proceeds of specific taxes for specific purposes is generally criticized in public finance theory (Musgrave and Musgrave 1989) and is rather uncommon in practice (European Commission 2010c). Usually revenues from specific taxes are not reserved for specific expenditures but are used to finance general public expenditures. The most important objection against earmarking tax revenues is that it causes budgetary inflexibility and rigidity as the reallocation of public funds to more efficient purposes, should the initial spending purpose become obsolete, is rendered more difficult. Furthermore, if the international tax is the only financing source for a specific international public good, only taxes with stable and reliable revenues in the short and the long run are meaningful financing instruments.

When used to finance international public goods, however, earmarking may have specific advantages which outweigh potential downsides. First of all, earmarking may increase the acceptance of international taxes by taxpayers. Furthermore, it should be considered that the international public goods to be financed by international taxes represent long-term challenges requiring financing sources which are available in the long run. Earmarked tax can represent such long-term financing sources guaranteeing – in contrast to other financial sources, particularly (voluntary) contributions agreed on and granted for a limited timespan only – predictable and reliable public funds.

To avoid the potential disadvantages of earmarking, international taxes and the purposes for which they are used should be evaluated regularly. Moreover, the provision of international public goods should rather rest on a mix of financing sources, where international taxes are complemented by at least one additional financial source whose revenues can be adjusted flexibly to financial needs (see, for example, the system of self-generated resources of the EU which contains one revenue source – the GNI-based own resource – which is set yearly to cover the difference between the predetermined expenditures and the revenues stemming from other sources).

Uneven Cross-country Distribution of the Tax Base

An uneven distribution of the tax base across participating countries, which would result in an equally uneven distribution of the tax burden across countries, might lead to resistance of those countries raising a large share of the total revenue of the tax. This problem may be illustrated by the case of taxes on the financial sector in general and of a financial transaction tax in particular. Considering that the quantitative weight of the financial sector differs markedly across countries,[21] it is obvious that it won't be easy to reach a consensus within the EU alone, let alone within a larger supranational context as the G20 represents. The average share of the financial sector in total value-added in Japan reached 5.6 per cent in 2008, only slightly more than in the EU 27, where it amounted to 5.3 per cent in 2008. However, there are considerable cross-country differences within the EU: member states with above-average shares are Luxembourg (28.9 per cent), Ireland (10.3 per cent), the United Kingdom (9.6 per cent), Portugal (9 per cent), and Cyprus (8 per cent). In Australia, Canada, and the United States the financial sector accounted for about 8 per cent of total value added in 2008, a significantly higher share compared to Japan and the EU. The financial sector taxes discussed by the IMF (Claessens, Keen and Pazarbasioglu 2010) and the European Commission (2010d) would thus affect individual countries and regions differently. Revenues from a general financial transaction tax, for example, would be concentrated in the United Kingdom and Germany, according to the estimates by Schulmeister, Schratzenstaller and Picek (2008): at a tax rate of 0.01 per cent and under the assumption of a medium transaction reduction scenario, tax receipts would amount to 3.1 per cent of GDP in the United Kingdom and 0.5 per cent of GDP in Germany. It has to be pointed out in this context, however, that the regional concentration of potential revenues of a general financial transaction tax does not mean that taxpayers in the UK and Germany would be burdened over-proportionately, as these financial places are used not only by domestic, but to a considerable degree also by foreign residents. Unfortunately due to a lack of data, the volume of total transactions and therefore of potential revenues cannot be allocated to the users' countries of residence.

A possible solution to overcome potential resistance of single countries might be to grant all countries a certain share of the revenues they raise within their jurisdictions, which would also provide an incentive for effectively implementing and enforcing the respective international tax. At the same time it can be assumed that taxes which are not enforceable at a national level, as a general financial transaction tax, would be supported by all countries involved regardless of the regional distribution of the potential tax revenues, as long as each country benefits directly (in form of a share in total revenues) or indirectly (e.g., in form of reduced contributions to the EU budget). In any case the considerations above suggest that the introduction of new taxes should be much easier than assigning existing ones to the supranational level, because the latter option can be expected to inspire a debate about cross-country distribution effects due to the different weight of the affected taxes on national budgets.

Who Should Be in Charge of Implementing and Enforcing International Taxes?

A question of eminent importance not only from a technical/administrative but from a political point of view is who should be in charge of deciding on the introduction of international taxes as well as on their tax base and rate, and of implementing and enforcing them. Or to put the question differently: does an effective implementation of international taxes require a world parliament with democratic legitimacy?

Currently no supranational institutions exist with the power to tax and to enforce taxation. Tax sovereignty is regarded as one of the most, or even the most fundamental element of national sovereignty which national governments and parliaments are extremely reluctant to give up. This reluctance is mirrored, for example, in the unanimity principle in tax matters anchored in the EU Treaty according to which all decisions in tax matters require an affirmative vote by all member states. International (economic) institutions, which according to some proposals should be assigned sovereignty in the realm of international taxes (e.g., the IMF or the EU), lack democratic legitimacy. Stiglitz (2006) correctly criticises the fact that international economic institutions are 'undemocratic and opaque' (ibid.: 153) and characterised by 'smokestack structures' (ibid.: 154) which do not allow for any influence of important actors and stakeholders on decision making. At EU level the European Parliament, even after the recent reform of the EU Treaty, still cannot be regarded as an adequate substitute for national democratic parliamentary control. This does not imply, however, that the current political framework conditions would necessarily preclude the introduction and effective implementation of international taxes. As long as tax sovereignty remains completely at the level of nation states, the introduction of international taxes would require their cooperation. Some thought must be given to the design of an adequate institutional framework for tax collection and allocation to international public goods, including incentives to cooperate and sanctions for non-cooperative behaviour of individual countries. In the long run, the increasing emergence and acuteness of global problems might bring about supranational political structures and institutions with sufficient democratic legitimacy to take over some tax sovereignty from nation states.

Coordination with Other Policy Instruments

As diverse regulatory frameworks and agreements are emerging to cope with global challenges (e.g., the Kyoto Protocol to combat climate change, or the currently discussed measures for financial market regulation) and also other monetary instruments (e.g., the European emission-trading system, ETS) are applied, the need to coordinate these frameworks and policy instruments with international taxes is intensified. This involves the evaluation of the pros and cons of individual policy instruments and regulatory approaches in a comparative perspective as well as a comprehensive evaluation to identify potential feedbacks and inter-linkages, as a central prerequisite of their coordinated use, so that synergies can be exploited on the one hand and counterproductive effects can be avoided on the other.

Use of Revenues

Not the least problem is to reach an agreement between the countries involved about the qualitative structure and the quantitative supply of international public goods and the required amount of revenues from international taxes. Such an agreement may be hindered by different country-specific benefits from an international public good. Furthermore there are competing potential purposes for which the revenues from international taxes may be used – see the example of the EU where EU taxes are discussed as a revenue instrument to finance the EU budget as well as more global concerns like climate change and development. There may also be different assessments concerning the magnitude and urgency of global challenges, e.g., climate change, and the total benefits of international public goods, e.g., development aid.

Conclusion

This rather policy-oriented chapter is aimed at establishing a research agenda to improve the theoretical and empirical foundations for international taxes, departing from the observation that academic work in this field is lagging far behind the political discussion and that political initiatives in favour of international taxes are considerably retarded by this lack of a solid scientific basis. The author is convinced, however, that despite all potential problems and open questions associated with international taxes they should and most certainly will play a larger role in the future. And, even as an economist, one can hardly reject the conclusion of the Landau Report: 'The creation of a global tax is more a political than an economic or technical issue' (Groupe de travail sur les nouvelles contributions financières internationales 2004).

Notes

1. Often the terms 'global public goods' and 'international public goods' are used inter-changeably. We prefer the latter one which does not suggest that practically all countries worldwide need to be involved. Analogously, we prefer the term 'international taxes' to the term 'global taxes'.

2. One exception is the tax competition/harmonisation literature where a few authors have dealt with the implications of the existence of international public goods for international tax cooperation; see, e.g., Bjorvatn and Schjelderup (2002) or Kammas and Philippopoulos (2010).

3. See *Global Public Policies and Programs: Implications for Financing and Evaluation*, edited by Gerrard, Ferroni and Mody (2001) and *The New Public Finance*, edited by Kaul and Conceicao (2006).

4. See the volume edited by Ul Haq, Kaul and Grunberg (2006) which was followed by a rather voluminous theoretical and empirical literature – mostly rather sceptical – dealing with financial transaction taxes in general and the Tobin Tax in particular.

5. See, e.g., the recent European Commission Staff Working Paper on 'Innovative financing at a global level' (European Commission 2010c).

6. See, e.g., the so-called Landau Report (Groupe de travail sur les nouvelles contributions financières internationales 2004).

7. For a comprehensive presentation of the various types and properties of international public goods see Barrett (2008).

8. Meanwhile, several authors and the European Commission itself have established catalogues with criteria and principles for EU taxes. Our catalogue on the one hand is more general and comprehensive so that it can be applied to international taxes in general and not only to EU taxes; on the other hand it does not consider specific criteria relevant particularly in the debate about EU taxes (see, e.g. the catalogue compiled by Begg [2011]).

9. See Musgrave (1983), Gordon (1983), Inman and Rubinfeld (1996), or McLure (2001).

10. This catalogue is an extended version of the criteria elaborated in Schratzenstaller and Berghuber (2007).

11. Also called 'global common goods' in the Landau Report (Groupe de travail sur les nouvelles contributions financières internationales 2004).

12. These criteria are also applied by the European Commission (2010c).

13. One could also think of the agreed and coordinated implementation of a new tax across the whole of the EU, for which member states set the tax rate and the tax base, or of the complete harmonisation of a national tax; with revenues in both variants flowing into national budgets: obviously, these options can hardly be labelled as EU taxes.

14. See for a more detailed discussion of the problems associated with the current system of self-generated resources Schratzenstaller and Berghuber (2007) or Begg (2011).

15. For details see Schratzenstaller and Berghuber (2007).

16. However, there are also several EU countries with only short episodes of taxing air tickets due to fierce resistance from airlines and the tourism industry: in the Netherlands, a flight ticket tax introduced in 2008 was abolished in 2009; Denmark and Malta repealed their ticket taxes in 2007 and 2008, respectively; in Sweden a proposal for a ticket tax was withdrawn in 2006, in Belgium in 2008.

17. At the Paris Conference 'Solidarity and Globalisation: Innovative Financing for Development and Against Pandemics' in 2006, France along with twelve other countries (from the EU only Cyprus, Luxembourg and the United Kingdom) committed themselves to introduce an air ticket tax in the near future to finance development and health issues. France is the only EU country which in fact introduced the tax; the UK increased their flight ticket tax several times during the past years but in contrast to their commitment in Paris revenues are still just used to bolster the federal budget.

18. It should be noted that the European Commission (2010c) is rather sceptical about the allocative efficiency of a general financial transactions tax: 'The effect of such a tax on price volatility, including more persistent deviations from fundamental equilibrium levels, is unclear. Raising the price of transactions would affect the price finding mechanism and could have negative effects on the allocative efficiency of financial markets' (ibid.: 52).

19. See for a recent meta-analysis De Mooij and Ederveen (2008).

20. See for an overview De Santis and Stähler (2008).

21. See for the following figures European Commission (2010c).

Notes on Contributors

Douglas Bamford is a researcher in the Politics and International Studies department at the University of Warwick in the UK. His research interests are liberal political philosophy, egalitarianism, and taxation.

John Christensen directs the international operations of the Tax Justice Network. His researches into the role of tax havens in the global economy started in 1985 and have included twelve years working in the British tax haven of Jersey, where he served as economic adviser to the government from 1987 to 1998. His work in building a global tax justice movement is funded by the Joseph Rowntree Charitable Trust, an independent organisation committed to funding radical change towards a better world.

Dieter Eissel is Emeritus Professor of Political Science at Giessen University in Germany. His research interests and publications are concentrated mainly on economic and social policy, the EU, regional and local policies; he has conducted numerous research projects, including cooperation with several European universities, regional and local authorities; he is a member of the International Advisory Board of two British journals and co-editor of the series *Regionalisierung in Europa*. He is a member of the Academy of Science of Mongolia and lectures at European and Asian universities.

Paolo Ermano is Assistant Lecturer in the Department of Economics at the University of Udine in Italy, having studied at the universities of Trieste, Piedmont and Turin, as well as at Stirling in Scotland. His current teaching is in the area of public service management. He has recently organised a course in economics under the auspices of the Banca Etica, which is open to all comers. His research focuses on issues of distribution and taxation in economic theory.

Miguel Glatzer is Assistant Professor of Political Science at La Salle University, Philadelphia, USA. His research focuses on the politics of globalisation, democracy and inequality in comparative perspective as well as social policy in authoritarian regimes. He is the co-editor of *Politics Matters: Globalization and the Future of the Welfare State* (University of Pittsburgh Press, 2004) as well as *Portugal: Strategic Options in a European Context* (Lexington Books, 2003) and has also published in the journal *South European Society and Politics*.

Caren Grown is Professor of Economics at the American University in Washington D.C. Her research interests are focused on the gender dimension of economic development and feminist economics. Her recent work has involved comparative studies of gender and taxation in developing countries. She is currently Senior Gender Advisor at the US Agency for International Development. She is also Associate Editor of *Feminist Economics*.

George Irvin is a retired professor of economics and for many years worked at the Institute of Social Studies in The Hague. He is now Professorial Research Fellow in Development Studies in the School of Oriental and African Studies at the University of London. His most recent publications include *Super Rich: The Rise of Inequality in Britain and the United* (Polity, 2008) and *Regaining Europe: An Economic Agenda for the 21ˢᵗ Century* (Palgrave Macmillan, 2006).

Yusuf Kaçar is lecturer in Accountancy in the Social Science Vocational College at Marmara University, Istanbul, Turkey. His main areas of research are the funding of political parties and issues relating to accounting for tax justice. He is also on the editorial board of the *Journal of Marmara Social Research*.

Jeremy Leaman is Senior Lecturer in the School of Social, Political and Geographical Sciences at Loughborough University, UK, with a primary research focus on German and European political economy. He is currently completing a study of taxation policy in Europe. Recent publications include *The Bundesbank Myth* (Palgrave, 2001) and *The Political Economy of Germany under Chancellors Kohl and Schröder* (Berghahn, 2009). He is also managing editor of the *Journal of Contemporary European Studies* and a member of the Euromemorandum Group.

Dries Lesage is Professor of Globalisation and Global Governance at the Ghent Institute for International Studies, Ghent University. His main research interests are the global governance architecture, the G8 and G20, as well as global taxation and energy governance. He has published on international tax governance in journals such as *Oxford Development Studies, Studia Diplomatica* and *Development Policy Review*.

Olatunde Julius Otusanya is a lecturer in Accounting at the University of Lagos, Nigeria. He obtained his Master's and Doctoral degrees in Accounting from the University of Lagos and the University of Essex respectively. He has published a number of articles and monographs. His research interests include financial crime, tax evasion and tax avoidance, the role of professionals in anti-social practices and corporate social responsibility. He has received several research grants and awards.

Paul Sagar is currently a PhD candidate at the University of Cambridge, working primarily on eighteenth century moral and political philosophy. Prior to graduate study he undertook extensive archival research for the Tax Justice Network, investigating the historical emergence of Britain's offshore tax haven network. He has co-edited *Fight Back!*, a collection of writings emerging from the UK student protests of late 2010 (Open Democracy, 2011), has written for *The Guardian* website, and is a regular contributor to UK politics blog *Liberal Conspiracy*.

Margit Schratzenstaller has held the position of Senior Researcher (Public Finance) at the Austrian Institute of Economic Research (WIFO) in Vienna, Austria since April 2003. Her research interests are (European) budget and tax policy, international tax competition and harmonisation, fiscal federalism, gender budgeting. She is a member of the Austrian Federal Debt Committee and lecturer at the University of Vienna. She is currently also co-editor of *Intervention: European Journal of Economics and Economic Policies*.

Nick Shaxson is a British author, journalist and an Associate Fellow of Chatham House, the Royal Institute of International Affairs in London. He is best known for his investigative books *Poisoned Wells* (2007) and *Treasure Islands* (2011). He is a full-time writer and researcher for the *Tax Justice Network*. He has written extensively on global business and politics for the *Financial Times*, Reuters, the *Economist* and its sister publication the *Economist Intelligence Unit*, *International Affairs* and *Foreign Affairs*.

Imraan Valodia is Professor of Economics and Senior Research Fellow in the School of Development Studies, University of KwaZulu-Natal, South Africa. His research interests include the informal economy, gender and economic policy, as well as trade and industrial development, areas in which he has published widely. With Caren Grown, he coordinated an eight-country international comparative study on gender and taxation.

Alberto Vega is a doctoral candidate in Law at Universitat Pompeu Fabra (Barcelona, Spain). He has also been a guest research student at the Max Planck Institute for Intellectual Property, Competition and Tax Law (Munich, Germany) and at the University of Heidelberg (Germany). His research interests include international tax law, comparative tax law and the economic analysis of law.

Attiya Waris is Senior Lecturer in the Department of Commercial Law at the University of Nairobi in Kenya and a Visiting Lecturer in the Law School at the National University of Rwanda. Her research interests include work on tax law combined with poverty alleviation, development and human rights with specific reference to developing countries.

Bibliography

Archival Sources

Bank of England Archives, un-coded file marked 'Bahamas – Start Date 1934, Completion Date 1965'.

The National Archives, Public Record Office, File T295/587 - *Overseas tax havens: balance of payments and tax problems.*

The National Archives, Public Record Office, File T295/588 - *Overseas tax havens: balance of payments and tax problems.*

The National Archives, Public Record Office, File T295/892 - *Balance of payments and tax problems resulting from the setting up of overseas 'tax havens'.*

The National Archives, Public Record Office, File T295/1013 - *Balance of payments and tax problems resulting from the setting up of overseas 'tax havens'.*

The National Archives, Public Record Office, File T317/1452 - *Tax havens and tax concessions for development schemes in the Turks and Caicos Islands and other dependant territories.*

The National Archives, Public Record Office, File T317/1453 - *Tax havens and tax concessions for development schemes in the Turks and Caicos Islands and other dependant territories.*

The National Archives, Public Record Office, File T328/1157 - *Balance of Payments aspects of tax questions (including use of Falkland Islands as a tax haven).*

Secondary Sources

AAPPG (2006) 'The Other Side of the Coin: The UK and Corruption in Africa', Report by the Africa All Party Parliamentary Group, March 2006, London.

Abdulrazaq, M.T. (1993) *Nigerian Tax Offences and Penalties.* Ilorin: Batay Law Publications Limited, Nigeria.

————— (2002) 'Tax Avoidance', in CITN (ed.), *CITN Nigerian Tax Guide Statutes*, pp. 675–85. Lagos: Chartered Institute of Taxation in Nigeria.

Accountancy Age (2005) 'Corporate Tax Dodgers Contribute to World Poverty'. Available at <http://www.accountanchage.com/articles/print/2142242> (accessed 10 October 2006).

Accounting Standards Board (2010) 'Response to the European Commission'. Available at <http://circa.europa.eu/Public/irc/markt/markt_consultations/library?l=/account-ing/country-by-country/public_authorities/accounting_standards/_EN_1.0_&a=d> (accessed 3 September 2010).

Acemoglu, D., S. Johnson and J.A. Robinson (2001) 'The Colonial Origins of Comparative Development: An Empirical Investigation', *American Economic Review* 91(5): 1369–401.

Acemoglu, D. and J.A. Robinson (2006) *Economic Origins of Dictatorship and Democracy*. Cambridge: Cambridge University Press.

Adema, W. and M. Ladaique (2009) 'How Expensive is the Welfare State?', OECD Social, Employment and Migration Working Paper 92. Paris: OECD.

Akanni, O.P. (2007) 'Oil Wealth and Economic Growth in Oil Exporting African Countries', AERRC Research Paper 170. Nairobi: African Economic Research Consortium.

Akinsanya, A.A. (1986) 'Nigeria and the Multinational', in G.O. Olusanya and R.A. Akindele (eds), *Nigeria's External Relations*. Ibadan: University Press Ltd.

Alm, J., R. Bahl and M.N. Murray (1991) 'Tax Base Erosion in Developing Countries', *Economic Development and Cultural Change* 39(4): 849–72.

Altman, Z.D. (2006) *Dispute Resolution under Tax Treaties*. Amsterdam: IBFD.

Altshuler, R. and H. Grubert (2005) 'The Three Parties to the Race to the Bottom: Host Countries, Home Countries and Multinational Companies', unpublished paper (March).

Andrews, William D. 1974. 'A Consumption-Type or Cash Flow Personal Income Tax', *Harvard Law Review* 87(6): 1113–188.

Arbeitsgruppe Alternative Wirtschaftspolitik (Alternative Economic Policy Working Group) (2010) 'Memorandum 2010. Sozial-ökologische Regulierung statt Sparpolitik und Steuergeschenken'. Cologne: Papyrossa.

Arecelus, F.J., B. Sharma and G. Srinivasan (2005) 'The Human Development Index Adjusted for Efficient Resource Utilization' World Institute for Development Economics Research (WIDER), United Nations University.

Aristotle (1976) *The Ethics of Aristotle: The Nicomachean Ethics*. Harmondsworth/New York: Penguin.

Arrow, K.J. and A.C. Fischer (1974) 'Environmental Preservation, Uncertainty and Irreversibility', *Quarterly Journal of Economics* 88: 312–19.

Atkinson, A.B. (2003): 'Income Inequality in OECD Countries: Data and Explanations', CESifo Working Paper 881, Munich: Centre for Economic Studies.

Atkinson, Anthony and Thomas Piketty (2007) *Top Incomes over the Twentieth Century: A Contrast between Continental European and English-speaking Countries*. Oxford: Oxford University Press.

Atkinson, R.D. (2007) 'Expanding the R&E Tax Credit to Drive Innovation, Competitiveness and Prosperity', *The Journal of Technology Transfer* 32: 617–28.

Auerbach, Alan J. (2009) 'Income or Consumption Taxes?', in R. Krever and J.G. Head (eds), *Tax Reform in the 21st Century*, pp. 147-65. Alphen aan den Rijn: Kluwer Law International.

Ault, H.J. (2009) 'Reflections on the Role of the OECD in Developing International Tax Norms', *Brooklyn Journal of International Law* 34: 757–81.

Ault, Hugh J. and David F. Bradley (1990) 'U.S. Taxation of International Income', in A. Razin and J. Slemrod (eds), *Taxation in the Global Economy, A National Bureau of Economic Research Project Report*. Chicago: University of Chicago Press.

Autorité des Normes Comptables (2010) 'Letter to the IASB, 6 September 2010'. Available at <http://www.ifrs.org/NR/rdonlyres/E50ABE46-73AF-4A18-8794-A308A2E1AE79/0/CL140.pdf> (accessed 15 September 2010).

Avi-Yonah, Reuven S. (2000) 'Globalization, Tax Competition, and the Fiscal Crisis of the Welfare State', *Harvard Law Review* 113(7): 1573–676.

Ayanwale, A.B. (2007) 'FDI and Economic Growth: Evidence from Nigeria', AERRC Research Paper 165. Nairobi: African Economic Research Consortium.

Babawale, T. (2006) 'Nigeria in the Crises of Governance and Development: A Retrospective and Prospective Analysis of Selected Issues and Events'. Working Paper for IKEJA. Lagos: Political and Administrative Resource Centre.

Backhaus, J. (2002) 'Fiscal Sociology – What For?', *American Journal of Economics and Sociology* 61(1): 55–77.

Bahl, R.W. and R.M. Bird (2008) 'Tax Policy in Developing Countries: Looking Back – and Forward', *National Tax Journal* LXI (2): 279–301.

Baiocchi, G. (2001) 'Participation, Activism, and Politics: The Porto Alegre Experiment and Deliberative Democratic Theory', *Politics & Society* 29(1): 43–72.

Baistrocchi, E.A. (2008) 'The Use and Interpretation of Tax Treaties in the Emerging World: Theory and Implications', *British Tax Review* 4: 352–91.

Bakan, J. (2004) *The Corporation: The Pathological Pursuit of Profit and Power*. London: Constable and Robinson Ltd.

Baker, R. (1999) 'The Biggest Loophole in the Free Market System', *The Washington Quarterly* 22(4): 29–46.

Baker, R.W. (2005) *Capitalism's Achilles Hell: Dirty Money and How to Renew the Free Market System*. New Jersey: John Wiley and Sons.

Bakre, O.M. (2006a) 'Tax Avoidance, Capital Flight and Poverty in Nigeria: The Unpatriotic Collaboration of the Elite, the Multinational Corporations and the Accountants: Some Evidence', paper presented at the University of Essex Tax Workshop, Essex Business School, University of Essex, UK, July.

——— (2006b) 'The Spoil of Oil: How Multinationals and Their Professionals Advisers Drain Nigeria of Much Needed Resources', *Tax Justice Focus* 2(3): 4–5.

——— (2007) 'Money Laundering and Trans-organised Crime in Nigeria: Collaboration of Local and Foreign Capitalist Elites', School of Accounting, Finance and Management Working Paper 07/03. University of Essex, UK: School of Accounting, Finance and Management.

Bamford, Douglas (2010) 'The NARC Conception of Comprehensive Income', unpublished manuscript.

Bamford, Douglas (forthcoming) *Rethinking Tax: An Introduction to the CLIPH-Rate Tax*. London: Searching Finance.

Banco de Portugal (2009) 'The Portuguese Economy in the Context of Economic, Financial and Monetary Integration'. Lisboa: Banco de Portugal, Economics and Research Department.

Barrett, S. (2001) 'Financing Global Public Goods', in C.D. Gerrard, M. Ferroni and A. Mody (eds), *Global Public Policies and Programs: Implications for Financing and Evaluation*, pp. 93–203. Washington DC: World Bank.

——— (2008) *Why Cooperate? The Incentive to Supply Global Public Goods*. Oxford: Oxford University Press.

Barsh, R.L. (1991) 'The Right to Development as a Human Right – Results of the Global Consultation', *Human Rights Quarterly* 13(3): 322–38.

Basok, T. and S. Ilcan (2006) 'In the Name of Human Rights: Global Organizations and Participating Citizens', *Citizenship Studies* 10(3): 309–27.

BDI (Bundesverband der deutschen Industrie) (ed.) (2008) 'Systemkopf Deutschland Plus. Die Zukunft der Wertschöpfung am Standort Deutschland', BDI-Drucksache No. 405, January. Available at <www.bdi.eu> (accessed 15 April 2010).

Begg, Ian (2011) 'An EU Tax – Overdue Reform or Federalist Fantasy?' Working Paper, International Policy Analysis Bonn: Friedrich-Ebert-Stiftung International Policy Analysis.

Beinhocker, E.D. (2006) *The Origin of Wealth*. Boston,MA: Harvard Business School Press.

Belloc, M. and P. Vertova (2004) 'How Does Public Investment Affect Economic Growth in HIPC? An Empirical Assessment', Working Paper 416. Siena: Department of Economics, University of Siena.

Bergh, A. and M. Karlsson (2010) 'Government Size and Growth: Accounting for Economic Freedom and Globalization', *Public Choice* 142: 195–213.

Bernardi, Luigi and Paola Profeta (eds) (2004) *Tax Systems and Tax Reforms in Europe*. London: Routledge.

Bertrand, M. and S. Mullainathan (2000) 'Do CEOs Set Their Own Pay? The Ones Without Principals Do', National Bureau of Economic Research Working Paper 7604. Washington DC: NBER

Bessard, Pierre (2008) *Das europäische Steuerkartell und die Rolle der Schweiz*. Zurich: Liberales Institut.

Bieler, Andreas and Adam David Morton (2004) 'A Critical Theory Route to Hegemony, World Order and Historical Change: Neo-Gramscian Perspectives in International Relations', *Capital and Class* 81(1): 85–113.

Bird, Richard M. and Jack M. Mintz (2003) 'Sharing the International Tax Base in a Changing World', in S. Cnossen and H.-W. Sinn (eds), *Public Finance and Public Policy in the New Century* (The CESifo Seminar Series), pp. 405-46. Cambridge, MA: MIT Press.

Bittker, Boris (1967) 'A "Comprehensive Tax Base" as a Goal of Income Tax Reform', *Harvard Law Review* 80(5): 925–85.

Bjorvatn, K. and G. Schjelderup (2002) 'Tax Competition with International Public Goods', *International Tax and Public Finance* 9(2): 111–20.

Blanchflower, D. (2011) 'Enough of These Ridiculous Rate Rise Calls', *New Statesman* (online), 16 February. Available at <http://www.newstatesman.com/blogs/david-blanchflower/2011/02/mervyn-king-growth-inflation> (accessed 19 February 2011).

BMAS (Federal Ministry of Labour and Social Affairs) (ed.) (2009) *Statistisches Taschenbuch*. Berlin: BMAS.

———— (2010) *Statistisches Taschenbuch*, Berlin: BMAS.

BMF (Federal Ministry of Finance) (2008) *Die Wichtigsten Steuern im Internationalen Vergleich, 2008*. Berlin: BMF.

——— Monthly Reports (various).

———— (2011) 'Results of Tax Assessment', no. 11. Berlin: BMF.

Boix, C. (2003) *Democracy and Redistribution*. Cambridge: Cambridge University Press.

Bonney, R. (1999) *The Rise of the Fiscal State in Europe, c 1200–1815*. Oxford: Oxford University Press.

Borges, Antonio (1991) 'A Economia Portuguesa de 1985 a 1991 – Estabilizacao, Crescimento, Reformas Estruturais e Equidade', in Marcelo Rebelo de Sousa et al. (eds), *Portugal em Mudanca*, pp. 41–103. Lisboa: Imprensa Nacional – Casa da Moeda.

Boucher, B. and Y. Bramoullé (2010) 'Providing Global Public Goods under Uncertainty', *Journal of Public Economics* 94(9–10): 591–603.

Boxell, James (2011) 'Majority Hostile to Business Tax Avoidance', *Financial Times* (online), 11 February. Available at <http://www.ft.com/cms/s/0/fc2cfeda-35f9-11e0-b67c-00144feabdc0.html#axzz1HvuDL9Ou> (accessed 11 February 2012).

Bratton M., R.B. Mattes and E. Gyimah-Boadi (2005) *Public Opinion, Democracy, and Market Reform in Africa*. Cambridge: Cambridge University Press.

Brennan, G. and J.M. Buchanan (1980) *The Power to Tax: Analytical Foundations of a Fiscal Constitution*. Cambridge: Cambridge University Press.

Brett, E.A. (1973) *Colonialism and Underdevelopment in East Africa: The Politics of Economic Change 1919–1939*. Nairobi: Heinemann.

Brewer, Mike, Carl Emerson and Helen Miller (2011) *IFS Green Budget*. London: Institute for Fiscal Studies.

Brewer, Mike, Alissa Goodman, Alistair Muriel and Luke Sibieta (2007) 'Poverty and Inequality in the UK: 2007', IFS Briefing Note 73. London: Institute for Fiscal Studies.

Briggs, A. (1961) 'The Welfare-State in Historical-Perspective', *Archives Europeennes de Sociologie* 2(2): 221–58.

British Institute of Directors (2010) 'How Competitive is the UK Tax System?' London: British Institute of Directors.

Brittain-Catlin, W. (2005) *Offshore: The Dark Side of the Global Economy*. New York: Farrar, Straus and Giroux.

Brooks, K. (2007) 'Tax Treaty Treatment of Royalty Payments from Low-Income Countries: A Comparison of Canada and Australia's Policies', *eJournal of Tax Research* 5(2): 168–97.

——— (2009) 'Inter-Nation Equity', in R. Krever and J.G. Head (eds), *Tax Reform in the 21st Century*, pp. 471–498. Alphen aan den Rijn: Kluwer Law International.

Brooks, Richard (2011) 'The Principles of Tax Policy', written evidence to UK Parliament. Available at <http://www.publications.parliament.uk/pa/cm201011/cmselect/cmtreasy/memo/taxpolicy/m46.htm> (accessed 11 December 2011).

Brown, Alexander (2009) *Ronald Dworkin's Theory of Equality: Domestic and Global Perspectives*. Basingstoke: Palgrave Macmillan.

Brown, E. Cary and Luis M.C.P. Beleza (1976) 'Some Long-Run Goals of Tax Reform in Portugal', in The German Marshall Fund of the United States and Fundacao Calouste Gulbenkian, *Conferencia Internacional Sobre Economia Portuguesa*.

Brown, G. and N. Sarkozy (2009) 'For Global Finance, Global Regulation', *Wall Street Journal*, 9 December.

Brown, J. (2010) 'Personal Taxes and Distributional Impact of Budget Measures', Institute for Fiscal Studies Working Paper. London: Institute for Fiscal Studies.

Brown, N.J. and P. Quiblier (eds) (1994) *Ethics and Agenda 21: Moral Implications of a Global Consensus*. New York: United Nations Environmental Programme.

Bruce, Robert (2008) 'IASB: Barriers Fall as New World Order Fast Emerges', *Financial Times* (online), 25 March. Available at <http://www.ft.com/cms/s/0/f0d2ff38-f7a6-11dc-ac40-000077b07658,s01=1.html#axzz1HvuDL9Ou> (accessed 5 May 2010).

Bruton, H.J. and C. Hill (eds) (1996) *The Evaluation of Public Expenditure in Africa*. Washington, DC: World Bank.

Buchanan, J. (1954) 'Social Choice, Democracy, and Free Markets', *The Journal of Political Economy* 62: 114–23.

Budlender, D. (2000) 'The Political Economy of Women's Budgets in the South', *World Development* 28(7): 1365–78.

———— (2003) 'The Debate about Household Headship', *Social Dynamics* 29(2): 48–72.

Budlender, D., D. Casale and I. Valodia (2010) 'Gender and Taxation in South Africa', in Caren Grown and Imraan Valodia, *Taxation and Gender Equity: A Comparative Analysis of Direct and Indirect Taxation in Developing and Developed Countries*, pp. 206–32. London and New York: Routledge.

Buiter, Willem (2008) 'Blockade the Tax Havens', *Financial Times Maverecon Blog*, 20 February.

Bundesverband der Deutschen Industrie (BDI) (2011) 'Stellungnahme. Konsultation zur länderspezifischen Berichterstattung von multinationalen Unternehmen'. Available at <http://circa.europa.eu/Public/irc/markt/markt_consultations/library?l=/accounting/country-by-country/registered_organisations/bundesverband_deutschen/_DE_1.0_&a=d> (accessed 5 June 2011).

Business Europe (2010) 'Letter to the European Commission of 22 December 2010'. Available at <http://circa.europa.eu/Public/irc/markt/markt_consultations/library?l=/accounting/country-by-country/registered_organisations/businesseurope2/_EN_1.0_&a=d> (accessed 3 Februay 2011).

Byrne, D. and S. Ruane (2008) 'The UK Tax Burden: Can Labour Be Called the "Party Of Fairness"?' Compass Thinkpiece 40. London: Compass.

Cable, Vince (2009) 'The Offensive Secrecy of Tax Havens', *The Guardian* (online), 23 September. Available at <http://www.guardian.co.uk/commentisfree/2009/sep/23/tax-havens-g20/print> (accessed 24 September 2012).

Cadbury 2008 Annual Report and Accounts (2008) 'Focused on Performance: Delivering Against Our Plan', pp. 1–148. Available at <www.cadbury.com>.

Cain, P.J. and A.G. Hopkins (1993) *British Imperialism – Crisis and Deconstruction 1914–1990*. Harlow, Essex: Longman.

Cameron, David (1978) 'The Expansion of the Public Economy: A Comparative Analysis', *American Political Science Review* 72: 1243–61.

Campbell, J.L. (1993) 'The State and Fiscal Sociology', *Annual Review of Sociology* 19: 163–85.

Caney, Simon (2006) *Justice Beyond Borders: A Global Political Theory*. Oxford: Oxford University Press.

Carrier, J. and I. Kendall (1986) 'Categories, Categorizations and the Political-Economy of Welfare', *Journal of Social Policy* 15: 315–35.

Cavaco Silva, Anibal (1999) 'Political Economy and the Equity-Policy Agenda', in Vito Tanzi, Ke-young Chu and Sanjeev Gupta (eds), *Economic Policy and Equity*. Washington, DC: International Monetary Fund.

———— (2001) *Cronicas de Uma Crise Anunciada*. Lisboa: Editorial Noticias.

CDF Secretariat. (2009) 'CDF Review Taskforce'. Available at <http://www.cdfreview.org/index.php?option=com_content&task=view&id=20&Itemid=1> (accessed 25 September 2009).

Chakraborty, P., L. Chakraborty, K. Karmakar and S. Kapila (2010) 'Gender and Taxation in India', in C. Grown and I. Valodia (eds), *Taxation and Gender Equity: An Analysis of Direct and Indirect Taxes in Developing and Developed Countries*, pp. 94–118. London: Routledge.

Chang, Ha-Joon (2010) 'Is Industrial Strategy Back?', *The Guardian* (online), 9 June 2010. Available at <http://www.guardian.co.uk/business/audio/2010/jun/09/the-business-podcast-industrial-strategy> (accessed 9 June 2012).

Chapman, A. (1996) 'A Violations Approach for Monitoring the International Covenant on Economic, Social and Cultural Rights', *Human Rights Quarterly* 18(1): 23–66.

Checchi, D. (2001) 'Education, Inequality and Income Inequality', STICERD Distributional Analysis Research Programme Papers 52. London: Suntory and Toyota International Centre for Economics and Related Disciplines, LSE.

Chiapello, Eve and Karim Medjad (2009) 'An Unprecedented Privatisation of Mandatory Standard-setting: The Case of European Accounting Policy', *Critical Perspectives on Accounting* 20(4): 448–68.

Christensen, J. and S. Kapoor (2004) 'Tax Avoidance, Tax Competition and Globalisation: Making Tax Justice a Focus for Global Activism', *Accountancy Business and the Public Interest* 3(2).

Christian Aid (2005) 'The Shirt off their Backs: How Tax Policies Fleece the Poor', Christian Aid report, online. Available at <http://www.christianaid.org.uk/images/the_shirts_off_their_backs.pdf> (accessed 6 March 2010).

———— (2006) 'UK Profits From Sub-Saharan Africa Despite Aid and Debt Pledges', *Christian Aid News*. Available at <http://www.christianaid.org.uk/news/media/pressrel/060705p.htm> (accessed 12 June 2010).

———— (2008) 'Death and Taxes: The True Toll of Tax Dodging', Christian Aid report, online. Available at <http://www.christianaid.org.uk/images/deathandtaxes.pdf> (accessed 15 May 2008).

———— (2009) 'False Profits: Robbing the Poor to Keep the Rich Tax-Free', Christian Aid report, online. Available at <http://www.christianaid.org.uk/Images/false-profits.pdf> (accessed 15 April 2009).

Christians, A.D. (2010a) 'Global Trends and Constraints on Tax Policy', *University of British Columbia Law Review*, forthcoming. Available online at Social Science Research Network: <http://ssrn.com/abstract=1445433> (accessed 8 September 2010).

———— (2010b) 'Networks, Norms and National Tax Policy', *Washington University Global Studies Law Review* 9(1): 2–36.

———— (2010c) 'Taxation in a Time of Crisis: Policy Leadership from the OECD to the G20', *Northwestern Journal of Law & Social Policy* 5(5): 19–40.

Chweya, L. (2006) 'Constituency Development Fund: A Critique', *The African Executive*.

CITN (Chartered Institute of Taxation of Nigeria) (2002) *CITN Nigerian Tax Guide and Statutes*. Lagos: Chartered Institute of Taxation of Nigeria.

Claessens, Stijn, Michael Keen and Ceyla Pazarbasioglu (2010) 'Financial Sector Taxation: The IMF's Report to the G-20 and Background Material', Washington, DC: IMF.

Cobham, A. (2005) 'Tax Evasion, Tax Avoidance and Development Finance', Queen Elizabeth House Working Paper Series 129. Available at <http://www3.qeh.ox.ac.uk/pdf/qehwp/qehwps129.pdf> (accessed 6 March 2010).

Cohen, G.A. (1989) 'On the Currency of Egalitarian Justice', *Ethics* 99(4): 906–44.

———— (2008) *Rescuing Justice and Equality*. Cambridge, MA: Harvard University Press.

Collignon, S. (2007) 'The Three Sources of Legitimacy for European Fiscal Policy', *International Political Science Review* 28(2): 155–84.

Commission on Human Rights (1977) 'The Right to Development'. New York: United Nations.

Confederation of British Industry (CBI) (2010) 'Response of the Confederation of British Industry'. Available at <http://circa.europa.eu/Public/irc/markt/markt_consultations/library?l=/accounting/country-by-country/individuals_other/confederation_cbi-enpdf/_EN_1.0_&a=d> (accessed 25 August 2010).

Connolly, W. (ed.) (1984) *Legitimacy and the State*. Oxford: Blackwell.

Constituency Development Fund (2007) 'Minister Appoints CDF Chairman'. Available at <http://consultation.boundarycommissionforengland.independent.gov.uk/> (accessed 25 August 2010).

Cooper, George (1985) 'Taming of the Shrewd: Identifying and Controlling Income Tax Avoidance', *Columbia Law Review* 85(4): 657–725.

Cooper, R.N. (2001) 'Financing International Public Goods: A Historical Overview and New Challenges', in C.D. Gerrard, M. Ferroni and A. Mody (eds), *Global Public Policies and Programs: Implications for Financing and Evaluation*, pp. 15–26. Washington DC: World Bank.

Council of Europe (1953) 'European Convention on Human Rights'. Rome: Council of Europe. Available at <http://conventions.coe.int/Treaty/Commun/ListeTraites. asp?MA=3&CM=7&CL=ENG> (accessed 16 September 2010).

Council of the European Union (2010) 'Council Conclusions on Tax and Development – Cooperating with Developing Countries in Promoting Good Governance in Tax Matters'. Available at <http://www.financialtaskforce.org/wp-content/uploads/2010/07/ Council-of-the-European-Union-June-2010.pdf> (accessed 14 June 2010).

———— (2011) 'Conclusions on Tackling the Challenges on Raw Materials and in Commodity Markets'. Available at <http://www.consilium.europa.eu/uedocs/cms_ Data/docs/pressdata/en/intm/119744.pdf> (accessed 10 March 2011).

Court, J.F. (1992) 'Some Reflections on the Experience of the UN Model in Tax Treaties Between Developed and Developing Countries', in A.H. Figueroa (ed.), *Double Taxation Treaties Between Industrialised and Developing Countries: OECD and UN Models, A Comparison*, pp. 15–19. Deventer, the Netherlands: Kluwer.

Crouch, C. (2008) 'After Privatised Keynesianism', Compass Thinkpiece 41. Available at <http://clients.squareeye.com/uploads/compass/documents/CTP41 KeynesianisamCrouch.pdf> (accessed 5 May 2010).

Cullison, W.E. (1993) 'Public Investment and Economic Growth', *Economic Quarterly* 79(4): 19–33.

Dagan, T. (2000) 'The Tax Treaties Myth', *New York University Journal of International Law and Politics* 32(939): 2–53.

Darity, W. Jr. and P.A. Mason (1998) 'Evidence on Discrimination in Employment: Codes of Colour, Codes of Gender', *The Journal of Economic Perspectives* 12: 63–90.

Dasai, M.A., C.F. Foley and J.R. Hines (2006) 'The Demand for Tax Haven Operation', *Journal of Public Economics* 90(3): 513–31.

Daunton, M. (1994) 'The Entrepreneurial State 1700–1914', *History Today* 44(5): 11–17.

———— (2001) *Trusting Leviathan: The Politics of Taxation in Britain 1799–1914*. Cambridge: Cambridge University Press.

Davies, R.B. (2004) 'Tax Treaties and Foreign Direct Investment', *International Tax and Public Finance* 11(2): 775–802.

De Mooij, R.A. and S. Ederveen (2008) 'Corporate Tax Elasticities: A Reader's Guide to Empirical Findings', *Oxford Review of Economic Policy* 24(4): 680–97.

De Santis, R.A. and F. Stähler (2008) 'Foreign Direct Investment and Environmental Taxes', ECB Working Paper 921. Frankfurt: European Central Bank.

Deloitte, J. (2010) 'Letter to the European Commission of 21 December 2010'. Available at <http://circa.europa.eu/Public/irc/markt/markt_consultations/library?l=/account-ing/country-by-country/individuals_other/be-deloitte_enpdf/_EN_1.0_&a=d> (accessed 2 January 2011).

The Democrat's Diary (2005) 'Africa's Battle with Corruption', in *Perspectives on Western Foreign Policy*, 11 July. Available at <http://www.democratsdiary.co.uk/2005/07/africa battle-with corruption_11> (accessed 10 November 2006).

Deutscher Gewerkschaftsbund (DGB) (2010a) 'Response to the European Commission'. Available at <http://circa.europa.eu/Public/irc/markt/markt_consultations/library?l=/ accounting/country-by-country/registered_organisations/gewerkschaftsbund/_ DE_1.0_&a=d> (accessed 22 September 2010).

——— (2010b) 'Sparpaket: Bundesregierung setzt falsches Signal', DGB-Bundesvorstand, Abteilung Wirtschafts-, Finanz- und Steuerpolitik, *klartext* Nr. 19/2010, 11 June.

Dietsch, Peter and Thomas Rixen (2012) 'Tax Competition and Global Background Justice', *Journal of Political Philosophy* (early view online version).

Dischinger, M. and N. Riedel (2008) 'Corporate Taxes and the Location of Intangible Assets within Multinational Firms', Munich Discussion Paper 2008/15. Munich: University of Munich, Department of Economics.

Dixon, J. and R.P. Scheurell (2002) *The State of Social Welfare: The Twentieth Century in Cross-national Review*. Westport, CN: Praeger.

Dorling, D. (2010) *Injustice: Why Social Inequality Persists*. London: Policy Press.

Downs, Anthony (1957) *An Economic Theory of Democracy*. New York: Harper and Row.

Dworkin, Ronald (2000) *Sovereign Virtue*. Cambridge, MA: Harvard University Press.

Eckhard, Hein and Achim Truger (2008) 'Fiscal Policy in the Macroeconomic Policy Mix: A Critique of the New Consensus Model and a Comparison of Macroeconomic Policies in France, Germany, the UK and Sweden from a Post-Keynesian Perspective', IMK Working Paper 3/08. Düsseldorf: Hans Böckler Foundation Available at <www.imk-boeckler.de>.

Economist Intelligence Unit (2002) 'Country Report: Portugal'. London: EIU.

——— (2003) 'Country Report: Portugal'. London: EIU.

——— (2004) 'Country Report: Portugal'. London: EIU.

——— (2005) 'Country Report: Portugal'. London: EIU.

——— (2006) 'Country Report: Portugal'. London: EIU.

——— (2007) 'Country Report: Portugal'. London: EIU.

——— (2008) 'Country Report: Portugal'. London: EIU.

——— (2009) 'Country Report: Portugal'. London: EIU.

Edwards, Christopher and Daniel Mitchell (2008) *Global Tax Revolution: The Rise of Tax Competition and the Battle to Defend It*. Washington, DC: Cato Institute.

Eissel, Dieter (1997) 'Reichtum unter der Steuerschraube? Staatlicher Umgang mit hohen Einkommen', in E.-U. Huster, *Reichtum in Deutschland. Die Gewinner der sozialen Polarisierung*, pp. 127–57. Frankfurt am Main: Campus.

Eissel, D. (2006) 'Verteilungspolitik, soziale Gerechtigkeit und Wirtschaftskrisen', in Angelika Beier, Kai Eicker-Wolf, Stefan Körzell and Achim Truger (eds), *Investieren, Sanieren, Reformieren? Die Wirtschafts- und Sozialpolitik der Schwarz-roten Koalition*. Marburg: Metropolis.

——— (2008) 'Inequality and Poverty as a Motor for Growth and Prosperity?', *Journal of Contemporary European Studies* 16(1): 9–23.

Elson, D. (2006) *Budgeting for Women's Rights: Monitoring Government Budgets for Compliance with CEDAW*. New York: UNIFEM.

Engen, E.M. and J. Skinner (1996) 'Taxation and Economic Growth', *National Tax Journal* 49: 617–42.

Erhard, L. (1957) *Wohlstand für Alle*. Munich: ECON.

Eriksson, T. and M. Jantti (1997) 'The Distribution of Earnings 1971–1990 in Finland', *European Economic Review* 41: 1763–79.

Esping-Andersen, G. (1990) *The Three Worlds of Welfare Capitalism.* Cambridge: Polity.

Euromemorandum Group (2011) *Euromemorandum 2010/11: Confronting the Crisis: Austerity or Solidarity?*, Available at <http://www.euromemo.eu/euromemorandum/euromemorandum_2010_11/index.html>.

Europa (2012) 'Statement by the EC, ECB and IMF on the Third Review Mission to Portugal', Memo/12/142, Brussels. Available at <http://europa.eu/rapid/pressReleases-Action.do?reference=MEMO/12/142>.

European Commission (1998) 'Financing the European Union', Commission Report on the Operation of the Own Resources System, 1998. Brussels: European Commission.

—— (2004) 'Financing the European Union', Commission Report on the Operation of the Own Resources System, 2004. Brussels: European Commission.

—— (2005) 'New Sources of Finance for Development. A Review of Options', Commission Staff Working Document 2005, SEC(2005)467. Brussels: European Commission.

—— (2008) 'Taxation Trends in the European Union'. Luxembourg: European Commission.

—— (2009a) 'Economic Forecast: Spring 2009'. Luxembourg: European Commission, DOI 10.2765/80609.

—— (2009b) 'General Report on the Activities of the European Union 2009', SEC(2010)18. Luxembourg: European Commission.

—— (2009c) 'Taxation Trends in the European Union 2009', Luxembourg: European Commission Available at <http://ec.europa.eu/taxation_customs> (accessed 15 September 2009).

—— (2010a) 'Taxation Trends in the European Union 2010'. Brussels: European Commission.

—— (2010b) 'European Economic Forecast: Autumn 2010', Commission Staff Working Document. Brussels: European Commission. Available at <http://ec.europa.eu/economy_finance/publications/european_economy/2010/pdf/ee-2010-7_en.pdf> (accessed 15 September 2010).

—— (2010c) 'Innovative Financing at a Global Level', Commission Staff Working Document, SEC(2010)409final. Brussels: European Commission.

—— (2010d) 'Financial Sector Taxation', Commission Staff Working Document, SEC(2010)1166/3. Brussels: European Commission.

—— (2010e) 'The EU Budget Review', COM(2010)700. Brussels: European Commission.

—— (2010f) 'Communication from the Commission to the European Parliament, the Council and the European Economic and Social Committee. Tax and Development. Cooperating with Developing Countries on Promoting Good Governance in Tax Matters', COM(2010)163 final. Brussels: European Commission.

—— (2011a) 'Taxation Trends in the European Union 2010'. Brussels: European Commission.

—— (2011b) 'The Distributional Effect of Austerity Measures: A Comparison of Six EU Countries', EU Social Observatory: Research Note 2. Brussels: EUSO.

European Parliament (2007) 'Resolution of 14 November 2007. International Accounting Standards (IFRS 8)'. Available at <http://www.europarl.europa.eu/sides/getDoc.do?pubRef=-//EP//TEXT+TA+P6-TA-2007-0526+0+DOC+XML+V0//EN&language=EN> (accessed 10 September 2010).

————(2008) 'Resolution of 23 September 2008. Follow-up to the Monterrey Conference of 2002 on Financing for Development'. Available at <http://www. europarl.europa.eu/sides/getDoc.do?pubRef=-//EP//TEXT+TA+P6-TA-2008-0420+0+DOC+XML+V0//EN> (accessed 10 September 2010).

———— (2010a) 'Resolution of 10 February 2010. Promoting Good Governance in Tax Matters'. Available at <http://www.europarl.europa.eu/sides/getDoc. do?type=TA&reference=P7-TA-2010-0020&language=EN> (accessed 10 September 2010).

———— (2010b) 'Resolution of 25 March 2010. The Effects of the Global Financial and Economic Crisis on Developing Countries and on Development Cooperation'. Available at <http://www.europarl.europa.eu/sides/getDoc.do?pubRef=-//EP//TEXT+TA+P7-TA-2010-0089+0+DOC+XML+V0//EN> (accessed 9 September 2010).

———— (2010c) 'Resolution of 15 June 2010. Progress Towards the Achievement of the Millennium Development Goals: Mid-term Review in Preparation of the UN High-level Meeting in September 2010'. Available at <http://www.europarl.europa.eu/sides/getDoc.do?pubRef=-//EP//TEXT+TA+P7-TA-2010-0210+0+DOC+XML+V0//EN> (accessed 10 September 2010).

———— (2011) 'Resolution of 8 March 2011. Cooperating with Developing Countries on Promoting Good Governance in Tax Matters. Available at <http://www. europarl.europa.eu/sides/getDoc.do?pubRef=-//EP//TEXT+TA+P7-TA-2011-0082+0+DOC+XML+V0//EN&language=EN> (accessed 4 April 2011).

Eurostat (2010) 'Government Finance Statistics 2010'. Luxembourg: Eurostat.

———— (2011) 'Government Finance Statistics 2011'. Luxembourg: Eurostat.

Evans, Chris (2009) 'Containing Tax Avoidance', in R. Krever and J.G. Head (eds), *Tax Reform in the 21st Century*. Alphen aan den Rijn, the Netherlands: Kluwer Law International.

Evans-Pritchard, Ambrose (2005) 'Poland's Single Tax-Rate is "Wake-Up Call for the Chancellor"', *Daily Telegraph*, 16 March.

Ezeoha, A.E. and E. Ogamba (2010) 'Corporate Tax Shield or Fraud? Insight from Nigeria', *International Journal of Law and Management* 52(1): 5–20.

Fahnbulleh, M. (2006) 'In Search of Economic Development in Kenya: Colonial Legacies and Postindependence Realities', *Review of African Political Economy* 33(107): 33–47.

Falola, T. and M. Heaton (2008) *A History of Nigeria*. Cambridge: Cambridge University Press.

Fasoto, F. (2005) 'Contentious Issues in Tax Policy and Administration in Nigeria', Joint Tax Board, First National Tax Retreat Proceedings, Ikeja, pp. 26–42. Lagos: Joint Tax Board.

Federal Government of Nigeria (1999) 'Constitution of the Federal Republic of Nigeria 1999'. Lagos: Federal Government Press, Nigeria.

Federal Minister of Finance (2010) 'Results of the Working Group on Tax Assessment', May 2010. Lagos: FMF.

Federal Republic of Nigeria (1999) 'Law of the Federation 1999'. Available at: <http://www.nigeria-law.org/LFNMainPage.htm> (accessed 10 March 2008).

Federal Statistical Office (2006) 'Datenreport 2006'. Wiesbaden: FSO.

———— (2008) 'Datenreport 2008'. Wiesbaden: FSO.

———— (ed.) (2009) 'Yearbook 2009'. Wiesbaden: FSO.

———— (ed.) (2011a) 'Yearbook 2011'. Wiesbaden: FSO.

_____ (2011b) 'Datenreport 2011', Wiesbaden: FSO.

Fernandes Ferreira, Rogerio (1976) 'Commentario', in The German Marshall Fund of the United States and Fundacao Calouste Gulbenkian, *Conferencia Internacional Sobre Economia Portuguesa*. Michigan: University of Michigan Press.

Fernandez, R. and R. Rogerson (1996): 'Income Distribution, Communities, and the Quality of Public Education', *The Quarterly Journal of Economics* 3: 135–64.

Ferrero, Raul (1983) 'Study of the New Economic Order and the Promotion of Human Rights', UN Doc E/CN.4/Sub.2/1983/24. New York: United Nations.

Ferroni, M. and A. Mody (2002) 'Global Incentives for International Public Goods: Introduction and Overview', in M. Ferroni and A. Mody (eds), *International Public Goods: Incentives, Measurement, and Financing*, pp. 1–29. Washington, DC: World Bank.

Figueroa, A.H. (1992) 'Comprehensive Tax Treaties', in: A.H. Figueroa (ed.), *Double Taxation Treaties Between Industrialised and Developing Countries: OECD and UN Models, A Comparison*, pp. 9–13. Deventer, the Netherlands: Kluwer.

Financial Times Editorial (2010) 'A Taxing World', *Financial Times* (online), 21 December. Available at <http://www.ft.com/cms/s/0/60a37860-0d3e-11e0-82ff-00144feabdc0.html#axzz1HvuDL9Ou> (accessed 22 December 2010).

Fiscer, J.A.V. and B. Torgler (2006) 'The Effect of Relative Income Position on Social Capital', *Economics Bulletin* 26: 1–20.

Fleming, J. Clifton Jr., Robert J. Peroni and Stephen E. Shay (2001) 'Fairness in International Taxation: The Ability-to-Pay Case for Taxing Worldwide Income', *Florida Tax Review* 5(4): 299–356.

Frey, B.S. and R. Jegen (2001) 'Motivation Crowding Theory: A Survey Of Empirical Evidence', *Journal of Economic Survey* 15: 589–611.

Frick, J.R. and M.M. Grabka (2009) 'Gestiegene Vermögensungleichheit in Deutschland', *DIW- Wochenbericht* 4: 54–67.

Friedman, M. (1962) *Capitalism and Freedom*. Chicago: Chicago University Press.

Fuchs, M. (1985) *Soziale Sicherheit in der Dritten Welt: Zugleich eine Fallstudie Kenia*. Baden Baden: Nomos.

Fukuda-Parr, S., T. Lawson-Remer and Susan Randolph (2008) 'Measuring the Progressive Realization of Human Rights Obligations: An Index of Economic and Social Rights Fulfilment', University of Connecticut Department of Economics Working Paper Series. University of Connecticut: DigitalCommons@UConn.

G20 (2010) 'The G20 Toronto Summit Declaration', 26–27 June 2010. Available at <http://www.g20.utoronto.ca/2010/to-communique.html> (accessed 10 September 2010).

Galbiati, Roberto and Giulio Zanella (2011) 'The Tax Evasion Social Multiplier: Evidence from Italy'. Available at <www2.dse.unibo.it/zanella/papers/taxevasion.pdf>.

Ganghof, Steffen (2004) 'Progressive Income Taxation in Advanced OECD Countries. Revisiting the Structural Dependence of the State on Capital', paper given at the American Political Science Association Conference, 1–5 September 2004, Chicago.

_____ (2006) *The Politics of Income Taxation*. Colchester: European Consortium for Political Research.

_____ (2008) 'The Politics of Tax Structure', in Ian Shapiro, Peter Swenson and Daniela Donno (eds), *Divide and Deal: The Politics of Distribution in Democracies*. New York: New York University Press.

Ganji, M. (1969) 'The Realization of Economic, Social and Cultural Rights: Problems, Policies, Progress', UN Doc E/CN.4/1108/Rev.1. New York: United Nations.

Genschel, Philipp, Achim Kemmerling and Eric Seils (2011) 'Accelerating Downhill: How the EU shapes Corporate Tax Competition in the Single Market', *Journal of Common Market Studies* 49(3): 585–606.

Gerrard, C.D., M. Ferroni and A. Mody (eds) (2001) *Global Public Policies and Programs: Implications for Financing and Evaluation*. Washington, DC: World Bank.

Giddens, A. (1990) *The Consequences of Modernity*. Stanford, CA: Stanford University Press.

Gideon, Y. (1990) 'Tax Evasion under Differential Taxation, The Economics of Income Source Misreporting', *Journal of Public Economics* 43(2): 327–37.

Gikonyo, W. (2008) *The CDF Social Audit Guide*. Open Society Initiative for East Africa. Nairobi: OSEIA.

Giles, C. (2011) 'Slower Growth Seen as Inflation Buster', *Financial Times*, 16 February. Available at <http://www.ft.com/cms/s/0/3279a6ee-3a0c-11e0-a441-00144feabdc0. html#axzz1EDbJnmWK> (accessed 5 April 2011).

Global Financial Integrity (2009) 'Transparency Key to Curtailing Abusive Offshore Tax Schemes', Press Release, GFI. Available at <http://www.gfip.org/index. php?option=com_content&task=view&id=153&Itemid=70> (accessed 15 August 2010).

Global Witness, Care, Save The Children UK, Open Society Institute, Transparency International UK, Cafod, PWYP (2005) 'International Accounting Standard 14. Segment Reporting. 2005 update', submission to the International Accounting Standards Board. Available at <http://www.taxresearch.org.uk/Documents/IAS14Final. pdf> (accessed 7 September 2010).

Goldscheid, R. (1962) 'A Sociological Approach to Problems of Finance', in R.A. Musgrave and A.T. Peacock (eds), *Classics in the Theory of Public Finance*, pp. 202–13. London: Macmillan and Company.

Goode, Richard (1977) 'The Economic Definition of Income', in Joseph A. Pechman (ed.), *Comprehensive Income Taxation*, pp. 1–30. Washington, DC: Brookings Institute.

Gordon, R.H. (1983) 'An Optimal Taxation Approach to Fiscal Federalism', *Quarterly Journal of Economics* 98(4): 567–68.

Gradin C., C. del Rio and O. Canto (2006) 'Poverty and Women's Labour Market Activity: The Role of Gender Wage', ECINEQ Working Paper, 2006-40. Palma de Mallorca: ECINEQ.

Graf, W.D. (1988) *The Nigerian State: Political Economy, State Class and Political System in the Post Colonial Era*. London: James Currey.

Gravelle, J.G. (2009) 'Tax Havens: International Tax Avoidance and Evasion', *National Tax Journal* 62(4): 727–53.

Greenpeace (2008) 'Conning the Congo', Logging Sector Review, online. Available at <http://www.greenpeace.org/raw/content/international/press/reports/conning-the-congo.pdf> (accessed 20 August 2008).

Gregg, Paul and Emma Tominey (2004) 'The Wage Scar from Youth Unemployment', Centre for Market and Public Organisation Working Paper Series No. 04/097. Bristol: CPMO.

Gregory, M. and R. Jukes (2001) 'Unemployment and Subsequent Earning: Estimating Scarring among British Men 1984–94', *Economic Journal* 3(475): 607–25.

Group of Experts on the UN Programme on Public Administration and Finance (1997) 'Political, Social and Economic Realities in Developing Countries and in Countries with Economies in Transition'. New York: United Nations.

Groupe de travail sur les nouvelles contributions financières internationals (2004) 'Rapport à Monsieur Jacques Chirac'. Paris: Groupe de travail sur les nouvelles contributions financières internationals.

Grown, C. and I. Valodia (eds) (2010) *Taxation and Gender Equity: An Analysis of Direct and Indirect Taxes in Developing and Developed Countries*. London: Routledge.

Grubert, H. (2003) 'Intangible Income Intercompany Transactions, Income Shifting, and the Choice of Location', *National Tax Journal* 56(1): 221–42.

Grubert, H. and J. Mutti (1991) 'Taxes, Tariffs and Transfer Pricing, in Multinational Corporate Decision Making', *Review of Economic and Statistics* 73(2): 285–93.

Guellec, D. and B. Van Pottelsberghe de La Potterie (2003) 'The Impact of Public R&D Expenditure on Business R&D', *Economics of Innovation and New Technology* 12: 225–43.

Ha, Byung-jin, Caroline McInerney, Steven Tobin and Raymond Torres (2010) *Youth Unemployment in Crisis*. Geneva: International Institute of Labour Studies.

Hampton, M.P. (1994) 'Treasure Islands or Fool's Gold: Can and Should Small Island Economies Copy Jersey?' *World Development* 22(2): 237–50.

——— (1996a) 'Exploring the Offshore Interface: The Relationship between Tax Havens, Tax Evasion, Corruption and Economic Development', *Crime, Law and Social Change* 24: 293–317.

——— (1996b) *The Offshore Interface: Tax Havens in the Global Economy*. London: MacMillan.

Hans-Boeckler-Stiftung (2010) 'Finanzpolitik, Kostspielige Steuersenkungen', Boeckler-Impuls No. 6/2010, 21 April 2010. Dusseldorf: Hans-Boeckler-Stiftung. Available at <http://www.boecklerimpuls.de> (accessed 15 June 2010).

Harris, Peter (1996) *Corporate/Shareholder Income Taxation and Allocating Taxing Rights between Countries: A Comparison of Imputation Systems*. Amsterdam: IBFD Publications.

Harvey, D. (1989) *The Conditions of Postmodernity*. Oxford: Basil Blackwell.

Hayek, F.A. (1944) *The Road to Serfdom*. Chicago: University of Chicago Press.

——— (1945) 'The Use of Knowledge in Society', *The American Economic Review* 35(4): 519–30.

——— (1960) *The Constitution of Liberty*. London: Routledge.

Heller, P.S. (1974) 'Public Investment in LDC's With Recurrent Cost Constraint: The Kenyan Case', *Quarterly Journal of Economics* 88(2): 251–77.

Henry, C. (1974) 'Investment Decisions under Uncertainty: The Irreversibility Effect', *American Economic Review* 64: 1006–12.

Hills, J., M. Brewer et al. (2010) *An Anatomy of Economic Inequality in the UK: Report of the National Equality Panel*. London: Government Equalities Office.

Hince, J.R. Jr. and E.M. Rice (1994) 'Fiscal Paradise: Foreign Tax Havens and American Business', *Quarterly Journal of Economics* 109(1): 149–82.

Hines, R. James Jr. and Lawrence Summers (2009) 'How Globalization Affects Tax Design', NBER Working Paper No. 146664. Cambridge, MA: NBER.

Hobson, John M. (2003) 'Disappearing Taxes or the "Race to the Middle"? Fiscal Policy in the OECD', in Linda Weiss (ed.), *States in The Global Economy: Bringing Domestic Institutions Back In*. Cambridge: Cambridge University Press.

Holmes, S. and C.R. Sunstein (1999) *The Cost of Rights: Why Liberty Depends on Taxes*. New York: W.W. Norton.

Horner, F.M. (2001) 'Do We Need an International Tax Organization?', *Tax Notes International* 24: 179–87.

Horton, T. and H. Reed (2010a) 'Where the Money Goes: How We Benefit from Public Services'. London: Trades Union Congress. Available at <http://www.tuc.org.uk/extras/wherethemoneygoes.pdf> (accessed 29 August 2010).

——— (2010b) 'The Distributional Impact of the 2010 Spending Review', *Radical Statistics* 103: 13–24.

Howard, C. (1993) 'The Hidden Side of the American Welfare State', *Political Science Quarterly* 108(3): 403–36. Available at <http://ec.europa.eu/development/icenter/repository/COMM_COM_2010_0163_TAX_DEVELOPMENT_EN.PDF> (accessed 16 June 2010).

Ifo-Institut (2008) 'The EEAG Report on the European Economy 2008'. Munich: Ifo. Available at <www.cesifo-group.de/ pls/guestci/download/ EEAG Report 2008/ EEAG-2008.pdf> (accessed 15 September 2009).

IMF (International Monetary Fund) (2007) 'World Economic Outlook'. Washington, DC: IMF.

——— (2011) 'Revenue Mobilization in Developing Countries', document prepared by the Fiscal Affairs Department. Washington, DC: IMF.

Inman, R.P. and D. Rubinfeld (1996) 'Designing Tax Policy in Federalist Economies: An Overview', *Journal of Public Economics* 60(3): 307–34.

International Accounting Standards Board (2010) 'Extractive Activities', Discussion Paper DP/2010/1. London: IASB.

Irish, C.R. (1974) 'International Double Taxation Agreements and Income Taxation at Source', *International and Comparative Law Quarterly* 23(2): 292–316.

Irvin, G. (2009) 'Now's the Time for a Tobin Tax', *The Guardian*, 11 December 2009. Available at <www.guardian.co.uk/commentisfree/2009/dec/11/tobin-tax->.

——— (2010) 'Rebuilding Social Democracy in Twenty-first Century Britain', *Soundings* 45(Summer): 6–67.

Irvin, G., D. Byrne, R. Murphy, H. Reed and S. Ruane (2009) 'In Place of Cuts: Tax Reform to Build a Fairer Society', Compass pamphlet. London: Compass.

Irvin, G., H. Reed and Z. Gannon (2010) 'The £100bn Gamble on Growth without the State'. London: Compass. Available at <http://www.compassonline.org.uk/ publications/item.asp?d=3265>.

Isaac, T.M.T. and P. Heller (2003) 'Democracy and Development: Decentralized Planning in Kerala', in A. Fung and E.O. Wright (eds), *Deepening Democracy: Institutional Innovations in Empowered Participatory Governance*, pp. 77–110. London: Verso.

Jerome, A. and J. Ogunkola (2004) 'Foreign Direct Investment in Nigeria: Magnitude, Direction and Prospects', paper presented to the African Economic Research Consortium Special Seminar Series, Nairobi.

Johannson, A., C. Heady, B. Brys and L. Vartia (2008) 'Taxation and Economic Growth', OECD Economics Department Working Paper No. 620. Paris: OECD.

Jones, Adam (2011) 'IASB Urges US to Adopt New Accounting Rules', *Financial Times*, 10 March. Available at <http://www.ft.com/cms/s/0/dfc2eae6-4b45-11e0-b2c2-00144feab49a.html#axzz1HvuDL9Ou> (accessed 11 March 2011).

Jones, Adam and James Fontanella-Khan (2011) 'New Dehli Pressed over IFRS Accounting Standards', *Financial Times* (online), 16 January. Available at <http://www.ft.com/cms/s/0/16785760-219d-11e0-9e3b-00144feab49a,s01=1.html#axzz1HvuDL9Ou> (accessed 17 January 2011).

Jowett, J. and P. Wintour (2008) 'Cost of Tackling Global Climate Change has Doubled, Warns Stern', *The Guardian*, 26 June.

Joyce, Robert, Alastair Murie, David Phillips and Luke Sibieta (2010) *Poverty and Inequality in the UK: 2010*. London: IFS.

Julius, A.J. (2006) 'Nagel's Atlas', *Philosophy & Public Affairs* 34(2): 176–92.

Kammas, Pantelis and Apostolis Philippopoulos (2010) 'The Role of International Public Goods in Tax Cooperation' *CESifo Economic Studies* 56(2): 278–99.

Kapoor, S. (2005) 'Plugging the Leaks: A Very Short Paper on Curbing Capital Flight, Tax Avoidance and Tax Evasion for International Policy Dialogue', organised by InWEnt and the Federal Ministry for Economic Cooperation and Development (BMZ). Available at <http://www.new-rules.org/docs/kapoor4.pdf> (accessed 28 March 2006).

Kato, Junko (2003) *Regressive Taxation and the Welfare State*. Cambridge: Cambridge University Press.

Kaufman, Nancy H. (1998) 'Fairness and the Taxation of International Income', *Law & Policy International Business* 29(2): 145–204.

Kaul, I. and P. Conceicao (2006) 'The Changes under Way. Financing Global Challenges through International Cooperation behind and beyond Borders', in I. Kaul and P. Conceicao (eds), *The New Public Finance: Responding to Global Challenge*, pp. 28–70. Oxford: Oxford University Press.

Kaul, I., I. Grunberg and M.A. Stern (eds) (1999) *Global Public Goods: International Cooperation in the 21st Century*. New York: Oxford University Press.

Kelley, D. (2000) 'A Life of One's Own: Individual Rights and the Welfare State', in H.J. Steiner and P. Alston (eds), *International Human Rights in Context: Law, Politics, Morals*. Oxford: Oxford University Press.

Kemp, L.J. (1982) 'The Use of Captive Insurance Companies', *Multinational Business* 1: 1–8.

Kenya National Audit Office (2006–7) 'The Report of the Controller and Auditor General Together with the Appropriation Accounts Other Public Accounts and the Accounts of the Funds of 2006–2007'. Nairobi: Government of Kenya.

Khoo, J. (2007) 'China's Evolution as a Capital Exporter: A Shift in Tax Treaty Policy?', *Hong Kong Law Journal* 37(3): 891–918.

Killian, S. (2008) 'Taxing Thought: Ireland, Tax Competition and the Cost of Intellectual Capital', *Accountancy Business and the Public Interest* 7(1): 70–91.

Kosters, B. (2004) 'The United Nations Model Tax Convention and its Recent Developments', *Asia-Pacific Tax Bulletin* 5(1): 4–11.

Kwamboka, E. (2009a) 'Constituents Sue MP over Fund Misappropriation', *The Standard* (online).

——— (2009b) 'Court Allows Otuoma to Access CDF Kitty', *The Standard* (online).

Lansley, S. (2008) 'Do the Super-Rich Matter?' Touchstone Pamphlet No. 4, TUC. London: Trades Union Congress.

Lawanson, A.O. (2007) 'An Econometric Analysis of Capital Flight from Nigeria: A Portfolio Approach', AERRC Research Paper 166. Nairobi: African Economic Research Consortium.

Lazear, E. and K. Shaw (2007) 'Wage Structure, Raises and Mobility. International Comparisons of the Structure of Wages within and across Firms', NBER Working Paper 13654. Cambridge, MA: NBER.

Leaman, J. (2009) *The Political Economy of Germany under Chancellors Kohl and Schröder*. New York: Berghahn.

——— (2010) 'Youth Unemployment Policy in Britain and Germany. A Comparison of "Third Way" Approaches', in J. Leaman and Martha Wörsching (eds), *Youth in Contemporary Europe*. London: Routledge.

Lefranc, A., N. Pistolesi and A. Trannoy (2009) 'Equality of Opportunity and Luck: Definitions and Testable Conditions, with an Application to Income in France', *Journal of Public Economics* 93: 1189–207.

Leigh, D. (2009), 'The Tax Gap', *The Guardian*. Available at <http://www.guardian.co.uk/business/series/tax-gap> (accessed 16 September 2010).

Lenin, V.I. (1939) *Imperialism: The Highest Stage of Capitalism. A Popular Outline*. London: International Publishers Co., Inc.

Lesage, Dries, David McNair and Mattias Vermeiren (2010) 'From Monterrey to Doha: Taxation and Financing for Development', *Development Policy Review* 28(2): 155–72.

Levin-Waldam, O. (2003) 'The Minimum Wage and the Cause of Democracy', *Review of Social Economy* XLI: 487–510.

Lewis, J. (2000) *Empire State-Building: War and Welfare in Kenya 1925–52*. Oxford: James Curry.

Lucifora, C. and R. Simmons (2003) 'Superstar Effects in Sport. Evidence from Italian Soccer', *Journal of Sports Economics* 4: 35–55.

Machuhi, E. (2009) 'Kenya: Rights Activists Denied CDF Records', *Nation* (online).

MacLean, R. (2005) *Encyclopedia of African History*, ed. K. Shillingdon, Volume 1, pp. 693–99.

MacNamara, William and Christopher Thompson (2011) 'Shell Chief's Warning on Dodd-Frank', *Financial Times*, 2 March. Available at <http://www.ft.com/cms/s/0/f5dcb758-450a-11e0-80e7-00144feab49a.html#axzz1HvuDL9Ou> (accessed 3 March 2011).

Mankiw, N.G., M.C. Weinzier and Yagan D. Ferris (2009) 'Optimal Taxation in Theory and Practice', *Journal of Economic Perspectives* 23: 147–74.

Manso Palazuel, E. (2006) 'The Influence of Earnings on Income Distribution in the United States', *The Journal of Socio-Economics* 35: 710–26.

Mapesa, B.M. and T.N. Kibua (2006) 'An Assessment of the Management and Utilisation of the Constituency Development Fund in Kenya', Discussion Paper Series. Nairobi: Kenya Institute of Policy Analysis and Research.

Mario de Carvalho, A. (1976) 'Comentario', in The German Marshall Fund of the United States and Fundacao Calouste Gulbenkian, *Conferencia Internacional Sobre Economia Portuguesa*. Michigan: University of Michigan Press.

Marmor, Theodore, Jerry Mashaw and Philip Harvey (1990) *America's Misunderstood Welfare State: Persistent Myths, Enduring Realities*. New York: Basic Books.

Martens, J. (2007) 'The Precarious State of Public Finance: Tax Evasion, Capital Flight and Misuse of Public Money in Developing Countries – and What Can be Done about It', Global Policy Forum Report. Available at: <http://www.globalpolicy.org/eu/en/publ/martens_precarious_finance_%20207> (accessed 2 September 2010).

Mathiason, Nick (2009) 'OECD Close to Forcing Multinationals to Reveal Tax Bills', *The Guardian*, 23 June. Available at <http://www.guardian.co.uk/business/2009/jun/23/uk-multinationals-tax-avoidance> (accessed 29 August 2010).

McAuslan, P. and J. McEldowney (eds) (1985) *Law, Legitimacy, and the Constitution: Essays Marking the Centenary of Dicey's Law of the Constitution*. London: Sweet & Maxwell.

McCaffery, Edward J. (2002) *Fair not Flat: How to Make the Tax System Better and Simpler*. Chicago: Chicago University Press.

McKinsey Global Institute (2008) 'Mapping Global Capital Markets', Chapter 2. San Francisco: McKinsey Global Institute Available at <www.mckinsey.com/mgi/reports/pdfs/Mapping_Global/MGI_Mapping_chapter_2.pdf> (accessed 15 June 2009).

McLure, C.E. (2001) 'The Tax Assignment Problem: Ruminations on How Theory and Practice Depend on History', *National Tax Journal* 54(2): 339–63.

Mellor, Mary (2010) *The Future of Money. From Financial Crisis to Public Resource.* London: Pluto Press.

Meltzer, A.H. and S.F. Richard (1981) 'A Rational Theory of the Size of Government', *Journal of Political Economy* 89: 914–27.

Miller, David (2001) 'Distributing Responsibilities', *Journal of Political Philosophy* 9(4): 453–71.

Mirrlees, J.A. (1971) 'An Exploration in the Theory of Optimal Income Taxation', *Review of Economic Studies* 38: 175–208.

Mitchell, A. and P. Sikka (2005) *Taming the Corporations.* Basildon, UK: Association for Accountancy and Business Affairs.

Mitchell, A. et al. (2002) *No Accounting for Tax Havens.* Basildon, UK: Association for Accounting Business Affairs.

Molina, Núria and María José Romero (2011) 'Turning CSO Demands On Tax Justice Into Binding European Law' Report by the Financial Task Force. Available at <http://www.financialtaskforce.org/2011/02/18/turning-cso-demands-on-tax-justice-into-binding-european-law> (accessed 15 February 2011).

Monbiot, G. (2011) 'We Know What to March Against on 26 March; Here's What to Protest For', *The Guardian*, 6 March.

Mooij, Ruud A. and Gaëtan Nicodème (2008) 'Corporate Tax Policy and Incorporation in the EU', CPB Netherlands Bureau for Economic Policy Analysis, The Hague.

Moore, M. and L. Rackner (2004) 'The New Politics of Taxation and Accountability in Developing Countries', *Institute of Development Studies Bulletin* 33(3). University of Sussex: IDSB.

Mouvement des Entreprises de France (Medef) (2010) 'Response to the European Consultation'. Available at <http://circa.europa.eu/Public/irc/markt/markt_consultations/library?l=/accounting/country-by-country/registered_organisations/fr_medef1_enpdf/_EN_1.0_&a=d> (accessed 17 August 2010).

Müller-Armack, A. (1947) *Wirtschaftslenkung und Marktwirtschaft.* Hamburg: Kastell.

Mumford, A. (2001) *Taxing Culture: Towards a Theory of Tax Collection Law.* Burlington, VT: Ashgate.

——— (2008) 'Towards a Fiscal Sociology of Tax Credits and the Fathers' Rights Movement', *Social and Legal Studies* 17(2): 217–35.

Murphy, Liam and Thomas Nagel (2002) *The Myth of Ownership. Taxes and Justice.* Oxford: Oxford University Press.

Murphy, R. (2003) 'A Proposed International Accounting Standard Reporting Turnover and Tax by Location'. Available at <http://visar.csustan.edu/aaba/ProposedAccstd.pdf> (accessed 15 August 2009).

——— (2009a) *The Missing Billions.* London: Trades Unions Congress.

——— (2009b) 'Country-by-Country Reporting; Holding Multinational Corporation to Account Where They Are', Financial Integrity and Economic Development. Washington: Task Force on Financial Integrity and International Development.

Musgrave, Peggy (2000) 'Consumption Tax Proposals in an International Setting', *Tax Law Review* 54(1): 77–100.

——— (2002) *Tax Policy in the Global Economy: Selected Essays of Peggy B. Musgrave. Studies in Fiscal Federalism and State–Local Finance.* Cheltenham, UK: E. Elgar.

———— (2006) 'Combining Fiscal Sovereignty and Coordination', in I. Kaul and P. Conceição (eds), *The New Public Finance: Responding to Global Challenges*. Oxford: Oxford University Press.

Musgrave, R.A. (1959) *The Theory of Public Finance: A Study in Public Economy*. New York: McGraw-Hill.

———— (1992) 'Schumpeter's Crisis of the Tax State: An Essay in Fiscal Sociology', *Journal of Evolutional Economics* 2: 89–113.

———— (1983) 'Who Should Tax, Where and What?', in C.E. McLure (ed.), *Tax Assignment in Federal Countries*, pp. 2–19. Canberra: Australia University Press.

———— (2002) 'Equity and the Case for Progressive Taxation', in J.J. Thorndike and Dennis J. Ventry Jr. (eds), *Tax Justice: The Ongoing Debate*. Washington, DC: Urban Institute Press.

Musgrave, Richard A. and Peggy B. Musgrave (1972) 'Inter-nation Equity', in R.M. Brid and J.G. Head (eds), *Modern Fiscal Issues: Essays in honour of Carl S. Shoup*, pp. 63–85. Toronto: University of Toronto Press.

———— (1989) *Public Finance in Theory and Practice*, 5th edition. New York: McGraw Hill.

Mutti, J.H. and H. Grubert (2007) 'The Effect of Taxes on Royalties and the Migration of Intangible Assets Abroad', NBER Working Paper Series 13248. Cambridge, MA: NBER.

Nagel, Thomas (1975) 'Review: Libertarianism without Foundations', *The Yale Law Journal* 85(1): 136–49.

———— (2005) 'The Problem of Global Justice', *Philosophy & Public Affairs* 33(2): 113–47.

Nairn, T. (1997) *Faces of Nationalism*. London: Verso.

Ndirangu, M. (2007) 'Probe Ordered into Laikipia CDF Cash misuse claims', *Daily Nation*.

Nelson J. (1996) *Feminism, Objectivity, and Economics*. New York: Routledge.

Newton, Scott (2010) 'The Sterling Devaluation of 1967, The International Economy, and Post-War Social Democracy', *The English Historical Review* CXXV(515): 912–45.

Nickel, J. (1987) *Making Sense of Human Rights: Philosophical Reflections on the Universal Declaration of Human Rights*. Berkeley: University of California Press.

Nickell, S. (2004) 'Employment and Taxes', CEP Discussion Paper dp0634. London: LSE Centre for Economic Performance.

Nigerian Revenue Law Report (1998–1999) 'Shell Petroleum International Mattschappij B. V. v FBIR, Appeal No. FHC/L/CS/1A 96', *NRLR* 1: 63–82.

NNPC (2008) 'Development of Nigeria's Oil Industry', NNPC Official Report. Available at <http://www.nnpcgroup.com/development.htm> (accessed 9 January 2009).

Nonet, P. and P. Seznick (2000) *Law and Society in Transition: Towards Responsive Law*. New Brunswick: Transaction Publishers.

North, D.C. and J.J. Wallis (1982) 'American Government Expenditures: A Historical Perspective', *American Economic Review* 72: 336–40.

Nozick, Robert (1974) *Anarchy, State, and Utopia*. Oxford: Blackwell.

Nyaga, N. (2008) 'Why MPs Are So Cagey: CDF and the Politics of Transition', *Daily Nation*.

O'Leary, N.C. and P.J. Sloane (2004) 'The Return to a University Education in Great Britain', IZA Working Paper 1199. Bonn: IZA.

Ocaya-Lakidi, D. (1977) 'Manhood, Warriorhood and Sex in East Africa', in A.A.A. Mazrui (ed.), *The Warrior Tradition in Modern Africa*, pp. 134–65. Leiden: E.J. Brill.

Ochieng, W.R. (1985) *A History of Kenya*. London: Macmillan.

Ochieng, W.R. and R.M. Maxon (1992) *An Economic History of Kenya*. Nairobi: East African Educational Publishers.

OECD (1998) 'Harmful Tax Competition. An Emerging Global Issue'. Paris: OECD.

———— (2001) 'Economic Survey: Portugal'. Paris: OECD.

———— (2003) 'Economic Survey: Portugal'. Paris: OECD.

———— (2006a) 'Revenue Statistics 2006', OECD Press Release, Berlin, 11 October.

———— (2006b) 'Economic Survey: Portugal'. Paris: OECD.

———— (2008a) 'Growing Unequal? Income Distribution and Poverty in OECD Countries'. Paris: OECD.

———— (2008b) 'Revenue Statistics 1965–2007'. Paris: OECD.

———— (2009a) 'The OECD's Current Tax Agenda 2009'. Available at <http://www.oecd.org> (accessed 15 March 2010).

———— (2009b) 'Revenue Statistics 1965–2008'. Paris: OECD.

———— (2010a) 'Global Forum on Transparency and Exchange of Information for Tax Purposes, A Background Information Brief'. Paris: OECD.

———— (2010b) OECD Model Tax Convention on Income and Capital, Condensed Version. Paris: OECD.

———— (2010c) 'Issues Paper. Domestic Resource Mobilisation for Development: The Taxation Challenge'. Paris: OECD.

———— (2010d) 'Tax Policy Reform and Economic Growth', OECD Tax Policy Studies No. 20. Paris: OECD.

———— (2011) Growing Income Inequality in OECD Countries: What Drives it and How Can Policy Tackle it? Paris: OECD.

Office for National Statistics (2009) 'Social Trends 39'. London: HMSO.

Olson, M.J. (1982) *The Rise and Decline of Nations: Economic Growth, Stagflation, and Social Rigidities*. New Haven: Yale University Press.

———— (1969) 'The Principle of "Fiscal Equivalence": The Division of Responsibilities among Different Levels of Government', *American Economic Review* 59(2): 479–87.

Omonso, G. (2008) 'Police to Quiz 17 over CDF Cash', *Daily Nation*.

Omonso, G. and D. Ng'etich (2008) 'Fund Manager got Death Threats', *Daily Nation*.

O'Neill, O. (1996) *Towards Justice and Virtue: A Constructive Account of Practical Reasoning*. Cambridge: Cambridge University Press.

O'Rawe, M. (1999) 'The United Nations: Structure Versus Substance (Lessons from the Principal Treaties and Covenants)', in A. Hegarty and S. Leonard (eds), *Human Rights: An Agenda for the 21st Century*, pp. 15–33. London: Cavendish.

Osaghae, E.E. (1998) *Crippled Giant: Nigeria since Independence*. Bloomington: Indiana University Press.

Ostrom, E. (2005) *Understanding Institutional Diversity*. Princeton: Princeton University Press.

Otusanya, O.J. (2010) 'An Investigation of Tax Evasion, Tax Avoidance and Corruption in Nigeria', Unpublished Doctoral Thesis, University of Essex, United Kingdom.

Overesch, M. (2009) 'The Effects of Multinationals' Profit Shifting Activities on Real Investments', *National Tax Journal* 62(1): 5–23.

Oxfam (2000) 'Tax Heaven: Releasing the Hidden Billions for Poverty Eradication', Oxfam GB Policy Paper. Available at <http://www.oxfam.org.uk/whatwedo/issues/debt-aid/tax-heaven.htm> (accessed 25 November 2005).

———— (2004) *Paying the Price: Why Rich Countries Must Invest now in a War on Poverty*. Oxford: Oxfam International.

Oxhorn, P., J.S. Tulchin and A. Selee (eds) (2004) *Decentralisation, Democratic Governance and Civil Society in Comparative Perspective*. Washington, DC: Woodrow Wilson Centre Press.

Paine, Thomas (2009 [1791]), *The Rights of Man*, ebook. Available at <http://ebooks. adelaide.edu.au/p/paine/thomas/p147r/>.

Pak, S.J. (2006) 'Estimates of Capital Movements from African Countries to the U.S. through Trade Mispricing', paper presented at the Workshop on Tax, Poverty and Finance for Development, Essex Business School, University of Essex, July.

Pak, S.J. and S.J. Zdanowicz (2002) 'An Estimate of 2001 Lost US Federal Income Tax Revenue due to Over-invoiced Imports and Under-invoiced Exports', Working Paper. Penn State University: Trade Research Institute.

Palan, R. (2002) 'The Havens and the Commercialization of State Sovereignty', *International Organisation* 56(1): 151–76.

——— (2003) *The Offshore World: Sovereign Markets, Virtual Places and Nomad Millionaires*. Ithaca: Cornell University Press.

Palan, R., R. Murphy and C. Chavagneux (2010) *Tax Havens: How Globalisation Really Works*. Ithaca: Cornell University Press.

Palley, T. (2009) 'America's Exhausted Paradigm: Macroeconomic Causes of the Financial Crisis and Great Recession', Report for New America Foundation. Washington, DC: New America Foundation.

Pampel, F.C. and J.B. Williamson (1989) *Age, Class, Politics, and the Welfare State*. Cambridge: Cambridge University Press.

Panitch, Leo (1993) 'Beyond the Crisis of the Tax State', in Allan Maslove (ed.), *Fairness in Taxation*, pp. 135–59. Toronto: University of Toronto Press.

Paus, Lisa and Axel Troost (2011) 'A European Clearing Union – The Monetary Union 2.0', Working Paper for Federal Finance Committee, Bundestag, Germany. Available at <http://www.solidarische-moderne.de/de/article/154.die-europaeische-ausgleich-sunion-die-waehrungsunion-2-0.html>.

Payne, A. (1991) 'Britain and the Caribbean', in P. Sutton (ed.), *Europe and the Caribbean*, pp. 13–36. London: MacMillan.

Pechman, Joseph A. (ed.) (1977) *Comprehensive Income Taxation*. Washington, DC: Brookings Institute.

Phillips, Kevin (2008) *Bad Money, Reckless Finance, Failed Politics, and the Global Crisis of American Capitalism*. London: Penguin.

Picciotto, S. (1992) *International Business Taxation: A Study in the Internationalization of Business Regulation*. New York: Quorum Books.

——— (2007) 'Tackling Tax Havens and "Offshore" Finance', paper presented at a seminar on Money Laundering, Tax Evasion and Financial Regulation, Transnational Institute, Amsterdam, 12–13 June. Available at http://www.globalpolicy.org/nations/launder/havens/2005/09shirts.pdf (accessed 13 June 2010).

Pierson, P. (2000) 'Increasing Returns, Path Dependence, and the Study of Politics', *American Political Science Review* 94: 251–67.

Piketty, T. (2003) 'Income Inequality in France, 1901–1998', *Journal of Political Economy* 111: 1004–42.

Piotrowska, Joanna and Werner Vanborren (2008) *The Corporate Income Tax Revenue Paradox: Evidence in the EU*, European Commission/Taxation and Customs Union: Working Paper Nr 12-2007.

Pissarides, C.A. (1998) 'The Impact of Employment Tax Cuts on Unemployment and Wages. The Role of Unemployment Benefits and Tax Structure', *European Economic Review* 42: 155–83.

Prasad, Monica and Yingying Deng (2009) 'Taxation and the Worlds of Welfare', Luxembourg Income Studies Working Paper Series, Working Paper No. 480. Luxembourg: LIS.

PricewaterhouseCoopers (2010a) 'Letter to the European Commission of 21 December 2010'. Available at <http://circa.europa.eu/Public/irc/markt/markt_consultations/library?l=/accounting/country-by-country/registered_organisations/pricewaterhouse_1/_EN_1.0_&a=d> (accessed 15 January 2011).

——— (2010b) 'Tax Transparency: Communicating the Tax Companies Pay'. Available at http://www.pwc.co.uk/eng/publications/tax_transparency.html (accessed 15 January 2011).

Profeta, Paolo and Simona Scabrosetti (2010) *The Political Economy of Taxation*. Cheltenham: Edward Elgar.

Przeworski, A., M. Alvarez, M. Cheibub and F. Limongi (2003) *Democracy and Development: Political Institutions and Well-being in the World*. Cambridge: Cambridge University Press.

Publish What You Pay (2010) 'Letter to the European Commission of 22 December 2010'. Available at <http://circa.europa.eu/Public/irc/markt/markt_consultations/library?l=/accounting/country-by-country/individuals_other/eu_pwyp2_enpdf/_EN_1.0_&a=d>.

Putnam, B.H. (1915) 'Maximum Wage-Laws for Priests after the Black Death, 1348–1381', *The American Historical Review* 21: 12–32.

PWYP (2010) 'Letter to the European Commission of 22 December 2010'. Available at <http://circa.europa.eu/Public/irc/markt/markt_consultations/library?l=/accounting/country-by-country/individuals_other/eu_pwyp2_enpdf/_EN_1.0_&a=d> (accessed 14 January 2011).

Ramesh, R. (2010) 'How to Bridge the Divide between Health and Wealth', *The Guardian*, 23 June.

Rawls, J. (1971) *A Theory of Justice*. Cambridge, MA: Harvard University Press.

——— (1999a) *A Theory of Justice*, revised edition. Oxford: Oxford University Press.

——— (1999b) *The Law of People, with the idea of Public Reason Revisited*. Cambridge, MA: Harvard University Press.

——— (2001) *Justice as Fairness: A Restatement*, ed. Erin Kelly. Cambridge, MA: Harvard University Press.

Reese, P.D. (1988) 'United States Tax Treaty Policy toward Developing Countries: The China Example', *UCLA Law Review* 35(2): 369–98.

Reisen, H. (2004) 'Innovative Approaches to Finance: The Millennium Development Goals', OECD Development Centre Policy Brief, 2004, No. 24. Paris: OECD.

Republic of Kenya (1965) 'African Socialism and its Application to Planning in Kenya'. Nairobi: Government Printers.

——— (1988) 'The Constitution of the Republic of Kenya', 1988. Nairobi: Government Printers.

——— (1992) 'The Constitution of the Republic of Kenya', 1992. Nairobi: Government Printers.

——— (2004) 'The Constituency Development Fund Act'. Nairobi: Government Printers.

———— (2007) 'The Constituency Development Fund (Amendment) Act'. Nairobi: Government Printers.

Richardson, G. (2006) 'Taxation Determinants of Fiscal Corruption: Evidence across Countries', *Journal of Financial Crime* 13(3): 323–38.

Rixen, T. (2008) *The Political Economy of International Tax Governance*. Basingstoke, UK: Palgrave Macmillan.

———— (2011) 'Tax Competition and Inequality – The Case for Global Tax Governance', in T. Farer and T.D. Sisk (eds), *Global Governance: A Review of Multilateralism and International Institutions*. Boulder, CO: Lynne Riener.

Rixen, T. and P. Schwarz (2008) *Bargaining over the Avoidance of Double Taxation: Evidence from German Tax Treaties*. Berlin: WZB Economics and Politics Seminar Series.

Roberts, A.D. (ed.) (1986). *The Cambridge History of Africa*, Volume 5. Cambridge: Cambridge University Press.

Roberts, K. (1984) 'Theoretical Limits to Redistribution', *Review of Economic Studies* 51: 177–95.

Robinson, M. (1998) 'Corruption and Development: An Introduction', in Mark Robinson (ed.), *Corruption and Development*, pp. 1–14. London: Frank Cass.

Rodrik, Dani (1997) *Has Globalization Gone Too Far?* Washington, DC: Institute for International Economics.

———— (1998) 'Why Do More Open Economies Have Bigger Government?', *Journal of Political Economy* 106: 997–1032.

Roemer, John E. (1996) *Theories of Distributive Justice*. Cambridge, MA: Harvard University Press.

Romonet, I. (1997) 'Disarming the Markets', *Lemonde Diplomatique*, December. Available at <http://www.mondediplo.com/1997/12/leader> (accessed 10 August 2006).

Ronzoni, Miriam (2009) 'The Global Order: A Case of Background Injustice? A Practice-Dependent Account', *Philosophy and Public Affairs* 37(3): 229–56.

Rosa, Mario Joao Valente and Paulo Chitals (2010) *Portugal: Os Numeros*. Lisbon: Fundacio Francisco Manuel dos Santos.

Rosen, S. (1981) 'The Economics of Superstars', *American Economic Review* 71: 167–83.

Ruggie, John Gerard (1987) 'International Regimes, Transactions and Change: Embedded Liberalism in the Postwar Economic Order', *International Organization* 36(2): 379–415.

Sabine, B.E.V. (1980) *A Short History of Taxation*. London: Butterworths.

Sandford, Cedric (2000) *Why Tax Systems Differ. A Comparative Study of the Political Economy of Taxation*. Bath: Fiscal Publications.

Sandler, T. (2001a) 'On Financing Global and International Public Goods', The World Bank Policy Research Working Paper, No. 2638. Washington, DC: World Bank.

———— (2001b) 'Financing Global and International Public Goods', in C.D. Gerrard, M. Ferroni and A. Mody (eds), *Global Public Policies and Programs: Implications for Financing and Evaluation*, pp. 183–92. Washington, DC: World Bank.

Sandmo, A. (2003) 'Environmental Taxation and Revenue for Development', WIDER Discussion Paper, No. 2003/86. Bergen: World Institute for Development Economics Research.

Sarkozy, Nicolas (2011) 'Lettre adressée à Bono, en réponse à sa tribune du Monde daté du 29 janvier 2011'. Available at <http://www.elysee.fr/president/les-actualites/communiques-de-presse/2011/lettre-adressee-a-bono-en-reponse-a-sa-tribune-du.10545.html?search=Bono&xtmc=bono&xcr=> (accessed 30 January 2011).

Sawyer, A.J. (2009) *Developing a World Tax Organization: The Way Forward*. Birmingham: Fiscal Publications.

Schlunk, Herwig J. (2006) 'A Lifetime Income Tax', *Virginia Tax Review* 25(4): 939–76.

Schmidt-Traub, G. (2009) 'The Millennium Development Goals and Human Rights-based Approaches: Moving towards a Shared Approach', *International Journal of Human Rights* 13(1): 72–85.

Schratzenstaller, M. and B. Berghuber (2007) 'Alternative Financing Sources for the EU Budget', *Austrian Economic Quarterly* 12(1): 34–50.

Schulmeister, Stephan, Margit Schratzenstaller and Oliver Picek (2008) 'A General Financial Transaction Tax: Motives, Revenues, Feasibility and Effects', Österreichisches Institut für Wirtschaftsforschung, Research Study, March.

Schumpeter, J.A. (1954) *History of Economic Analysis*. London: Allen & Unwin.

——— (1991) 'The Crisis of the Tax State', in R. Swedberg (ed.), *The Economics and Sociology of Capitalism*, pp. 99–140. New Jersey: Princeton University Press.

Seidman, Laurence (1997) *The USA Tax: A Progressive Consumption Tax*. Cambridge, MA: MIT Press.

Sen, Amartya (2000) *Development as Freedom*. Oxford: Oxford University Press.

Senator Carl Lenin Report (2007) 'Statement of Senator Carl Levin on Introducing the Stop Tax Haven Act, Part I', US Senate Floor Statement. Available at <http://levin.senate.gov/senate/statement.cfm?id=269514> (accessed 20 June 2008).

Shaxson, Nicholas (2011) *Treasure Islands: Tax Havens – The Darkest Chapter in Economic History since the Slave Trade*. London: Bodley Head.

Sheffrin, Steven (1996) 'Perceptions of Fairness in the Crucible of Taxation Policy', in Joel Slemrod (ed.), *Tax Progressivity and Income Inequality*. Cambridge: Cambridge University Press.

Shelton, N. (2004) *Interpretation and Application of Tax Treaties*. London: Lexis Nexis Tolley.

Shillingdon, K. (ed.) (2005) *Encyclopedia of African History*, Volume 1, pp. 693–99. Boca Raton, FL: CRC Press.

Shue, H. (1996) *Basic Rights: Subsistence, Affluence, and U.S. Foreign Policy*. Princeton: Princeton University Press.

Sikka, P. (2003) 'The Role of Offshore Financial Centres in Globalization', *Accounting Forum* 27(4): 365–99.

——— (2005) 'Corporate Tax Avoidance and Global Economic Development', seminar paper presented at the International Trade and Law Institute. Available at <http://visar.csuctan.edu/aaba/sikka17Jan2005.html> (accessed 11 October 2006).

——— (2008a) 'Enterprise Culture and Accountancy Firms: New Masters of the Universe', *Accounting, Auditing and Accountability Journal* 21(2): 268–95.

——— (2008b) 'Globalization and Its Discontents: Accounting Firms Buy Limited Liability Partnership Legislation in Jersey', *Accounting, Auditing and Accountability Journal* 21(3): 398–426.

Sikka, P. and M. Hampton (2005) 'Tax Avoidance and Global Development: An Introduction', *Accounting Forum* 29(3): 245–48.

Sikka, P. and C. Haslam (2006) 'Transfer Pricing and its Role in Tax Avoidance and Flight of Capital: Some Theory and Evidence', paper presented for discussion at the 'Interdisciplinary Perspectives on Accounting' Conference, Cardiff, UK, July.

Sikka, P. and Willmott, H. (2010) 'The Dark Side of Transfer Pricing: Its Role in Tax Avoidance and Wealth Retentiveness', *Critical Perspectives on Accounting* 21(5): 342–56.

Silva Lopes, Jose da (2004) *A Economia Portuguesa no Seculo XX*. Lisboa: Imprensa de Ciencias Sociais.

——— (2005) 'Financas Publicas', in Pedro Lains and Alvaro Ferreira da Silva (eds), *Historia Economica de Portugal, Vol III*. Lisbon: Imprensa de Ciencias Sociais.

Simons, Henry Calvert (1938) *Personal Income Taxation: The Definition of Income as a Problem of Fiscal Policy*. Chicago: University of Chicago Press.

Slemrod, Joel and Jon Bakija (2000) 'Does Growing Inequality Reduce Tax Progressivity? Should It?' NBER Working Paper 7576. Cambridge, MA: NBER.

Smeeding, T. (2002) 'Inequality and the Rich Countries of the G-20: Evidence from the Luxembourg Income Study', Luxembourg Income Study Working Paper 320. Luxembourg: LIS.

Smith, Adam (1904) *An Enquiry into the Nature and Causes of the Wealth of Nations*, Volume II. London: Grant Richards [original edition 1776].

Smith, Rhona (2007) *Textbook on International Human Rights*. Oxford: Oxford University Press.

Solt, F. (2008) 'Economic Inequality and Democratic Political Engagement', *American Journal of Political Science* 52: 48–60.

Sonja, O.R. (2003) 'Tax Avoidance Activities of US Multinational Corporations', *Contemporary Accounting Research* 20(4): 805–33.

Sørensen, P.B. (2006) 'Can Capital Income Taxes Survive? And Should They?' *CESifo Economic Studies* 53(2): 172–228.

Stark, Jürgen (2009) 'Solide Staatsfinanzen für nachhaltiges Wachstum', *Frankfurter Allgemeine Zeitung*, 30 October.

Stefan Bach, Giacomo Corneo and Viktor Steiner (2009) 'From Bottom to Top: The Entire Income Distribution in Germany', *The Review of Income and Wealth* 55(2): 303–33.

Steiner, H.J., P. Alston and R. Goodman (eds) (2007) *International Human Rights in Context: Law, Politics, Morals*. Oxford: Oxford University Press.

Steurle, C. Eugene (1995) 'Incentives, Disincentives and Efficiency Issues', in David Bradford (ed.), *Distributional Analysis of Tax Policy*. Washington, DC: AEI Press.

Stewart, Heather (2011) 'Britain Backs "Publish What You Pay" Rule for Oil and Mining Firms in Africa', *The Observer*, 20 February. Available at <http://www.guardian.co.uk/business/2011/feb/20/george-osborne-oil-mining-africa> (accessed 22 February 2011).

Stigler, G.J. (1971) 'The Theory of Economic Regulation', *The Bell Journal of Economic and Management Science* 2: 3–21.

Stiglitz, J.E. (2006) 'Global Public Goods and Global Finance: Does Global Governance Ensure that the Global Public Interest is Served?', in J.P. Touffot (ed.), *Advancing Public Goods*, pp. 149–64. Paris: The Cournot Centre for Economic Studies Series.

Stotsky, J. (1997) 'Gender Bias in Tax Systems', *Tax Notes International* 9(June): 1913–23.

Strange, S. (1996) *The Retreat of the State: The Diffusion of Power in World Economy*. Cambridge: Cambridge University Press.

Stratfor (2012) 'Special Series: European Economies at Risk – Portugal', 16 March 2012. Available at <http://www.stratfor.com/analysis/special-series-european-economies-risk-portugal> (accessed 17 March 2012).

Subrahmanyam, G. (2004) *Schizophrenic Governance and Fostering Global Inequalities in the British Empire: The UK Domestic State Versus the Indian and African Colonies, 1890–1960*. Chicago: American Political Science Association.

338 | *Bibliography*

Surrey, S.S. (1978) 'United Nations Group of Experts and the Guidelines for Tax Treaties Between Developed and Developing Countries', *Harvard International Law Journal* 19(1): 1–66.

SVR (Sachverständigenrat zur Begutachtung der gesamtwirtschaftlichen Entwicklung, Council of Economic Advisors) (2008) 'Jahresgutachten 2008/09'. Wiesbaden: SVR. Available at <http://www.sachverstaendigenrat-wirtschaft.de> (accessed 21 June 2010).

——— (2009) 'Jahresgutachten 2009/2010'. Wiesbaden: SVR. Available at <http://www.sachverstaendigenrat-wirtschaft.de> (accessed 21 June 2010).

——— (2011) 'Jahresgutachten 2011/2012'. Wiesbaden: SVR. Available at <http://www.sachverstaendigenrat-wirtschaft.de> (accessed 20 December 2011).

Swank, Duane (2002) *Global Capital, Political Institutions, and Policy Change in Developed Welfare States*. Cambridge/New York: Cambridge University Press.

Szeflet, M. (2000) 'Clientelism, Corruption and Catastrophe', *Review of African Political Economy* 85: 427–41.

Tabellini, G. (2003) 'Principles of Policymaking in the EU: An Economic Perspective', *CESifo Economic Studies* 49(1): 75–102.

Tait, Nikki (2011) 'EU Plans New Transparency Rules for Mining Groups', *Financial Times*, 20 March. Available at <http://www.ft.com/cms/s/0/bd92440e-530f-11e0-86e6-00144feab49a.html#axzz1HvuDL9Ou> (accessed 22 March 2011).

Tanzi, V. (1999) 'Is There a Need for a World Tax Organization?', in A. Razin and E. Sadka (eds), *Economics of Globalization, Policy Perspectives from Public Economics*, pp. 173–86. Cambridge: Cambridge University Press.

——— (2000) 'Globalization, Technology Development, and the Work of Fiscal Termites', IMF Working Paper 00/181. Washington, DC: International Monetary Fund.

——— (2004) 'Foreword: Common Pressures to Reform European Tax Systems', in Luigi Bernardi and Paola Profeta (eds), *Tax Systems and Tax Reforms in Europe*. London: Routledge.

Tanzi, V. and Luc de Wulf (1976) 'A Distribuicao da Carga Fiscal por Grupos de Rendimento em Portugal', in The German Marshall Fund of the United States and Fundacao Calouste Gulbenkian, *Conferencia Internacional Sobre Economia Portuguesa*. Michigan: University of Michigan Press.

Task Force on Financial Integrity and Economic Development, Christian Aid, Tax Justice Network, TUC, Tax Research UK (2010) 'Taxing Banks. A Joint Submission to the International Monetary Fund'. Norfolk: Tax Research LLP.

Tax Justice Network (2005) 'Tax Us if You Can', A TJN Briefing Paper, September 2005. Available at: <http://www.taxjustice.net/cms/upload/pdf/tuiyc_-_eng_-_web_file.pdf> (accessed 21 June 2010).

——— (2006) 'Global Tax Justice: A Task for Nordic Co-operation', Briefing Paper. Available at <http://blogi.kaapeli.fi/tjnnordic/doc/Mission_Statement/index_html> (accessed 4 November 2006).

——— (2007) 'Tax Havens Cause Poverty'. Available at <http://www.taxjustice.net/cms/front_content.php?idcat=2> (accessed 19 July 2008).

Tax Research LLP and Tax Justice Network (2010) 'Response to the European Commission'. Available at <http://www.taxresearch.org.uk/Documents/ECTransSubmission.pdf> (accessed 13 September 2010).

Therborn, Goran (2009) 'The Killing Fields of Inequality', *Soundings* 42: 20–32.

Thomson, R. (2009) 'Tax Policy and the Globalization of R&D', Intellectual Property Research Institute of Australia Working Paper 01/09. Melbourne: IPRIA.

Tobin, J. (1978) 'A Proposal for International Monetary Reform', *Eastern Economic Journal* 4(3–4): 153–59.

Tomlinson, J. (1996) 'Cultural Globalisation Placing and Displacing the West', *European Journal of Development Research* 8(2): 22–35.

Toynbee, Polly (2011) 'Tory Free Market Hurricane Will Blow our NHS Apart', *The Guardian* (online). Available at <http://www.guardian.co.uk/commentisfree/2011/jan/17/free-market-bill-blow-nhs-apart?>.

Trade Union Congress (TUC) (2008) 'The Missing Billions: The UK Tax Gap', Touchstone Pamphlet 1

——— (2010) 'The Corporate Tax Gap', Working Paper. Available at <http://www.tuc.org.uk/extras/corporatetaxgap.pdf> (accessed 13 January 2011).

Trichet, Jean-Claude (2010a) Interview, *Financial Times*, 9 September.

——— (2010b) 'Stimulate No More – It Is Now Time for All to Tighten', *Financial Times*, 22 July.

Tse, C.Y. (2002) 'Monopoly, Employment and Wages', *Labour Economics* 9: 681–97.

Ul Haq, M., I. Kaul and I. Grunberg (2006) *The Tobin Tax: Coping with Financial Instability*. Oxford: Oxford University Press.

United Nations (1945) 'Charter of the United Nations'. New York: United Nations.

——— (1976) 'Declaration of Principles and Programme of Action of the World Employment Conference'. New York: United Nations.

——— (1979) 'Report of the World Conference on Agrarian Reform and Rural Development', UN Doc. A/54/485. New York: United Nations.

——— (1985) 'Study by the Secretary General on Popular Participation', UN Doc. E/CN.4/1985/10. New York: United Nations.

——— (1990) 'Global Consultation on the Right to Development as a Human Right'. New York: United Nations.

——— (1995) 'Copenhagen Declaration on Social Development', World Summit for Social Development. Copenhagen: United Nations.

——— (2001) 'Recommendations of the High-level Panel on Financing for Development'. New York: United Nations.

——— (2001a) 'Model Double Taxation Convention between Developed and Developing Countries'. New York: United Nations Department of Economic and Social Affairs

——— (2004) 'Resolution on the Permanency of Sovereignty over Natural Resources'. New York: United Nations.

United Nations Department of Economic and Social Affairs (2001a) 'United Nations Model Double Taxation Convention between Developed and Developing Countries', ST/ESA/PAD/SER.E/21. New York: United Nations.

United Nations General Assembly (1966) 'International Covenant on Economic, Social and Cultural Rights'. New York: United Nations.

——— (1974) 'Charter of Economic Rights and Duties of States'. New York: United Nations.

——— (1986) 'Declaration on the Right to Development'. New York: United Nations.

United Nations International Children's Fund (2007) 'Eyes on the Budget as a Human Rights Instrument'. New York: United Nations.

US Department of Commerce (1993) 'International Business Practices'. Darby, PA: Diane Publishing.

US General Accountability Office (2005) 'Tax Shelters: Services Provided by External Auditors'. Washington, DC: GAO.

US Senate Sub-Committee on Investigations (2006) 'Offshore Abuses, the Enablers, the Tools and Offshore Secrecy', Minority and Majority Staff Report. Available at <http://hsgas.senate.gov/_files/TaxHvnAbRPT> (accessed 18 August 2006).

—— (2008) 'Tax Haven Banks and U.S. Tax Compliance', Staff Report, July 2008. Available at <http://hsgac.senate.gov/public/_files/071708PSIReport.pdf> (accessed 16 June 2010).

—— (2010) 'Keeping Foreign Corruption Out of the United States: Four Case Histories', PSI Staff Report, April. Washington, DC: US General Accounting Office.

Uzoigwe, G.N. (2004) 'Nigeria to 1960: An Overview', in L.A. Nwachuku and G.N. Uzoigwu (eds), *Troubled Journey Nigeria Since the Civil War*, pp. 1–19. Lanham, MD: University Press of America Inc.

Valodia, I. (2010) 'Policy Conclusions', in C. Grown and I. Valodia (eds), *Taxation and Gender Equity: An Analysis of Direct and Indirect Taxes in Developing and Developed Countries*, pp. 299–312. London: Routledge.

Van Oranje, Mabel and Henry Parham (2009) 'Publishing What We Learned. An Assessment of the "Publish What You Pay" Coalition', Online Monograph. Available at <http://eiti.org/files/Publishing%20What%20We%20Learned.pdf>.

Varian, H.R. (1980) 'Redistributive Taxation as Social Insurance', *Journal of Public Economics* 14: 49–68.

Verdi Bundesvorstand (2010) 'Wirtschaftspolitik aktuell, nr.12', May 2010. Available at <http//wipo.verdi.de> (accessed 12 September 2010).

Vickrey, William (1972) *Agenda for Progressive Taxation*. Clifton, NJ: Augustus M. Kelley.

—— (1994) *Public Economics*. Cambridge: Cambridge University Press.

Visco, Vincenzo (1992) 'Fiscal System and Fiscal Reform in Italy in the 1990s', in G. Galeotti and M. Marrelli (eds), *Design and Reform of Taxation Policy*, pp. 113–49. Dordrecht: Kluwer.

Walters, M. (2001) *Globalization*. London: Routledge.

Watt, Nicolas (2009) 'Brown Targets Switzerland in Tax Haven Crackdown', *The Guardian*, 19 February.

Webb, Dominic (2010) 'The Economic Recovery and the Budget Deficit', House of Commons Library Research: Key Issues for the New Parliament 2010.

Webber, C. and A. Wildavsky (1986) *A History of Taxation and Expenditure in the Western World*. New York: Simon and Schuster.

Weber, M. (1972) *Economy and Society*. London: Routledge.

Weldon, D. (2011) 'The Danger of Spending Cuts: Some Advice from the IMF'. Available at <http://duncanseconomicblog.wordpress.com/2011/02/15/the-dangers-of-spending-cuts-some-advice-from-the-imf/> (accessed 3 March 2011).

Whisenhunt, W. (2002) 'To Zedillo or Not to Zedillo: Why the World Needs an ITO', *Temple International and Comparative Law Journal* 16(2): 541–60.

White House (2010) 'Statement by the Press Secretary on Transparency in the Energy Sector', 23 July. Available at <http://www.whitehouse.gov/the-press-office/statement-press-secretary-transparency-energy-sector> (accessed 10 September 2010).

Wijnen, W.F.G. and M. Magenta (1997) 'The UN Model in Practice', *Bulletin for International Fiscal Documentation* 12: 574–85.

Wilensky, H.L. (1975) *The Welfare State and Equality: Structural and Ideological Roots of Public Expenditures*. Berkeley: University of California Press.

Wilkinson, Richard and Kate Pickett (2009) *The Spirit Level: Why More Equal Societies Almost Always Do Better*. London: Allen Lane.

Willmott, H. and P. Sikka (1997) 'On Commercialisation of Accountancy Thesis: A Review Essay', *Accounting, Organisations and Society* 22(8): 831–42.

Wolf, Martin (2005) *Why Globalisation Works*. London/New Haven, CT: Yale University Press.

Wolf, M. (2011) 'Britain's Experiment in Austerity' *Financial Times*, 8 February. Available at <http://www.ft.com/cms/s/0/5e5a6d1e-33c9-11e0-b1ed-00144feabdc0.html#axzz1EDbJnmWK> (accessed 9 February 2011).

World Bank (2009) 'Participation and Civic Engagement'. Available at <http://web.world-bank.org/WBSITE/EXTERNAL/TOPICS/EXTSOCIALDEVELOPMENT/EXTP CENG/0,,menuPK:410312~pagePK:149018~piPK:149093~theSitePK:410306,00> (accessed 24 September 2009).

———— (2010) 'Letter to the IASB of 30 July 2010'. Available at <http://www.ifrs.org/NR/rdonlyres/0068A751-5E77-495A-A986-DA776A40779F/0/CL55.pdf> (accessed 10 September 2010).

Zelenak, Lawrence (2009) 'Tax Policy and Personal Identity Over Time', *Tax Law Review* 62(3): 333–75.

Zero Tolerance (2006) 'Public Officials and the War against Corruption', *The Official Magazine of Nigeria's Economic and Financial Crimes Commission*, 1 July.

Index